second edition

COUNSELING: PHILOSOPHY,
THEORY AND PRACTICE

second edition

COUNSELING: PHILOSOPHY, THEORY AND PRACTICE

DUGALD S. ARBUCKLE

BOSTON UNIVERSITY

allyn and bacon, inc.
boston, massachusetts

The author wishes to thank the following for permission to reprint copy-righted materials:

AMERICAN ACADEMY OF PSYCHOTHERAPISTS, Philadelphia, Pa.

For quotations from: the tape, *Loretta*, A.A.P. Tape Library, 6420 City Line Avenue, Philadelphia.

AMERICAN PERSONNEL AND GUIDANCE ASSOCIATION, Washington, D.C.

For: Richard S. Dunlop, "Letters and Comments," *Personnel and Guidance Journal* 47: 71–77 (September, 1968); copyright (1968) by the American Personnel and Guidance Association; reproduced by permission of the publishers and author.

For excerpts from: Dugald S. Arbuckle, "Current Issues in Counselor Education," *Counselor Education and Supervision*, 7: 244–252 (Spring, 1968); "Counselor, Psychologists, Social Workers: Let's Ecumenalize," *Personnel and Guidance Journal*, 45: 532–538 (February, 1967); "A Question of Counselor Function and Responsibility," *Personnel and Guidance Journal*, 47: 341–346 (December, 1968); "Counselors, Admissions Officers, and Information," *The School Counselor*, 16: 164–170 (January, 1970); and "The School Counselor: Educator, Psychologist or What," *The School Counselor*, 14: 132–138 (January, 1967). Copyright (1968, 1967, 1968, 1970, and 1967, respectively) by the American Personnel and Guidance Association.

NATIONAL CATHOLIC GUIDANCE JOURNAL, 2001 Riverside Avenue, Minneapolis, Minn.

For quotations from: Dugald S. Arbuckle, "Values, Ethics and Religion in Counseling," *NCGJ* 13: 5–17 (Fall, 1968).

MCGRAW-HILL BOOK COMPANY, New York, N.Y.

For excerpts from: Dugald S. Arbuckle (Ed.), *Counseling and Psychotherapy: An Overview* (New York: McGraw-Hill Book Company, 1967), Chapter 1.

PRENTICE-HALL, INC., Englewood Cliffs, N.J.

For quotations from: Arthur Burton (Ed.), *Case Studies in Counseling and Psychotherapy*, © 1959, Prentice-Hall.

And from: William Evraiff, *Helping Counselors Grow Professionally: A Casebook for School Counselors*, © 1963, Prentice-Hall.

Library of Congress Catalog Card Number: 79–111092

Printed in the United States of America

Second printing . . . December, 1971

to Peg

contents

preface

This book is a revision of *Counseling: Philosophy, Theory and Practice,* but it is even more of a new book than a revision. In simple statistical terms, about one-half of the pages in the book are new, about one-quarter have been modified and changed, and about one-quarter are almost as they were. Most of the latter, however, are examples, excerpts, and quotes. There are now fifteen chapters instead of twelve, and the new material in the chapters ranges from 100 per cent to 0 per cent.

Statistics concerning page numbers, however, do not tell the more human aspect of the revision of a book. Student reactions in the past few years have given me the strong impression that modifications in my thinking about counseling have been well ahead of modifications in my writing, or—I would like to think—student interpretations of my writing. I have tried to make clear in this book what I have felt for some time, namely, that I hold to no dogma or methodology or procedure as being the answer in counseling. Thus it makes little sense to talk about kinds of counseling, since counseling is a reflection of the person of the counselor. The more the counselor operates on the basis of the rightness of dogma, the less human he is, and the less capable, therefore, of establishing a meaningful human relationship with another person.

Thus there have been additions, and some modifications, in the section dealing with the philosophy of counseling, and of man and his nature, but these are more in the way of refinements. The major change, in the form of deletions and additions, occurs in the sections dealing with *The Counselor* and *The Nature of Counseling.* In a way, I suppose, I have tried to align more closely my philosophy of counseling with my perception of the counselor and the counseling process in which he is involved.

The book is written for anyone who is involved in a human relationship with another person, but it centers primarily in the educational milieu, and, more specifically, on the school counselor. I have tried to keep it up-to-date, and modifications were being made continually up to the point of completing the last part of this book—this preface.

What I have written has been, to a great extent, the product of my relationships with people I have known as students and clients. They have been my teachers, and for this I thank them.

DSA

counseling

part 1

THE PHILOSOPHY
OF COUNSELING

chapter 1

RELIGION, SCIENCE, AND MAN

The individual who is known as a professional counselor might range all the way from someone who has just completed several semester hours of training, to someone whose name might happen to be Rogers or Freud or Menninger or May, but all would be likely to agree that whatever counseling might be, it at least involves two human beings, and thus man and his nature is a proper subject of concern. Counseling is also an expression of human values and human attitudes, and as the counselor is working and relating and experiencing with another person, he is giving a fairly clear picture of his own personal philosophical concept of man, his nature, and his function on earth. It would seem logical, then, that the first question that should be examined is the question of why we do what we do, rather than how we do it. The "why" is the philosophical rationale for whatever one does as a counselor, and this chapter will attempt to examine the impact of religion and science on current developments in counseling and psychotherapy.

Neither organized religion nor science has been noted historically for its dedication and commitment to the welfare of individual man, but it is from religion and science that the counselor develops his own philosophy regarding the nature of man, and thus, the nature and purpose of counseling. It would be reasonable to hope that this philosophy, whether it be geared primarily in the direction of religion or the direction of science, or somewhere in between, is at least pro-human rather than anti-human. Let us note, then, the perception of man that is held by science and by religion.

RELIGION AND MAN

Man, in his present form (give or take a little), has been around for some time—about five million years, some anthropologists say, and it is likely that his living, for an important segment of that time, has had as a part of it what would be described today as religion. In that brief span of history which is recorded, man has had his gods, and he likely had them in some form in much of that greater part of his history which is unrecorded. On the more recent pages of history four great religious leaders appeared within less than two thousand years of each other. From an anthropological point of view, Moses, Mohammed, Christ, and Buddha were all born, and lived, and died within the same day, and one must assume that man's development must have had something to do with their joint appearance on the earthly scene. In the several centuries since their day, a significant proportion of the world's organized religions has become centered around these four giant figures, and as long as man has need to differentiate and separate his identity from that of his brother, it is likely that "I am a Jew" and "I am a Christian" will be enough to separate one from another. It is likely too that the debate and the dissension and the violence that have centered around the attempt to answer the question of just who these men were, and what they believed, what they said, and what they did, will continue for some time. It may be just as well for organized religion that tape recorders were not available several thousand years ago. Human beings being what they are, we can assume that there would be some discrepancy between these people as they actually were and the images of them that have been developed.

The Greeks looked at life rationally, and the Greek citizen could have his religion and his reason. The Christian religion, however, was based on faith, and even more important for the future of man in the centuries that lay ahead, he *had* to believe or be guilty of heresy. For much of the Western world, philosophy became *religious* philosophy. It was concerned with the other world rather than with this world, and with man's relation to God rather than with man. Aquinas became the official Christian spokesman for the separation of reason from faith, and truth was that which came from God, rather than the product of reason.

Science, at least as we know it today, was a rather modern up-start, and it has been engaged in an almost constant struggle with organized religion. The counselor, particularly one of somewhat humanistic leanings, may periodically find himself in line of fire from both sides! In many ways, this struggle has been primarily one of faith (believe what I tell you) against reason (believe what your mind says is true); a struggle of truth against truths; a struggle of the absolute against the relative; a struggle of answers against questions. Ironically enough, both religion and science have expressed their love of man and their concern for him, yet both would appear to have been concerned generally with bits and pieces of him, although they may, of course, have felt that these bits and pieces were man. [Thus, in the Western world, the Christian church has generally exerted no great social effort for the benefit of man, and has appeared more concerned with getting him into the next world than with helping him in the current world, which is the only one that man can know.] The church has always been concerned about the soul of man, but it has too frequently ignored the rest of him. Religion and science have struggled against each other, and yet, so often, neither appeared to have known and understood the real existential living-in-being man. To the church he was a soul, preparing for the glory to come; to the scientist, he was a set of behaviors to be examined. For both, he was someone to be controlled and manipulated and directed for the good of someone other than himself. To both, he was one who could not be trusted. Freud was anti-religious, and yet the psychological body of man, as developed by Freud, bears a striking resemblance to the spiritual body of man of the church of the day.

The stresses and strains that are shaking the Christian church today are directly related to the increasing involvement of many members of the clergy in the human and social issues of the day. As the church becomes more concerned with people and their problems, it becomes more humanized and thus is more subject to criticism and attack. When a prince of the church, clad in magnificent robes, carried on the backs of his subjects, makes some statement about the after life, that is one thing; when an aged celibate man, whose own sexual life has been definitely atypical, tries to tell a virile young couple about their proper sexual behavior, that is something else again!

Although Tillich[1] was later to argue that the man whose will is in

---

[1] Paul Tillich, *The Protestant Era* (Chicago: The University of Chicago Press, 1948).

bondage must have the power of self determination, since a being without the power of self determination has no capacity for decision at all, organized religion has generally shared with science a deterministic view of man. Thus while science may talk about natural laws' being lawful and determined, religion will talk about universal truths' being ultimately determined by some divine will or some supreme supernatural being. In both situations, man is obviously not in control; he is being controlled.

It would probably be safe to say that most religions—those of Moses, and Buddha, and Christ, and Mohammed—were at least to some extent a protest of man against his suppression and his misery and his fear and his anxiety. They were movements, and all of the major original religious figures, known and unknown, were heretics against the current ruling order. Christ and Socrates shared the same fate, and they were guilty of the same offense, heresy against the state. It is ironic that the revolutionary individualism of Christ should have become symbolized so quickly by the dogma and conservatism of an organized church named after him. Kaufmann points this out when he says:[2]

> What is ironical . . . is that Jesus' dissatisfaction with all formulas and rules should have given way within one generation, to an attempt, not yet concluded, to determine the most precise dogmas.

And again:[3]

> The point is not just that religion tends to become repulsive when it prospers, or that religion is at its best in times of persecution . . . but whether religion is a pious name for conformity or a fighting name for non-conformity. The men who conducted the Greek heresy trials, the Inquisition, and the witch hunts, who went on crusades and to holy wars, were conformists, men of the crowd, true believers. The Hebrew prophets were not.

Religion and the church need not, of course, be synonymous, and one might pose a reasonable argument as to why "religious" and "religion" need not be synonymous. Most individuals, growing up in a "religious" culture, generally assume that if one is religious he must have a denominational title, and they would probably be disturbed if someone said, "Yes, I think I'm religious, but I don't know that I fit

---

[2] Walter Kaufmann, *The Faith of a Heretic* (New York: Doubleday & Co., 1961), p. 233.
[3] *Ibid.*, p. 264.

any particular title or name." For many citizens, agnostic and atheistic mean the same thing, and both are nasty words! Most, too, would probably think that one's devoutness is measured by the extent to which he accepts the dogma of the particular creed that he professes, although very rarely would this dogma have anything to do with man's relations with man. Affiliation with a particular denomination often tends to encourage and facilitate withdrawal and segregation, and the building of parochial walls. This, in turn, tends to make it more difficult to see all men as one's brothers, just as does the stress on any differences between men. There is no particular difference in the element of the denial of one's fellows when one is told, "Don't ever forget you are an American, not an Indian," or "a white man, not a black man," or "a Jew, not a Baptist." They are all equally vicious, and it is particularly tragic when, in the name of religion, one must learn to spurn and suspect, and if necessary to kill, one's fellows. "Love" is a word that organized religions have used profusely, but they have practiced love less frequently.

On the other hand, man as seen by various people who probably consider themselves religious, in a current cultural sense, is by no means the same fellow. We may contrast, for example, this somewhat broad perspective of religion of Progoff:[4]

> The psychological dimension of religion is the dimension of lived experience in which religion is not a dogma but a fact of life and of accomplishment for persevering effort. . . .

with this astonishingly parochial version of one who happens to be a psychoanalyst:[5]

> The historical defect in human psychological understanding has been spanned by the vision of religion; the historical inadequacy of human responsibility has been remedied by the heroic in military life. Without religion, society would have lost its capacity for faith; without military life men would have failed to give embodiment to hope and its accompanying social morality.

On the other hand, Curran, who is a man of the cloth, also feels that man must search for his own answers.[6]

---

[4] Ira Progoff, "The Psychological Dimension of Religion," *Journal of Existential Psychiatry* 3:166–178 (Fall, 1962).
[5] Paul Rosenfels, *Psychoanalysis and Civilization* (New York: Library Publishers, Inc., 1962), pp. 34–35.
[6] Charles A. Curran, "Some Ethical and Scientific Values in the Counseling Therapeutic Process," *Personnel and Guidance Journal* 39:15–20 (September, 1960).

It would restore again the possibility of starting out . . . on a thrilling personal pursuit of oneself in a fierce and independent search for reasonable self values and yet allow that one would ultimately come, by this process, not to violent rebellion and anarchy, but to ancient and secure traditional values.

Curran is existential in that he would see man taking the lonely road of choice in search of his self, and the measure of his existentialism might be seen in the extent to which he would freely allow man to make his search, and to move in directions that might not be toward those "ancient values" that Curran apparently feels *must* be there.

It is often difficult too, to try to determine just what is meant by the often vague and somewhat amorphous term "God." In much of the culture, God has become a requisite, and for many Americans, God is something of a status symbol. Fromm has a related thought when he says:[7]

If there is anything to be taken seriously in our profession of God, it is to recognize the fact that God has become an idol. Not an idol of wood or stone like our ancestors worshiped, but an idol of words, phrases, doctrines. . . . We consider people to be "religious" because they say that they believe in God. Is there any difficulty in *saying* this?

Many counselors would see God as being in the person, and of the person. Wheelis comments:[8]

But freedom is not fortuity, does not war with continuity, means only that we make out of past and present something new, something which is not a mechanical unfolding, and cannot have been foretold, that no law limits how far we may go, how wide, how deep. We are gods because we create.

Sartre, who could hardly be considered to be denominationally "religious," says:

The best way to conceive of the fundamental project of human reality is to say that man is the being whose project is to be God. . . . To be man means to reach toward being God. Or, if you prefer, man fundamentally is the desire to be God.[9]

---

[7] Eric Fromm, *Beyond the Chains of Illusion* (New York: Pocket Books, Inc., 1962), p. 169.

[8] Allen Wheelis, "To Be a God," *Commentary* 36:125–134 (August, 1963).

[9] Jean-Paul Sartre, *Existentialism and Human Emotions* (New York: The Wisdom Library, 1957), p. 63.

Gary describes vividly some of the gods (many would say devils) that reside within all of us. Probably all of us have heard their voices:[10]

First comes Totoche, the god of Stupidity, with his scarlet monkey's behind, the swollen head of a doctrinaire and a passionate love for abstractions; he has always been the Germans' pet, but today he prospers almost everywhere, always ready to oblige; he is now devoting himself more and more to pure research and technology, and can be seen frequently grinning over the shoulders of our scientists; with each nuclear explosion his grin grows wider and wider and his shadow looms larger over the earth; his favorite trick is to hide his stupidity under the guise of scientific genius, and to enlist support among our great men to ensure our own destruction.

Then there is Merzavka, the god of Absolute Truth and Total Righteousness, the lord of all true believers and bigots; whip in hand, a Cossack's fur cap over one eye, he stands knee-deep in a heap of corpses, the eldest of our lords and masters, since time immemorial the most respected and obeyed; since the dawn of history he has had us killed, tortured and oppressed in the name of Absolute Truth, Religious Truth, Political Truth, Moral Truth; always with a capital "T" raised high above our heads, like a scaffold. One half of the human race obsequiously licks his boots, and this causes him immense amusement, for well he knows that there is no such thing as absolute truth, the oldest trick to goad us into slavery or to drive us at each other's throats; and even as I write these words, I can hear above the barking of the seals and the cries of the cormorants the sound of his triumphant laughter rolling toward me from the other end of the earth, so loud that even my brother the ocean cannot raise his voice above it.

Then there is Filoche, the god of Mediocrity, full of bilious scorn and rabid prejudice, of hatred and petulance, screaming at the top of his voice, "You dirty Jew! You nigger! Jap! Down with the Yanks! Kill the yellow rats! Wipe out capitalists! Imperialists! Communists!"— lover of holy wars, a Great Inquisitor, who is always there to pull the rope at a lynching, to command a firing squad, to keep the jails full; with his mangy coat, his hyena's head and his deadly breath, he is one of the most powerful of the gods and the most eagerly listened to; he is to be found in every political camp, from right to left, lurking behind every cause, behind every ideal, always present, rubbing his hands whenever a dream of human dignity is stamped into the mud.

And Trembloche, the god of Acceptance and Servility, of survival at all costs, shaking with abject fear, covered with goose flesh, running with the hare and hunting with the hounds; a skilled persuader, he knows how to worm his way into a tired heart, and his white reptilian snout always appears before you when it is so easy to give up and to remain alive takes only a little cowardice.

---

[10] Romain Gary, *Promise at Dawn* (New York: Harper & Row, Publishers, 1961), pp. 5–6.

The more one feels that counseling is related to, or aligned with, philosophy, the more likely it is that he feels it is also related to religion; whereas the more he feels that counseling is an empirical science, the more likely it is that he will question the necessity of counseling's becoming involved with religion. On the other hand, most counselors would agree with Becker when he writes:[11]

> [Thus psychology and religion, which entered into a state of legal separation during the early part of this century in order to allow psychology to thrive as a science unfettered by doctrinal restraints, have fallen in love again, and are at least cohabiting if not fully married to each other because of the influence of psychotherapy on psychology.]

Certainly the basic principles of operation of the counselor often appear to bear a remarkable resemblance to the basic principles of the operation of the Christian and Jewish cultures. Statements regarding the integrity and rights of the individual are found as often in religious literature as they are in counseling literature. In fact, it would almost seem that if John Smith, Christian, and Mart Cohen, Jew, were to *practice* to the *n*th degree the basic principles of their religions as regards their relationship with their fellow men of all faiths and sizes and colors, then there might not be much difference between their relationship with another human being and the relationship between a counselor and a client. It is when one gets to what people actually do, in the name of their religion, or supposedly because of their religion, or for their religion, that one might say "Well, if this is what you must be or if this is what you must do—and if this is synonymous with your religion, then there is a big gap between the practice of your religion and the practice of counseling."

In an article on this subject Cole has this to say:[12]

> If this interest in psychotherapy does no more than muzzle the minister its worth will be beyond measure. The contrast between the approaches of parson and psychiatrist to troubled human beings is sharp and cutting. The psychotherapist, even if he is a psychoanalyst, the most directive of the new secular priesthood, listens and listens and listens, with an angelic fear of treading too heavily on an already trampled psyche. He waits for weeks before he essays a highly tentative diagnosis and he allows the patient to come to his own insights

[11] Russell J. Becker, "Links Between Psychology and Religion," *The American Psychologist* 13:566–568 (October, 1958).
[12] William Graham Cole, "Couch and Confessional," *The Nation*, September 20, 1958, pp. 147–150.

into the nature of his problems and their solution. The minister, dealing with the same individual, talks and talks and talks!

The minister wants to persuade the troubled parishioner to see his problem in terms of a particular theological formulation. And that is precisely what the analyst does not want. . . .

Thus, if the psychotherapeutic binge now being enjoyed by the clergy does no more than influence them to talk less and listen more, the results will be startling. Further, if ministers can learn the importance of focusing on how people feel rather than on what they say, then counseling will be more effective. For the Bible is at one with the new depth psychology in regarding all human behavior, including conversation, as symptomatic, as springing from the inner wells of emotion. "As a man thinketh in his heart, so is he."

What Cole is saying here is not that religion is in the way of counseling, but rather that some individuals who are called clergymen operate, in the name of religion, in ways that could hardly be called therapeutic.

Mann stresses another problem of the religious counselor when he says:[13]

In the meantime, the clergyman employed in clinical work will have to stand guard against his own need to trespass upon the apparent theological insufficiencies of the patient. Otherwise, he will reap the bitter fruits of his compulsion: a rebellious patient who will not return for counseling, or a submissive devotee who has temporarily buried his pathology under the superficial signs and symbols of religion.

Because in recent years the role of the clergyman as a counselor has been increasingly stressed, counseling is becoming a familiar term to the clergyman, rabbi, and priest-to-be. On the other hand, if the counselor is primarily a clergyman it means that he may view his function as a counselor in a somewhat different light than does the professional secular counselor. On the Catholic side of this question, for example, Bier says:[14]

As a Catholic, I consider this care to be first of all of a spiritual nature and to be exercised through the spiritual ministrations of the priest. . . . a clergyman would think of himself as being dedicated principally to the religious care of those entrusted to him.

---

[13] Kenneth W. Mann, "Religious Factors and Values in Counseling: A Symposium," *Journal of Counseling Psychology* 6:255–274 (Winter, 1959).
[14] William C. Bier, "Goals in Pastoral Counseling," *Pastoral Psychology* 10:10 (February, 1959).

And Moynihan has this to say:[15]

> Pastoral counseling primarily involves education and re-education, a realization of how a problem may be solved through the means at hand in a given religion, be it prayer, the sacraments, conferences and retreats, whereby a new outlook on life is reached, new motivations are reached, and the basis of character modification through a change of will is developed. The primary function of the pastoral counselor is the care of the souls entrusted by ecclesiastic jurisdiction to his ministration, and since this is a spiritual function, the means he employs will be primarily spiritual.

[Judaism has not moved into the area of pastoral counseling to the same degree as has Christianity, one of the reasons being that a rabbi is viewed somewhat differently from the priest or the clergyman. First and foremost they are teachers. This is the essence of their being. In light of this situation, the obvious problem of the rabbi as a counselor is expressed by Schnitzer.[16]

> The usual and accepted role of the rabbi may not be readily adapted to the requirement of the professional counselor who listens and helps people to help themselves.]

It is in the Protestant area that pastoral counseling has probably found its greatest support. Fairly typical of the comments of Protestant clergymen would be those of Hiltner.[17]

> Broadly speaking, the special aim of pastoral counseling may be stated as the attempt by a pastor to help people help themselves through the process of gaining understanding of their inner conflicts. Counseling is sometimes referred to as emotional re-education, for in addition to its attempting to help people with a problem immediately confronting them, it should teach people to help themselves with other problems.

And Wise adds the thought:[18]

> Counseling is essentially communication and as such it is essentially a two directional process. It is not what the counselor does for or to the

---

[15] James F. Moynihan, "The Counselor and His Religion," *Personnel and Guidance Journal* 36:328 (January, 1958).

[16] Jeshaia Schnitzer, *New Horizons for the Synagogue* (New York: Bloch Publishing Co., 1956), p. 16.

[17] Seward Hiltner, *Pastoral Counseling* (New York: Abingdon Press, 1949), p. 19.

[18] Carrol A. Wise, *Pastoral Counseling—Its Theory and Practice* (New York: Harper & Row, Publishers, 1951), p. 63.

counselee that is important; the important thing is what happens between them. The pastor needs to know himself as well as the dynamic processes of personality as they find expression in the counselee.

Even in these few examples of the expressed attitudes of clergymen who are leaders in the area of pastoral counseling, there are noticeable differences between the secular counselor and the clerical counselor.

There are many traits and characteristics that are usually associated with organized religion, and, to a greater or lesser degree, with those who are the spokesmen for religion. Let us look at some of these traits that would appear to be somewhat contradictory to a philosophy of counseling, and that might be considered to hinder the development of a therapeutic relationship between counselor and client.

1. The desire to convert and to change—usually to the religion of the counselor, and to his particular denomination of that religion—is a trait of many clergymen, if not an outright obligation that the clergyman has to his particular church. Many religious denominations even have particular orders whose primary purpose is to convert people to see the truth and the light. "The truth and the light," of course, are the way the particular denomination sees them, even though quite a different truth and light from those accepted by another religion. Whether an individual who feels within him a burning responsibility to persuade all people to feel and to think the way he does could be considered a counselor is a question. Such a setting would surely contradict the concept of the acceptance of the right of the individual to be as he is and to hold the values that he holds, the right to be a free man and to develop his own system of values. It may be a moot theological question whether the "true" Christian, or whether the X denomination—which, in its own mind, represents the "true" Christianity—can operate in a philosophical area such that they would, in effect, be saying that other Christian denominations, or other non-Christian religions, might have the true answers. If this is the case, one might push a little further and say, "Well, since, you do not *know* if you have answers, and since others might be just as right as you, then what difference does it make what denomination of Christian I might be, or whether I am a Christian at all, or instead a Jew or a Buddhist?" What it boils down to might be the simple question: can a good and devout Christian say that he might, in later years, in a later period of the world's history, be shown to be quite wrong in his religious beliefs? Certainly church leaders appear to find no problem in disagreeing

with the church's earlier pronouncements regarding, say, Galileo and Bruno, the question of the sun or the earth as the center of the universe, and the question of evolution.

Actually, there would appear to be little difference between those who would speak of relative truths and the more theologically oriented who feel that there is a God's truth, but are willing to accept the possibility that the current version of *the* truth may not be the correct Godly version. If the church of earlier years had accepted this philosophy, there would have been little reason for it to jail Galileo and burn Bruno. This too, of course, would remove from the church the major reason for the existence of heresy; at least one could hypothesize that the doubter might be closer to God's truth than the devout! The acceptance of the possibility of human (if not Godly) error also removes the major reason for the existence of different branches and denominations of religions. Thus, as the leaders of the Eastern and the Western branches of the Catholic church meet and talk with each other, and cautiously say, "We should not be so far apart—we are not *that* different," they are doing what is also being done by various Protestant denominations, by Protestants and Catholics, and by Christians and Jews. And the closer they become, of course, the more absurd their centuries-long self-segregation becomes. And it may be, eventually, that there will be no point in saying, "I am a Methodist" or "I am a Catholic" or "I am a Jew." All one will need to say is, "I am a human being, and you are my brother."

Certainly many of the concepts of religion are quite akin to those of counseling. The Judeo-Christian heritage stresses the worth and the dignity of the individual man, and it puts on the shoulders of man the responsibility for his actions.

Curran[19] describes some of the relationships between counseling and religion as "parallels." The first parallel is the commitment of self of both the counselor and the religious person. The second parallel has to do with communion—the religious person "communes" with God, whereas the client and the counselor "communicate" together. A third parallel relates to the urge of the religious person to "do better" for himself because of the love and acceptance and understanding of him by God; so too the client is urged to movement and growth because he knows he is understood and accepted, and is thus freer to become.

White speaks much like a counselor when he says:[20]

---

[19] Charles A. Curran, "Religious Factors and Values in Counseling: A Symposium," *Journal of Counseling Psychology* 6:266–270 (Winter, 1959).
[20] Victor White, *God and the Unconscious* (London: Harvill Press, 1953), p. 166.

We Catholics ask of psychotherapy, not to make us good, not to tell us what to do or not to do in order to be good, nor to make us "normal" in accord with any given norm, however estimable; but only to help us to achieve greater freedom through a better knowledge of our necessities and compulsions. We must decline to be "made" anything by psychotherapy; we want to be helped to be able to make or mar ourselves.

On the other hand, the *meaning* of religion, like that of every other aspect of living, must be measured by what it does rather than by what it says. If the Christian counselor who, when some topic about religion is being discussed, feels toward his Jewish client, "*I* am right," then he is probably saying not only "*You* must be wrong," but also, "*I* must be right." The problem, then, rests: is it possible to be accepted by your church as a good and devout and faithful member, and be able to say to yourself, "I think I'm right, but it doesn't really matter too much if it turns out that I am wrong, and you are right, as well you might be." If he can feel this way, then it might be possible for him to be completely acceptant of an individual whose value system, as well as religion, differed sharply from his own. If he cannot feel this way, it would be rather difficult for him to accept another individual when he is saying to himself, "You are, of course, quite wrong."

2. Another area where counseling and religion might find themselves to be uneasy bedfellows is in dealing with the question of sin, original or otherwise. A generally accepted psychological tenet is that it is not so much the actual "sinning," but the acceptance of the belief that we have sinned that causes problems and troubles of the mind. A person may become neurotic not because of his sins, but because he feels that he has sinned. Is the person who wears a hair shirt, or scourges himself, or pays penance, indicating the depth of his religious belief, or is he rather indicating his lack of capacity to accept himself as he is? And does he thus appease himself by doing something to atone for his sins, and, in the meantime, do nothing whatsoever to really change this self that is such that he must continue to sin, and to punish himself for sinning?

It might be, too, that one should distinguish between the social and the religious mores of a Judeo-Christian society. Can we compare the feeling of sinfulness that the Jew might have in committing adultery (which would also be breaking a social law), and that which he might feel because he did not eat Kosher foods (which would be a religious custom, limited only to those Jews who accepted this particular concept)? Every counselor has had as clients individuals who are highly disturbed because they cannot intellectually accept some of the "sinful" acts of their religion as being sinful, and yet who cannot dismiss them. They may be torn between being what they feel is intellectually dishonest but secure, or being intellectually honest and uneasy. The Jew who does not eat Kosher foods, the Catholic who uses contraceptive devices, the Mormon who drinks coffee, the Seventh Day Adventist who works on Saturday—these individuals are sinning according to their religion, but not according to their society. If a person accepts such acts easily or rejects them easily, then he has no problem; but the unhappy one is the person who can do neither.

There are even good citizens who almost seem to be being scared into Heaven because they are afraid that if they do what they want to do, then they will go to Hell. Preparing for Heaven in this manner seems a most unhappy way of spending one's years on earth; and yet there is a strong segment in nearly every religious denomination—more in some than others, of course—where a basic tenet seems to be "You have sinned, and only by living the life that we say you should live will you have any chance of ever seeing the promised land." Surely, this is rather a negative way to do good. Are we good to our neighbors only because of our guilt feelings? It would seem that an ideal and realistic society will be one where such authoritarian and autocratic means for control are not necessary. We know, as a matter of fact, that such means of control are actually useless, and in the long run no control at all. In a free and democratic society, the individual accepts his responsibility for his own behavior without any pressures, subtle or otherwise. He does not steal his neighbor's belongings because he has *no need to steal,* even though he may have a very real need for his neighbor's belongings.

As long as a person can be acceptant, however, of his particular religion's "sins," and not do what he is not supposed to do, or if he can, on the other hand easily reject them as sins, then he has no psychological trouble. If, however, these sins begin to be imposed as sins on others who do not see them as sins, what then? Laws preventing the sale of merchandise on Sunday or preventing the dissemination of information on contraceptive devices are good examples of supposedly "social" laws that are actually religious laws, and are imposed on some who do not accept them as religious laws.

If a person believes too that he is basically a sinful creature, through no fault of his own other than having been born, then he begins his life as a guilty creature. This too would seem to be an insecurity-breeding way of introducing the young to life—the idea that a person must somehow get off his back sins for which he has no responsibility, other than by being a human being. Does man have potential for good and a tendency to evil, or does he have, to start, potential for good and potential for evil, but tendency, if there must be tendency one way or the other, for good rather than evil? This latter point, however, would be in the realm of belief. The empiricist might well say that man, at the beginning, has his various potentialities, but he has no tendencies until he is born, or at least, to play it safe, until he is conceived.

[The problem of sins and sinning may also raise problems for the theologian as a counselor, since a client, in talking with a clergyman about sins he has committed, knows that the clergyman must consider them sins, and therefore cannot be acceptant to them. Hence the client will assume, almost certainly, that the clergyman cannot be acceptant of him as a person.] This situation is illustrated by a statement by Moynihan,[21] who says, "While the pastoral counselor cannot permit anything which is contrary to the laws of God and nature, what he may legitimately permit is the opportunity for the client to talk out any kind of situation or motivation which may have led him to contemplate such a course of action." This point of view indicates that the pastoral counselor must surely be in a somewhat conflicting situation, and that his acceptance is of the most limited type. If the Catholic pastoral counselor does not feel free as an individual to accept the decision of the Catholic client to use contraceptive devices, if the Jewish pastoral counselor does not feel free as an individual to accept the decision of his Jewish client to eat non-Kosher foods, if the Methodist pastoral counselor does not feel free as an individual to accept the decision of his Methodist client to use alcoholic beverages, if the Mormon pastoral counselor does not feel free as an individual to accept the decision of his Mormon client to drink coffee, and if all four feel that as the arm of their respective churches they must be non-acceptant of the client's right to do these things, then surely their acceptance is most limited, and surely, as therapists, they are handicapped.

Such a situation, of course, occurs to some extent with every counselor, since clients frequently discuss various deviations which are not acceptable, and might even be considered criminal, by their culture; and the client may have some beginning uneasiness as to the extent to which the counselor will be acceptant of him and his actions. Thus a Lesbian client once said to me, "I feel okay talking to you like this when I think of you as a counselor, but when I think of your title

---

[21] James F. Moynihan, "Symposium: The Counselor and His Religion," *The Personnel and Guidance Journal* 36:327–331 (January, 1958).

as Professor of Education, I don't feel so good!" At least the client may not know how the secular counselor feels about these things; but he does know, in his own mind at least, that the theological counselor is the arm of a powerful organization that says, "This is a sin that you should not have committed."

Mowrer has spoken out in defense of sin as being of therapeutic value:[22]

> Therefore, we can and should show him all the love and charity within our souls, and do not need in the least to play a punitive role. But this is very different from saying that we should dispute or brush aside his assertions of guilt or minimize the reality of his need for deliverance. Several members of the group expressed the conviction that much of our present would-be therapeutic effort is useless and even harmful because we so actively *oppose* the patient's own most substantial psychological realities and his brightest prospects for change and recovery, i.e., his conviction of guilt and sense of sin. Perhaps the patient is not so wrong, not so "crazy" as some of our own theories have been!

In a later, thought-provoking article, Mowrer discussed at length the problems of sin and psychotherapy.[23]

3. Another problem that finds its way into any discussion of religion and counseling is that concerned with morality and virtue. If religion thinks of itself, as it appears to, as the custodian of man's moral values, then it is speaking in terms of absolutes, a stand that poses a knotty set of problems in a nation where there are many religions, and therefore many sets of values, each set being somebody's "absolutes." Roessler has some interesting comments on this subject. In comparing a personal morality with a "codified" morality, he writes as follows:[24]

> Personal morality is defined in positive terms. Feelings become a reliable guidance to action which enhances and enriches both self and others. . . . By contrast, codified moralities are most often preponderantly prohibitions, because they are frequently based on a pessimistic view of man's nature. . . .

---

[22] O. Hobart Mowrer, "Judgment and Suffering: Contrasting Views," *Faculty Forum* No. 10, October, 1959.
[23] O. Hobart Mowrer, " 'Sin', the Lesser of Two Evils," *The American Psychologist* 15:301–304 (May, 1960).
[24] Robert Roessler, "A Psychiatrist's View of Morality," *The Humanist* 18:333–339 (November–December, 1958).

Like good law, such morality is centered in the needs of men rather than in the sometimes arbitrary demands of institutionalized codes. Because it is so centered, it is tailor-made. . . .

It is a morality of dynamic rather than static quality, changing with ever-changing circumstances and the ever-changing person. It is ceaselessly fluid, completely or almost completely adapted to the requirements of the complex moment. . . .

Personal morality is morality without absolutes. . . . Another characteristic of personal morality is. its tolerance for the behavior of others. . . .

The person capable of choice . . . does not function in spite of circumstances but because of them and in concert with them. . . .

It seems to me that codified moralities may have a predominantly negative effect on self-realization and thereby on society. If they are characterized preponderantly by an absence of "roots in man's nature," if they are inherently inflexible and narrow, if they are absolute—then they will serve neither the needs of the individual nor those of the society comprised of individuals. Fortunately for man, such systems either die because of their lack of pragmatic value, or they are ignored in action as they deserve to be.

This probably points to one of the dilemmas that religion faces when it begins to be involved in the problems of man's behavior. Neither man nor his society, nor the needs of the individual man nor those of the collective society, have much resemblance to what they were several thousands of years ago. The "moralities" of then do not fit the "moralities" of today any more than the sins of yesterday are the sins of today. We may argue that they should be, but if we go on the basis of the way man operates, then he simply does not accept them. If we assume that there should be some relationship between a man's behavior and his morality, then those individuals who are most closely related to a religion or to a church should be our most moral citizens (in the sense of being acceptant of their responsibility toward their neighbors, their love of their fellow man, and their defense of the rights of others). I know of no evidence to indicate that this is so. Theoretically, one might assume that among the graduates of religious schools there should be less in the way of immoral behavior, but there is no evidence to indicate that this is so. We might assume that the person who goes to his synagogue or church every Sunday should be a better man than the one who does not; but, again, there is no evidence that this is so.

The counselor is very much concerned with love and acceptance, and his love and acceptance of an individual client is not of a limited nature. The client finds in the counselor an individual who may gradually help him to feel, "I *really* am being accepted—me—as I am." Although he may not say it to himself, somewhere in his feelings may possibly come a sense that he is experiencing a non-wanting and a non-demanding love, from a counselor who wants nothing from the client, not even for him to be anybody else other than the person he himself wants to be. This is surely the love that was preached by the great and original men of many religions, and it is the love that must encompass man's morality. But is it the love that man over the centuries has really believed that he was getting from his religion; or did he feel rather that he was being measured and judged, and then possibly forgiven, but not loved? It might even be that what we are saying is: has the Christian, over the centuries, been Christian, and has the Christian Church, over the centuries, been Christian? Has it really practiced what is written in the books? Has it been moral in its concern for the welfare of the individual man, or has it been more concerned with the welfare of the Church as a massive organization? On this point Becker writes:[25]

> It need hardly be argued that the patience involved in spending 50 or 100 or 200 hours with a single individual plus the depth of permissiveness, acceptance and respect involved in the therapist's capacity to be open to the emotional complexities of another person's life provide a new definition of what "caring" for another person means, of what charity or true "love" means, of what creative personal relationships may be, of what the ethical demands of religion upon daily living are. . . . What we have in the evolving field of psychotherapy is a new conception of the ethic of love and a new understanding of the worth of persons that has grown up largely outside of organized religion.

Thus it is probably correct to say that clergymen and counselors are both *concerned* with the morality of man, but that different religions represent different codified systems of morality, whereas the counselor tends to operate on a basis of personal morality. Thus there is no clash of one absolute with another, one truth with another, a clash that surely must occur if the counselor feels and believes that *his* set of truths and moral values is the only *true* set of truths and moral values.

---

[25] Russell J. Becker, *op. cit.*

4. Another question that involves religion and its role in counseling has to do with the extent to which religion stands for authority and the control of human behavior rather than the acceptance of human behavior. There would probably be general agreement that religion has been a major factor in the control of human behavior over the centuries, and probably most people would agree that some form of control has been necessary. If, however, we talk in terms of the development of a free and democratic society, and think of the counselor as one who operates in a free and democratic society, with the rights of the individual paramount in his mind, there will possibly be a clash between the individual and the church trying to impose its controls for what it sincerely believes is the good of the individual. Ostow[26] refers to the various devices by means of which behavior can be influenced, and the way in which organized religion has made use of these devices. One method is imitation, the lives of saints and religious heroes being described in religious literature for the express purpose of inviting imitation. Second is by the communication of affect, accomplished on an individual-to-individual basis, by congregations worshipping together and sharing the same feelings, by religious rituals, by sacred objects, by religious art. Religion also intervenes in the pursuit of instinctual gratification, and thus exercises control by promising rewards for good behavior and threatening frustration and injury for bad behavior. The invoking of obedience is a primary concern of religion, and God and his surrogates are seen as parental figures who require and deserve obedience, while human beings are seen as refractory children. Religion also exploits human susceptibility to signs of vulnerability, and weakness, innocence, humility, and suffering are displayed constantly. Ostow refers too to the encouragement, by religion, of a controlled regression, whereby the individual becomes more compliant to religious authority and hence to religion's effort to control human behavior to the end of social stability.

Thus, as clergymen become more involved in counseling, this is a problem that they must face. If they basically represent an organization that is trying to control human behavior, then they enter the counseling relationship with a handicap, just as does the teacher, the policeman, the judge. All of these may be splendid people, consciously concerned with the improvement of the human lot, but they cannot function completely as counselors because they have other obligations that clash with their basic obligation, as counselors, to the individual.

---

[26] Mortimer Ostow, "The Nature of Religious Controls," *The American Psychologist* 13:571–574 (October, 1958).

5. A final issue of some concern to the problem of counseling and religion is the matter of faith and belief. [A therapist can be thought of as a man of science, whereas a clergyman has been traditionally considered a man of faith.] It might be, however, that in recent years each one has been affected somewhat by the other, with the clergyman beginning to become more of a man of science and the therapist beginning to become more of a man of faith—a movement that has probably been good for all concerned. It should not be unempirical to say that the counselor who does not have faith in the capacity of his client to find an answer to his problems is not going to have much success in helping the client to find the strengths that the counselor does not believe exist. [The person with strength is the one who has faith in himself, and the individual should originally derive this solidarity from his parents. If he does not, the counselor in a school system is probably the next person who will have the job of trying to help him to achieve some confidence in himself; but the counselor himself *must believe* if he is ever to help the client to believe.]

There is no question about the fact that religion has traditionally given the individual a faith, but it may be that this in too many cases was a faith in somebody else's doing something for him and looking after him. Although such a faith may have led to stability of a sort, it gave the individual a strength deriving from his belief in the strength of someone or something else. A responsible member of a free society must come to have faith in himself, and man's greatest rationalization throughout the ages has probably been the statement, "It is God's will." It has been, in a way, a comforting thought, but man would never have pulled himself out of the caves if he had accepted all of his misfortunes as God's will, never to be tampered with. Man became a forward-moving creature when he could really look at himself, blame himself for his own mistakes, and at the same time have confidence in his capacity to move ahead. Thus the counselor needs more faith— faith in the capacity of the individual client actually to learn, with his help, how to move ahead. The clergyman needs the same sort of faith—possibly less of the faith in someone else—and more faith in himself, not just as an arm of the church, but as a human being with human responsibilities toward his fellows that may even transcend his responsibilities toward his church.

On the other hand, all of this need not in any way detract from the therapeutic possibilities of faith, since faith in one's self often comes from faith in someone else. Throughout the ages, miracles have been testimony to the power of faith. It is not so much *what* one believes in, as it is that one deeply *believes* that something positive, or negative, will happen. Converts are sometimes good examples of the power of faith; a Jew who becomes a Catholic may find tremendous new strengths because of his faith in his new religion, while at the same time a Catholic who becomes a Methodist, and a Methodist who becomes a Jew will also find tremendous new strengths in their respective new religions. It is obviously not the religion, per se, that has the effect, but rather what the individual sees in it.

Another example of the power of faith is seen in various experiments, in which placebos containing inert substances have been given to some patients as having curative powers, while the same substance is given to other patients as something that has doubtful curative powers. The general procedure has been used in a variety of ways, and in most cases there is a significant difference in the improvement of those individuals who *have a belief in what they are taking*. The druggist could likely substitute placebos in half of his aspirin bottles, and it would be doubtful if those who benefit from aspirin would benefit any less. An excellent discussion of the power of faith is presented in a paper by Frank.[27]

These then, would appear to be some of the issues that face the counselor who is also involved in religion, either as a lay individual or as a theologian. Organized religion has already moved into the field of counseling, and discussions of issues such as those raised in this section are becoming commonplace in seminaries and schools of theology. Both counseling and religion, and thus, in the long run, man, should benefit from this rapprochement.

SCIENCE AND MAN

Science, like religion, is a rather large word, and takes in a rather broad area. One may wonder whether man, as an existential being, has greater likelihood of growth under the autocracy of religion or under the autocracy of science—or, possibly, in a humanistic, existential society in which man is viewed as the center and the reason for being. Some might ask, of course, cannot humanism and existentialism exist in a religious or a scientific society, or in a society that is religious-scientific, if such a thing is possible? It would certainly seem that in somewhat modern Western times, the Greek society was one in which

---

[27] Jerome D. Frank, "The Dynamics of the Psychotherapeutic Relationship," *Psychiatry* 22:17–39 (February, 1959).

man reached a high point of being. His existential being was realized to a high degree, and he was seen as a reasoning man, living on this earth. In the many dark centuries that followed, however, man all but disappeared. He was viewed by the Christian church as a soul, with faith as the primary asset and reason as the primary sin. His purpose on earth was not to live, but to prepare for the hereafter. With the Renaissance, the light began to shine once again on reason, and science began the movement that is accelerating to this day. Increasingly, however, to science man became a thing, and as medicine graduated from the barber pole to the status of a profession it too saw man as a part of a thing—namely, a disease. The psychologist, striving for status, kept within the scientific fringe, and tended to see man as a problem. It is somewhat intriguing to note that the basic underlying theme of today's "new," "dynamic" "revolution in psychiatry" is the dawning realization that it is just possible that man is a total being after all—he is not a soul, or a thing, or a disease, or a problem.[28] He is a total existential being, and he should be considered as such.

[It would appear, then, that science today tends to view man in a deterministic fashion, and that the humanism that is to be found in the existential view of man is not too visible in the determinism of modern science.] Science tends to be somewhat skeptical about philosophy, and some of the initial reaction to Rogers was probably caused by his raising some very basic questions about the nature of man, questions that challenged some of the basic assumptions of the psychology of Freud and the religion of various denominations.

Psychiatrists and psychologists whose full-time job was a service relationship have not generally functioned as scientists,[29] but until the advent of Rogers, counseling and psychotherapy were generally accepted, professionally, as scientific pursuits. Rogers' careful elaboration, through the years, of Client-centered psychotherapy, however, has brought to the fore the question of the relationship of counseling to philosophy. For many of the more empirical psychologists, philosophy was, and is, a meaningless word, and I have heard Rogers described more than once somewhat scornfully as "nothing but a philosopher." The psychologist as a scientist is by no means all wrong, of course, in being somewhat suspicious of the philosopher, who may sometimes be too prone to accept on "faith." History presents a dismal

---

[28] *See* Karl A. Menninger, *The Vital Balance* (New York: The Viking Press, 1963).
[29] *See* Dugald S. Arbuckle, "Counseling: Philosophy or Science," *Personnel and Guidance Journal* 39: 11–19 (September, 1960).

picture of what happens when people do not insist on asking "why" or on wanting some evidence before they accept a doctrine as the truth, to be followed blindly. The scientists do not want the faith that makes one say, "I know that I can see a new body in the heavens, but my faith says it cannot be there, so it cannot be there." This is the sort of faith that has made religion the enemy of science.

Typical of the negative reaction to the philosophically oriented concept of the counselor are two letters written in reply to an article by Rogers called "Persons or Science? A Philosophical Question."[30] One of the letters states:[31]

> Rogers' article was painful in its implication for those who are now struggling for scientific method to clarify our present state of development. It could be more harmful to the graduate student who is looking for leadership in this field. How can such an integration as Rogers' which reifies science, glorifies mute feelings of ignorance by calling them personal subjective values, and abounds in infallible premises be looked upon as typical of the clinician's or psychologist's viewpoint. . . .

Another letter writer, commenting on the same article, says:[32]

> Comment on Rogers' article is irresistible, yet difficult and saddening. . . . Yet what graduate student could get by with such talk of "the essence of therapy," "the subjective and the objective person," "the scientific versus the experimental viewpoint," etc.? . . . The greatest disservice that Dr. Rogers does for psychotherapy seems to be his insistence on something mystical in the therapeutic process. There is nothing mysterious about the source of this mysticism. . . . There is another trace of mysticism in his seeming naïveté about learning. What happens in therapy, he says, is a type of learning that cannot be taught. . . .

In the article that evoked the above comments Rogers had pointed out some of the basic questions of the scientist as compared with those of the experientialist. The questions asked by the scientist might be as follows:

1. How can you know that this account, or any account given at a previous or later time, is true? How do you know that it has any

---

[30] Carl R. Rogers, "Persons or Science? A Philosophical Question," *The American Psychologist* 10:267–278 (July, 1955).
[31] Letter in "Comment," by George F. Castore, *The American Psychologist* 11:154–155 (March, 1956).
[32] Letter in "Comment," by Richard A. Lake, *The American Psychologist* 11:155 (March, 1956).

relationship to reality? If we are to rely on this inner and subjective experience as being the truth about human relationships or about ways of altering personality, then Yogi, Christian Science, dianoetics, and the delusions of a psychotic individual who believes himself to be Jesus Christ are all true, just as true as this account.

2. Any experience that can be described at all can be described in operational terms. Hypotheses can be formulated and put to test, and the sheep of truth can thus be separated from the goats of error.
3. Implicit in the description (by the experientialist) of the therapeutic experience seems to be the notion that there are elements in it that *cannot* be predicted—that there is some type of spontaneity or (excuse the term) free will operative here. Why not at least *aim* toward uncovering the causes of all *behavior*?
4. Why must the therapist challenge the one tool and method that is responsible for almost all of the advances that we value—namely, the method of science?

In reaction to these thoughts of the scientist, Rogers has the therapist responding as follows:

1. Science has always to do with the other, the object. It never has anything to do with the experiencing me.
2. Because science has as its field the "other," the "object," everything it touches is turned into an object. This has never presented a problem in the physical sciences, but in the biological sciences it has caused certain difficulties. It is in the social sciences, however, that it becomes a genuinely serious issue. It means that the people studied by the social scientists are always objects. In therapy, both client and therapist become objects for dissection, but not persons with whom one enters a living relationship.
3. When science transforms people into objects, it has another effect. The end result of science is to lead toward manipulation. If we know how learning takes place, we use that knowledge to manipulate persons as objects. It is not too strong a statement to say that the growth of knowledge in the social sciences contains within itself a powerful tendency toward social control, toward control of the many by the few. An equally strong tendency is toward the weakening or destruction of the existential person. When all are regarded as objects, the subjective individual, the inner self, the person in the process of becoming, the unreflective consciousness

of becoming, the whole inward side of living life, is weakened, devalued, or destroyed.

4. Is not ethics a more basic consideration than science? In the physical sciences it took centuries for the ethical issue to become crucial. In the social sciences the ethical issues arise much more quickly because persons are involved. But in counseling the issue arises most quickly and most deeply. We should think long and hard before we give up the values that pertain to being a person, to experiencing, to living a relationship, to becoming, that pertain to one's self as a process, to one's self in the existential moment, to the inward subjective self that lives.

This article has been referred to at some length because it poses this problem of the counselor and the scientist as succinctly as any with which I am familiar, probably because its author is the one who has raised this problem as an issue more than any other contemporary counselor. In pondering how to solve this dilemma, Rogers concludes his article by saying "If I am open to my experience, and can permit all of the sensing of my intricate organism to be available to my awareness, then I am likely to use myself, my subjective experience, *and* my scientific knowledge, in ways which are realistically constructive."

Over a decade later, Carkhuff and Berenson expressed much the same feeling when they referred to counseling as an:[33]

> approach that emphasizes a process culminating in a moment-to-moment, fully sharing process—a process born not only of the emotional resources of both parties to the relationship, but also of the deepest and broadest understanding of existing knowledge, and complemented by anything that will work for the client.

Patterson refers to something totally different from this, when, in discussing the counselor's responsibility in rehabilitation, he effectively describes what is all too often thought of as the scientific method in counseling.[34]

> He *determines* the eligibility of clients as clients and the feasibility of their rehabilitation; he *appraises* the client's vocational potential and the probability of his success; he *evaluates* the suitability of various

---

[33] Robert R. Carkhuff and Bernad G. Berenson, *Beyond Counseling and Psychotherapy* (New York: Holt, Rinehart and Winston, 1967), p. 233.
[34] C. H. Patterson, "The Counselor's Responsibility in Rehabilitation," *Journal of Rehabilitation* 24:7–11 (January–February, 1958).

jobs; he *interviews* the client *toward realistic* (as defined by himself) goals; he *develops* a vocational rehabilitation plan with all its parts; he *carries out* the plan, implementing and administering its various aspects; he *makes referrals* to related services. One might ask: What is the client doing all this time? Too often he is literally doing nothing, except what he is told to do by the counselor.

The possible reason that the client is doing nothing is that he is viewed as an object, a piece of material, to be manipulated by the counselor who has the knowledge and the know-how not possessed by the client. Patterson wrote this as a protest against the all too prevalent concept of vocational counseling, but surely it describes frighteningly what happens when the client becomes lost as a person, as a human being, and is treated as one who is not to be accepted and understood as he is, but rather must be manipulated and modified until he becomes another faceless creature.

The function of science is to determine what is, and, as a result of this determination, to predict what might be. Such a scientific prognosis is based on evidence and facts; it is not concerned with values, with what ought to be. Generally this has not been a problem for the medical doctor, since man's physical body is not concerned with what ought to be either. A leg is smashed; there are certain proven techniques which have shown themselves to be superior over others in the mending of the broken leg. The leg does not ask, "Why should I mend?" or "What difference will it make if I do mend?" or "How did I come to get into this situation which resulted in a broken leg?" Thus as long as the medical doctor functioned as a surgeon, he could well be scientific. But as soon as he began to work with the owner of the leg, a human being who had a mind, his organic scientific knowledge began to fail him.

This circumstance probably posed no problem for the earlier medical doctor, who actually knew very little other than how to use his few skills and dispense his few medicines; however, if he was an intelligent individual, concerned with human values, then he probably functioned very much as a philosopher and a counselor. When Freud appeared on the scene with the first studied presentation of counseling and psychotherapy, it was presented as a science, although Freud[35] was probably thinking of the dangers of the "too scientific" approach when he said, "Cases which are thus destined at the start to scientific

---

[35] Sigmund Freud, "Recommendations for Physicians on the Psychoanalytic Method of Treatment," *Collected Papers, II* (London: Hogarth Press, 1925), pp. 326–327.

purposes and treated accordingly suffer in consequence; while the most successful cases are those in which one proceeds, as it were, aimlessly, and allows oneself to be overtaken by any surprises, always presenting to them an open mind, free from any expectations." Freud was no doubt influenced by his medical background, and with his generally anti-religious point of view, it is little wonder that there was not much in the way of a philosophical approach to his psychotherapy. It should be noted, too, that then as now philosophy tended to be related to religion. While this is obviously true, it is not correct to assume, as some theologians do, that in order to be a philosopher one must be allied with a denominational religion. Some of the greatest minds in philosophy have been, and are, looked at with some suspicion by the more orthodox of their brethren, and the narrowness of philosophical breadth of some individuals may be correlated with their concept of religion as a set of dogmas, mostly telling man what not to do.

Thus, in a way, man moved into the study of the psychological and philosophical nature of man, with very little in the way of knowledge about the former, and a general bias or suspicion toward the latter. To some degree this condition still holds today, with the psychologist, as the newcomer in the field, taking on many of the characteristics of the medical profession, even while he strives with might and main to prove that he is different, as obviously he is.

The theologian has not generally been considered to be very scientific, being, rather, a man of faith. As he moves into the therapeutic arena, however, will he tend to become more scientific, and if he does, what will this attitude do to his faith? Although one might agree with Walters[36] that "existential anxiety is properly the object of priestly concern, while pathologic anxiety is the concern of the psychotherapist," I cannot accept the implication that existential anxiety is not the concern of the psychotherapist. This very example might be an excellent indication of the difference between the counselor and the psychotherapist as scientists and as philosophers. If the counselor is concerned only with the pathological, and this is often thought of as the logical concern of the medical doctor and the clinical psychologist, then he can probably remain as the empirical scientist. Once, however, he becomes concerned with the more "existential" aspects of anxiety (and how could one be a counselor without having this concern?), then he has entered the realm of philosophy. Certainly it is not man's

---

[36] Orville S. Walters, "Metaphysics, Religion and Psychotherapy," *Journal of Counseling Psychology* 5:243–252 (Winter, 1958).

acts that cause him stress and strain so much as it is the guilts, the anxieties, the fears, the frustrations that have come to be associated with these acts. An individual is not disturbed by the physical act of masturbation until he learns that it is bad for him to masturbate, or that something dreadful will happen to him if he does; one is not distressed about hating a miserable parent unless one has learned that one is supposed always to love one's parents; one is not concerned about killing one's fellows as long as he knows that they are his enemy and must be killed, and that he will be rewarded for the act. These are surely matters of values that bring in questions about who we are, what we are around for, what is right, and what is wrong. And these are questions for which it is difficult to pose clear-cut empirical answers. One might be scientific in his attempts to evaluate what happens as a result of his counseling, what might happen if he does this instead of that, what happens if a certain variable (difficult to isolate in the social sciences) is introduced, and so on; but how scientific can one be in actual relationship with the client? And this, after all, is what counseling is.

Certainly the organic aspects of counseling can be scientific. Neither the patient nor the medical doctor is in the realm of philosophy when both are involved in a brain lobotomy or an electro-shock, or in the injection of various drugs. Here one can be somewhat pragmatic, and on the basis of statistical evidence, say that he will proceed thus and so with this helpless patient, with no involvement on his part; and he knows the statistical odds that this, instead of that, will happen.

The traditional case study approach, revered by social workers, might also be considered to be somewhat scientific, since it tends to be an investigation of what is, without the personal involvement of the client, and without the personal involvement and intrusion of the values and ideas and thoughts and feelings of the counselor, other than those that are based on evidence. Again, however, when the social worker becomes a counselor, she is no longer working *on* a case, but *with* a human being, and again the question arises. How scientific can you be in the actual close personal relationship between client and counselor, or does the very "scientificness" of one's approach render you less effective?

Many of the techniques and methods of counseling might logically be described as scientific. Thus, diagnosis is an empirical means of assessment of an individual or his problems. The whole process of analysis and interpretation can really be defended only on the basis of a scientific validation of their use. Thus it would probably be correct to say that counseling, as it is allied with or descended from medicine or psychology, will tend to have a strongly scientific tinge; and certainly many counselors, in their descriptions of counseling, would refer to it as "the science of. . . ."

Probably all counselors would agree that if counseling is to have the status of a profession, then its practitioners cannot say that they operate on faith and intuition, or that they need no evidence of whether the client is better or worse off because of their ministrations. This is surely the road to quackery, and counseling already has more than its share of quacks. On the other hand, if one thinks of counseling as basically a human relationship between two individuals, rather than as things the counselor does with or to the client during the relationship, then he enters the realm of the more subjective, the realm of human feelings.

One may wonder, too, if even the science of physics is as exact as it might appear to be, in that while it may be laws of nature that are being examined and studied, it is *man* who is involved in the examining. He sees what he sees, and what he sees depends on certain assumptions and suppositions. As May says:[37]

> Every scientific method rests upon philosophical presuppositions. These presuppositions . . . determine not only how much reality the observer with this particular method can see . . . they are indeed the spectacles through which he perceives, but also whether or not what is observed is pertinent to the real problem, and therefore whether the scientific work will endure. It is a gross, albeit common, error, to assume naively that one can observe facts best if he avoids all preoccupation with philosophical assumptions. All he does, then, is mirror uncritically the particular parochial doctrines of his own limited culture. The result in our day is that science gets identified with isolating factors and observing them from an allegedly detached base—a particular method which arose out of the split between subject and object made in the seventeenth century in Western culture and then developed into its specialized compartmentalized form in the late nineteenth and twentieth centuries.

Much the same thought is expressed by Rogers:[38]

> Science exists only in people. Each scientific project has its creative inception, its process, and its tentative conclusion, in a person or

---

[37] Rollo May, *Existence* (New York: Basic Books, 1961), p. 149.
[38] Carl R. Rogers, *On Becoming a Person* (Boston: Houghton Mifflin Company, 1961), p. 216.

persons. Knowledge—even scientific knowledge—is that which is subjectively acceptable. Scientific knowledge can be communicated only to those who are subjectively ready to receive its communication. The utilization of science also occurs only through people who are in pursuit of values which have meaning for them.

And by Walters:[39]

The therapist usually conceives of himself, and is often represented as the detached, dispassionate scientist. A more realistic view would see him as an involved participant with an interest in the outcome, following a sectarian psychotherapeutic doctrine or combination of doctrines, the selection, and practice of which are tinctured by his own basic philosophy of life.

Einstein was also thinking of the human aspect of science when he wrote:[40]

For the scientific method can teach us nothing else beyond how facts are related to, and conditioned by, each other. . . . Yet it is equally clear that knowledge of what *is* does not open the door to what *should be.*

As was Burtt:[41]

In its most general historical meaning the word "science" simply denotes the search for some orderly pattern in the world around us; its aim is to conquer the contingency and chance that initially confront us wherever and as far as it can. But it is evident when we think about it that this aim, merely as such, is quite ambiguous and indeterminate. Many different kinds of order are discoverable; in fact, everything that one experiences is related with some measurable degree of regularity to an indefinite number of other things. Accordingly, what sort of order is discovered depends primarily on the sort that scientists aggressively look for, and what they look for depends in turn on the further ends which, consciously or unconsciously, they want their explanations to serve.

The question has also been raised whether predictions obtained in the past, based on units larger than the electron, occurred because

---

[39] Orville S. Walters, "Metaphysics, Religion and Psychotherapy," *Journal of Counseling Psychology* 5:243–252 (Winter, 1958).
[40] Albert Einstein, *Out of My Later Years* (New York: Philosophical Library, 1950), pp. 21–22.
[41] E. A. Burtt, "The Value Presuppositions of Science," in Paul C. Obler and Herman A. Estrin (Eds.), *The New Scientist: Essays on the Methods and Values of Modern Science* (New York: Anchor Books, 1962), p. 282.

one could predict the future behavior of an electron or because laws of statistics come into play when we deal with appreciable lumps of matter.[42]

Thus science is neither as exact nor as objective as is sometimes assumed, and the parents of the counselor, science and religion, may not be as far apart as one would imagine.

[42] J. W. N. Sullivan, *The Limitations of Science* (New York: Mentor Books, 1961), p. 72.

chapter 2

DETERMINISM, PHENOMENOLOGY, AND EXISTENTIALISM

The counselor and his counseling is directly affected, in a broad and total sense, by science and religion. The two broad philosophical concepts of both science and religion that have had the most impact on counseling and psychotherapy would appear to be determinism and existentialism, with phenomenology bearing some relationship to each. Many would tend to view determinism as being scientific, and existentialism as philosophic, but I would view them both as being philosophic, since they deal directly with man and his nature.

DETERMINISM

Empirical science is deterministic, and man usually appears as a rather hapless and helpless creature, fated to be buffeted around during a rather miserable existence by various forces—the id, the culture, and others—over which he has no direction and no control. Orwell[1] paints his society as an example of what might happen to man, but Skinner's version is painted objectively as the inevitable fate of man. As a determinist, Skinner assumes that behavior is lawful and determined. As his hero says:[2]

---

[1] George Orwell, *1984* (New York: Harcourt, Brace and Co., 1949).
[2] B. F. Skinner, *Walden Two* (New York: The Macmillan Co., 1948), p. 273.

. . . democracy . . . isn't, and can't be, the best form of government, because it's based on a scientifically invalid conception of man. It fails to take account of the fact that in the long run *man is determined by the state.* A *laissez-faire* philosophy which trusts to the inherent goodness and wisdom of the common man is incompatible with the observed fact that men are made good or bad, and wise or foolish by the environment in which they grow.

This is the world of the empirical scientist, and in it the existential man, the living being, is nowhere to be seen. A counselor with such a concept would probably be acceptant of the statement by Michael and Meyerson[3] that "the phenomenon with which counselors deal, then, is behavior. . . ." They would probably share the apparent lack of concern of the same writers when they say:[4]

Parents, educators and guidance workers make no bones about their earnest intention to create and maintain the "good" behavior that is valued and approved of by the culture and to eliminate "bad" behavior to the maximum degree of which they are capable.

. . . For most of those to whom society entrusts the guidance of others influencing or inducing people to behave in ways that society says are "good" ways is an accepted goal, and the critical question is "How can we 'motivate' a person so that he does behave, 'wants' to behave, and 'enjoys' behaving in good ways?"

The behavioral scientist would probably subscribe to the above, possibly with some variations, but in general he would tend to feel not only that man lives in a lawful and determined world, but that man is a bit of that lawful and determined world. Man is the product of his culture, and any such ideas as freedom and choice are subjective and sentimental myths. Man is "fated" to be what he is, and there is little or nothing that he can do about it. Man becomes another creature, or possibly not even a creature, but rather another thing, to be manipulated and directed by someone to do something for somebody. The manner in which one becomes a manipulator instead of the manipulated is also determined. This is a sort of womb-to-tomb philosophy of life, in which man has given up the risks of freedom, and instead has accepted, as inevitable, the security of the autocrat. In a way, it accepts what Fromm has described as the authoritarian ethic, which:[5]

---

[3] Jack Michael and Lee Meyerson, "A Behavioral Approach to Counseling and Guidance" *Harvard Educational Review* 32:383–402 (Fall, 1962).
[4] *Ibid.*
[5] Erich Fromm, *Man for Himself* (New York: Rinehart & Winston, 1947), p. 10.

. . . denies man's capacity to know what is good or bad; the norm giver is always an authority transcending the individual. . . . Materially . . . authoritarian ethics answers the question of what is good or bad primarily in terms of the interests of the authority, not the interests of the subject.

Hobbs* is another who accepts a psychological version of man's limited and determined "choice." He describes it as follows:[6]

> Within the limitations of the situation . . . the individual scans the situation and tries out various responses symbolically until there emerges into prominence (or until time runs out) a response that fits into his expectations of establishing a more satisfactory state of affairs. He makes the response, or better, the response is made which is most important at the time when the response is required.

Freud would certainly appear to have been deterministic, at least from the point of view of his scientific theories about man and his behavior in which man appeared to be pretty much a victim of forces beyond his control, forces which he spent his life striving to suppress and direct. On the other hand, one has only to read Freud to sense the humaneness of the man above and beyond his theories, a feeling which is borne out by Ludwig Binswanger in his *Sigmund Freud: Reminiscences of a Friendship.*

Some writers have adopted a more relative attitude on determinism which is illustrated by Samler, who, although he wonders whether in the study of man we may have carried over the postulates of a science that may not be applicable to organisms that have self-awareness and self-understanding, states that ". . . a degree of self-determinism is available and should be called upon . . ." and ". . . there is a measure of basic freedom of choice available to the individual, and that within limits he can move in a given direction. . . ."[7]

Fromm describes our movement toward this deterministic concept of society in this way:[8]

---

* Some of the following material, and excerpts in Ch. 3 and Ch. 4 are taken from Chapter One in Dugald S. Arbuckle (Ed.), *Counseling and Psychotherapy: An Overview* (New York: McGraw-Hill Book Co., 1967).
[6] Nicholas Hobbs, "Science and Ethical Behavior," *The American Psychologist* 14:217–225 (May, 1959).
[7] Joseph Samler, "An Examination of Client Strength and Counselor Responsibility," *Journal of Counseling Psychology* 9:5–11 (Spring, 1962).
[8] Fromm, *op. cit.*, p. 248.

Our moral problem is man's indifference to himself. It lies in the fact that we have lost our sense of the uniqueness and significance of the individual, that we have made ourselves into instruments for purposes outside of ourselves, that we experience and treat ourselves as commodities, and that our own powers have become alienated from ourselves. We have become things, and our neighbors have become things. The result is that we feel powerless and despise ourselves for our own impotence. Since we do not trust our own power, we have no faith in man, no faith in ourselves or in what our own powers can create. We have no conscience in the humanistic sense, since we do not dare to trust our judgment. We are a herd believing that the road we follow must lead to a goal since we see everybody else on the same road. We are in the dark and keep up our courage because we hear everybody else whistle as we do.

It would, of course, be extremely naive to assume that one can live his individual life, in the company of other individuals, past, present, and future, without being affected by them. It is equally obvious that, to a great extent, we live in a determined world. But there is a vast difference between the individual who knows and feels and believes that he *is* the master of his fate, that in the long run he *can* choose, even though, because of circumstances, that choice might be infinitesimally small, and the individual who has not this conviction. Man always, even in the most oppressive of circumstances, possesses the small, thin wedge of freedom, and if we feel that education is a process or a means by which one can become what he is, and if we believe that learning is growing into greater depths of freedom and creativity, then the counselor must surely be one who does not accept the concept of the determinism of man. The counselor, we could hope, would be sympathetic to the protest of Scher when he says:[9]

> Life for most of us so-called normals is a constant struggle to scorch the feelings of richest life, to render ourselves unconscious, stamp out individuality, and all in the name of normality. Better a bit more abnormality than this living death we call normal living.

If the counselor is willing to accept the deterministic concept of the nature of man, and of course many are, it would seem that he must be willing to accept his function as that of a manipulator of the individual for the pre-determined "good" of some current body or organization of people who are no longer individuals. It would also seem

---

[9] Jordon M. Scher, "Vivacity, Pathology, and Existence," *Journal of Existential Psychiatry* 3:205–210 (Fall, 1962).

that he must, in some respects at least, be the enemy of the free man, since he is surely saying to man that he has no rights as an individual, that he has no integrity as a human personal entity, that his only purpose is, like the cows in the field, to serve the pre-determined state.

Such a determined counselor would see his function as helping the client to adjust and fit more comfortably into the already established societal order, and in this sense he could probably work as comfortably in a totally autocratic country as in a country with a relatively high degree of individual freedom. He would not likely agree with Carkhuff and Berenson who see society as the enemy when they say:[10]

> Society is not organized to free man's creative potential but rather to maintain or render man impotent or maintain him with minimal potency. . . . In its rules and regulations and in the role models which it presents for emulation, society replaces the individual experience with a collective experience. Man cannot create with someone else's experience.

This, of course, may be considered a somewhat exaggerated point of view, but it reflects my own deep concern for the extent to which the counselor might become the servant of the scientific state, which, rather than helping the individual to grow to greater freedom as an individual, may manipulate and control him so that he becomes a numb and voiceless instrument. The attack on the freedom of the individual occurs, of course, in our current "free" world as well as in our "slave" world, and in that part of the world that is considered to be in somewhat of a limbo. Probably no better example in the United States could be found than in the fact that a citizen who makes use of a constitutional right such as the Fifth Amendment is considered, by some, to be "guilty" of un-Americanism, and this, of course, is a minor restriction compared to those that entrap the individual in some of the new "people's democracies." Americans might well wonder if some of the freedoms that they now possess, freedoms that were written in the books of the past, would be as easily written in the books of today's America. The people of the "free" new nations might well be concerned about the paucity of the guarantees of individual freedom that are being written into their books of the present.

---

[10] Robert R. Carkhuff and Bernard G. Berenson, *Beyond Counseling and Psychotherapy* (New York: Holt, Rinehart and Winston, 1967), p. 219.

PHENOMENOLOGY

Phenomenology is somewhat different from determinism, but is nevertheless related to it in its concept of man and his behavior, and both might be considered to be part of the behavioral science concept of man. Phenomenological psychology is by no means new, and in a way it grew up with psychology. Descartes, in the early seventeenth century, was probably the first phenomenological psychologist, and his approach was simply to study the mind through the immediate experience as it appears at the conscious level. This was, of course, long before the unconscious became postulated as the major aspect of the mind, and the maker of human behavior. A century later, in Ireland, Berkeley was arguing much the same way—that is, that perception is reality, that what we perceive is real. Currently, the phenomenological approach is best described in a book by Combs and Snygg. They refer to the phenomenological approach to psychology as seeking:[11]

> . . . to understand the behavior of the individual from his *own* point of view. It attempts to observe people, not as they seem to outsiders, but as they seem to themselves. . . .

Combs and Snygg would also appear to be deterministic in their phenomenological approach to human behavior, although their means of determinism would not be the same as those of empiricist Skinner or therapist Freud. They say, ". . . let each one of us look at his behavior as we actually see it at the moment we are behaving. At once, we find lawfulness and determinism."[12] And again, ". . . The concept of complete determinism of behavior by the perceptual field is our basic postulate. . . . All behavior . . . is completely determined by, and pertinent to, the perceptual field of the behaving organism."[13]

However, although phenomenologists Combs and Snygg would apparently feel that what one does, what one sees, what one chooses, and where one goes—in fact all human behavior—are determined by the phenomenal or perceptual field, they would not likely say "Yes" to the question raised by Levine and Kantor, who ask: "Is man only a hapless and hopeless organism, a servant to his surroundings and a

---

[11] Arthur W. Combs and Donald Snygg. *Individual Behavior* (revised) (New York: Harper & Row, Publishers, 1959), p. 17.
[12] *Ibid.*, p. 17.
[13] *Ibid.*, p. 20.

prisoner of his passions?"[14] They do say, however, ". . . man [is] neither so completely responsible for his behavior as the first view . . . nor, on the other hand so willy-nilly at the mercy of his environment as the second. . . . He is part controlled by and in part controlling of his destiny."[15] In this regard they agree with Shoben, who is critical of what he feels to be an oversimplification of determinism into a fatalism of events and a neglect of the self-determining quality of human character.[16]

One can be phenomenological in his approach and still be deterministic, whereas one cannot be deterministic and existentialist. There would seem, however, to be little difference between the concept of the phenomenal self and that of the existentialist self, since both operate within the perceptual field. Combs indicates his own feeling of the primacy of the *self* over the *field,* which is, of course, the opposite of the deterministic point of view, when he says, ". . . the perceptual field is usually organized with reference to the behaver's own phenomenal self," and ". . . the phenomenal self is both product of the individual's experience and product of whatever new experience he is capable of."[17] The degree of determinism, however, depends on the primacy of the field over the self. If one feels that one's actions are determined by the phenomenal field, of course, he has no choice, and he can hardly be held "responsible" for his actions. Combs would seem to at least be somewhat acceptant of this deterministic concept when he describes the term "conflict" as:[18]

> . . . a term of external description. It is an outsider's description of what he observes. The behaver himself does not experience conflict. He experiences threat to self maintenance from one or more differentiations of his self which he is unable to accept at that moment . . . may . . . even be described by the individual as "conflict." In so doing, however, he is making an external observation of his behavior just as any outsider would.

May[19] apparently feels no necessity of a phenomenological concept also being deterministic and thinks of phenomenology, the first

---

[14] L. S. Levine and R. E. Kantor, "Psychological Effectiveness and Imposed Social Position," *Personnel and Guidance Journal* 40:418–425 (January, 1962).
[15] Combs and Snygg, *op. cit.,* p. 310.
[16] E. J. Shoben, "New Frontiers in Theory," *Personnel and Guidance Journal* 32:80–83 (October, 1953).
[17] Combs and Snygg, *op. cit.,* p. 146.
[18] *Ibid.,* p. 185.
[19] Rollo May, *Existential Psychology* (New York: Random House, Inc., 1961), p. 26.

stage in the existential psychotherapeutic movement, as being the endeavor to take the phenomena as given. Nor does Rogers, who sees a goal of human development:[20]

> . . . as being a *basic congruence* between the phenomenal field of experience and the conceptual structure of the self . . . the establishment of an individualized value system having considerable identity with the value system of any other well adjusted member of the human race.

Again, however, it is important to note that Rogers's "unconditional acceptance" is not dependent on the "considerable identity" of the value system of the self with the value system of some other "well adjusted" members of the human race. This *may* or *may not* happen, but it is the self, the transcendent self, the self-in-being, that is the determiner of the congruence.

Thus we might even say that it may be that an acceptance of the phenomenological field theory of human behavior might make it easier to see determinism as the fate of mankind; yet, on the other hand, the existentialist accepts the phenomenological concept without in any manner feeling that this means the dominance of the field in which the self operates over the self. In fact, one could hardly hold to an existential concept without being acceptant of the basic phenomenological approach to reality and to the self.

EXISTENTIALISM

There is a more humanistic, a more individualistic concept, however, in which man is viewed as the creator of his culture. It exists for him, not he for it. This existential concept views man as *being;* life is now, and man is as he is. Determinism may say, "You cannot be what you are, you must not be what you are, you simply cannot *be,*" but the existentialist would say that human existence is *being,* and that man is the being who is there.

Existentialism, as a factor in counseling in the United States, is interesting in that it is primarily a European product, and it is philosophical rather than psychological in nature. It is also interesting to note that the current psychological involvement in existentialism has been primarily brought about by practicing counselors and psycho-

---

[20] Carl R. Rogers, *Client-centered Psychotherapy* (Boston: Houghton Mifflin Company, 1951), p. 532.

therapists, rather than by psychological theoreticians. There are also, of course, many differences among the major figures of existentialism, such as Sartre, Heidegger, Kierkegaard, Jaspers, and Frankl, and the range of religion that they represent extends from atheist to theologian.

Here are a few of Sartre's thoughts on existentialism:[21]

> . . . by existentialism we mean a doctrine which makes human life possible, and, in addition, declares that every truth and every action implies a human setting and a human subjectivity.

And again:[22]

> Not only is man what he conceives himself to be, but he is also what he wills himself to be after this thrust toward existence. . . . Man is nothing else but what he makes of himself. Such is the first principle of existentialism.

And again:[23]

> There can be no other truth to take off from than this: I think, therefore I exist.

For Sartre, man is free, man *is* freedom. If we accept the concept that existence does precede essence, then there can be no determinism. Man can be what he will.

The existentialist is anti-deterministic in that he sees the person as transcending both himself and his culture. May describes existential thought in this way:[24]

> Existentialism means centering upon the *existing* person; it is the emphasis on the human being as he is *emerging, becoming*. . . . Traditionally in Western culture, existence has been set over against *essence*, the latter being the emphasis on immutable principles, truth, logical laws, etc. that are supposed to stand above any given existence.

Maslow is speaking about the existential self as he describes his authentic person as one who:[25]

---

21 Jean-Paul Sartre, *Existentialism and Human Emotions* (New York: The Wisdom Library, 1957), p. 10.
22 *Ibid.,* p. 15.
23 *Ibid.,* p. 36.
24 Rollo May, *op. cit.,* p. 16.
25 A. H. Maslow, in Rollo May, *op. cit.,* p. 55.

. . . not only transcends himself in various ways; he also transcends his culture. He resists enculturation. He becomes more detached from his culture and his society. He becomes a little more a member of his species and a little less a member of his local group.

Van Kaam describes a basic aspect of existentialism when he says:[26]

> Existential psychology . . . insists on the free responsibility and the spontaneous creativity which remain the unique and fundamental characteristics of existence. It retains awareness of the limits of freedom revealed by deterministic psychologies, yet it transcends determinism by its recognition of man's radical freedom.

And again:[27]

> The main characteristic of the human existant is that he exists, literally stands out in a world of meaning. Subject and world, self and world are correlatives . . . the counselee is best understood from his personally lived and experienced universe.

Lyons[28] comments that "existentially one always begins within human subjectivity; it is the given framework and source . . . ," and Howland[29] states that "To put it in existential terms, a part of being always consists of 'having been.' 'Having been' is a kind of immortality in that it can never be destroyed or taken away."

The self, the person-in-being as seen by the existentialist, is not one who is subject to empirical prediction and control. Ostow expresses this anti-deterministic concept when he says:[30]

> If religion, then, has failed to obtain complete control over human behavior, if its effect is merely one of influence and modulation, it is not because of poor technique, but because of the ultimate independence of the human spirit and the essential autonomy of the instinctual apparatus.

---

[26] In a statement at an Arden House conference, January, 1963.

[27] Adrian Van Kaam, "Counseling from the Viewpoint of Existential Psychology," *Harvard Educational Review* 32:403–415 (Fall, 1962).

[28] Joseph Lyons, "The Problem of Existential Inquiry," *Journal of Existential Psychiatry* 4:142 (Fall, 1963).

[29] Elihu S. Howland, "Nostalgia," *Journal of Existential Psychiatry* 3:197–204 (Fall, 1962).

[30] Mortimer Ostow, "The Nature of Religious Controls," *The American Psychologist* 13:571–574 (October, 1958).

As does Frankl:[31]

A real person is not subject to rigid prediction. Existence can neither be reduced to a system or deduced from it.

Freedom, is the core of existential thought. This may be expressed as Sartre's consciousness as freedom, Jasper's existence as freedom, Kierkegaard's self as freedom, or Tillich's concept of man as freedom. They are all saying the same thing—that I am free, that where I go and what I do depends on me, not on the forces outside of me or even on the forces which I may have internalized as a part of me. I, and I alone, always have the ultimate choice, and this choice I am free to make. The very fact that one is alive means that he has the potential to be free, but one is never free to live, of course, until he is free to die.

Effectively expressing this point of view is Rogers[32] when he talks of freedom as essentially an inner thing, something which exists in the living person quite aside from any of the outward choice of alternatives which we so often think of as constituting freedom. And Frankl:[33]

. . . everything can be taken from a man but one thing: the last of the human freedoms—to choose one's own attitude in any given set of circumstances.

And Buber:[34]

He who forgets all that is caused and makes decisions out of the depths . . . is a free man, and destiny confronts him as a counterpart of his freedom. It is not his boundary, but his fulfillment.

And May:[35]

No matter how great the forces victimizing the human being, man has the capacity to *know* that he is being victimized, and thus to influence in some way how he will relate *to* his fate. There is never lost that kernel of the power to take some stand, to make some decision, no matter how minute.

[31] V. E. Frankl, "On Logotherapy and Existential Analysis," *American Journal of Psychoanalysis* 18:28–37 (No. 1, 1958).
[32] Carl R. Rogers, "Learning to Be Free," an unpublished paper.
[33] V. E. Frankl, *From Death Camp to Existentialism* (Boston: Beacon Press, 1955), p. 65.
[34] M. Buber, *I and Thou* (Edinburgh: T. & T. Clark, 1937), p. 53.
[35] May, *op. cit.*, p. 41.

This movement toward freedom is also the core of the therapeutic process, and May is really describing the process of counseling when he says:[36]

> The patient moves toward freedom and responsibility in his living as he becomes more conscious of the deterministic experiences of his life. . . . As he becomes more conscious of the infinite deterministic forces in his life, he becomes more free. . . . Freedom is thus not the opposite to determinism. Freedom is the individual's capacity to know that he is the determined one . . . and thus to throw his weight on the side of one particular response.

Although determinism may be a fact of the physical world, it is man who completes that world, and it is man who makes of the world whatever reality he may wish it to become. Thus the growth that occurs in counseling might be considered to be the process, the experience, and the learning to be free. Rogers[37] refers to the qualities of a growth-facilitating or freedom-promoting relationship as being:

1. The element of congruence—the therapist being what he is. The feelings the therapist is experiencing are available to his awareness, and he is able to live them and be them and communicate them if need be.
2. The counselor's warmth and acceptance of what is in the client—the counselor's willingness to be whatever feeling is going on in him at the moment—the unconditional positive regard.
3. Empathic understanding—the sensing and perceiving of the feelings from the inside, as they seem to the client.

Freedom may not be the opposite of determinism, but one does not find the concept of freedom in a deterministic society. The existentialist would feel that the individual may live in a physical world which is, in a sense, determined, but the human individual, the existential self, the spirit of man is not bound by any set of determined chains. Man basically *is* free, and any man can come to learn and to grow and to become the free person he is. This is the purpose of counseling—to help the individual to loose himself from his deterministic shackles and to come to realize and to see what he has always had—choice and freedom.

---

[36] Rollo May, "Freedom and Responsibility Re-examined," unpublished paper given at Chicago, 1962 APGA Convention.
[37] Carl R. Rogers, *On Becoming a Person* (Boston: Houghton Mifflin Company, 1962), pp. 61–62.

Being free is difficult, and one cannot be free without continually running the risk of losing one's person. The struggle to be free, too, is often much more intense and complicated at the inner self-level than is the struggle against overt and obvious forces of oppression. If education results in real understanding, it can widen one's horizon of freedom, and the counselor must be concerned about the extent to which the educational experience helps to free each child.

Although one could hardly be both deterministic and existential, neither can be considered as absolute terms. Skinner might be considered to represent the deterministic end of a continuum, where man would appear to be a nothing, manipulated and controlled for the furtherance of the ends of some faceless and unknown "group," whereas Sartre would represent the other end of the continuum, which would see man as supreme, responsible for his own actions, answerable only to himself. Such a man lives in a world in which things and events have not been determined by him, but the human self is the determiner of the reaction to these events, and the human self will determine the manner and the mode in which man will live and grow and die.

The existential view of man could not accept the concept that the ends might justify the means, since the human person and his world of reality cannot be separate, and they are not tomorrow, but today. Thus the world of work for the child is a very real world of work. However, it is not something in the vague future; it is today. A "stay-in-school" campaign will seem a little pointless to a child, when, from his reality, nothing has changed, either in his view of the world or in its view of him.

Nor would the existentialist help to maintain, for the child, the myth of equality, at least in the sense that every young American child has the same chance. Even worse, of course, is the attendant myth that inequality and difference are synonymous with inferiority. Having a dark skin instead of a white skin, being a male instead of a female, having an IQ of 90 instead of 140, these may be very real outer restrictions, but the existentialist operates with what *is*, and thus, in a very real sense, helps to change what is. Excellence is within the reach of all, but excellence is an inner concept of self, and it is the excellence that is missing in many of our fellows because we have alienated them from us, and we have helped them to come to believe that they are small people. They have not transcended their culture, and their fight against it seems hopeless, because they have become enculturized and entrapped by it.

Choice, too, becomes an inner, relative matter. The child who can be helped to choose really freely to stay in school has immediately removed from himself some of the restrictions and impositions of that school, even though there has been no outer change of either curriculum or teachers. The very fact of choice is freedom, and this immediately changes the outer world around us. Man may live in a determined world, but he is not determined. Choice of a job, after all, in the sense of "I want to be able to choose any job I want" has always been an illusion. It is unfortunate that some American children come to view freedom and choice as "something I can do to someone," rather than as a continuing struggle by one to maintain his integrity and his responsibility. For many children, choice becomes more and more restricted, but the real restriction comes in the sense that they have allowed themselves to come to believe that they are determined victims of a determined world. ⟦Freedom and choice have nothing to do with outer restrictions. They are an inner matter, a matter of the self—of the spirit, if you will.⟧ The man who kills is usually less free than his victim; the man who hates is less free than the man who loves.

In education, the existential view is being expressed by Mathewson,[38] when he says ". . . in the form of education which emphasizes development of individual potential and adaptability, narrow forms of information acquirement may cease to remain at the center of the educational target," and by Murphy,[39] who comments that "the teacher must help the learner to believe in his own individuality and his capacity to learn." Vanderberg[40] also points out an existential view in commenting that education is the process of becoming oneself, that freedom is restricted when pupils are treated as objects, and that the authentic teacher thinks only in terms of the interactions of individuals who have achieved different degrees of becoming themselves.

EXISTENTIALISM, COUNSELING, AND PSYCHOTHERAPY

It is unfortunate, but probably unavoidable, that psychotherapy has come to have certain tags and handles, and these carry with them the

---

[38] Robert H. Mathewson, *Guidance Policy and Practice* (New York: Harper and Row, Publishers, 1962), p. 374.
[39] Gardner Murphy, *Freeing Intelligence Through Teaching* (New York: Harper and Row, Publishers, 1961), p. 47.
[40] D. Vanderberg, "Experimentalism in the Anesthetic Society: Existential Education," *Harvard Educational Review* 32: 155–187 (Spring, 1962).

obvious implication of a "method" of psychotherapy. It is probably just as safe to assume that Rogers was not thinking of a method of counseling when he used the term "nondirective" and later "client-centered" as it is to assume that there is really only one Rogerian, namely Carl Rogers, as there was only one Freudian, Sigmund Freud. What is too often missed is that "client-centered" means literally, not just figuratively, what it says: It refers to a human relationship which is centered on one of the two people involved, the client. And the client-centered concept of man, and of the counseling relationship, is very much an existential point of view. This, it might be pointed out, is not the traditional doctor-patient relationship of medicine, nor is it the somewhat similar doctor-patient relationship as it is carried over into much of the traditional pre-Rogers psychotherapy. In much of this, as in much of counseling today, at best only lip service is paid to the concept that the client must be the central figure and the deciding agent as far as any choice or decision is concerned.

Thus, Gendlin[41] describes three recent modifications in client-centered therapy as: (1) Basic therapist attitudes, rather than any specific "client-centered" behaviors, are essential therapeutic factors. (2) Necessary are genuine spontaneity and expressiveness of the therapist—an undefensive transparency and genuineness of the therapist as the person he is, free of professional or personal artificiality. (3) Experiencing (the preconceptual feeling process) constitutes therapy rather than verbal self-expression.

Thus, philosophically, the existential version of the human relationship appears to be very similar to the therapeutically oriented version of the client-centered counselor. Titus, for example, describes existentialism thus:[42]

> Existentialism is an emphasis on the uniqueness and primacy of existence in the sense of the inner, immediate experience of self-awareness. . . . The most meaningful point of reference for any person is his own immediate consciousness.

This would not appear to differ much from Rogers' description of the counseling relationship:[43]

---

[41] Eugene T. Gendlin, "Client-centered Developments and Work with Schizophrenics," *Journal of Counseling Psychology* 9:205–212 (Fall, 1962).
[42] Harold H. Titus, *Living Issues in Philosophy* (New York: American Book Co., 1959), p. 292 (4th Ed., 1964).
[43] Carl R. Rogers, "Learning to be Free," an unpublished paper.

I launch myself into the therapeutic relationship, having a hypothesis, or a faith, that my liking, my confidence, my understanding of the other person's inner world will lead to a significant process of becoming. . . . I enter the relationship . . . as a person. . . . I risk myself. . . . I let myself go . . . my reaction being based (but not consciously) on my total organismic sensitivity to this other person.

In a somewhat similar manner, May describes the existential approach to pychotherapy:[44]

[I]t is not a system of therapy, but an attitude toward therapy, not a set of new techniques but a concern with the understanding of the structure of the human being and his experience that must underlie all techniques.

This appears to be what therapist Gendlin describes as he writes:[45]

As I express my present feeling and my vague images of what may be happening between us now, a very personal quality enters into my expressions. I am giving words to my ongoing experiencing with him. There is a quality of personal risk and openness in my saying these things. . . . The client lives in a responsive context made up of my person and my openly expressive interaction with him. Yet, his side of the interaction might be quite tentative, implicit, until he wishes to make it explicit as his.

It would thus seem that at least the client-centered counselor and the existential therapist are talking much the same language when they discuss man, the person-in-being, and the counseling relationship, the process of becoming. It should be noted too, that existentialism is primarily a product of European philosophers, rather than psychotherapists. The earlier existentialists, Kierkegaard (some would add Marx and Nietzsche), Sartre, Heidegger, Marcel, Jaspers, Maritain, and Buber, were and are tremendous beings, and while they lived fully, and wrote extensively about man, they wrote from a philosophical and theistic or atheistic point of view. It may be, in a living and experiencing way, they knew more about man than they knew man. Their modern American counterpart might be Tillich, whereas May would appear to be an American therapist who has an existential approach to man. This might be one reason: the older non-therapist

---

[44] May, *op. cit.*, pp. 18–19.
[45] Eugene T. Gendlin, "Client-centered Developments and Work with Schizophrenics," *Journal of Counseling Psychology* 9:205–212 (Fall, 1962).

existentialist had a somewhat more pessimistic and deterministic view-point of man, and the more optimistic point of view of Rogers would appear to be shared more by therapist May than by theologian Tillich. Again, we note here that religion, at least in a formal and doctrinaire sense, appears to be more a part of the make-up of Tillich and Curran, somewhat less of May and Van Kaam, and still less of Rogers.

Thus I would view counseling in a humanistic and existential sense. It is not as pessimistic as existential philosophy would appear at times to be. It is phenomenological in the sense that the phenome-nological world of the individual is the world of reality for the indi-vidual, but it is not phenomenological in a deterministic sense. This forward looking, humanistic, existential concept of man as a free, self-evolving, self-actualizing Being would seem to me to be a good base on which to develop the practice of counseling and psychotherapy.

The basic human problem is never the overt issue, but the individual concept of the degree to which that issue controls and domi-nates and determines his life. Deprivation becomes crucial and con-trolling only when it is of the *inside* as well as of the outside. In a way, the counselor would help the child who is having difficulties in school to make his school experience more real, not in the sense that it would become any more pleasant, but rather that it is there, and he is there, and he can make reality out of the unpleasant as well as the pleasant. One does not have to run; one runs only because one chooses to.

While this counselor may be the provider of information, he is not the sort of counselor described by the United States Department of Labor,[46] who would appear to be overwhelmingly a center of infor-mation. I would question the effectiveness of information in actually helping a child who is already alienated from this group, one who has the outer characteristics of failure, and who has likely come to believe them, one who is hostile and afraid of self. This person, surely, needs the warmth of human closeness; he needs acceptance of him as he is; he needs to live close to security and freedom so that he can eventually come to know, and to believe, that they are within his grasp too.

Nor would he be the sort of counselor described by Federal manpower employment legislation, in which the counselor both "coun-sels" and "selects." One of these actions would seem to contradict the other.

Counseling is not helping the client either to adjust to society or

---

[46] *Counseling and Employment Services for Youth* (Washington, D.C.: Depart-ment of Labor, November, 1962).

to fight it. It is helping him to come to see who he really is, and what he has and what he does not have; what he can do easily, what he can do with difficulty, and what he probably cannot do at all. This might, I suppose, be called self-actualization, and the person comes to see that the struggle for being is really the struggle to have people take him as he is, rather than accepting the culture's version of him. This obviously is a process of living and experiencing; it is a far cry from the rather simple telling and directing, and since it involves a good deal of personal sharing, we can assume that the counselor himself must be one who sees himself as a free human being, one who has personally achieved a high level of self-actualization.

Thus the counselor, as a human being, is more important than the counseling, just as every child and adult is more important as a human being than the title that purports to describe him. Whatever the current status of the client might be, he still has strength, he still has the potential for freedom, and although many things on many fronts must be done to help him, the counselor is the one who, now, *should* be able to offer him what he needs most. This is a close sharing of a human relationship with one who has for him a high regard; one who can offer him acceptance, but one who has no guarantees, no answers; one who can help him to see freedom, but freedom with risk; one who can help him to come to see that freedom and self integrity are the same thing, that they are within the grasp of each of us, and that we are the ones to determine whether we wish to hold them tightly or let them fall.

chapter 3

A PHILOSOPHICAL BASE
FOR COUNSELING

All humans operate from some philosophical base, even though the great majority of humans may do very poorly in attempting to articulate it. Our mode of human operation also obviously reflects our human values. Let us look here, then, at the general question of human values, and I will then present what I at least perceive as the philosophical concepts on which I base my operation as a counselor.

HUMAN VALUES

A value is not something which is apart from a person. Values are human products, and they exist only in a human community. Usually, a "value" implies a judgment, but the same act may have as many different values placed upon it as there are people who are involved in it. A generally accepted cultural concept is that certain "values" are better than others, and an equally acceptable concept is that values can, and should, be taught. The questionable assumption here is that the teacher somehow is the possessor of a value which is not possessed by the learner and that it is the function of the teacher to teach this better value (his) to the learner, who either does not have this value or has a "wrong" one. This concept detaches the value from the person so that just as one can be taught how to drive, one can be "taught" morality, virtue, and courage. This concept also makes possible the widely accepted tenet in counseling that "I like him but I don't like what he is doing." It obviously implies that the counselor should, and must, have as part of his value system a feeling of the rightness of his ways *for others*, an obligation to impose this rightness on others, and an assumption that this rightness can be imposed (taught) to others. Although these assumptions are questionable from an existential point of view, they are, nevertheless, widely held.

Mueller,[1] for example, has indicated her feeling that not only can one teach ethics, but the "counselor" must teach ethics as he "counsels." She may be describing a Dean of Women, but hardly a counselor[2] when she says:[3]

> In discipline the counselor is teaching emotional stability, moral judgment, self reliance and self control. . . . The balance between force and sympathy is achieved by first exhausting every resource of counseling and persuasion and only then turning to punitive action.

There would appear here, again, to be a concept of a detachment of the human act from the person, the idea that values are some form of appendices that one "learns" by being taught. There is an absence of the feeling that values, being a part of the person, can only come through an experiencing and a living and a human relationship. Close human contact with a patient and compassionate person may help another person to free himself so that he, too, may move in the direction of patience and compassion. He may thus "learn," from a counselor, from a teacher, from a friend, but he has not been taught. History would surely bear witness to the futility of the attempt by one person to "teach" his value system to another person.

Most counselors would probably agree with Samler[4] when he says, "It ought not to be irreligious to propose that if value commitment and promulgation work in bringing about lasting client change in desirable direction then it provides its own justification." The questions

---

[1] Kate H. Mueller, "Theory for Campus Discipline," *Personnel and Guidance Journal* 36:302–309 (January, 1958).
[2] See Mary Elizabeth Reeves and Dugald S. Arbuckle, "The Counseling Attitudes of Deans of Women," *Personnel and Guidance Journal* 41:438–441 (January, 1963).
[3] Kate H. Mueller, *Student Personnel Work in Higher Education* (Boston: Houghton Mifflin Company, 1961), pp. 356–357.
[4] Joseph Samler, "An Examination of Client Strength and Counselor Responsibility," *Journal of Counseling Psychology* 9:5–11 (Spring, 1962).

that do remain, however, are "what value commitment?" and "what desirable direction?"

Ferree[5] also leaves these questions unanswered when he raises what would appear to be a contradiction, when he calls for "a clear commitment on the part of the counselor to certain values which he in turn seeks to foster in his counselees . . . ," indicates that the counselor is to "promote in his counselee what is not already there," and states that "it may involve deliberate effort on the part of the counselor to change the basic nature of the person." Can the counselor actually have such values as "tolerance and respect for others and a capacity to listen well," and at the same time seek to foster values in his client? Can one be acceptant while he is seeking to eliminate from the individual certain values that are not of the "right" kind? It may be, of course, that Ferree, as an educational philosopher, has a somewhat hazy idea of the unique function of the counselor, and sees him somewhat as a classroom teacher. The counselor who has not moved well along the road of psychological freedom himself may have a difficult time in helping another to traverse a road that is strange to him, and the individual who sees his role as that of practically forcing his particular value system, teaching his values, if you will, to the client, is surely showing a most limited version of acceptance. The autocrat, after all, could agree totally with Samler's and Ferree's words!

In a way, Lowe has provided an answer to this question when he says:[6]

> We conclude that differences in value orientations cannot be resolved, each orientation having adherents whose beliefs should be respected. We suggest that each counselor have an understanding of the values both of himself and others and that his values be known by all who are personally affected by his professional behavior.

Simply by being the person he is, in a close human relationship, the counselor is making obvious some of his own value patterns. The fact that he is always acceptant of generally unacceptable material, the fact that he does not criticize, measure, or evaluate, the fact that he centers his complete attention on the client and never on himself, the fact that he shows unwavering patience and kindness—these are surely a display of the person, and are almost certainly transmitted in some

---

[5] George Ferree, "Psychological Freedom as a Counseling Objective," *Counselor Education and Supervision* 3:13–18 (Fall, 1963).
[6] C. Marshal Lowe, "Value Orientations—An Ethical Dilemma," *The American Psychologist* 14:687–693 (November, 1959).

degree to the client, who, more likely than not, will hold the therapist in trust and admiration. This situation is well described by Rosenthal:[7]

> It may be that the therapist communicates his values to the patient in many unintended, subtle ways, even when trying to avoid doing so. The patient, who is often sensitized to the therapist's every word and inflection, may be able to receive these communications, and because of his trust, admiration, and respect, may permit himself to be influenced by them.

Somewhat along the same line, Wolff[8] reported that while only 6 percent of a group of therapists who were being studied regarded change of values as a goal in therapy, 48 percent believed that therapy did directly transmit or develop value concepts in the patient.

Williamson expresses a deterministic feeling of human limitation when he appears to view the counselor as one whose outside-of-me values control him, rather than one whose inner self is expressed in terms of his values:[9]

> Rather is counseling . . . value-oriented and not open-ended both regarding goals sought through aspirations and strivings of both counselor and student within their counseling relationship.

This concept also implies a striving by the counselor to achieve for the client something, some answer, some right path or goal that is external to the client, and possibly to the counselor. This is almost like the counselor's cheating on his income tax returns and then trying to convince the client who has been cheating on exams that the virtue of honesty is something that he should practice. Actually, this "virtue" is real for neither client nor counselor, and it is unlikely that any change is going to take place in either one. On the other hand, we might hypothesize that if the counselor is a "no-cheating" sort of fellow, in his living-being, regardless of any words, then he will see no point in trying to press this on the client. And the client, in turn, might possibly internalize, or at least let stir around inside him, the idea that this might be something worth incorporating so that it becomes a part of his being. People who believe feel no particular pressure to convince

---

[7] D. Rosenthal, "Changes in Some Moral Values Following Psychotherapy," *Journal of Consulting Psychology* 19:431–436 (December, 1955).

[8] W. Wolff, "Facts and Value in Psychotherapy," *American Journal of Psychotherapy* 8:466–486 (July, 1954).

[9] Edmund G. Williamson, "Value Orientation in Counseling," *Personnel and Guidance Journal* 36:520–528 (April, 1958).

others that they should believe the same way. It is likely that the evangelist is very concerned with who he is and where he is going, and that this is why he continually tries to convince others that they should follow him. He neither respects nor trusts the other to find his own right way. If his religion includes compassion and gentleness and love toward his fellow man, he spends his time preaching it rather than practicing it.

The concept that one can separate a person from his values is a very common one in counseling. It is almost as if one could view a human act and the person who commits it as two separate entities. One might feel that the act of robbery, the taking away of another person's belongings so that one can further his own interests, is questionable. But when a counselor is relating with another fellow human who has committed the act of robbery, he cannot divorce the person from the act. Part of the person is the fact that he has committed a robbery, and since we accept the client as he is, the unrelated fact of robbery, or what the counselor may think about it, has no relation to the therapeutic interaction whatsoever. It is the person, all of him, with whom we are concerned, and the various bits and pieces, by themselves, mean nothing. The existential counselor, however, would not view acts at any time as detached from human beings, so that a question such as, "Well, do you mean that you don't think that robbery is bad?" really isn't a question because robbery, per se, really doesn't mean anything. It is only when it becomes a part of an individual's human behavior that it means something, and the counselor, being concerned with the person, is not particularly aware of the "goods" or the "bads" of the individual's actions.

This is probably also why practically every act that is labeled "bad" by someone is labeled "good" by someone else. Robin Hood's thieving was considered wonderful by those who were the recipients of his loot, but not by those from whom he stole! Americans think affectionately of the "robber barons" who were the ancestors of some of our most illustrious current figures, political and otherwise!

Patterson[10] expresses this somewhat separatist, and nonexistential, point of view when he states that "while the counselor may judge the attitudes, standards or actions of his client in terms of his own or prevailing standards, he does not judge the client himself. . . ."

Shoben[11] also expresses the "doing something to somebody" atti-

---

[10] C. H. Patterson, *Counseling and Psychotherapy: Theory & Practice* (New York: Harper & Row, Publishers, 1959), p. 72.
[11] E. J. Shoben, "New Frontiers in Theory," *Personnel and Guidance Journal* 32:80–83 (October, 1953).

tude when he comments that "the field is committed to the development of responsible individuals capable of maintaining and advancing a democratic society." The existentialist would be more concerned with helping the individual to come to be able to release and use the potential that he has, and he would have less concern about whither the "inner man" would go. He would help the person to grow to freedom, and while a product might be a "democratic society," this would be somewhat meaningless, since in today's world we have earnest people who are sure they have "democratic societies" in such countries as China, Yugoslavia, Ghana, and Russia. Shoben, of course, means *his* concept of a democratic society, and doubtless many of us would share this concept very closely with him. [But can we not, at least in a counseling relationship, operate on the assumption that the client who has learned to be free will help to develop a society in which all may live their lives to the utmost, with respect for the rights and the integrity of their fellows, since they respect their own rights and integrity?]

[While we could agree that the counselor might as well admit that he has his own values, it is important to distinguish between those values that are a part of the make-up of the inner self of the counselor, and are shown in his patience, his compassion and his acceptance of the client, and values of judgment and evaluation. The counselor who feels that "robbery," per se, is "bad," is not actually very far removed from the counselor who feels that the client who has robbed is "bad," who in turn is not too far removed from the individual who feels that the person who has robbed is bad and should therefore be punished. While such individuals may be being existential in the sense that they are saying, "You, and you alone must be responsible for your deeds," they are not existential in the sense that they are not getting close to, or being understanding of, the existential self.] They may be observing it, but they are living it.

Curran expresses more of a trust in the person-in-being when he indicates that we should seek a personal integration that is also an integration with the whole civilization that has produced us. This might then:[12]

> . . . free us from the more recent, possibly Kantian, ethical concept that all personal values must be imposed from without which has come not to mean either by parents, society or even more threatening and

---

[12] Charles A. Curran, "Some Ethical and Scientific Values in the Counseling Therapeutic Process," *Personnel and Guidance Journal* 39:15–20 (September, 1960).

dangerous, by the state. It would restore again the possibility of starting out . . . on a thrilling personal pursuit of oneself in a fierce and independent search for reasonable self-values and yet allow that one would ultimately come by this process, not to violent rebellion and anarchy, but to ancient and secure traditional values.

This might represent a somewhat theistic existential point of view, in that while Curran trusts the individual to determine for himself how he will move and when and where he will move, he believes that there are, somehow, already established answers and values that the individuals will come to find. The individual does not develop and create his own answers, but moves toward pre-established answers. In this case, in Curran's mind, these are likely established by some deity or God. Curran also indicates the interesting concept that somehow the "ancient" values are more "secure," and, we can assume, somehow better, than more recent values. Were the ancient and traditional values of the Romans more secure, and better, than some of the values that were being advanced by a heretic named Christ? Were the ancient and traditional values of the Greeks more secure than those of the heretic Socrates? The nontheistic existentialist would probably feel, with Curran, that the individual must find his own way. With Curran, he would have faith that the individual could find his own way. But he would differ with Curran in that he would have no preconceived concept of where the individual might end, or what his values might become. They might be like those of yesterday, or they might be like those of tomorrow, but man lives his life, and creates his values. He never goes back to what once was, although he may become like what once was.

In a sense, Curran would seem to have his "man" attempting to discover pre-existent truths and values, to somehow become congruent with what already is, and in this sense, of course, he is expressing the view of determinism. For him, what is, was, but for the existentialist, what is, is. Life is today, now, not yesterday, and we move away from yesterday, not toward it, even though we may yearn for this return to the womb.

One cannot discuss values and freedom, and living, without also taking into consideration that closely allied experience that eventually comes to all—death. The free man of the existentialist, the human being who is never merely a victim of a pre-determined culture, the person-in-being who is the maker of his values, being free to live, is also free to die, and it would seem that no person can really be free to live if he is afraid to die. Feifel expresses this feeling when he comments that:[13]

> . . . the willingness to die appears as a necessary condition for life. We are not altogether free in any deed as long as we are commanded by an inescapable will to live. . . . Life is not genuinely our own until we can renounce it.

Sartre relates freedom with death when he says, "The very act of freedom is therefore the assumption and creation of finitudes: if I make myself, I make myself finite and hence my life is unique."[14]

It is ironic, and sad, that one of the basic feelings that many individuals learn from their "religion" is fear, particularly fear of death. Feifel,[15] for example, found, in a study of his patients, that the religious person, as compared with the nonreligious person, was personally more afraid of death. There must be untold millions of Christians who spend much of their lives trying to guarantee their entry to Heaven, but, since they feel that they are not the ones who control their destiny, are never quite sure whether God is approving or disapproving. They thus seek as much as they can in the way of assurances that there is a Heaven, and that they, and a few of their chosen fellows, are the ones who will be there. The old and hoary joke about each group in Heaven having to be segregated behind walls so that they might not discover that there are other peoples in Heaven too is not a joke to many. Many "devout" Christians cannot accept doubt and uncertainty as a part of their religion. They must know, particularly about the rewards and punishments of the hereafter, and this might logically tend to make them somewhat self-centered in their actions toward others. The one who does not know about the future, and will, with certainty, face this uncertainty, even to the point of dying to defend a fellow human, is indeed showing a far higher level of altruism and compassion.

The existential man would live his life of freedom and responsibility and would not have to "know" about what happens after death. If his reason conflicted with some religious fairy stories, he would not be too disturbed since his life is now, and he would live this the best he could. The rest he could accept, without fear, as the unknown.

---

[13] Herman Feifel, in Rollo May (Ed.), *Existential Psychology* (New York: Random House, Inc., 1961), p. 71.
[14] Jean-Paul Sartre, *Existentialism,* Translated by B. Freeman (New York: Philosophical Library, 1947), p. 545.
[15] Feifel, *op. cit.,* p. 68.

Not all would agree that this is a valid picture of the existentialist. Kaufmann, for example, feels that not one of the existentialists has grasped the most crucial distinction that makes all the difference in facing death, and he quotes Nietzsche in *The Gay Science:* "For one thing is needful: that a human being attain his satisfaction with himself—whether it be by this or by that poetry and art; only then is a human being at all tolerable to behold."[16] It would appear, however, that this is just what the existentialist does believe: The person is as he is; satisfaction must come from within; man is able to be free; man is able to choose and so, to himself, becomes "tolerable to behold." Whether he is tolerable to others is of secondary importance. He must first be tolerable to himself, and it would surely seem that most people who are intolerable of their self are the ones who find others intolerable. One person becomes a heretic to another person because that person has not yet learned the life of the free man and is thus afraid.

For the counselor, then, several points might be noted on this question of human values:[17]

1. It is surely obvious that one can hardly be a human being without values. Indeed, the values of the person *are* the person, although one may argue that at any one moment the values that a person is exhibiting are not necessarily the authentic values of that person. But for the moment they are his values, and they are the best answer to the question, "Who is he? What is he like?" It is interesting to note that one of the earlier criticisms of the so called "non-directive" counseling of Carl Rogers, was that the very concept of non-direction by the counselor meant that the counselor possessed no values. One may wonder about the values of an individual which are such that another person who says, "I do not direct or advise or tell the other how to live his life" is assumed to possess no values whatsoever! The very statement of deep feeling of the lack of either ability or right to direct the way of life of another is a very definite indication of a value that is a part of the individual. So, of course, is the feeling that one could not have any values if you were not quite certain about how others should live their lives!

2. Thus being alive, being a member of the human species, being one of the homo-sapiens means that one does possess values, and the rather simple question of "Where do these come from?" is not quite as

---

[16] Walter Kaufmann, *The Faith of a Heretic* (New York: Doubleday and Co., 1961), p. 383.
[17] *See* Dugald S. Arbuckle, "Values, Ethics and Religion in Counseling," *National Catholic Guidance Conference Journal,* 13:5–17 (Fall, 1968).

simple as it appears. To a tremendous degree, of course, our values are the values that we have learned, and we usually learn them from the people and the organizations who have most control and most influence over us. Only recently a clergyman took some offense when I commented that for the vast majority of us, our race, our nationality, our sex and our religion were but accidents of birth. He had no concern about the first three, but he was bothered by the thought that religion too, might be no more than an accident of birth. And yet, was it any more than an accident of birth that Emmanuel Ginsburg, a Jew living in Germany in the 1930's, was in a few years to die in a concentration camp at Dachau, his sole sin being that he happened to be born of Jewish parents, while Fritz Brandenburg, the blond Aryan who beat him to death, secure in the confidence of his own superiority, had as his sole and doubtful asset the fact that he was born of Christian parents? It was an accident of birth that one was a Jew and one was a Christian, but it was cultural conditioning that made it possible for the German people, and for Fritz Brandenburg, as one of them, to feel pleased about the murder of Emmanuel Ginsburg, and millions of his fellow Jews. It is a rather grim and ghastly indictment of the values of at least some Christians when one remembers that some German Christians suffered real guilt feelings over the eating of meat on Fridays, but their sleep was not at all disturbed by the murder of the Jewish people. Closer to home, many American Christians have calmly accepted their role as the superior ones, although their values are such that some Christians are assumed to be more superior than others. Some probably feel that one is not a really *real* Christian unless one is a Catholic, or maybe a Baptist, or maybe a Seventh Day Adventist. Then of course, color of skin is sometimes important, and until recently the white Christian felt that he was just a little bit better a Christian than his brother whose skin was dark. Then too, our Christian values have showed in our attitude toward male and female Christians. Women have minimal power in most organized Christian churches, and while our values wouldn't let us say so, we have tended to regard them as second class citizens. Imagine the shock of some of our brethren if, on getting to heaven, they were welcomed by a God who had a dark skin and who was obviously a female! We, at least, however, have the virtue of consistency in that the devil is usually portrayed as a light skinned male!

All of this, of course, is intellectual madness. And indeed, our conditioning has often moved us in the direction of madness. The dreadful and the bestial things that man has done to man over the centuries he has learned to do, but he was not destined to do. And the question must be: how much do we allow ourselves to be the victims of our culture? To what extent are we passively acceptant of the dogma of yesterday as being the light of tomorrow, which will surely mean that there will be no tomorrow. The blind unthinking irrational obedience to dogma, religious or no, can lead to nothing but destruction. Aquinas solved, or at least quietened for the time, the struggle between faith and reason, with faith taking precedence over reason, but that struggle is intensified today. For anyone who views himself as religious, a crucial question must be, "Can I not be faithful and rational too? Can I not be faithful and ask 'Why?' Can I not be faithful and at the same time disagree with something that was said long ago?" Increasing numbers of individuals, lay and clerical, are answering these questions in the affirmative, but we cannot have it both ways. We cannot say, "Yes, I believe in change, but I want things to stay in the same comfortable way they have always been." If we believe in change, then we have no certainty as to what lies on the other side of the door that we are slowly opening.

Lee and Pallone,[18] for example, in discussing the clash between counseling concepts and the Catholic concept of morality, make the comment that, "Nowhere can this clash be more clearly seen than in the case of the client whose problems are materially (as contrasted to formally) sinful (e.g. masturbation)." The word "sinful," however, is a human value judgment, whereas masturbation is a physical act. Must the Catholic counselor, for ever and ever, operate on the belief that masturbation, no matter by whom, under what circumstance, is an act of sin? The psychotic patient, who, for quite obvious psychological reasons, openly masturbates in front of a group of visiting experts; the little child, who in his exploring, discovers how to have a pleasant physical feeling, and thus masturbates; and the disturbed girl, who after every sexual encounter with a man, can only find sexual satisfaction by masturbation—*must* the counselor actually believe that all of these people are guilty of sin? Then, too, one might wonder what leeway one has in a definition of sin. Curran,[19] for example does not think of sin as worthlessness, but rather as the absence of desirable goodness. Even here, of course, there is judgment, and it is someone

---

18 James Michael Lee and Nathaniel J. Pallone, *Guidance and Counseling in the School* (New York: McGraw-Hill Book Co., 1966), p. 99.
19 Charles A. Curran, "Religion—Its Relation to Counseling" in Dugald S. Arbuckle, *Counseling and Psychotherapy: An Overview* (New York: McGraw-Hill Book Co., 1967), pp. 62–63.

else who has made the blanket judgment that a certain act does not indicate "desirable goodness." Curran,[20] too, shows an acceptance of what might be described as both a religious and psychological dogma when he states that "There is in man the mystery of evil: a tendency toward disorder and even viciousness." It is not so much that such dogma is right or wrong, it is simply that judgments have been made without empirical evidence one way or the other. In the first example a descriptive term is given to a physical act; in the second example a statement is made about human behavior. Since such statements are accepted by some, not by others, cannot the counselor at least be open, and not be compelled to believe? How can the counselor communicate to the client "You must determine the meaning of life for yourself," if he cannot allow himself this freedom, but feels, "I must believe, because I was told it is so."

Just as nationalistic and racial dogma teaches superiority, and thus the inferiority of those of other nationalities and races, so often does religious dogma teach the inferiority of others. If the Catholic Church is the sole possessor of "absolute truth," it is very clear that the majority of mankind does not possess the truth. Although the scholarly theologian might not agree, many Jewish children, I believe, are taught from the *amidah,* as part of their religious dogma, that they are the selected, if not the chosen people. The Mormons are taught that black people represent those unhappy individuals who are paying for their sins, and they can thus never become members of the ruling circle of the Mormon church. These are beliefs which deny to others the right of individual dignity and freedom. They are representative of the conditioned value structure of the individuals who, against their own reason and rationality, feel that they *must* hold to them in order to be true to the faith.

3. But the question then arises: are these values, these conditioned products, the real basic human values of the particular human being? It would seem reasonable to assume that the more one learns that he cannot be who and what he is, the more artificial he becomes as a person. His whole being exemplifies a lack of congruence; he cannot be open and spontaneous and honest. His life becomes, possibly, somewhat like the beginning counselor who cannot let himself go, and must carefully surround himself with methodology and technique. He will say that he does what he does because he is thus and so. There is a high level of security in this procedure, since one never

<hr>

[20] *Ibid.*

need accept responsibility for what one does. The price one pays, of course, is heavy, and the face of such a person does not reflect the inner man, but is rather the mask which has been molded in the desired contours: desired, that is, by others rather than by the self.

A clash will come if this inner self rebels against the conditioned front, and very often this is what the client is saying when he comes to see the counselor. "I am not who I wish to be, and I want to do something about it." As Johnson[21] says, "Cultural values may, however, contradict real experienced values, and thus the individual is thrown into conflict." The struggle is one in which the person tries to become more trusting of this own experiencing, his own feelings; the meanings he gives to actions and situations are closer to being *his* meanings rather than those of someone else. Such a person is open to continual change, and he has no need to hold blindly to any values. In this sense he does not have a value *system*, because there is no system. His values are open to change as he lives and experiences, deeply, his life. He is free to allow his experiences of living to modify and change his self, and he has no preconceived concepts into which his experiences must fit. There is thus honesty toward self, rather than alienation from self, and individual freedom becomes a reality.

SOME PHILOSOPHICAL CONCEPTS

Each counselor, as a member of the human species, should ask of himself, "What are the philosophical concepts on which I base my operation as a counselor?" This is the answer which I would give to that question:

1. A basic tenet is that man is the determiner of the culture. This in no way detracts from the obvious fact that man is, to a tremendous degree, a conditioned product of his culture. But man came first, and it is man who produces the culture. Cultural change does not just happen; it is a human product. Thus man *can* be one who has some say in his fate, or he *can* be one who, willy-nilly, accepts his role as the product of a kindly or vengeful culture. With the more pious this culture is often seen in terms of a supernatural deity (it is God's will), whereas with the more secular it is simply seen as fate (that's the way it is). A less determined and more existential view would see man as having to accept his responsibility of choice and decision. Attitudes

---

[21] Ernest L. Johnson, "Existentialism, Self-Theory, and the Existential Self," *Personnel and Guidance Journal* 46:53–58 (September, 1967).

toward race and religion and sex and ethnic background may mean that one person is the recipient of more human abuse than is another, but this does not mean that that individual cannot have some say in how he feels and what he does about that which others do to him. No human can ever, with total accuracy, say, "I did it because I had to. . . ." Somewhere along the line one has to agree that a choice was made, and in this case the choice was to do what "I didn't want to do"; it is never accurate to say straightforwardly that "I didn't want to do it." One never has to do what one does not wish to do; it is very simply a question of what penalty one is willing to pay for doing what one wishes to do. A more accurate statement than "I didn't want to do it," would be "I was unwilling to pay the price for doing what I wanted to do, and for this reason I am doing what I am doing." Very often, of course, the price that one refuses to pay is minimal—the loss of a pay raise, getting a low grade instead of a high grade, criticism instead of praise from one who might have been a friend; occasionally the price may be major, such as jail or death.

Such a philosophy, of course, makes life more Spartan, since one cannot easily rationalize one's behavior toward one's fellows. When one comfortably says, "Well, I can see that I dislike my white (or black) brothers because of my conditioning," the existential reply is: "So what? What are you going to do now? Are you going to keep on disliking them because of your conditioning, or are you going to ask yourself how stupid can you be? No one *has* to dislike a someone just because of a difference in the color of his skin. Are you going to accept the responsibility of either staying the way you are, or making some change in your attitude? You *do* have a choice. What is it going to be?"

Man, then, cannot excuse himself because of a harsh Nature or a capricious God. He is born with certain assets and certain liabilities, and one must be cautious about assuming that what appear to be many assets and liabilities, or vice versa, are actually so. It is not what one has that is the major determiner of the future for the vast majority of mankind, but rather what one does with what one has, and this ability to deal with one's life is an indication of a high level of individual freedom.

2. If one is nothing but a victim of the culture, to be tossed hither and thither by the whims of nature, then any concept of individual freedom is, of course, simply a happy illusion. On the other hand, if one conceives of human freedom as an individual matter, to be determined by each individual, then total freedom, for each human

being, is a real possibility. It is a goal which may never be achieved, but it is a worthy goal toward which one might dedicate his life. When I am the one to determine the extent to which I am free, then the oppressor, either subtle or manifest, can never chain me, even though I may be shackled. The other may have the external power to kill me, but never quite to totally destroy me.

Children soon learn from their parents, from the school, and from the church, that freedom is an external matter which is determined by someone else, and that they thus have no control over their individual freedom. It would seem to be of crucial importance that the school, while accepting the legal and practical dependence of the child, helps him to develop individual freedom within the very real limitations which surround him. A child may be forced to experience a certain educational curriculum, but he does have the freedom to affect, in some way, just what he gets out of that educational experience. A child may have little or no control over the kind of teacher he happens to have, but he can control his reactions to that teacher, and the individual freedom of some children is such that they can actually learn from a poor teacher. Such a child is one who is having some effect on what is learned, rather than being totally dependent on the teacher, and thus, of course, learning little or nothing from a poor teacher.

The freedom, then, to become, the freedom to be. This is the real freedom, and for this, of course, the individual must be willing to pay a price. In some societies, such as that of the United States, the price the individual must pay is often quite modest, because other generations have already paid a heavy price. But even in the United States, and other so-called "free" countries, one must be willing, if necessary, to pay a very high price for the maintenance and strengthening of one's individual freedom. Such a person is free to live and free to die, he is free to love and free to hate, he is free to experience sorrow and free to experience ecstasy. Despite all the uncontrollable factors which push in and upon him, he is the one who determines the extent to which he is free, and in this way, of course, he will always be free. He is the maker of the culture, not its victim.

3. The worth and the dignity of the human individual is an obvious addition to these two basic tenets. The government is the servant and the organized voice of the people, not its master. In a free society one obeys a law simply because this is a rule or a regulation of human behavior which the majority of the citizens have found to be desirable. In a truly free society there will obviously be a minimum of such laws, since a truly free individual will have no need to impose

himself on others or do things which will be obviously destructive to a large number of his fellows. The more autocratic the society, the more laws that are necessary to control the population, and the mark of a decaying free society is the increase in the number of laws, usually stressing what one cannot do.

Even in a relatively free society such as that of the United States, the individual still must come first. In a sense, in a free society the individual owes the state nothing, nor, of course, does the state owe him anything. In the long run the law of one's conscience must take precedence over the law of the land, and in the United States today we see an increasing number of responsible citizens, who have contributed much to their fellow man, deliberately violating a law of the land, because they cannot, in all conscience, obey it. When this happens, all those who value individual freedom should be concerned, and the crucial question is not so much how can one stop the dissenter, but rather, is something possibly wrong with some of the laws of the land, in that responsible and caring citizens openly defy them and break them.

For the counselor and the teacher this tenet simply means that the child comes first. The school is there for the benefit of the child; its purpose is to serve him, not to enslave him. The only reason for the existence of a school is the children who populate it. The positive development of each individual child, as an individual, should be the goal of the school, rather than the mass production of a number of human robots, which is the necessary goal of any school in an autocratic society.

4. Philosophically, it would seem that we can make more out of our lives, that we can live our lives more fully, if we live in a world of today rather than a world of yesterday or tomorrow. For some humans, life would appear to be predominantly based on what has gone, and we hear much about "how it used to be," or "the good old days," or "now, when I was young." All of this is understandable, but it is wasteful of life, since what is gone *is* gone, and, in a way, this living in yesterday is a culturally acceptable form of schizophrenia. It is a running away rather than a running back. It is a refusal to face the only real issues of living—namely the issues of now and today. The individuals who live for tomorrow are much the same, and their life today is as if there were no today, only a tomorrow. A powerful motivater of this attitude has been the Christian religion. It has tended traditionally to place more importance on life in the next world rather than life in the only world we will know during our lifetime—the one

we live in now. The Hebrew prophets would appear to have been more concerned with the life of man on earth today than were the Christian apostles, and in the some 2,000 years of the Christian church, it has hardly shown a consistent concern with the lot of man on this earth, today. Indeed, it has frequently allied itself with a corrupt and autocratic state to impede the development of individual man.

This existential concept of stress on life today does not mean that one ignores the lessons of the past, nor does he ignore the fact that man will have a tomorrow. But the only life we know on this earth is the life we live today, and it is this life which should be the center of attention. It is of little point to say that there is racial and religious prejudice in America because of thus and so which happened some time ago. Nor do the pious meandering platitudes that "things will be better in the next century if we will just be patient and wait" mean much to the victim of prejudice. The time we live is today, now, and for each one of us the basic question is not "What did you do yesterday?" or "What do you plan to do tomorrow?" but rather "What are you doing *now?*"

5. While we all know, in a cognitive sense, that we are creatures of mind and emotion, we often appear, particularly in educational institutions, to ignore this as a philosophical tenet of operation. As one goes up the educational ladder, emotions would appear to be considered to be of less and less importance in the learning process. The university student is generally considered, by the great majority of professors, as a cognitive creature, capable of reacting in a totally rational manner to all issues, questions, and problems, intellectual or otherwise. Thus teaching becomes more important than learning, and the university teacher is acceptable as long as he knows what he is talking about; whether he is able to communicate and thus help the student to learn something would often appear to be of minimal importance. The result is that a good grade often bears little relationship to the ability to think and reason, with feeling, but it indicates rather a high level ability to retain data, often quite meaningless.

If a human being is accepted as a creature of mind and emotion, then the teacher and the counselor are as sensitive to what the child feels as they are to what the child thinks. When the teacher screams, "Sit down and learn your lesson," it is surely obvious that the child is learning a lesson, but not the lesson that the teacher has insisted he must learn. All counselors are doubtless aware of situations in which the client has, for example, come to understand intellectually the absurd reasons behind his feelings of guilt, but still feels guilty. One does not think oneself out of certain basic and well-entrenched human feeling. One must feel and experience the feeling before one can change the feeling. The ineffectiveness of simple knowing in problems of human behavior is well illustrated by the racial and religious prejudice of those who, in an intellectual sense, "know better," but still carry with them strong feelings of prejudice toward others. Thus, if human behavior is to change for the better, if man is to realize his full development as a self-actualized creature, a basic tenet of operation must surely be the acceptance of man as a creature who feels as well as thinks. Indeed, the progress of mankind is probably more dependent on what one feels about what he thinks than what he thinks about what he feels. The ability of man to offer a non-possessive and non-demanding love to his fellow man is a better indication of his membership in the human species than is his high-level intellectual prowess.

part 2

THE COUNSELOR

chapter 4

THE COUNSELOR AS A PERSON

Many and varied are the lists of virtues that should be possessed by that, apparently, paragon of virtue known as the counselor. If, indeed, there were some human creature who possessed all of these characteristics to a high degree, a client would probably find the development of a warm relationship with him a difficult thing, since he would be so far removed from the world in which the client lived. Some years ago, Pepinsky and Pepinsky stated, with some justification, that if the counselor were to possess all the characteristics that supposedly should be his, then he would be better equipped for divine than for vocational guidance![1] And yet, in a more serious vein, could one say that Gould is wrong when he writes, "a teacher (or a counselor) is a person with a sense of immortality, for to leave a vestige of oneself in the development of another is a touch of immortality. Through this we find an impelling and sufficient reason for living. Through this we live far beyond our span of years."[2]

It might even be that Ruskin, in discussing great men, was talking about the counselor as he could be, when he said ". . . the first great test of a truly great man is his humility. I do not mean, by

---

[1] Harold B. Pepinsky and Pauline N. Pepinsky, *Counseling: Theory and Practice* (New York: The Ronald Press Company, 1954), pp. 139–140.
[2] As quoted by C. Gilbert Wrenn in "Status and Role of the School Counselor," *The Personnel and Guidance Journal* 36:182 (November, 1957).

humility, doubt of his own power, or hesitation in speaking his own opinions; but a right understanding of the relation between what *he* can do and say, and the rest of the world's sayings and doings."[3]

It should be noted, too, that when I am discussing the counselor, I am obviously talking about the counselor as I see him, involved in counseling as I see it. Actually, these perceptions do not appear to differ too much from those appearing in policy statements that were adopted at the annual convention at San Francisco, in March, 1964, by the American Personnel and Guidance Association, the American School Counselors Association, and the Association for Counselor Education and Supervision. A revised edition of the standards for the preparation of secondary school counselors was accepted at the Dallas convention in March of 1967. The adopted policy statement of the American School Counselors Association, for example, states that:

> *School Counselor* is a term used in this policy statement to designate a counselor working in a secondary school setting, concerned with and accepting a responsibility for assisting all pupils, and having as his major concern the developmental needs and problems of youth. Counseling is perceived as involving a dynamic relationship between counselor and counselee, and thus the school counselor accepts the responsibility of involving himself in the lives of pupils with clear and humble knowledge of the implications.

Since such stated definitions of counseling differ little from what I would refer to as either counseling or psychotherapy, it seems logical to refer to studies that may use the word "therapist" or "psycho-therapy," even though some counselors and some counselor educators recoil in horror whenever these terms are mentioned. I will also refer to studies involving psychiatrists, since quite frequently, in modern schools, we find school counselors and psychiatrists working quite closely together with the same clientele. This clientele, while it consists of "normal" individuals in the sense that most of them do not suffer any abnormal personality disorientation, does, nevertheless, have problems and questions and difficulties and anxieties and concerns that cannot be alleviated by other personnel in the school. It is the counselor who provides the needed service, and it is about this person that we speak in this chapter.

---

[3] A. H. R. Ball (Ed.), *Ruskin as Literary Critic* (Cambridge: The University Press, 1928), pp. 248–249.

THE PERSONALITY OF THE COUNSELOR

If counseling becomes identified as a distinct and unique professional occupation, then it is likely that the counselor will also be identified as a unique and professional individual. Currently, however, we still have numerous definitions, concepts and ideas about counseling and counselors, and it would probably be more valid to talk about the personalities of counselors rather than the personality of the counselor. However, because of an optimistic nature, I retain the heading that is used above.

The major sources of information about the person of the counselor are the ideas and opinions of the theorists and practitioners, and various studies which tend to imply that the person known as the counselor does have certain characteristics which differentiate him from the general population. Over twenty years ago, for example, the National Vocational Guidance Association issued a publication on Counselor Preparation that referred to the general characteristics of counselors as being: a deep interest in people, patience, sensitivity to the attitudes and reactions of others, emotional stability and objectivity, a capacity for being trusted by others, and respect for the facts.[4]

Hamrin and Paulson reported a study in which counselors themselves listed the traits necessary for counseling, in order of frequency, as understanding, sympathetic attitude, friendliness, sense of humor, stability, patience, objectivity, sincerity, tact, fairness, tolerance, neatness, calmness, broadmindedness, kindliness, pleasantness, social intelligence, and poise.[5] This study would have been more interesting if there could have been some indication of the extent to which clients felt that these counselors possessed the traits that they themselves said were essential for good counseling.

Rogers[6] has stated that the counselor should (1) be sensitive to human relationships; (2) have an objective attitude and an emotionally detached attitude—in short, a capacity for sympathy that is

---

[4] National Vocational Guidance Association, *Counselor Preparation* (Washington, D.C., 1949).

[5] S. A. Hamrin and B. B. Paulson, *Counseling Adolescents* (Chicago: Science Research Associates, 1950).

[6] Carl R. Rogers, *Counseling and Psychotherapy* (Boston: Houghton Mifflin Company, 1942).

not overdone; (3) have respect for the individual and an ability and willingness to accept the child as he is, giving him freedom to work out his own solutions; (4) understand himself, and his emotional limitations and shortcomings; (5) know human behavior.

An earlier summation of the evidence and research on the question of who counselors are and what they should be is to be found in the classic volume by Jones,[7] and a summation by Cottle.[8]

Weitz[9] has pointed out three traits that he considers essential for counseling effectiveness: security, a sense of self-acceptance; sensitivity, the capacity of generalizing one's own feelings of self-acceptance to the acceptance of other people; and objectivity, the capacity to distinguish between objective and symbolic behavior, and yet understand the intimate relationship between the two.

In the last few years, what would at least appear to be an interesting change has occurred in the various "should be" articles that are written about counselors. Older articles by counselors and counselor educators, such as some of those just mentioned, tended to refer to broad and general characteristics of what might be generally described as "good" people. Those referring to more specific aspects of human behavior tended to be written by psychologists or therapists. Today, however, this stress on the more psychological aspects of the human being of the counselor is to be found in almost all of the literature. Emphasis is placed on the counselor's ability to look at, and to understand and accept *his* self, as well as the self of the other person.

For example, a few years ago Hobbs was less representative than now, when he stated that:[10]

> The life style of the counselor is perhaps as important as his competencies, and whereas one would expect a multiplicity of life styles among counselors, there are two ingredients which I would hope our training programs would uniformly foster. One of these we might call a sense of time or dimensionality; the other is creativity, and the two may turn out to be different faces of the same coin.

---

[7] A. J. Jones, *Principles of Guidance* (New York: McGraw-Hill Book Co., Inc., 1951), pp. 542–583.
[8] William C. Cottle, "Personal Characteristics of Counselors: I," *The Personnel and Guidance Journal* 31:445–450 (April, 1953).
[9] Henry Weitz, "Counseling as a Function of the Counselor's Personality," *Personnel and Guidance Journal* 35:276–280 (January, 1957).
[10] Nicholas Hobbs, "The Compleat Counselor," *Personnel and Guidance Journal* 36:594–602 (May, 1958).

So was Wyatt, when he was warning about the temptations encountered by the therapist:[11]

> (a) The gratification of his instinctual needs in the disguise of therapeutic activity which is likely to follow along the repetition of certain subjective patterns of his own development; (b) indulgence in the narcissism which the therapeutic situation amply occasions.

More representative, today, are Stone and Shertzer, when they say:[12]

> The true professional knows not only who he should be but also what he is. . . . All too many counselors invest their energy in arguing what they should be without stopping to look at what they are both personally and professionally. . . . The counselor who waits upon an externally supplied solution to his questions "Who am I?" and "What do I do?" does a disservice to himself and to the profession.

And Appell, when he comments:[13]

> The most significant resource a counselor brings to a helping relationship is himself. It is difficult to understand how a counselor unaware of his own emotional needs, of his expectations of himself as well as others, of his rights and privileges in relationships, can be sensitive enough to such factors in his counselee. More than that, it would seem that he needs to experience himself as a person of worth and of individuality before he can afford another such privileges. Indeed, in a most profound sense, the greater his congruence, the freer he can be in assisting others to actualize themselves.

School counselors Boy and Pine[14] describe the counselor's personal problems as discovering his professional identity, freeing himself of himself, developing a humanistic attitude, being professionally secure, counselor anxieties, transference and counter-transference. They comment that "the school counselor must be sensitive to his own desires to 'wrap up a case' and to how much such an attitude can

---

[11] Frederick Wyatt, "The Self-Experience of the Psychotherapist," *Journal of Consulting Psychology* 12:83–87 (February, 1948).
[12] Shelley C. Stone and Bruce Shertzer, "The Militant Counselor," *Personnel and Guidance Journal* 42:342–347 (December, 1963).
[13] Morey L. Appell, "Self-Understanding for the Guidance Counselor," *Personnel and Guidance Journal* 42:143–148 (October, 1963).
[14] Angelo V. Boy and Gerald J. Pine, *Client-Centered Counseling in the Secondary School* (Boston: Houghton Mifflin Company, 1963), pp. 188–202.

influence him to prod the client instead of allowing him to proceed at his own rate in solving a problem."[15]

Williamson,[16] while talking in a rather odd way about the counselor as technique, indicates that the counselor's philosophy of human development should show through his behavior, that his efforts at relating effectively with the student must issue from his own acceptance of himself as he is, and his behavior should be such as to be identified as the carrying on of his own "independent intellectual life," both in his own technical field and in the broad literature of human cultures.

Van Kaam,[17] in describing the ideal therapist, sees the crucial human characteristics as flexibility, acceptance, gentleness, and sincerity. Boy and Pine[18] see the role of the counselor as being basically an extension of his essence as a person, and they describe such roles as the concessionary counselor (who defines his function in terms of what is best for him); the mechanistic counselor (who is frequently a former teacher who is conditioned to answering questions); the guidance counselor (in which two distinctly separate processes are confused); the vocational counselor (where traditionally one attempted to match the man to the job).

Nor are such statements limited to individuals. In a joint report by the New York State Counselors Association and the New York State Association of Deans and Guidance Personnel, essential personal competencies of the counselor are described as:[19]

> . . . a knowledge of self: needs, values, strengths, and weaknesses.
> . . . an understanding and acceptance of individual differences: intellectual, personal, physical, cultural, and socio-economic.
> . . . the capacity to relate to and work with others.
> . . . skill in communicating with others.
> . . . the ability to recognize a need for continual personal and professional development.

---

[15] *Ibid.*
[16] E. G. Williamson, "The Counselor as Technique," *Personnel and Guidance Journal* 41:108–111 (October, 1962).
[17] Adrian Van Kaam, *The Art of Existential Counseling* (Wilkes-Barre, Pa.: Dimension Books, 1966), pp. 140–149.
[18] Angelo V. Boy and Gerald J. Pine, *The Counselor in The Schools* (Boston: Houghton Mifflin Co., 1968), pp. 44–56.
[19] *An Exploration of the Role and Preparation of the Counselor in the Secondary School.* A Report of the Professional Advancement Committee of the New York State Counselors Association and the Professional Development and Research Committee of the New York State Association of Deans and Guidance Personnel, 1963.

⎰The report of the Committee on Professional Preparation and Standards of the American Personnel and Guidance Association, accepted at the annual convention in San Francisco in March, 1964, described as basic qualities of the effective counselor a belief in each individual, a commitment to individual human values, alertness to the world, open-mindedness, understanding of self, and professional commitment.⎱ A statement of policy for secondary school counselors was accepted by the American School Counselors Association at the same convention. It described the counselor as follows:

> The counselor is dedicated to the idea that most pupils will enhance and enrich their personal development and self-fulfillment by means of making more intelligent decisions if given the opportunity to experience an accepting, non-evaluating relationship in which one is helped to better understand himself, the environment he perceives, and the relationship between these. Counseling is essentially such a relationship. The school counselor views himself as the person on the school staff with the professional competencies, behavioral science understandings, philosophical orientation, and position within the school necessary to provide such help to pupils.

These, then, are thoughts and ideas, by individuals and organizations, as to who the counselor should be, and they are important in that they will play a major role in the development of the counselor of tomorrow. Is this the way, however, that the counselor is today? Let us look at some of the evidence that describes the counselor as he is today. There is, obviously, no such thing as a "counselor"—he comes in many sizes and shapes. There are, however, certain similarities among professional counselors, and there are certain differences that may be caused by their orientation, their background, where they were educated, and the sort of education they experienced. Arbuckle[20] made a study of certain differences between student counselors who were chosen by their fellows as potential counselors and those who were rejected by their fellows. Those who were chosen by their fellows as individuals they would like to have as counselors showed a higher degree of confidence (as measured by the Heston Personality Inventory) than those who chose them. They were more normal in that they scored lower on the Hypochondriasis, Depression, Paranoia, Hysteria, Schizophrenia, Social I.E., and Psychasthenia scales (as measured by the Minnesota Multiphasic Personality Inventory). They showed a

[20] Dugald S. Arbuckle, "Client Perception of Counselor Personality," *Journal of Counseling Psychology* 3:93–96 (Summer, 1956).

higher degree of interest in such areas as social service, persuasive, literary, and scientific activities (as measured by the Kuder Preference Record). On the other hand, those students who were rejected by their fellows as potential counselors indicated less in the way of home satisfaction than those who chose them. They were more abnormal in that they scored higher on the Hypochondriasis, Paranoia, Hysteria, Schizophrenia, Psychopathic Deviate and Hypomania scales. There were no significant differences in interest areas.

Several years later, in a somewhat similar study, forty participants in an NDEA Guidance Institute judged each other as potential counselors. The nine "most chosen" participants were compared on a number of variables with the nine "least chosen." Most chosen participants had a higher academic performance, somewhat more appropriate Strong scores, and less dogmatism as indicated on the Rokeach scale.[21]

In another study using an NDEA Institute population, the criterion for "good" or "bad" counselor was supplied by the staff ranking the student counselors in the order in which they would hire them as counselors. Using this criterion, the perceptual organization of effective counselors was significantly different from that of less effective counselors. The more effective counselors tended to perceive from an internal rather than external frame of reference; they perceived in terms of people rather than things; they perceived people as able rather than unable, dependable rather than undependable, friendly rather than unfriendly, worthy rather than unworthy, identified rather than unidentified; they perceived their self as enough rather than not enough, revealing rather than not revealing; they perceived their purpose as freeing rather than controlling, altruistic rather than narcissistic, in larger rather than smaller meanings.[22]

Using an audio scale, O'Hern and Arbuckle[23] found that student counselors in seven summer NDEA Guidance Institutes who were considered to be most sensitive as counselors were significantly younger, they had attained a lower educational degree, and they had been employed fewer years than those who were considered to be least sensitive. These results raise some questions about certain assumptions

---

[21] Buford Stefflre, Paul King, and Fred Leafgren, "Characteristics of Counselors Judged Effective by Their Peers," *Journal of Counseling Psychology* 9:335–340 (Winter, 1962).
[22] Arthur W. Combs and Daniel W. Soper, "The Perceptual Organization of Effective Counselors," *Journal of Counseling Psychology* 10:222–226 (Fall, 1963).
[23] Jane S. O'Hern and Dugald S. Arbuckle, "Sensitivity: A Measurable Concept?" *Personnel and Guidance Journal* 42:572–576 (February, 1964).

having to do with counselor effectiveness! In an earlier study by Abeles,[24] somewhat related results were found when it was determined that the differences between student counselors rated by supervisors as more or less promising were in values and interests rather than in ability and general adjustment.

Truax, Carkhuff and Douds[25] appear to be satisfied that enough evidence has been produced to indicate that the three therapist characteristics that determine the depth of self-exploration on the part of the client are therapist empathic understanding, therapist non-possessive warmth, and therapist self-congruence or transparency.

Comrey described some of the differences among samplings of American Psychological Association members with different professional interest areas.[26] Those with interests in counseling and guidance thought that more psychologists lived up to their standards of what a psychologist should be than not; they judged religion to be more of a positive force in their lives than the others; they liked group projects; they liked administrative work in psychology; they liked psychotherapy; they liked teaching; they wanted to spend more time with their families; they wanted to do something for society; they wanted to help people who needed help; they were less productive in research articles than other groups; they had spent less of their time in positions where they had to do research; they believed that most institutions placed too much emphasis on research; they believed that less emphasis should be placed on research in training clinical psychologists; they were less interested in doing research; they attended either few or many professional meetings; they neither liked nor disliked competitive situations; they devoted either few or many weeks to vacation from professional work; they were less interested in sex; they liked a job where forty hours per week were devoted to teaching and preparation; they liked a well-paid teaching position in a small college.

On the other hand, predominant among those with interests in psychotherapy were some of the following attitudes: they allowed the expressed interests of graduate students to determine the content of a graduate course; they liked the idea of doing counseling and guidance; they wanted to help people who needed help; they had less resentment

---

[24] N. Abeles, *A Study of the Characteristics of Counselor Trainees* (doctoral dissertation, University of Texas, 1958).

[25] Charles B. Truax, Robert R. Carkhuff, and John Douds, "Toward an Integration of the Didactic and Experiential Approaches to Training in Counseling and Psychotherapy," *Journal of Counseling Psychology* 11:240–247 (Fall, 1964).

[26] Andrew L. Comrey, "Publication Rate and Interests in Certain Psychologists," *The American Psychologist* 11:314–322 (July, 1956).

than others of a colleague who was a homosexual or an adulterer; they spent neither very little nor an excessive number of evening hours on professional work; they neither strongly liked nor disliked competitive situations; they expected to reach a higher income; they found it less unpleasant than many to be alone; they believed that life in our society is too competitive; they found mathematics distasteful; they were most interested in having quite a lot of money; research was not their forte.

In an interesting article on neurotic interactions between counselors and clients, Lawton[27] refers to some of the therapist's insecurities as being expressed in the following ways. The therapist tends to dominate the patient because of his fear that he will lose control of the relationship; he competes with other significant authority figures in the life of the patient; he showers the patient with excessive love and attention, going to extreme lengths to prevent marriage failure (his attitude seems to be, "This marriage must succeed"); he functions as the child of the patient, misses him when he is away and welcomes him back with a sigh of relief and pleasure; he indicates a sort of Pygmalion complex, in the sense that he needs to make the patient like the therapist; he resents the patient's demands; fearing the patient's hostility, he tries to appease him; he is unable to stand the patient's tension and anxiety. On this latter point, Lawton points out, this sort of anxiety is likely to result in glittering pseudo-optimism: "Don't worry; everything will be all right!"

In the same paper Lawton points to the seductive role of the more immature therapists. Verbal wooing may take the form of calling the patient by his first name too soon or without ascertaining the patient's wishes; of using affectionate or meaningful intonation of words; engaging in long, cozy telephone conversations; talking, explaining, interpreting excessively; asking for deep material too soon or too obviously. Non-verbal seduction of the patient may take such means as visiting the patient's home at the request of the patient whenever the latter undergoes an emotional emergency connected with transference; giving affectionate or meaningful glances; putting an affectionate hand on the patient's shoulder or giving a parental pat; allowing the patient to telephone regularly after hours or to see the therapist at times not ordinarily office hours; charging the patient a fee which the patient feels is lower than called for in a particular situation and letting the patient know that this is done because the therapist

---

[27] George Lawton, "Symposium on Neurotic Interaction in Marriage Counseling," *Journal of Counseling Psychology* 5:28–33 (Spring, 1958).

likes him; regularly overrunning the usual and conventional time limits for sessions.

In another paper from the same symposium, Harper[28] lists still other neurotic interactions among counselors as being the pose of objectivity, the overemphasis on likeability, and the effort on the part of the counselor to show that he is a good fellow, just like everyone else.

A study of Fiedler indicated that there was less in the way of differences among expert counselors of supposed different orientations than there was among inexperienced counselors of supposedly similar orientations.[29] The expert counselors were close together in their ability to understand the client's meanings and feelings; their sensitivity to the client's attitudes; their warm interest in the client without emotional involvement.

On the other hand, there would seem to be no doubt that counselors do use different techniques and methods. Strupp, for example, made a study of Rogerian and psychoanalytically oriented psychotherapists, and while the differences tended to diminish among the more experienced as compared with the less experienced, there were, nevertheless, significant differences.[30] For example, with the Rogerian psychotherapists, 75.5 percent of the responses were of a restating, clarifying, reflecting type, whereas only 14.2 percent of the psychoanalytically oriented psychotherapists used this type of response; 9.8 percent of the responses of Rogerians were of an exploring nature, asking for clarification, or expressing feeling, while 35.6 percent of the responses of non-Rogerians were of this type.

In a later study, Strupp gave evidence of differences in the attitudes of psychoanalytic and client-centered counselors, as indicated by their reactions to the showing of a sound film of a first interview.[31] The client-centered counselors judged the prognosis with therapy to be more favorable than the members of the psychoanalytic group; a larger proportion of the Rogerian counselors than of the others professed a positive attitude toward the client; Rogerians either declined to specify

---

[28] Robert A. Harper, "Symposium on Neurotic Interaction in Marriage Counseling," *Journal of Counseling Psychology* 5:33–38 (Spring, 1958).

[29] Fred Fiedler, "Quantitative Studies on the Role of Therapists' Feelings Toward Their Patients," in O. Hobart Mowrer (Ed.), *Psychotherapy: Theory and Research* (New York: The Ronald Press Company, 1953), p. 296.

[30] Hans H. Strupp, "An Objective Comparison of Rogerian and Psychoanalytic Techniques," *Journal of Consulting Psychology* 9:1–7 (February, 1955).

[31] Hans H. Strupp, "An Objective Comparison of Rogerian and Psychoanalytic Therapists in an Initial Interview," *Journal of Consulting Psychology* 22:265–274 (August, 1958).

attitudes and behaviors that the therapist should encourage in therapy with his patient or stressed the expression of feelings, while the others stressed such things as a sense of responsibility, increased socialization, and relating feelings and symptoms to interpersonal situations. Conversely, psychoanalytic therapists were more likely to discourage attitudes and behaviors such as intellectualization, obsessive ruminations, self-pity, self-depreciation, helplessness, refusal to accept responsibility, demanding attitudes, and acting out; Rogerians tended to say they would discourage nothing or leave it to the patient. No member of the Rogerian group advocated strictness by the therapist, as contrasted with more than one third of the members of the psychoanalytic group, who considered strictness therapeutically desirable. Rogerians commented on the patient's feelings and attitudes, but in contrast to the others, paid less attention to such clues as gestures, bodily movements, manner of speaking, the patient's past and present interpersonal relations with his mother, wife, brother, or father. In terms of the handling of the transference problem Rogerians recommended understanding, clarification, and reflection; analytically oriented therapists preferred an interpretive approach. Rogerians were more definite in their assertion that they would have conducted the interview in a different manner. They dissociated themselves from the therapist's approach, tending to evaluate his performance as inadequate; the analytic therapists considered his performance reasonably adequate. Over 75 percent of the Rogerians said that they would have spent somewhat less or considerably less time in obtaining data on the patient's life history than did the film therapist; almost one half of the analytic group said that they would have devoted somewhat more or considerably more time. The majority of the Rogerian therapists described their attitude toward the therapist in the film as negative, whereas most analytically oriented therapists professed a positive or neutral attitude.

Another interesting picture of counseling methodology was obtained in a study by Arbuckle and Wicas[32] that tended, among other things, to indicate that there was as much disagreement among counselors who received their training for the doctorate in the same institution as there was among those who received their doctorates in different institutions. Thus, among the members of the jury that was used in the study, the four experts who had the greatest number of

---

[32] Dugald S. Arbuckle and Edward Wicas, "The Development of an Instrument for the Measurement of Counseling Perceptions," *Journal of Counseling Psychology* 4:304–312 (Winter, 1957).

"client-centered" responses had received their doctorates at, respectively, the University of Chicago, Columbia University, the University of Minnesota, and Harvard University. There was no significant difference in the degree of "client-centeredness" or the responses of four members of the jury who received their training at Columbia, as compared with the four members who received theirs at Chicago.

The possession of a medical degree has historically come to be generally accepted as a requirement for competence in the matter of therapy of any kind, including psychotherapy and counseling. There is little or no actual relationship between the possession of such a degree and competence in psychotherapy, and medical doctors are the first to agree that their background gives them little in the way of understanding or skill when dealing with matters that are psychological. Many psychiatrists would agree with Colby, who tends to feel that his medical background was a hindrance rather than a help in his development into a capable psychotherapist.[33]

> Outstanding among educationally induced handicaps are detachment and dehumanization achieved in medical school. One tends to become interested almost entirely in diseases per se rather than in the people who have diseases. A once-active imagination may become stunted in the name of false scientific objectivity. The traditional medical single cause-and-effect concept of disease narrows the observation and sympathetic understanding of inter-human processes. . . . In the matters of treatment also, medical attention directs the axis of the student's interest toward mechanisms that can be seen and touched.

Freud, as the first outstanding "psychotherapist," stressed the fact that the possession of a medical degree had little or nothing to do with effectiveness as a psychotherapist. Freud's medical colleagues, however, paid no attention to this feeling, and medicine took over the responsibility for the study of human personality, conscious and unconscious. The effects of this will be noted in another chapter, but let it suffice to say that we are currently caught in the confusion of talking about "mental health," and "mental illness," when we are discussing problems and tensions and disturbances that are primarily the result of the psychological process of learning rather than the physiological process of being born.

Mowrer has this to say on the subject:[34]

---

[33] Kenneth M. Colby, *A Primer for Psychotherapists* (New York: The Ronald Press Company, 1951), pp. 20–21.
[34] O. Hobart Mowrer, " 'Sin,' the Lesser of Two Evils," *The American Psychologist* 15:301–304 (May, 1960).

We psychologists do not, I believe, object *in principle* to the type of authority which psychiatrists wish to exercise, or to our being subject to other medical controls, if they were truly functional. But authority and power ought to go with demonstrated competence, which medicine clearly has in the physical realm but, equally clearly, does not have in "psychiatry." Despite some pretentious affirmations to the contrary, the fact is that psychoanalysis, on which modern "dynamic" psychiatry is largely based, is in a state of virtual collapse and imminent demise. And the tranquilizers and other forms of so-called chemotherapy are admittedly only ameliorative, not basically curative. So now, to the extent that we have accepted the "illness" postulate and thus been lulled under the penumbra of medicine, we are in the ungraceful maneuver of "getting-out."

Since the possession of a medical degree is assumed by some to be an absolute prerequisite to the practice of psychotherapy, a book that takes a look at the applicants to medical schools is of much interest.[35] Kelly, discussing the results of an intensive testing and evaluation of one graduating class from one medical school, makes the following comments:[36]

Essentially, our medical students are persons who, if they were not becoming physicians, would be planning to become manufacturers, big businessmen, production managers, engineers; they are not the kind of people who would become teachers, ministers, social workers, i.e., professional persons interested in doing something for the good of mankind. As a group, the medical students reveal remarkably little interest in the welfare of human beings. . . . All of the evidence available to us leads to the conclusion that the *typical* young physician has little interest in cultural aspects of the society in which he lives, has very little sensitivity to or feeling for the needs of the community, and is generally not inclined to participate in community activities unless these contribute to his income. I am not saying this is true of all physicians; I am saying this is true of the model young man going into one medical school.

It is also pointed out that whereas a decade or so ago medical students tended to be A or B students, in recent years they have been drawn primarily from the ranks of the B students in the colleges.[37]

In this same report, too, Handler, discussing the results of psy-

---

[35] Helen Hofer Gee and John T. Cowles (Eds.), *The Appraisal of Applicants to Medical Schools* (Evanston: Association of American Medical Colleges, 1957).
[36] *Ibid.*, pp. 195–196.
[37] *Ibid.*, p. 13.

chiatric interviews with three classes of freshmen medical students, comments as follows.[38]

> Our impression was that the majority of the students we saw were quite conformist, emotionally constricted young men and women, given to internalizing their hostility either with depressive or compulsive traits for the most part, or sometimes with somatic manifestations. We felt that there was a high premium put on this in pre-medical competition, and, provided that it was not too extreme, we thought of this matter of conformity and constriction as actually one of the criteria of success both in premedical work and in getting through medical school.

On the basis of a more comprehensive study of data obtained from nearly 2,500 first-year medical students in twenty-eight medical schools, Gee describes the "average" entering medical student as a man who values the pursuit of scientific truth above all.[39] He values prestige and power next to theoretical values, but holds these values no higher than does the average college student. He is considerably less interested in economic and material gain than is the average college student, and somewhat more interested in the cultural aspects of community life. He is strongly motivated by needs to achieve and to work hard and persistently toward achievement of his goals. He is not prone to be motivated through altruistic love of his fellow man, it is true, but he is likely to want to understand why that fellow man behaves as he does, and is likely to be motivated by a desire to help him when he is in trouble and to treat him with sympathy and kindness. His interests cannot be characterized as being very much like those of social workers; they are more like those of physicians, osteopaths, and public administrators. But he is more likely to have the interests of a teacher or social worker or of an author-journalist than he is to have the interests of a businessman or farmer.

These various statements may be somewhat contradictory, but they are probably representative. They tend to raise at least some doubt as to the validity of the concept that the possession of a medical degree is a prerequisite for the practice of psychotherapy.

There is also evidence of a difference between psychiatric and psychological opinion regarding personality disturbances. Glosser[40] contacted 90 psychiatrists and 60 psychologists, and had a 56 percent

---

[38] *Ibid.*, p. 68.
[39] In a personal communication from Dr. Gee to the author.
[40] Harry J. Glosser, "Psychiatric Versus Psychological Opinion Regarding Personality Disturbances," *The American Psychologist* 13:477–481 (August, 1958).

return from the psychiatrists and a 61 percent return from the psychologists. Glosser's questionnaire consisted of 100 statements of opinion regarding psychological disturbances. On 81 percent of the items there was a virtual unanimity of opinion. On 63 of the 100 items, however, a higher percentage of psychologists than psychiatrists selected the "?" response indicating some doubt or skepticism of the validity of either a "yes" or "no" response. The psychiatrists leaned more strongly toward psychogenic than physiogenic concepts, generally opposing physiological, biological, and biochemical accounts of mental and personality disturbances. They expressed a favorable attitude toward the psychodynamics of Freudian and psychoanalytic theory. The psychologists were somewhat more inclined to accept the existence of underlying physiological disturbances in mental disorders. They were more inclined to oppose certain Freudian and psychodynamic concepts. They were somewhat more inclined to accept hereditary influences in the susceptibility of the individual to certain mental and personality disorders, and more strongly opposed to the view that therapy cannot exist without direction. On this latter item, the reaction to the statement, "Therapy cannot exist without direction; therefore, the nondirective method is not really therapy," for the psychiatrists was 32 percent "yes," and 44 percent "no," whereas the reaction of the psychologists was 8.3 percent "yes," and 70 percent "no." This is probably surprising to many psychiatrists and psychologists!

Wicas and Mahan[41] found that counselors who were rated high by their peers and supervisors achieved a pattern of scores that indicated that they were anxious, sensitive to the expectations of others and society, patient and non-aggressive in interpersonal relationships, and concerned about social progress, but always with appropriate self-control. On the other hand, the evidence also indicated the lack of high scores on measures of originality and venturousness; the rejection of contemplation and receptivity to inner experience; the danger that these counselors will not persist in the face of opposition; the highly conservative nature of their orientation to social problems.

Demos and Zuwaylif,[42] in a study whose interpretations were

---

[41] Edward A. Wicas and Thomas W. Mahan, "Characteristics of Counselors Rated Effective by Supervisors and Peers," *Counselor Education and Supervision* 6:50–56 (Fall, 1966).
[42] George D. Demos and Fadil H. Zuwaylif," Characteristics of Effective Counselors," *Counselor Education and Supervision* 5:163–165 (Spring, 1966).

later to be questioned, found that the Allport-Vernon-Lindzey Study of Values and the Kuder Preference Record did not discriminate between the most effective and the least effective counselors. On the Edwards Personal Preference Schedule, on the other hand, the most effective counselors indicated significantly more nuturance and affiliation, while the least effective counselors exhibited more autonomy, abasement and aggression.

It has been hypothesized that effective male counselors need to deviate from normal male norms in the direction of femininity, whereas effective female counselors need not deviate from the norms for women. In an interesting study on this subject, however, McLain[43] found that while male counselors did deviate significantly from the norms for men in general on three of six scales selected to measure femininity, the women counselors also scored significantly in the direction of masculinity on three factors! This tends to imply that in this particular study population, the male counselors possessed some of the feminine traits considered necessary for effective counseling, whereas the female counselors possessed certain male traits which are not considered to be necessary for effective counseling!

The ideal counselor has also been described as one who would be an actualizer rather than a manipulator. The characteristics of the actualizer are those of honesty, awareness, freedom and trust, as contrasted with those of deception, unawareness, control and cynicism. An intimate human relationship, such as occurs in counseling, would obviously have a very different effect with an actualizer as contrasted with a manipulator.

PERCEPTIONS OF COUNSELORS

The perceptions that counselors hold of themselves, and the way in which they are perceived by others is obviously of crucial importance, regardless of what studies say they are, or theorists say they should be. Rogers postulates a few of the questions that he, as a counselor, would ask of himself. These questions give an excellent picture of Rogers' concept of the personality of the counselor:[44]

---

[43] Edwin W. McLain, "Is the Counselor a Woman?" *Personnel and Guidance Journal* 46:444–448 (January, 1968).
[44] Carl R. Rogers, "The Characteristics of a Helping Relationship," *Personnel and Guidance Journal* 37:6–16 (September, 1958).

1. Can I *be* in some way which will be perceived by the other person as trustworthy, as dependable or consistent in some deep sense . . . ?
2. Can I be expressive enough as a person that what I am will be communicated unambiguously . . . ?
3. Can I let myself experience positive attitudes toward this other person—attitudes of warmth, caring, liking, interest, respect . . . ?
4. Can I be strong enough as a person to be separate from the other? Can I be a sturdy respecter of my own feelings, my own needs, as well as his? Can I own and, if need be, express my own feelings as something belonging to me and separate from his feelings? Am I strong enough in my own separateness that I will not be downcast by his depression, frightened by his fear, nor engulfed by his dependency?
5. Am I secure enough within myself to permit his separateness? Can I permit him to be what he is—honest or deceitful, infantile or adult, despairing or overconfident? Can I give him the freedom to be . . . ?
6. Can I let myself enter fully into the world of his feelings and personal meanings and see these as he does? Can I step into his private world so completely that I lose all desire to evaluate or judge it . . . ?
7. Can I receive him as he is? Can I communicate this attitude? Or can I receive him only conditionally, accepting some aspects of his feelings and silently or openly disapproving of other aspects . . . ?
8. Can I act with sufficient sensitivity in the relationship that my behavior will not be perceived as a threat . . . ?
9. Can I free him from the threat of external evaluation . . . ?
10. Can I meet this other individual who is in the process of *becoming*, or will I be bound by his past and by my past . . . ?

Two counselors, wondering about why they happen to be counselors, are, in a way, answering for themselves some of these questions. One of them says:

> The essence of democratic life is a person's individuality. In our society the individual can easily become the victim of the group. The individual finds it difficult to be himself, to be the master of his fate, because of the pressures of conformity that the group imposes upon him. The individual can become swallowed by the group. A person's individuality is consumed because of the neurotic need of the group for conformity. The individuality of the free thinker is the cornerstone of our democratic life. In a totalitarian state there is no room for individuality. In a democratic state the individual must be preserved. It is from the free thinking of an individual that a democracy thrives. I guess I'm a counselor because of a caring for the individual and the things that his free spirit can contribute to mankind. I desire to see the

individual function freely so that whatever he contributes to civilization will be a maximal contribution, an unrestricted contribution. Enlightened ideas that improve civilization come from men who are free enough to think and to create. I am a counselor because I think I can help men to be free. I am a counselor because I believe in democracy, and without the free-thinking individual who is master of himself there is no democracy. I feel that as a counselor I can help man to be free, and thus preserve democracy.

The other counselor, half a continent away, comments:

I see my function as a counselor as providing a growth-producing and non-threatening environment for the client. I see my function as establishing a relationship in which I can communicate understanding and acceptance. I am committed to the idea that nothing is more important to the individual than self-understanding. I can imagine no more worthwhile goals than to help my client and myself to achieve self-understanding.

Counselors, like other humans, are usually measured in somewhat subjective terms. Johnson, Shertzer, Linden and Stone,[45] for example, found that counselees, peers and supervisors reacted favorably to male counselors who were affable, friendly, likeable, accepting, capable and satisfied, and to females who were outgoing, confident, efficient and assertive.

In the long run, of course, it is the concept that the client has of the counselor that will determine the effectiveness of the counseling relationship. And the perceptions of counselors as to who they are are not always the same as the perceptions of clients. A study by Strowig and Sheets,[46] for example, indicated that students perceived counselors as counselors more negatively than as deans. This at least implies that students do not see the functions of counselors as they are perceived by counselors. In a study involving counselors and Upward Bound students, Grande[47] found that, to a greater extent than the Upward Bound students, counselors regarded the guidance program as an important element in the total value of the school; they believed that removal of the program would leave a serious void in the school

---

[45] Dorothy Johnson, Bruce Shertzer, James E. Linden and Shelley C. Stone, "The Relationship of Counselor Candidate Characteristics and Counseling Effectiveness," *Counselor Education and Supervision* 6:297–304 (Summer, 1967).

[46] R. Wray Strowig and Stanley E. Sheets, "Student Perception of Counselor Role," *Personnel and Guidance Journal* 45:926;931 (May, 1967).

[47] Peter P. Grande, "Attitudes of Counselors and Disadvantaged Students," *Personnel and Guidance Journal* 46:889–892 (May, 1968).

program, and that the guidance services needed to be expanded. On the other hand, to a greater degree than the counselors, the students felt that the guidance program was not essential, although it did have something to offer, that specialized guidance personnel were outsiders, and that the guidance program confused students and made them begin to doubt their individual judgments.

Here are some of the more positive perceptions of junior high school boys and girls about the counselor they have experienced:

"He's me . . . in some strange and mysterious way he's felt exactly the way I've felt about things."

"That's not complicated—he's simply someone to whom I can talk easily and honestly. He's someone I don't have to put on a front with."

"He's someone who *really* cares about me and what happens to me."

"He's a person who has the time to help me in dealing with my parents."

"He's not easily shocked—no matter what I tell him."

"I suppose—well—he's someone I can trust. He isn't always judging me—he's letting me judge myself."

"He's someone to whom I can turn when things pile up . . . someone who helps me deal with this business of living."

"He's someone who doesn't get mad when I tell him about my foolish plans for the future."

"He's someone who doesn't get bugged when he hears about kids and what they're like."

"He's someone who makes school tolerable . . . if I couldn't get together with him I'd have quit school a long time ago."

"I'm making my own decisions for the first time . . . whatever he did helped me to do this."

Students, in evaluating a counseling program, described counselors in this way:[48]

"I thought that my counselor really took an interest in me and my problems."

"I like to have a counselor because it gives me a chance to say things."

". . . I can talk on just about anything that is on my mind."

"They let you get things off your mind that you couldn't tell to anyone else."

". . . the counselor listens to me and my ideas and doesn't give out wisecracks like my teachers."

"The counselors are very understanding."

"He always listened to what I had to say first."

[48] Angelo V. Boy and Gerald J. Pine, *The Counselor in the Schools* (Boston: Houghton Mifflin Co., 1968), p. 305.

Not all student clients, however, see the school counselor in such a positive light. Here are a few comments from students who have experienced counseling:

> "I wouldn't go to the counselor because he is so dense."
> "Counselors have no wisdom. . . ."
> "He is just like my father. . . ." •
> "He stands up for the teachers and protects them. . . ."
> "Counselors tell the teachers what we say. . . ."
> "They just sit around and get paid for nothing. . . ."
> "I don't want to bother him . . . he probably has problems of his own. . . ."

THE VALUES OF THE COUNSELOR

The reaction of the counselor, then, to the issues of life and living would appear to be a reflection of the values which differentiate him as a human being. The counselor can be a powerful instrument in helping the individual to move and to change, and movement and change usually imply change in values. It would be reasonable to assume that there are certain values which should be a part of the counselor, and there are others which should have no part in his make-up.

Counselors with different values apparently differ in what they do well and what they do poorly, as one would expect. In a study by Watley,[49] for example, counselors with a trait-and-factor orientation differed significantly from those with a client-centered orientation in their ability to predict freshmen grades and persistence and success in an educational major. Thus if the ability to predict is considered to be an important characteristic of the counselor, it would appear that counselors whose values reflected a trait-and-factor orientation would be a better bet than those whose values reflected a client-centered orientation. A study by Barre,[50] on the other hand, tended to indicate that both clients and counselors agreed that counselors who showed high achievement needs, high original thinking, high vigor and low order needs are rated as being more helpful, facilitating a closer relationship, and showing empathy for their clients. Thus if a close empathic counselor-client relationship was considered to be critical, then

[49] Donivan J. Watley, "Counseling Philosophy and Counseling Predictive Skill," *Journal of Counseling Psychology* 14:158–164 (March, 1967).
[50] Carole E. Barre, "Relationship of Counselor Personality and Counselor-Client Similarity to Selected Counseling Success Criteria," *Journal of Counseling Psychology* 14:419–425 (September, 1967).

counselors of this kind would be a better bet. In a study of general counseling effectiveness, Whitely, Sprinthall, Mosher and Donaghy[51] found a high relationship between the effective counselor and cognitive flexibility, which refers to dimensions of open-mindedness, adaptability, and a resistance to premature closure in perception and cognition. In this study at least, the counselor who had a higher level of individual freedom, and was less a conditioned product of his culture, would appear to be more effective.

Few would disagree with Robb[52] that "the search for truth must be undergirded by a personal sense of intellectual honesty and openness. If these qualities of mind are not present, the possibility for self-delusion threatens our honest pursuit of the truth."

Thus it would seem that one might at least theorize that if we hold to the importance of individual freedom, and if we believe in a society in which the dignity and the rights of individual man are the primary reason for the existence of the state, then the values of the counselor might at least be characterized by the following:

1. An openness and a flexibility which means that the counselor is not the slave of any dogma, religious or secular, professional or personal. The belief of a person is a part of his experiencing and living, and his beliefs and values are open to change as circumstances and people change. The counselor does not believe because he has to, and he accepts personal responsibility for his beliefs. All his beliefs are thus laced with rationality, and he does not continue to believe what has intellectually been shown to be false.

2. The counselor accepts a belief as an area in which we may not know, in an empirical sense, and thus it is irrational to argue that one person's belief is right and that of another is wrong. In a religious sense this would mean that one could be devout and still accept the possibility of error, and this, in turn, would of course mean that religion would be an area of uncertainty rather than an area of certainty. "I believe" would never be confused with "I know," and there would be little point in closing one's mind to a colleague, or killing one's fellow man because of a differing belief, since one would accept the possibility that the colleague or the fellow man might be right.

Since belief is a matter of faith, it would seem logical to suggest

---

[51] John W. Whitely, Norman A. Sprinthall, Ralph L. Mosher, and Rolla T. Donaghy, "Selection and Evaluation of Counselor Effectiveness," *Journal of Counseling Psychology* 14:226–234 (May, 1967).

[52] J. Wesley Robb, "Self Discovery and the Role of the Counselor," *Personnel and Guidance Journal* 45:1008–1011 (June, 1967).

that the counselor, at least, should believe positively. Why not hold to
the belief that man *can* grow and develop, and that he has within him
the seeds of self-actualization rather than holding to the belief that
man is vicious and evil, and must spend his life battling the evil forces
that reside within him? A belief is not factual, but it is a fact that one
believes. When one views the other person and feels "You *can* do it,
you *can* stand up straight and tall, you *can* experience freedom," then
what happens in the human relationship *is quite different* than when
one views the other person as evil and hopeless and condemned. This
latter statement is a statement of fact, not of belief!

3. The counselor will personally exemplify a high level of personal freedom and self-actualization, and he will thus have no need to
impose on others. He may serve as a model, not to be imitated and
followed, but rather a model from which the other person can draw
strength and gradually develop his own concept of self, his own person, and thus become capable of experiencing a high level of personal
freedom.

The possession and awareness of values by the counselor need
not imply the need to impose these values on others. On the other
hand, it is likely that every counselor would feel there are certain
aspects of what might be called a value system that would bring
disaster upon the client, and he could not be acceptant of them as a
satisfactory way of life. A client might feel that heroin was a part of his
way of life, and was good for him, but surely few counselors would
agree. Most counselors, however, tend to be too imposing rather than
too acceptant of the values of others. Vance, for example, states
that:[53]

> . . . unless the counselor is aware of his own values and the ethics of
> his own profession, it is likely that he could accept any behaviorial
> goal as stated by the client . . . (and) . . . unless the counselor is
> aware of what he believes should constitute desirable and undesirable
> behavior, both for himself and for his client. . . .

And Sanborn says:[54]

> We operate in schools, and schools are developmental institutions.
> . . . What, in terms of behaviorial characteristics of students who go
> through your school, do you look for in order to determine whether
> you earn your salary or not?

[53] Barbara Vance, "The Counselor—An Agent of What Change?" *Personnel and
Guidance Journal* 45:1012–1016 (June, 1967).
[54] Marshal P. Sanborn, "Following My Nose Toward a Concept of a Creative
Counselor," *The School Counselor* 14:68–73 (November, 1966).

The dilemma is to be found in just what this means in terms of limits, and too frequently the limits are narrow indeed. This, surely, is the primary reason for the gap between the young and the old, between teachers and students, between parents and children, between black children and the white society. The counselor, at least, should be one member of society who does not feel that he must determine what constitutes good behavior and bad behavior for his clients. He should be free enough, and secure enough, so that he can trust them to come to decisions (with his help, possibly) that are best for them. These decisions may sometimes be similar to those he feels he would have made for himself in a similar situation, but they may sometimes be quite different. The more certain the counselor feels that "this is the best way for you," the more likely it is that he is an imposing agent of society, rather than an aid in the self-development of the individual.

chapter 5

FUNCTIONS OF THE COUNSELOR

The 1960's will probably be known as the decade in which major attention was centered on the function and education, as well as general professional status, of the school counselor. Among the major reasons for this attention was the passage of the National Defense Education Act in 1958, and the Education Professions Development Act in 1968; the publication in 1962 of Gilbert Wrenn's book, *The Counselor in a Changing World;* and the work on the various policy statements on the functions and education of the counselor, accepted in 1964 by the American Personnel and Guidance Association, the American School Counselors Association, and the Association for Counselor Education and Supervision. A new policy statement on the elementary school counselor appeared in 1966, and a revision of the policy statement on the education of secondary school counselors appeared in 1967. All of these statements continue to stress that further study is necessary.

For several years the stress in the NDEA Counseling and Guidance Institutes moved steadily from short-term summer institutes to full-year, and even two-year, institutes. Thus the number of short-term institutes dropped from 83 in 1960 to 34 in 1965, while the full-year institutes increased from 7 in 1960 to 24 in 1966. About this time, however, the Division of Educational Personnel Training, counter to the recommendations of professional organizations, began to change the stress back to short-term institutes, possibly because this had greater political, if not educational, impact!

By 1969 the authority for such programs came under the Education Professions Development Act, Part C (fellowships) and Part D (institutes). There were 46 institute and fellowship programs granted for the summer of 1969 and the academic year 1969–70, with the majority of these being fellowship programs for experienced teachers.

The fact that, for several years, each year 500 to 700 individuals have been receiving an academic year of full-time counselor education, at the master's and the post-master's level, is obviously bound to have a major impact on both the concepts of the functions of the counselor and the education of the counselor. Prior to the passage of the NDEA, the great majority of school counselors were products of a part-time education. Few will question the benefit of a full-time graduate education, with minimal financial worries, as compared to a part-time education, with a maximum of financial and other concerns.

There is still, however, as will be noted, a discrepancy between what counselors do, and what is generally accepted as their more professional function. It should be noted, too, that while there is some professional disagreement on various questions about counselor function, there is a very high level of agreement on what the counselor should *not* consider to be his function.

Much of what some counselors are doing they do simply because their professional education, and their professional sense of responsibility, is at such a low level that they do not understand, and are not concerned about, what they should do. Thus they function in the general role of lackeys or sweep-up boys who do all of the odds and ends about which neither the administrators, the teachers nor the janitors wish to be concerned. Some of the blame for this sort of situation probably lies at the door of the state department of education and, more specifically, at the door of the supervisor or director of guidance for the state. It is up to the state not only to continue to increase their professional certification requirements, but, even more important, to enforce the requirements already on the books. I hear quite frequently, from fairly authentic sources, of individuals who are employed as counselors for the most unprofessional of reasons, in various states. State departments may have good reasons why they cannot immediately take action about such situations, but they could at least indicate their awareness of the situation, and in some way try to make it clear to school committees and other citizens that their children are being cheated by having, in a critical position, individuals who have no professional preparation for their jobs. The professional organizations, too, might share some of the blame for this situation, since they could frequently give more support to state departments by looking at the quality of the apples in their own barrels. If, in any state, the primary requirement for achieving a top educational job in the state department of education is that one be a professional politician, then we can assume that the quality of leadership in the field of counseling in that state is going to be feeble.

Then, too, there are still too many schools where principals and superintendents are living in the past century, and are woefully inadequate in the provision of any leadership in the development of a modern school program, including the provision of counseling and other pupil personnel services. Some school administrators lack the courage to do anything other than attempt to maintain the status quo, and counseling services will find little support from them. It is reasonable to assume that the school should provide the educational leadership in any community; in some communities, if this is not forthcoming from the school, there is no other source. Lay leadership may sometimes retard education rather than improve it.

In such school systems there is little likelihood of the presence of a professional school counselor, and if one does happen to be in such a system, he will obviously work under serious handicaps. Nevertheless, changes are possible, as long as the counselor is discreet, and not too much the bull in the china shop—and, of course, as long as he does not allow the system to wear him down and gradually erode his professional integrity. I have seen effective counselors doing a splendid job in a miserable school.

That some counselors perform nonprofessional tasks is not always, however, due to ignorance, feeble state departments, or inadequate school administrators. Some such counselors have had a fair degree of professional preparation. Probably every counselor-educator knows of former students who have gone through his program and have, for some reason, apparently got nothing from the program, who operate now as if they had never had any professional preparation whatsoever. The fault here lies on the doorstep of the counselor preparation institution, which might of course have good reasons for saying that it cannot, after all, guarantee the professional competence of all of its graduates. Nevertheless, every time a graduate of a counselor education program shows on the job that he is functioning in an unprofessional manner, the institution must look at its program, and at its admissions policies, and feel that somehow, somewhere, it has not done the job that it should be doing.

Such counselors, then, whether they perform their questionable acts because of ignorance or because of their own weaknesses, are a menace to the profession of counseling, and there is still an unfortunately large number of such individuals in schools and colleges. Without protest, they do all sorts of things, such as functioning as a policeman (checking the corridors, checking the lunch room, checking the detention hall); or a disciplinarian (actually punishing children for fancied or real misdemeanors, reporting deviate behavior to the principal); or a prosecuting attorney (trying to get a child to admit that he has committed some offense, or get him into a verbal trap); or a spy (trying to get information from various sources, which is reported faithfully to the principal); or a bigot (giving all of his attention to the "better" children in the community, but none to those whose parents do not count for much). They also, in the supposed guise of counseling, give a display of their own ignorance—or more likely, their own neurotic needs—when, supposedly for the good of the child but almost certainly for their own ego satisfaction, they criticize children, they talk endlessly to them about how they should live their lives and what their behavior should be; they scold and they moralize; they talk and they talk and they talk; and they never listen, and they never understand, since they can hear nothing because of the noise of their own voices.

This, however, is the dismal side of the picture. Although one such person among the ranks of counselors can be considered as one too many, every counselor must be careful to distinguish the counselor whose job concept is an unprofessional one from the counselor whose job concept is different but by no means unprofessional. Probably the basic professional argument centers around the question of the extent to which the "counselor" is a *counselor* with the stress on the emotions and feelings as well as intellect; with emphasis on helping the irrational individual get to the point where he can use information as well as providing him with information; with stress on the counselor's working with a minority of the children, in a remedial sense, but with most of the children and with all of the teachers in a preventive sense.

There is also what might be called a sub-debate among counselors on the extent to which counseling is psychotherapy, and hence the extent to which the counselor should think of himself as requiring professional preparation so that he can function as a psychotherapist with most disturbed individuals who are not in need of institutionalization. Some counselors would feel that the distinction between those clients who may be referred to a psychiatrist and those who should not is a rather meaningless one, since what is really meant when one refers to psychiatry is psychotherapy; and the term psychiatrist is not a job description, but rather the name of a particular kind of psychotherapist who has had a particular kind of training which probably makes him more effective with some disturbed people, less effective than other kinds of psychotherapists with other kinds of disturbed people. These individuals would feel that the professional counselor should think of his ultimate training as fitting him to work effectively with most noninstitutionalized individuals. When a client is sent to an institution, it is not so much that he needs the services of a psychiatrist, as that he needs the services of a number of specialized workers—psychiatrists, psychologists, counselors, nurses, and others— and that he can get these total combined services only in an institution. Recent evidence shows, however, that even more important than certain services is the complete and unequivocal acceptance of the individual by all staff members in the institution. The evidence also tends to indicate that one of the reasons why some individuals must spend their years in an institution is that they are not accepted by the staff as worthy individuals; rather, they are looked upon as the schizoid, or the manic depressive, or some other name of a disturbance, but not as a person. Even the rational and secure individual does not respond well when, in going to a medical doctor for the treatment of some physical ailment, he is looked upon as a "case." The disturbed individual is much less capable of reacting in a positive manner when he is looked upon as a problem.

In any case, as of now, the functions of the counselor are far from being determined, and there is a good deal of debate and dissension as to just what they might be. Sharp differences are to be noted between what might be described as the psychological perception of the counselor's functions, the school's perception of the counselor's functions, and the professional conception of the counselor's functions.

THE PSYCHOLOGICAL PERCEPTION OF THE FUNCTIONS OF THE COUNSELOR[1]

Most counselors would probably agree that what the counselor does is primarily psychological in nature. We may talk in a broad sense of the counselor being one who understands children and their behavior, and is able to help them to become more effective individuals who can

---

[1] *See* Dugald S. Arbuckle, "The School Counselor: Educator, Psychologist or What," *The School Counselor* 14:132–138 (January, 1967).

make more sense out of their educational experience and their day-to-day living. Later, they will be able to make educational, vocational, and personal choices which will be best for them. Certainly all would agree that this process of learning is psychological in nature. It may be Super[2] saying "Students should be helped to understand their own needs and the available resources in these terms, and to see how these resources may be used to meet their peculiar needs," or Gaither, Hackman and Hay,[3] describing vocational counseling as "it . . . starts with the individual's perception of himself (realistic or not), and in succeeding interviews the counselee learns more about the world of work and how various fields of work can meet his needs," or Mathewson[4] pointing out that "information may be *disseminated* but it is not necessarily *assimilated* effectively by the individual or his parents and applied wisely to his individual case. For that to happen an individual needs to have a pretty good understanding of himself as well as a motivation toward a continuing process of connecting up a maturing self-definition with social requirements and opportunities." They are all, surely, describing a process which is basically psychological in nature, even though it is being performed in an educational setting.

There are, however, other specialized personnel in the schools whose functions are also psychological in nature, and there is a remarkable similarity when one examines the functions of school social workers, psychologists, and counselors.[5] Here, for example, are a few descriptions of functions, with a few key words removed:

No. 1: . . . will perform a counseling function with pupils as well as parents and teachers . . . will perform a consultative function with parents and with other school and community personnel . . . will perform a coordinating function in integrating the resources of the school and community. . .[6]

No. 2: Assists each pupil to meet the needs and understand himself in relation to the social and psychological world in which he lives. . . . Assist each pupil to meet the need to develop personal decision making competency. . . . Assist all members

---

[2] Donald E. Super, "Goal Specificity in the Vocational Counseling of Future College Students," *Personnel and Guidance Journal* 43:127–134 (October, 1964).

[3] James W. Gaither, Roy B. Hackman, and John E. Hay, "Vocational Guidance: On the Beach," *Vocational Guidance Quarterly* 11:75–79 (Winter, 1963).

[4] Robert H. Mathewson, "Manpower or Persons: A Critical Issue," *Personnel and Guidance Journal* 43:338–342 (December, 1964).

[5] *See* Dugald S. Arbuckle, "Counselor, social worker, psychologist: Let's Ecumenicalize," *Personnel and Guidance Journal* 45:532–538 (February, 1967).

[6] "Preliminary Statement: Joint ACES-ASCA Committee on the Elementary School Counselor," *Personnel and Guidance Journal* 44: 659–661 (February, 1966).

of the staff to understand the importance of the individual pupil. . . . Determine the influence of the school program on pupil educational and psycho-social development. . . . Inform other staff members of significant changes in the school and non-school environments which have implications. . . . Assist parents to understand the developmental progress of their child, his needs, and environmental opportunities . . . interpret to the community . . . promote in the community non-school opportunities . . . use community resources.[7]

No. 3: . . . understanding and providing help, within the program of the school, for children who are having difficulties in using the resources of the school effectively . . . an approach . . . based on his understanding of human behavior, his skill in relationship and interviewing, and his ability to use school and community resources.[8]

No. 4: . . . in all areas of personal and social maladjustment, as well as academic difficulties, physical deficiencies, and confusion regarding educational and vocational choices.[9]

No. 5: . . . psychological counseling and guidance with such specific activities as individual child guidance, individual parent counseling, student counseling groups, and parent discussion groups; consultation, with such activities as consulting with individual teachers, teacher discussion groups, research and educational development, and referral and community services; individual and psychological evaluation, including such activities as case study, examination, diagnoses, recommending, reporting, and follow-up procedures.[10]

No. 6: . . . educational diagnosis, educational remediation, personality diagnosis, and personality remediation.[11]

It might be difficult for an outsider to believe that these examples refer to what are considered to be "unique" functions of three different groups of professional workers. Even those who read these words may have some immediate difficulty in realizing that the first example describes the functions of the elementary school counselor, the second

[7] "Tentative Statement of Policy for Secondary School Counselors," *Personnel and Guidance Journal* 42:195–196 (October, 1963).
[8] J. C. Nebo (Ed.), *Administration of School Social Work* (New York: National Association of Social Workers, 1960), p. 17.
[9] Jean R. Pearman and A. H. Burrows, *Social Services in the School* (Washington, D.C.: Public Affairs Press, 1955), p. 4.
[10] Robert E. Valett, *The Practice of School Psychology* (New York: John Wiley and Sons Inc., 1963), pp. 7–8.
[11] May Alice White and Myron U. Harris, *The School Psychologist* (New York: Harper and Brothers, 1961), pp. 5–6.

those of the secondary school counselor. Examples three and four describe the functions of the school social worker, and the last two examples describe the functions of the school psychologist.

It is obvious from these definitions, which I think are fairly representative, and are at least "semi-official," that all three groups view themselves as working in the same milieu, namely the school and its immediate environment, and with the same basic population—the children, and those who most immediately affect them—teachers, parents, and the community. To varying degrees, all three see their functions as involvement in counseling, appraisal and consultation, with children, teachers, parents, and other school personnel, and various members of the community.

The psychiatric profession has generally shown little understanding of the school, and particularly of the functions of the school counselor, and one is almost tempted to say, after perusing the psychological literature, that the psychological version of the school counselor is that he is "the little man who isn't there."[12] In looking over the last two years' issues of the *Journal of Counseling Psychology*, for example, the articles which are centered around "counselors" refer almost without exception to either graduate students or college or university counselors.[13] The term "school counselor" is practically nonexistent in this particular sampling of the literature, as is the term "mental health." Thus the *Journal of Counseling Psychology* pretty much ignores the existence of the person known as the "school counselor."

In perusing the last two years of pages of the *American Psychologist*, I find six issues which discuss mental health and disturbed children and schools. Again, however, the school counselor is noticeable by his almost total absence. Mariner,[14] for example, in examining professional education in the mental health field describes the four professional groups which he sees as providing most of the professional psychotherapeutic help in this country, and then goes on to say, "There are, of course, others who supply such help—some clergymen, nurses, and even aides in certain psychiatric hospitals . . ." The school as an institution and the school counselor as a person are

---

[12] *See* Dugald S. Arbuckle, "The School Counselor as a Therapist." Unpublished paper.
[13] Such as: Andrew Thompson and Robert Zimmerman, "Goals of Counseling: Whose? When?" *Journal of Counseling Psychology* 16:121–125 (March, 1969).
[14] Allen S. Mariner, "A Critical Look at Professional Education in the Mental Health Field," *American Psychologist* 22:271–281 (April, 1967).

viewed as having nothing to do with the provision of therapeutic help for children. Brown and Long,[15] in a paper on psychology and community mental health, totally ignore the existence of the school and the school counselor. The staff people mentioned are psychiatrists, psychologists, and social workers, and there is not the slightest implication that the school might possibly have some concern with the psychological health of children.

Brayfield,[16] the editor of the *American Psychologist*, in a presentation before a House Committee on community mental health centers, makes only a fleeting reference to the school when he says, "The schools, the courts, the churches, business and industry are among the major social arenas in which the special perspective and special competencies of the center should find expression." In the development of sound psychological health, the school, which has all of the children of the land for a significant period of time, and whose business is people and learning, is, in Brayfield's mind, on a par with the courts, churches, business and industry! In mentioning "important recent advances in psychological treatment" he refers to a special project in Tennessee, developments in behavior therapy, and treatment programs based on work in ecological psychology, the school being one part of the ecological system.

Hobbs,[17] in discussing a school for emotionally disturbed children, refers in 1966 to a "training program to prepare a new kind of mental health worker, called a teacher-counselor . . . ," apparently unaware of the fact that a somewhat similar person, needed for all schools, was the basis for a book *Teacher Counseling*,[18] published in 1950. While he does mention the place of the liaison teacher in helping to maintain communication between the regular classroom and the special school, there is no reference to the school counselor. It seems strange that "teacher" should somehow be more involved in the therapeutic function in the school than "counselor"! Implicit here, too, is the idea that "emotionally disturbed children" are a special breed of children who do not belong in the regular school, and that school staff should not be expected to be able to work with such children.

---

[15] Bertram S. Brown and Eugene S. Long, "Psychology and Community Mental Health: The Medical Muddle," *American Psychologist* 23:335–341 (May, 1968).
[16] Arthur H. Brayfield, "Community Mental Health Center Programs," *American Psychologist* 22:670–673 (August, 1967).
[17] Nicholas Hobbs, "Helping Disturbed Children: Psychological and Ecological Strategies," *American Psychologist* 21:1105–1115 (November, 1966).
[18] Dugald S. Arbuckle, *Teacher Counseling* (Cambridge, Mass.: Addison Wesley Press, 1950).

Hersch,[19] in referring to a "revolution" in mental health, describes the revolution as an overthrow of the status quo and the centering of attention on the community and the population rather than the individual. Nowhere is the school or the counselor mentioned as having anything to do with this revolution. A paper by Bardon[20] probably sums up the attitudes expressed in these various psychological journals. He refers to an array of pupil personnel service workers who will perform the functions now carried out by the school psychologist, but not by the *new* school psychologist as he envisages him. Among these workers "will be psychodiagnosticians, test technicians, child development specialists, home and school counselors, elementary guidance workers." These workers he views as "technicians," trained at the bachelors, one-year and two-year graduate level, and they will be thought of as "educational specialists," not directly related with psychology per se.

These attitudes are generally reflective of the psychological literature, and of psychologists, and they are, possibly, one of the major reasons for the crawling pace of what we know as mental health. The school is apparently seen as a place where children are forced to go to be taught something which in some dim future will be of value to them. School counselors would appear to be viewed as a part of this teaching team, not unlike the teachers, and neither would appear to have any major interest or concern or involvement in the therapeutic growth of the child. But surely the school is overwhelmingly the obvious, the only place where prevention can really have meaning. Until the concept of the therapeutic classroom becomes an accepted and integral part of the daily education of every child, we will continue to have clinics and hospitals making their possibly gallant, but futile gestures, in attempting to stop the flood of disturbed children who will increasingly pour down upon them, and may eventually overwhelm all of us. But the psychologists, generally, continue to have their experimental classes, and do their bits and pieces of research, and the impact on what happens in the classroom, day by day, is infinitesimally small. If we are really seriously interested in the development of the psychologically healthy mind and body, rather than in the cure of diseases, then that institution which is supposed to be

[19] Charles Hersch, "The Discontent Explosion in Mental Health," *American Psychologist* 23:497–506 (July, 1968).
[20] Jack I. Bardon, "School Psychology and School Psychologists: An Approach to an Old Problem," *American Psychologist* 23:187–194 (March, 1968).

totally dedicated to human growth and development, namely, the school, is the major social institution where this can take place.

THE SCHOOL'S PERCEPTION OF THE COUNSELOR

And what of the school, and particularly the school counselor? Does it, and he, resent this casual dismissal, this assumption of the almost total lack of school involvement in the development and growth of the psychological health of the child? Do school people resent the assumption that they have little or nothing to do with that which relates to the psychological and the therapeutic? The evidence would tend to indicate that far from resenting these assumptions, a great many school people, including school counselors, possibly even the majority, agree with them.[21] Counselors, many of whom are former teachers, tend to retain their teacher identity, and see their major function as the provision of information and advice rather than the development of a therapeutic atmosphere, either individually or in groups, in an office or a classroom, so that most effective learning and development might take place.

Papers or articles or talks which suggest the possibility of the school counselor being involved in a therapeutic sense, usually produce a sharp, and sometimes quite violent reaction. Krueger,[22] for example, warns school counselors about the grave effects of taking seriously such terms as "relationship" and "acceptance." Venn,[23] in describing the training of the counselor, says that he must have "courses in school administration, curriculum development, and school guidance itself. He must be a teacher on assignment, like a school administrator, not a specialist from another profession working in the school." Sexton[24] says, ". . . the less we emphasize the psychological, the psychiatric, and anything therapeutic, the better the feeling the students will have toward counseling." O'Hara[25] turns the counselor

---

[21] *See* Roger F. Aubrey, "Misapplication of Therapy Models to School Counseling," *Personnel and Guidance Journal* 48:273–278 (December, 1969).

[22] Albert H. Krueger, "Letters and Comments," *Personnel and Guidance Journal* 45:1033–1044 (June, 1967).

[23] Kenneth Venn, "Letters and Comments," *Personnel and Guidance Journal* 46:73 (September, 1967).

[24] John M. Sexton, "A Reaction to the ASCA Statement of Policy for Secondary School Counselors," *The School Counselor* 12:132–135 (March, 1965).

[25] Robert P. O'Hara, "Counseling and Vocational Psychology" in Dugald S. Arbuckle (Ed.), *Counseling and Psychotherapy: An Overview* (New York: McGraw-Hill Book Co., 1967), p. 113.

into a teacher when he presumes enough openness in the client to accept information-giving as the role of the counselor. When I suggested in a paper that counselors, psychologists, and social workers might get together and be given the more generic name "school counseling psychologist,"[26] I was put in my place with a "riposte" by Paulson,[27] which ended with the statement, "School counselors and school social workers are justly proud of their own names." Brammer,[28] who had the temerity to write a paper entitled "The counselor is a psychologist," was dismissed with such statements as, "Pathetically, the few statements in this presentation that can be deemed valid by an objective observer of counselors' work . . ." and "Brammer's proposal to discard the guidance model for counselor education, is then, alarmingly absurd."[29]

Collins,[30] who is a Dean of Instruction, says that "junior college counselors are not psychiatrists, not clinical counselors, nor depth psychiatrists, and those who overtly or covertly hold to such pretensions should be disabused of them." Payne,[31] a past president of the American Association of School Administrators, comments that a number of his faculty "do not believe that a counselor can help them in their understanding of a pupil in a class situation unless the counselor has actually had classroom experience" and that ". . . in the normal working day of a school counselor he is usually expected to perform both services (counseling and disciplining)."

Hoyt,[32] a past president of the American Personnel and Guidance Association, is apparently acceptant of such ideas, when in referring to the counselor's functions, he says, ". . . he regards the principal as his administrative superior and as the one person responsible for the direction of the guidance program."

Such statements, often rejecting with an almost hysterical vehemence the concept of a psychological and therapeutic role for the

[26] Dugald S. Arbuckle, "Counselor, Social Worker, Psychologist: Let's Ecumenicalize," *Personnel and Guidance Journal* 45:532–539 (February, 1967).

[27] Blanche B. Paulson, "Riposte," *Personnel and Guidance Journal* 45:539–540 (February, 1967).

[28] Lawrence M. Brammer, "The Counselor is a Psychologist," *Personnel and Guidance Journal* 47:4–9 (September, 1968).

[29] Joseph L. Felix, "Who Decided That?" *Personnel and Guidance Journal* 47:9–11 (September, 1968).

[30] Charles C. Collins, "Junior College Counseling: A Critical View," *Personnel and Guidance Journal* 43:546–550 (February, 1965).

[31] J. Win Payne, "Impact of the ASCA Statement of Counselor Role," *The School Counselor* 12:136–139 (March, 1965).

[32] Kenneth B. Hoyt, "Guidance: A Constellation of Services," *Personnel and Guidance Journal* 40:695–699 (April, 1962).

school counselor, are by no means atypical, and may even reflect the view of the majority of school counselors. The position papers which have been produced over the past number of years by the American Personnel and Guidance Association, the Association for Counselor Education and Supervision, and the American School Counselors Association on the function and the role of the counselor could very well fit into a psychological and therapeutic pattern, but this is not functionally the way that the pattern turns out. In actual practice the school counselor fits almost totally into the teaching and education model, hardly at all into the psychological and therapeutic model. The majority of even the younger counselors, many of whom go out with a "things will be different" gleam in their eye, within a few years are fairly well incorporated into the system, and become acceptant of the so-called guidance concept of the school counselor. The basic concept of the counselor being primarily responsible for the welfare of the individual is soon lost, and the welfare of the system and the organization easily takes precedence.

PROFESSIONAL PERCEPTION OF THE COUNSELOR'S FUNCTION

In the past decade the professional organizations directly concerned with counseling would appear to have moved in the direction of the psychological rather than the educational, although, as has been just indicated, there is a good deal of resistance to this movement. Nevertheless, the stress is now being put on *school* counselor rather than *guidance* counselor, *learning* rather than *teaching, listening* rather than *telling, preventive* rather than *remedial,* and *developmental problems* rather than medical diseases. Probably most critical of all, the counselor is emerging as a professionally competent individual whose functions and professional education are quite different from those of the teacher and the administrator. In earlier descriptions of the functions of the counselor, he sounded much more like a teacher and educator. Tooker, for example, in 1957, listed the following job functions of the counselor:[33]

1. First of all, he is an educator. . . .
2. He has direct responsibility for individual counseling of students assigned to him. . . .

---

[33] Ellis D. Tooker, "Counselor Role: Counselor Training," *Personnel and Guidance Journal* 36:263–267 (December, 1957).

3. He often has responsibility for group methods in guidance. . . .
4. He is expected to establish relationships with great numbers of individuals, so that students will come to identify him as a person to whom they can turn for advice and help within the school setting. . . .
5. He is expected to be familiar enough with standardized tests of intelligence, achievement, aptitude, interest and personality so that he can utilize test results in the process of counseling. . . .
6. He is often given considerable responsibility in arranging transfers of students for both academic and personal reasons. . . .
7. He is called upon to help in such important projects as building and maintaining cumulative record systems. . . .
8. He is often expected to conduct follow-up studies of graduates and drop-outs. . . .
9. It is not unusual for him to be asked to function as a resource person in such educational projects as the setting up of systems of reporting to parents. . . .
10. He is usually expected to know current college admission procedures and to serve as adviser to both parents and students in this area.
11. He is expected to participate in school activities and to assume his share of extracurricular activities. . . .
12. He is expected to maintain a knowledge of and working relationships with local business and industry so that he may be in a better position to counsel students in the area of local vocational offerings. . . .
13. He is often expected to help in the sponsoring of guidance-related activities such as college nights, career days, and guidance committees. . . .
14. He is frequently called upon to provide leadership in broad areas where guidance aspects may seem remote. . . .

Almost two decades ago Pierson[34] commented that the school counselor was primarily an educator whose clients were students, parents, and teachers. About the same time, Mathewson[35] felt that the school should spend less time with poorly adjusted students and more time with teachers and parents.

In 1957, Wrenn felt that any discussion of counselor role should be based on the following assumptions:[36]

[34] George A. Pierson, "Aesop and the School Counselor," *Personnel and Guidance Journal* 32:326–329 (February, 1954).
[35] Robert H. Mathewson, "The General Guidance Counselor," *Personnel and Guidance Journal* 32:544–547 (May, 1954).
[36] C. Gilbert Wrenn, "Status and Role of the School Counselor," *Personnel and Guidance Journal* 36:175–183 (November, 1957).

1. The school counselor is an educator with special professional training at the M.A. level and beyond.
2. The school counselor is a generalist in a number of school functions
and may be a specialist in at least one type of service. The nature
of this specialization may vary with each counselor's unique personal qualification and with the specific emphasis on his professional
education.
3. The school counselor's clients include teachers, parents, and administrators as well as students.
4. The school counselor's skills should include not only those necessary
for the individual counseling relationship but those essential to
working effectively with groups.
5. The school counselor is concerned primarily with the normal growth
needs of students, more with personality development than with
problem crises.
6. The school counselor, because of the expectations of student,
teacher, administrator, must have a fairly high level of psychological sophistication in his professional education and in-service
development. . . .

Five years later, one of his four recommendations dealing with
the counselor was as follows:[37]

That the professional job description of a counselor specify that he
perform four major functions: (a) counsel with students; (b) consult
with teachers, administrators, and parents as they in turn deal with
students; (c) study the changing facts about the student population
and interpret what is found to school committees and administrators;
(d) coordinate counseling resources in school and between school and
community. From two-thirds to three-fourths of the counselor's time,
in either elementary or high school, should be committed to the first
two of these functions. Activities that do not fall into one of these four
areas neither should be expected nor encouraged as part of the counselor's regular working schedule.

It may be noted, in these later statements, that the counselor is
considered to be neither an "educator" nor a "teacher." He has his own
particular professional function, counseling, which he performs in an
educational environment, usually a school, and he is thus known as a
school counselor. It may also be noted that while he may work with
"most" children, he also works with children who may have problems,
primarily of a developmental nature.

There is more than a subtle difference in the 1964 policy state-

---

[37] C. Gilbert Wrenn, *The Counselor in a Changing World* (Washington, D.C.:
American Personnel and Guidance Association, 1962), p. 137.

ment accepted by the American School Counselors Association, and modified very little in the succeeding years. It stresses the fact that the majority of the school counselor's time should be devoted to individual or small group counseling, and describes his major professional responsibilities as the following:

1. Assist each pupil to meet the need to understand himself in relation to the social and psychological world in which he lives. This implies helping each pupil to understand his aptitudes, interests, attitudes, abilities, opportunities for self-fulfillment, and the interrelationships among these.
2. Assist each pupil to meet the need of accepting (defined as being able to behave consistent with) his aptitudes, interests, attitudes, abilities and opportunities for self-fulfillment.
3. Assist each pupil to meet the need to develop personal decision-making competency. Included is the responsibility of assuring that the pupil's opportunities for self-understanding and self-fulfillment are not restricted by the group consideration and processes inherent in schools.
4. Assist all members of the individual staff to understand the importance of the individual pupil and to provide information, material and consultative assistance aimed at supporting their efforts to understand pupils.
5. Determine the influence of the school program on pupil educational and psycho-social development, and to convey such information to other staff members.
6. Inform other staff members of significant changes in the school and nonschool environments which have implications for instruction, the psycho-social well-being of pupils, and to participate in related program development.
7. Assist parents to understand the developmental progress of their child, his needs, and environmental opportunities, for purposes of increasing their ability to contribute to their child's development.
8. Interpret to the community the importance of consideration for the individual and the contribution of the school counseling program to that end.
9. Promote in the community nonschool opportunities necessary for pupil development.
10. Use and/or promote community resources designed to meet unusual or extreme needs of pupils which are beyond the responsibility of the school.

The report accepted by the American Personnel and Guidance Association at its annual convention in 1964 described the role of counselors as follows:

1. The major responsibility of the counselor is to assist an individual through the counseling relationship to utilize his own resources and his environmental opportunities in the process of self-understanding, planning, decision-making and coping with problems relative to his developmental needs and to his vocational and educational activities.
2. The counselor also engages in related activities. For example, he makes effective use of the services of other professional personnel through referrals and consultation. He works with other persons in his employment environment in a manner which facilitates the achievement of desirable objectives for the benefit of the counselee. He may perform additional services for which he has the necessary preparation and the nature of which is such that they are logically his professional responsibility within the setting in which he works. However, he should not be expected to perform tasks which are inconsistent with his professional role as a counselor, or which are inappropriate for the social institution for which he works.
3. In all of his professional activities, the counselor maintains a high level of ethical practice in accordance with the Code of Ethics of the American Personnel and Guidance Association.
4. The counselor expects that in the employment setting in which he works conditions will be maintained which will enable him to work in a professional manner. These conditions include freedom to exercise his skills on a professional level, time to perform the counseling function, and adequate facilities.

As has been indicated, a joint ACES-ASCA committee, in 1966, described the major functions of the elementary school counselor as counseling with pupils as well as with parents and teachers; consulting with parents and other school and community personnel; coordinating and integrating the resources of the school and the community.

It is interesting to note that, over the years, one of the continuing struggles of the hundreds of committees deliberating on the counselor's functions is over the acceptance of the concept that the professionally competent person cannot be all things to all men. The functions of the counselor must have certain limitations if the counselor is to be professionally effective.

There would seem to be little doubt, however, that the counselor is gradually assuming a professional place in the sun. Counselors themselves view their functions in a much different manner than they did a decade or more ago. In a study conducted in the 1920s, Edgerton[38] found that counselors felt that their functions consisted of (a) interviewing students; (b) teaching classes in occupations; (c)

---

[38] A. H. Edgerton, *Vocational Guidance and Counseling* (New York: The Macmillan Co., 1926).

finding jobs for students and following them up; (d) administering tests; (e) doing research in the study of occupations.

At that time, as would be expected, the counselor's concept of his role was almost entirely vocational. Some years later, Cox[39] undertook an investigation of a group of counselors in secondary schools throughout the country. She found that their functions, in order of frequency, were: (1) work with parents; (2) educational-vocational-emotional guidance of pupils; (3) supervision of tests, both giving tests and interpreting test results; (4) cooperation with law enforcement agencies; (5) consultation with employers; (6) discipline; (7) placement; (8) coordinating the guidance program of the school; (9) home-room supervision; (10) cooperation with community guidance agencies; (11) teaching; (12) chaperoning parties and social needs; (13) follow-up of pupils who had left school.

This study tended to point up the increasing and conflicting functions that were supposedly performed by the counselor. About the same time, Wright,[40] in a report of an analysis by Minneapolis counselors of their function, indicated that the secondary school counselors felt that their job consisted of (1) checking credits for graduation and college entrance; (2) advising those students entering and those in military service; (3) interviewing and counseling failing students; (4) handling employment; (5) arranging group conferences; (6) writing letters of reference for pupils who were in school or who had left school; (7) conferring with students planning to withdraw from school; (8) doing clerical work; (9) conferring with teachers about pupils' problems.

Another study of high schools in the state of Washington indicated that counselors were expected to orient eighth graders; provide occupational information about colleges; provide a testing program for the four years, and assume the responsibility for recording the data; provide for social development; make adequate provision for exceptional students; arrange adequate occupational placement; do follow-up studies; evaluate the program for future improvement; and organize their time so as to be able to do individual counseling.[41]

While, as has been indicated, such concepts about counselor

39 Rachel D. Cox, *Counselors and Their Work* (Harrisburg: Archives Press, 1945).
40 Barbara H. Wright, "Minneapolis School Counselors Analyze Their Jobs," *Occupations* 24:214–219 (January, 1946).
41 Werner C. Dieckmann, "What Kind of Guidance and Counseling Programs in the Small School," *The Bulletin of the National Association of Secondary School Principals* 37:233–235 (November, 1952).

functions have by no means been totally abandoned, especially by school administrators, there are, nevertheless, definite indications of change. Shertzer and Stone[42] have stressed the importance of counselors' articulating their own identity, and of communicating their role to the public. Boy and Pine have indicated the functions that are outside the role of the school counselor. Their list is as follows:[43]

1. He does not have administrative duties such as, for example, providing parents with academic reports, issuing failure reports to parents, arranging for bus transportation. . . .
2. He does not have instructional, tutorial, proctorial, or supervisory duties. . . .
3. He does not discipline students.
4. He has no clerical tasks which prevent him from devoting his full effort to professional activities. . . .
5. He has nothing to do with the scheduling of classes or the arrangement of academic programs.
6. He does not check attendance or serve as a truant officer.

In a study of the job satisfactions of school counselors, Hansen[44] found that the most satisfying activities were working with teachers and providing guidance services to individual students. The least satisfying activities were administrative duties and paper work. Roemmich[45] found that counselor trainees considered their three most important tasks, out of a list of over one hundred, to be counseling students in accepting themselves as individuals, counseling students in expressing and developing awareness of feelings and values, and counseling students regarding potentials and limitations. Helping the pupil or patient to develop his capacities for candid and foresightful self-evaluation (but not necessarily helping him to determine or give content to his conclusions) is considered to be the crucial counselor function by Shoben.[46]

There have been, then, and there still are, conflicting concepts of

---

[42] Bruce Shertzer and Shelley C. Stone, "The School Counselor and His Publics: A Problem in Role Definition," *Personnel and Guidance Journal* 41:687–692 (April, 1963).
[43] Angelo V. Boy and Gerald J. Pine, *The Counselor in The Schools* (Boston: Houghton Mifflin Co., 1968), p. 289.
[44] James C. Hansen, "Job Satisfactions and Job Activities of School Counselors," *Personnel and Guidance Journal* 45:790–794 (April, 1967).
[45] Herman Roemmich, "Counselor Functions in Terms of Behavioral Tasks," *The School Counselor* 14:312–317 (May, 1967).
[46] Edward J. Shoben, Jr., "Personal Worth in Education and Counseling" in John D. Krumboltz (Ed.) *Revolution in Counseling* (Boston: Houghton Mifflin Co., 1966), p. 73.

functions, particularly at the operational level in the school.[47] Nor, of course, is this surprising. In many states, the state department of education shows little or no concern with the quality of counselor education programs. Professionalism is measured in terms of several semester hours of doubtful study in questionable institutions from instructors whose lack of understanding is clearly surpassed by their courage in teaching something about which they know nothing. Many state departments of education appear to believe that the counselor is really a teacher, and that certification carries with it the requirement of teaching experience—the assumption is that teaching experience somehow makes one a better school counselor. This is a highly debatable assumption, and evidence tends at least to point to the possibility that teaching gives one so many bad counseling habits that a major function of counselor education is to help former teachers to unlearn most of what they learned as teachers! No one will argue with the statement that the counselor should be aware of the day-to-day problems of teachers, and should be understanding of them; that he should understand the working of the school and its relations with parents and with the community; that he should be able to work with teachers, administrators and other professional workers in the school; that he should be able to work effectively with children. The question is: does several years of unsupervised teaching give any evidence of the competence of the individual in these areas? Would not an educational program of counselor education that would include carefully supervised experiences in these areas be a more valid measure of the effectiveness of the potential school counselor? This latter statement assumes, of course, that teaching and counseling are different functions.

In the long run, the professional competence of any worker is not determined at a political level, but by the professional workers in the particular professional discipline. We can hardly talk about the professional school counselor as long as we have fifty state versions of who he is, the only level of agreement being the generally low status of the counselor. At the same time hundreds of universities and colleges are all shouting their versions of counselor education, and it is truly phenomenal how so many institutions, with the advent of federal funding, suddenly discovered that they had counselor education programs. Actually, how many institutions, with the staff and facilities they now have, can be described as having a first rate counselor education program—twenty, forty, or the several hundreds who indicate

---

[47] *See* Dugald S. Arbuckle, "The Conflicting Functions of the School Counselor," *Counselor Education and Supervision* 1:54–59 (Winter, 1961).

to the U.S. Office of Education that they have a counselor education program?

The professional stamp of approval must be on counselor education programs just as it is on counselors. This approval of counselors should come from the institution rather than from the state department of education or, rather, the approval of the state department should come through the institution. Once a counselor education program has been approved by the professional organization as first rate, a graduate of that program should meet state certification requirements anywhere in the country. There should be no need to have state department detectives checking to see if he has had this course, this course and this course—never, of course, asking where and from whom he took the courses! This also means that institutions will have to be named, identified, and periodically checked to determine the calibre of their programs. One does not become a medical doctor, a dentist, a lawyer, or an architect by attending a few classes at almost any institution in the United States. There are certain institutions that have professionally acceptable medical schools and law schools and schools of engineering, and so there must soon be certain institutions which will be identified as having professionally acceptable programs of counselor education.

Once the school counselor becomes a graduate of one of the relatively few professionally acceptable counselor education programs, then we may see a rapid reduction in both the "part-timeness" of his education and the "part-timeness" of his function. There may even, for a time, be a reduction in the number of people who are entitled to the name "school counselor." This is not all bad, since the major problem in school counseling today is not lack of quantity, but lack of quality. Ideally we must try to increase the number of qualified school counselors, but it is better to have fewer qualified counselors than to have more unqualified counselors, and thus live under the illusion that numbers of bodies will satisfy our problem. This illusion appears to be somewhat acceptable in the field of education.

It would seem reasonable to say that there are three major professional groups in the modern American school—the teachers, the administrators, and the specialized service personnel. It is interesting to note that of all these groups, it is only the school counselor who is willing to accept the part-time, dual-role status. Other professional workers may spend only part of their time in the service of the school, but they are not part-time doctors, or part-time nurses, or part-time psychologists, or part-time psychiatrists. They are medical doctors, or nurses, or psychologists, or psychiatrists. Like pregnancy, "they are or they ain't," and there is no in-between status. We have no doctor-teacher, or nurse-principal, or psychologist-janitor, but we have thousands of teacher-counselors, or even more absurd, principal-counselors, and even, horror added upon horror, superintendent-counselors. Even worse, this schizophrenic fellow doesn't seem to mind this dual or triple status, and goes blithely walking off in several directions at the same time, quite unaware that one set of feet is falling over the other.

There are many tasks that must be carried out to continue the necessary functions of the school, and while all of these tasks may be defended as being needed to achieve the broad and immediate goals of the school, they are tasks that cannot be done by one person, even assuming that he had the time. This is so because of his inadequate knowledge and education, because of his lack of skills, because of his personality structure, and because certain functions clash with other functions. Thus, a perfectly good mathematics teacher might be a very poor English teacher because he doesn't know English, and isn't interested in it; a perfectly good English teacher may be a poor physical education teacher because he lacks the physical coordination necessary for this task; a principal may be effective because he is the sort of person who likes organizing and administering and directing and controlling. All of these people *may* become good school counselors if they have, or if they develop, an understanding of people and human behavior, if they are deeply but not too neurotically interested in working with individuals as individuals, and if they master the knowledges and the skills that are part of the repertoire of the school counselor. They *may*, it should be noted, become effective school counselors, but they cannot do so while they still retain their previous occupational functions, since effectiveness as a teacher or a principal may often be equated with ineffectiveness as a counselor. The particular problems of the teacher as a counselor will be covered in more detail in a later chapter.

COUNSELOR FUNCTION AND COUNSELOR RESPONSIBILITY[48]

Any occupation which considers itself to be "professional" must have some degree of consistency among its practitioners as to their concept of what their professional functions might be. Thus all would probably

---

[48] *See* Dugald S. Arbuckle "A Question of Counselor Function and Responsibility," *Personnel and Guidance Journal* 47:341–346 (December, 1968).

agree that the most crucial immediate problem is that counselors themselves share some general agreement as to who they are and what constitutes their professional functions and professional responsibilities. There is no question that there has been positive movement in this direction in the last decade, but there is still a glaring discrepancy between the counselor's perceptions of his functions and responsibilities, and the perceptions of the school administrator. We could probably assume, for example, that school administrators would not accept the following statement by Weitz: "It is interesting to note that the typical administrator not only cannot provide the kinds of guidance described here, but he also cannot separate the guidance and instructional functions in general administrative practice."[49] Nor would some accept the line separating the two as spelled out by Mathewson:[50]

> The crucial line separating the educational counselor from the administrative officer, the admissions officer, or the industrial personnel officer is that the counselor is primarily concerned with personal and not institutional or social needs, and is engaged in educative and interpretive functions, not selective, placement or recruitment functions.

Are counselors and administrators different persons, then, with different kinds of values? Does the difference in attitude arise because they are different as people, rather than because they represent a different occupational group? There is at least some evidence to suggest that this might be so. Chenault and Seegars,[51] for example, concluded after a study that counselors and principals were both essentially dominant persons, with principals leaning toward the competitive side of the continuum and counselors leaning toward the tolerant side. Principals would have liked their counselors to be firmer and more aggressive. Another study[52] indicated that, on the matter of values, counselors and administrators both ranked high on self-realization and altruism, and low on money and security, although adminis-

---

[49] Henry Weitz, *Behavior Change Through Guidance* (New York: John Wiley and Sons, 1964), p. 64.

[50] Robert W. Mathewson, "Manpower or Persons: A Critical Issue," *Personnel and Guidance Journal* 43:338–342 (December, 1964).

[51] Joann Chenault and James E. Seegars, Jr., "The Interpersonal Diagnosis of Principals and Counselors," *Personnel and Guidance Journal* 41:118–122 (October, 1962).

[52] Buford Stefflre and Fred Lergren, "Value Differences Between Counselors and Administrators," *Vocational Guidance Quarterly* 10:226–228 (Summer, 1962).

trators did rank higher than counselors on money. The most significant difference was the high evaluation placed on control by the administrators. Still another study,[53] comparing the attitudes of counselors with women deans', indicated that deans were more authoritarian, more persuasive, less sympathetic and less understanding than college counselors. In a study of needs, Kemp[54] concludes that the counselor, more than the principal, satisfies his need to understand how others feel about problems, to put one's self in the other's place, to form new friendships, to share with friends, and to say things so that he might discover the effect they will have on others. The principal, more than the counselor, satisfies his need to be successful, to solve difficult problems, to be recognized as an authority, to complete the undertaking, to persist with the problem although no progress is apparent, to do what is expected, to conform to custom, to tell others they have done well, to follow a plan, to organize details and have things run smoothly.

Knock and Cody,[55] in a study of counselor candidates, teachers, and administrators found that persons preparing for careers as school counselors appeared to be more student-centered than currently-employed school teachers and administrators. Fotiu[56] found that principals tended to be more satisfied than counselors about the current role of secondary school counselors. One of the results of a study by Sweeney[57] was the indication that principals see the counselor as a quasi-administrator, and they prefer more administrative type leadership among counselors.

Thus it would seem that, in general, the counselor and the administrator are two different kinds of people, and the professional responsibilities which they accept are a reflection of this difference. Let us note what school administrators appear to be saying about counselors and their functions:

1. There is a degree of suspicion, particularly among school administrators and some teachers, of things psychological and thera-

[53] Mary Elizabeth Reeves and Dugald S. Arbuckle, "The Counseling Attitudes of Deans of Women," *Personnel and Guidance Journal* 41:438–445 (January, 1963).
[54] C. Gratton Kemp, "Counseling and Need Structure of High School Principals and of Counselors," *Journal of Counseling Psychology* 9:326–328 (Winter, 1962).
[55] Garry H. Knock and John J. Cody, "Student-centeredness: A Comparison of Counselor Candidates, Teachers and Administrators," *Counselor Education and Supervision* 6:114–119 (Winter, 1967).
[56] Peter G. Fotiu, "Do Counselors and Principals Agree?" *The School Counselor* 14:298–303 (May, 1967).
[57] Thomas J. Sweeney, "The School Counselor As Perceived by School Counselors and Their Principals," *Personnel and Guidance Journal* 44:844–849 (April, 1966).

peutic. This very attitude might at least be one of the reasons why, for some children at least, the learning which takes place in school is minimal. While counselors might disagree on methodological procedures, there would be little argument about their therapeutic role, even if this may mean nothing more than providing a therapeutic milieu in which the student may be helped to learn and to grow. Some counselors may be more information-centered than others, but in their helping and caring relationship with students, all have a therapeutic involvement. Indeed, many teachers would be the first to say that if one is to be really involved with a student in the learning process, a therapeutic atmosphere is an absolute requisite. Most counselors, too, would see themselves as psychologists, at least in a generic sense, whether or not they might carry such a title. After all, they are concerned with people, and their behavior, and the learning process. This surely, is in the realm of psychology. The term psychiatric is often used with the other two, and this probably brings visions of a couch and a man with a beard and an Austrian accent! Actually, whether one uses the term psychological or psychiatric, it would seem that an understanding of some of the abnormalities of human behavior, and at least some degree of skill in counseling and diagnosis, would be minimal requisites for anyone who calls himself a school counselor.

2. The administrator often sees no apparent clash between differing functions and responsibilities. This is most often noted in the assumption that the disciplinary, the evaluative, and the authority roles of the teacher and the administrator in no way interfere with the functions and the responsibilities of the counselor. Many children, of course, are secure and solid enough so that evaluation and disciplinary action will have little effect on them. The rub, however, is that the children and adults who are like this are the ones whose evaluations are usually quite positive, and who are very seldom the recipients of disciplinary action. The individuals who are least equipped to take the blows and the discipline are the ones who most often receive them. All too frequently in schools the smiles, the approving nods, and the "That's good" go to those who least need it. In universities administrative deans still insist on talking about "educational" value and use phrases like "we're really trying to help the student" at hearings of various disciplinary boards at which punishment is being meted out. Surely this is, psychologically, plain nonsense. The administrator who, while disciplining the individual, is at the same time encouraging him to feel free to express his feelings might be accused of at least some degree of schizophrenia!

It would seem crucial that the counselor be viewed by his potential clientele not only as a caring and helping individual, but equally important, as one who does not have, and does not represent the authority of the institution. The counselor should represent the highest level of security in the institution, he should be an individual with whom another person can correctly feel, "I can be totally honest with this person, and I will not have to pay a price." Surely that statement cannot be made to the administrator if he has accepted any level of responsibility for the operation of the institution.

3. If there is no particular difference in the functions and the responsibilities of the counselor and the administrator, then it is not unreasonable to assume, as do many administrators, that there is no need for any special training or education for the counselor. If the counselor does not have a specialized function, quite different from those of the teacher and administrator, then obviously there is no need for a special program of education for counselors.

A professional individual, of course, in a school as elsewhere, does not ask his employer "What do you want me to do?" It is not a case of the individual being fitted to the job, but rather are the particular skills and capacities of the individual such that he can be effective in a certain task. If they are, he might consider accepting the position, if they are not, he obviously should not accept the position even if it were offered to him. It is difficult for me to believe that any professional school counselor, if asked by a potential employer, "Do you accept the responsibility of utilizing your authority to compel certain students to change their behavior?" would answer any other way than, "No, I do not." On the other hand, it would seem equally logical that a school administrator, if asked the same question, might respond, "Well, I hope we never have to compel a student to do anything, but if his behavior is disruptive, and counter to school policy, then yes, I might have to compel him to change his behavior or leave the institution."

On this same point there is also the assumption that the counselor's professional knowledge, as well as his professional skills, are not in any way different from those of the teacher or the administrator. This again, of course, is totally counter to the position taken by APGA, ACES, and ASCA, and these positions represent the attitude of, literally, thousands of counselors and counselor educators. The counselor, obviously, as part of his professional education, should know the school, and the people who work in the school, and the culture and the environment which affect the school. But he should not be expected to be as expert in his knowledge of school building construction as is the superintendent; he should not be expected to be as knowledgeable about the costs and the staffing of the various curricular programs in the modern high school as the principal; he should not be expected to know as much about the latest in the "new math" as does the elementary teacher; he should not be expected to know as much about the history of Europe as the history teacher. He should, however, be expert in problems dealing with human communication; he should know much about people and their behavior; he should have diagnostic capacities and skills; he should know much about the nonschool world of work and further education; above all he should be capable of relating in a positive way with individuals who resist and resent any attempt at human communication and closeness. In effect, his knowledge and his capacities must be different than those of the teacher and the administrator if he is going to have any right to the name of counselor.

WHAT TO DO

It would seem crucial, then, that certain full-time school personnel, in large numbers, accept the function of helping to evolve, for each child, the means by which he can develop to his full potential, he can grow and become, he can truly move towards the goal of an individually free, self-actualized human being. The professional title of those who perform this function is totally irrelevant. I only use the term school counselor because this person would appear to be the one who is now in the most strategic position in the school to accept this role. And it is naive, I think, to assume that the teacher can perform such a task. He can contribute, but this must be the primary responsibility of a person such as the counselor. What, then can be done?

1. From the moment the child enters the school, the primary concern should be with his psychological well-being, and knowledge and skills should be considered to be a means by which this state of psychological health might be reached. By the time the child reaches the school, his experiences may have been such that he has already achieved a high level of psychological health, or he may already be well on the way to a pattern of neurotic, or even psychotic living. This means that not only will the child be provided with adequate and supportive human relationships, individually and in groups, but it also means that a variety of positive and therapeutic experiences will be

provided. The classroom will obviously be one of the key places where these experiences will be provided, and the teacher is obviously one of the key people. The teacher herself need not be a counselor or a therapist, but children should not have to live with a damaging and destructive teacher, and such a teacher should be helped to modify her own self-concept or be removed. The school counselor as a therapist, then, will work individually or in small groups with children, he will help teachers and others to devise helpful and therapeutic experiences for the child, in the classroom and out, and he will accept the responsibility of doing something to modify the outside environment if it is destructive to the well-being of the child. He will also accept the responsibility of doing something to the school environment, including the curriculum and the teachers and the administration, if it is destructive to the well-being of the child.

2. The sharply felt alienation of the college and university student is a culmination of his frustration over years of alienation from his school experience. Increasingly, as he progresses through the grades, his school experiences have less and less of a relationship to his life and living. The school, in a way, becomes the unreal ghetto; particularly in a very large city, the ghetto is the school, not the outside community. The black parents who are increasingly pressing the city school bureaucracy for local and community control are simply insisting on bringing the school back to the reality of the community of which it *should* be a part. The school counselor, accepting the responsibility of his therapeutic role, will work for the *responsible* involvement of the parents in the educational experiences of their children, and thus prevent the totally irresponsible takeover of the schools by irresponsible individuals. The child can hardly have a positive and therapeutic experience in the school if this experience has no relationship to his out-of-school living.

3. Every effort will be made to develop experiences starting with what the child has and does not have, rather than imposing general experiences on a group of children, on the apparent assumption that individual differences are no more than a myth!

4. Counselor education programs will move in the direction of developing experiences, including the accumulation of knowledge, which will help to increase the level of humanization and self-actualization of the student counselor. A program can be rigorous and scholarly and still consider such things as compassion and patience and understanding as basic therapeutic attributes rather than well-worn clichés. This means that drastic changes must be made in admis-

sions criteria, in the evaluation of student effectiveness, and in the cognitive course offerings and their relationship to effectiveness in the actual process of counseling.

And all of this will be the primary responsibility of those individuals who work in the realm of human behavior and learning and change, and psychology and psychotherapy. They will be an integral part of the school staff, and there will be little need to bring in medical doctors who are familiar with hospitals and diseases and injuries to assist in helping the school staff to understand the behavior of children and the complications of the learning process. There will be no need, as was indicated in a local paper of an eastern city, to bring in psychiatrists to "focus on and understand the role and the importance of the teacher and the school environment in relation to the intellectual and emotional development of all children." If the basic school staff cannot do this, if the school does not accept its responsibility as the institution which centers on learning and the positive development of the individual, the institution in which is centered the major knowledge about people and their behavior, then the alienation and the rejection of the school by millions of current students will be little more than an introduction to what lies ahead.

Counselors, too, will no longer be described by this rather melancholy news item which was taken from a recent edition of a large city newspaper. Only the names are changed:

> John H. Porter . . . has been appointed director of guidance at Pendor High School. He is a graduate of Kim High School and the University of Oregon, where he was a biology major and a member of Phi Beta Kappa. He served for six years in the army with the rank of captain. He was stationed in Hawaii, as a weapons instructor. He retired from the service in 1961. He has taught summer school at Pendor, and science at Pendor Junior High, grades 7 through 9. He now teaches biology and chemistry and is the football coach. He is studying for his masters degree in biological sciences. Mr. Porter does all senior counselling (sic) and college placement at Pendor.

As long as this continues to be the background and professional preparation of the person called school counselor, we can hardly expect the counselor to educate the administrator as to the uniqueness of his functions and his responsibilities!

chapter 6

THE PROFESSIONAL EDUCATION
OF THE COUNSELOR

While it is true that there is now a professional version of the counselor's education, there is a good deal of debate about it, and in actual practice there is still confusion over who is being educated for what. Let us first look at what might be considered to be the professional version of the counselor's education, and then examine some of the dissension that swirls around it.

THE PROFESSIONAL VERSION OF COUNSELOR EDUCATION

Reference was made in the previous chapter to the three events of the 1960's that had a tremendous impact on concepts regarding the functions and the education of the counselor. The implementation of Title VB of the National Defense Education Act soon made it painfully clear that very few institutions had actually developed effective programs for counselor education. The number of institutions applying for contracts to conduct guidance and counseling institutes dropped off drastically when the U.S. Office of Education instituted a policy of requesting each institution that applied for a contract to present also an "Inventory of Institutional Resources." A perusal of these inventories made it clear that there were surprisingly few institutions that had more than one full-time staff member totally employed in the education of the school counselor. The answers to questionnaires sent

126

out by the U.S. Office of Education[1] indicate an interesting institutional interpretation of the request for courses offering "specific preparation for guidance and student personnel." Some of the courses mentioned by various institutions were, for example, "Correctional Arithmetic," "Parent Counseling in Speech," "Research in Education," "Theories of Language," "Intercultural Relations," "Modern American Family," "Introduction to Social Work," "Labor Problems," "Contemporary Problems in Education," and so on. Practically every course that one could think of in the area of education, psychology, measurement, sociology, and social service work was mentioned, and almost as many from almost every other area that might come under the heading of social sciences. Thus, institutionally, there was little agreement as to just what constituted the education of the counselor, although it is probably true that those institutions which might be regarded as the best known in the preparation of counselors had some similarity of experiences for their students.

It should be kept in mind, too, that an actual program for the professional education of the counselor is a rather new development, and the National Defense Education Act of 1958 had, and the Education Professions Development Act of 1968 will have a major impact on the professional education of counselors. The positive and negative aspects of these acts will be examined in Chapter 12. Earlier in the decade, as an increasing proportion of NDEA Title VB funds began to be diverted to academic year institutes (later to be changed by the U.S. Office of Education despite professional recommendations to the contrary), it became obvious that there were very few institutions in the country that could offer even an effective one-year program at the Masters level. There is no question that there are more and better programs of counselor education now than a decade ago because of federal involvement, but a vast amount of federal seed money was wasted in a futile attempt to build up inadequate programs. On the whole, the good programs became bigger and better, but the poor ones, after the federal money was removed, remained pretty much as they were.

Federal legislation also spurred the American Personnel and Guidance Association to greater action in providing some indication of just what did constitute an effective program of counselor education. With the U.S. Office of Education, and the American people, ready to provide tens of millions of dollars for the more effective education of

---

[1] *Preparation Programs and Course Offerings in School and College Personnel Work, 1959–60* (Washington, D.C.: U.S. Department of Health, Education and Welfare, Office of Education).

school counselors, it was rather embarrassing to discover that the professional organizations representing counselors and counselor educators apparently did not know just what constituted an effective program of counselor education. Eventually, however, these organizations, did press for action, and the acceptance of various policy statements in 1964 and 1967 did represent a real achievement. The three major organizations that were involved in these policy statements were the American Personnel and Guidance Association, the "parent" body, and two of its divisions, the American School Counselors Association and the Association for Counselor Education and Supervision.

In many ways, these policy statements are elaborations of the seven basic recommendations regarding counselor education presented in the Wrenn report in 1962:[2]

1. That state certifying agencies for counselors and graduate faculties in counselor education specify that, in addition to essential professional courses and experiences, two other major cores be required in the counselor education curriculum; one major core is in the field of psychology, another in the social and other behavioral sciences, the two combined to represent a minimum of from one-third to one-half of the course work required for certification.

2. That the minimal two-year graduate program in counselor education include: (a) two major cores in psychology and the social sciences as described in Recommendation 1; (b) adequate orientation in educational philosophy and school curriculum patterns; (c) applied or professional courses as described in the text to the extent of *not more* than one-fourth of the total graduate programs; (d) supervised experience in both counseling and planned group leadership to the extent of *not less* than one-fourth of the total graduate programs; (e) an introduction to the understanding and utilization of changing research concepts; (f) an introduction to the problems of ethical relationships and legal responsibilities in counseling.

3. That the graduate courses in counselor education be taught by faculty qualified in the respective areas involved, *i.e.*, psychology courses by psychologists; counseling theory and technique courses by faculty who are both qualified in psychology and experienced in counseling; social science courses by social scientists; occupational information, psychological measurement, and research courses by qualified scholars in the areas involved.

4. That supervised counseling experience be required in every pattern of counselor certification; that certification be granted only upon the satisfactory completion of this experience and the recommendation of the graduate faculty involved.

---

[2] C. Gilbert Wrenn, *The Counselor in a Changing World* (Washington, D.C.: American Personnel and Guidance Association, 1962), p. 161.

These statements, however, are broad and general enough so that they could apply to many other helping professional groups, especially school psychologists and school social workers. One might assume that what one does professionally is affected to a major degree by his professional education and training, but it would sometimes seem to be affected more by the depth and quality of his professional education than by the particular kind of education he experiences. One can hardly contrast function on the basis of professional education and professional competence. School counselor Jones may have taken two courses from two instructors who were themselves not accepted into any major advanced graduate program, while school social worker Espano is the graduate of a two-year program from one of the better schools of social work, and psychologist Zun has a doctorate degree from a program in school psychology considered to be the best in the country. Or the social worker may be a hooky cop with no professional education, just seniority, while both psychologist and counselor are graduates of approved two-year programs in their field. Or the counselor may hold a doctoral degree from one of the better counselor education programs in the country, while social worker and psychologist have a most skimpy professional education. Thus we can hardly go into any school, pick out a counselor, a psychologist, a social worker and refer to the differences in the functions of the three professional groups on the basis of the differences in the functions of these three individuals.

Let us assume, for the purpose of comparison, however, that each of the three is a graduate of a two-year program from an approved institution—one from a school of social work, one from a department of counselor education, and one from a department of psychology or a department of education. Would their professional education have been such to definitely equip them for *different* professional tasks? Many, probably most, of the professional educators in each of the three areas would probably answer this question in the affirmative, but one may wonder.

Casework, for example, is usually considered to be the special something that the social worker has that nobody else possesses. And yet, what is this mysterious casework:[3]

> . . . when casework is employed to help the individual achieve better social functioning it becomes a form of psychosocial therapy. It relies

---

[3] Florence Hollis, *Casework: A Psychosocial Therapy* (New York: Random House, 1964), pp. 29–30.

mainly on rational procedures closely allied to psychoanalytic techniques, augmented by methods of direct influence when diagnosis indicates that these will be more effective. Focus is always upon the person-situation gestalt, which is seen as an interacting balance of forces between the needs of the person and the influence upon him of the environment.

A psychologist (or a counselor) might take this to say that the social worker is really a psychologist (or counselor) who helps individuals or families by a therapeutic involvement with them, or by a modification of the outer environment, usually the home, if this is the major cause of the problem. On the other hand, the social worker might feel that the current movement in the education of both the psychologist and the counselor to increase their involvement in the total environment of the child, including the home, is trespassing on territory which she has considered as her own. Then too, we may note that the scope and standards of preparation in psychology for school counselors often read almost like the complete educational program at the doctoral level of one who might be called a school counseling psychologist.

Thus it would appear that the education and training of the psychologist, counselor, and social worker in the schools are not too far apart, and those graduates of at least minimal two-year programs in approved institutions function on the job in a somewhat similar manner. Their functions may differ but this is due less to the fact that they are a counselor or a social worker or a psychologist, than it is because they work with a different population, their own personal interests and motivations and personality patterns are different, and the clinical and practicum aspect of their professional education may have been in a different milieu with a different kind of population. Actually, even in a two-year program, and certainly in a doctoral program, while we could assume that there would be a particular base core of skill and knowledge, the population with whom the individual would work, and the milieu in which he would work would be the major factor determining the possible differences in professional education rather than the occupational title of the individual. One student might see his professional future in an occupation in which he would be working in a therapeutic relationship with developmental problems; another student might see himself working primarily in the area of clinical diagnosis and appraisal of atypical children; another might see himself as involved primarily with parents, and the milieu in which they live. Each one of these individuals could be called a psychologist, a counselor or a social worker and still remain within the framework of function as recommended by their professional organizations. Only the rigidity of the professional training program would prevent them moving in the direction of their greatest interest and motivation and competency.

EDUCATION OR TRAINING FOR WHAT?

It is fairly clear, then, that even at the professional level there is much confusion over who is being trained for what, and in the case of the school counselor this confusion is being compounded by the tremendous stress being placed, particularly by state and federal governments, on the human condition which, for want of a better name, is known as mental health.[4] Despite the peripheral indications of distress with the current status of mental health treatment, it rolls merrily on its way, gathering vast sums from those government officials who are developing the new society, with little evidence of concern as to what it is, where it is going, and why it is going where it is going. Medicine generally continues to loftily assume that mental health naturally is its business, despite the bothersome and irritating attacks being made by psychologists. In turn, psychologists appear to be more interested in pressing the attack for a larger share of the pie than asking the somewhat pragmatic question, "What exactly have either of you fellows got to do with this matter of mental health, and are you doing what you should be doing?"

There would seem to be no question that the human condition known as mental health is currently well entrenched under the wing of medicine. However, one of the results of this odd alliance is that medical men are becoming increasingly involved in non-medical problems, away from the hospital, or they are converting part of the hospital into something which bears a great resemblance to a school. Medical control is as much as anything else an historical accident. We might wonder what would have happened if Freud had been a Ph.D. professor in a university, instead of a medical doctor working with a hospital. Freud made clear his feeling that the fact that he was a medical man had little to do with his involvement with the human

---

[4] *See* Dugald S. Arbuckle, "Psychology, Medicine and the Human Condition Known as Mental Health," *Community Mental Health Journal* 2:129–134 (Summer, 1966). Parts of the following section in this chapter were first printed in that article.

psyche. Those who followed him accepted the medical man in a hospital concept when dealing with individuals whose difficulties were either primarily of the mind and the emotions or of the physical body.

While the ideas as to what should be done for the oft-quoted 19,000,000 Americans who suffer from poor mental health are changing rapidly, psychotherapy would still appear to be the major kingpin as far as treatment is concerned. A recent report of the Joint Commission on Mental Health[5] makes it clear that psychotherapy is the realm of the medical doctor, although some room is left for the psychologist. One might say that if you have "bad" mental health you go to a hospital, see a doctor, and "get" psychotherapy! What has happened, however, is that man, with certain kinds of human difficulties, has been asked to fit into an already established profession, medicine, and he has naturally been regarded as a fellow with a disease. Psychology, in trying to break into the circle, has imitated medicine, the only difference being that it insists on viewing man as a set of behavioral problems rather than a disease. The words of Blanck would appear to be appropriate for the current situation:[6]

> Considered and objective study of the question should involve the complete resources of all of the relevant departments of a university, both in the social and physical sciences. The best thinking of educators might lead, not to a decision in favor of either contender, medicine or psychology, but to the creation of a new discipline with undergraduate and postgraduate curricula appropriate to its specific goals.

Many voices, from medicine, from psychology, and from various other areas have been raised questioning the traditional "You have a disease and you must go to the hospital for treatment" concept. The medical practitioners, however, while they overtly accept the need for change, are actually often recommending a slightly different concept of medical treatment for an ill patient, while the clinical psychologist too frequently tries to get more control for himself by doing pretty much what his medical colleague has suggested. Mainord,[7] for example, states that "teaching the patient to believe that he is sick is to encourage him to become a passive recipient of whatever treatment

[5] Joint Commission on Mental Illness and Health, *Action for Mental Health* (New York: Basic Books, 1961).
[6] Gertrude Blanck, *Education for Psychotherapy* (New York: The Institute for Psychoanalytic Training, 1962).
[7] W. A. Mainord, *A Therapy* (Ft. Steilacoom, Washington, D.C.: Mental Health Research Institute Bulletin, 1962), pp. 85–92.

the physician recommends," and he describes a different approach. We might wonder, however, if a person is not sick, why he is in a "hospital" being "treated" by a "physician."

Eysenck[8] has been probably the consistent gadfly in the side of both medical and psychological psychotherapists. He feels that what little movement and change may have resulted from various treatments, in and out of hospitals, has had a learning theory basis, and has nothing to do with sickness. Szasz[9] is another who argues that those who are called mental patients are not sick in a medical sense, but they have learned a certain style of living, and it is this which must be changed if they are to change.

The disquiet with the current situation is expressed in many ways. Adams, for example, speaks against the current confusing terminology when he says:[10]

> If behavior can be systematically described in *behavioral* terms, there is no need for the confusing non-psychological analogies and metaphors which have long plagued the mental-health professions. It becomes unnecessary to borrow words from medicine, engineering, or electronics, to describe human relationships. This approach makes it possible to clarify fundamental principles which have long been concealed by inappropriate, misleading jargon.

Albee comments somewhat along the same line when he says:[11]

> In many ways, too, clinical psychologists, like well-treated slaves in other empires, have unconsciously adopted the values, the language and the manners of their owners' masters. . . . The depth of brain washing to which the present generation of clinical psychologists has been exposed is evidenced by the degree to which our thinking accepts without resistance the medical model and the primacy of medicine's responsibility for the field of mental disorder.

It may be, of course, that Adams voices the desire of the clinical psychologist to replace the disease orientation of medicine with the sets of behaviors orientation of clinical psychology. Bugental indicates

---

[8] H. Eysenck, *Behavior Therapy and the Neurosis* (New York: Pergamon Press, 1960).

[9] T. S. Szasz, *The Myth of Mental Illness* (New York: Hoeber-Harper, 1961).

[10] H. B. Adams, "Mental Illness of Interpersonal Behavior," *American Psychologist* 19:191–197 (March, 1964).

[11] G. Albee, "A Declaration of Independence for Psychology," *Bulletin of Psychologists Interested in the Advancement of Psychotherapy* (November, 1964).

an equal skepticism about the medical treatment concept when he says:[12]

> Certainly the point is that we cannot follow a pattern of esoterically diagnosing our patient's difficulties and writing prescriptions in Latin and an illegible scrawl, which the patient dutifully carries to the pharmacist for compounding and then takes with complete ignorance of the preparation or its intended effects. We are recognizing more and more that essential to the psychotherapeutic course is the patient's own responsible involvement in the change process.

On the other hand, he shows a much greater understanding of the gestalt man, and even suggests the heresy that "psychology can turn again to its parents, the humanities and philosophy, and from these take new strength to meet the challenge of our day."

The medical man shares the quandary of the psychologist, and each, to some degree, is bound by his own professional shackles. Switzer,[13] a psychiatrist, for example, refers to mental health as a public health problem, and stresses the thought that the best public health efforts are those that prevent illness. He refers to his own position as being in a residential treatment center. Yet at the same time the "dream" program that he advocates shows no relationship whatsoever to illness or medicine or hospitals except for the last few words, which actually contradict the rest of his statement:

> It would be a program composed of three intimately related areas of function: home, classroom, school activities, and guidance and counseling, parents, teachers, guidance and counseling personnel—all in constant communication with each other, all devoted to ever increasing understanding of what is needed for promotion of psychological growth, all striving for considerate action, all keenly aware of their own role, all respectful of the contributions of the others, all dedicated to the individual child within the group, all committed to conscious, conscientious, and organized effort toward prevention of mental and emotional illness.

Glasser[14] is another medical psychotherapist who, while dissatisfied with current psychiatric practice, still at least appears to feel that

---

[12] J. F. T. Bugental, "Humanistic Psychology: A New Breakthrough," *American Psychologist* 18:563–567 (September, 1963).

[13] R. E. Switzer, "Guidance and Counseling as a Force in the Prevention of Mental Illness," paper read at the convention of the Minnesota Counselors Association, Minneapolis, February, 1962.

[14] W. Glasser, *Reality Therapy* (New York: Harper and Row, 1965), p. 155.

the people with whom he works are patients in need of medical treatment. He says ". . . mental hygiene is stalled because our present psychiatric approach emphasizes mental illness rather than responsibility." But he apparently feels that the right approach is still "psychiatric." Again, he states, ". . . assuming . . . that the schools were willing to participate in a mental hygiene program, conventional psychiatric concepts would be totally inadequate for the job." Yet, interestingly enough, when he talks about his program, it would seem that he is functionally casting aside not only conventional *psychiatric* approaches, but conventional *medical* and *psychological* approaches as well.

Even while medicine and psychology argue over who is most effective in the helping relationship, heartening (or disheartening) evidence continues to accumulate indicating that a high level of medical or psychological knowledge and skill may not be necessary in order to be helpful in providing the human relationship to allow those individuals who are hospitalized as mentally ill to show growth and improvement. A study of Carkhuff and Truax describing the effects of lay group counseling on 80 hospitalized patients, is typical. They state:[15]

> The evidence points to uniformly significant improvement in the patients treated by lay group counseling when compared to control patients. The suggestion is that a specific but relatively brief training program, devoid of specific training in psychopathology, personality dynamics, or psychotherapy theory, can produce relatively effective lay mental health counselors.

Thus, we are today in a situation in which millions of people, who might previously have been considered to have their ups and downs, have now been convinced that they are ill, and that they need to go to a hospital for medical treatment, by medical doctors, so that their illness might be cured. Their illness, usually referred to as the lack of mental health, might thus be categorized as mental unhealthiness. It is generally considered to be basically the same as other diseases: measles, smallpox, syphilis—and the treatment is basically the same. The criticism of many psychologists is not so much aimed at the pattern of treatment as it is at the fact that it is medical doctors rather than psychologists who determine what should be done. In the meantime, a small fringe group of heretics, both medical doctors and

[15] R. R. Carkhuff and C. B. Truax, "Lay Mental Health Counseling," *Journal of Consulting Psychology* 29:426–431 (November, 1965).

psychologists, as well as representatives of other disciplines, feel that what must be done is something quite different from the disease or problem orientation of either medical personnel or psychologists.

Several sign posts might at least suggest the direction in which we should be moving. Let us note these briefly:

1. It would appear to be more appropriate, and empirically effective, to react to man in a more gestalt and in a more humanistic fashion. Man is a total being, and while it is questionable enough to treat a physically ill person as primarily a damaged heart, rather than as a human being suffering from a damaged heart, it is surely even more questionable to react to a person who has an over-abundance of fears, anxieties, loneliness, as a paranoid or a schizophrenic or a manic depressive, or as one who lacks mental health. Basically, then, man is neither a disease nor a problem; he is a total person, and we should surely react to an anxious man as a man who suffers from anxiety, to a lonely woman as one who suffers from loneliness, not to conditions known as anxiety and loneliness.

2. The vast majority of the people who fall under the category of mental unhealthiness have nothing wrong with them mentally, nor are they unhealthy in a physiological sense. Nor is the answer to their human difficulty a cure in the sense that you are sick if you have measles, and you are not sick when you are cured of measles. In fact, without the human traits that make up the "mentally unhealthy" person there would be no human person. One could not live without experiencing varying levels of fear and anxiety and loneliness and hostility. Man's human problem is not so much to cure a person of such feelings, but to help him to come to live so that they are a part of his living which tend to be more appropriate to his experiencing of the moment. One is hardly guilty of disproportionate feelings if he experiences fear when he feels he might die; his anxiety is hardly irrational if he is awaiting word as to whether or not he might get the job he has sought; a mother who has just lost her son would rather naturally be experiencing a feeling called grief.

Thus help is needed, but the help is not in the form of medicines or treatments, but rather help in learning to be someone who is not quite the same sort of person that he might be. The process one must go through is a process of learning, a process of learning to be one who can experience and live with and change one's feelings, rather than allowing himself to be mastered by one's feelings.

3. Currently, the center for the "treatment" of the mentally ill is a hospital, although the movement is to change the center of treatment

from the hospital to a more community-centered mental health center. Unfortunately, however, the change may be more of location than of attitude, and illness and treatment and disease are still the terms that are used in the supposed new centers. Actually, of course, the logical institution to house what are currently called mental health services is a school rather than a hospital, since we are concerned with human behavior and learning rather than with diseases, human organs and medicines. It is interesting to note that in the current stress on mental health the school has been given only a cursory glance. There is a sort of "Oh yes, it might fit in here somewhere" attitude. Even those school personnel who are most closely concerned with the children who may have problems and difficulties and tensions, developmental and otherwise, the school counselors, the school psychologists, the remedial services personnel, the school social worker, the school nurse—these individuals too are treated as if they are generally quite incapable of working with and helping those individuals who suffer from "mental illness." What is needed, instead of a mental health unit which operates on the hospital philosophy of disease and sickness and medical treatment, is an expansion of the school, mostly in the way of an expansion of the current pupil personnel services, and a greater understanding among teachers of what is involved in the development of personal difficulties among children, and what they can do about it.

Actually, if school social workers, psychologists and counselors have the professional competence organizations describe them as possessing, and all are rapidly approaching this stage, they are able to work quite effectively in a preventive and a helping manner with the vast majority of the children who will eventually make up the population described currently as being mentally ill. Even the current population of the mentally ill are more in need of re-education than they are in need of medical treatment, and the center which houses services for them should also be a school, but one which would be geared to an adult population whose learning is centered in doing something about their own behavior and attitudes and feelings. It would, in a sense, be a self-actualization center, and one of its units might well be a hospital to which those individuals who were medically sick would be sent for the appropriate medical treatment.

One of the reasons for the lack of capacity of many adults who are currently hospitalized as mentally ill is not what they had when they came in, but what they have experienced, and thus learned, since they have been in the institution. Many state institutions, even today, are fearfully depressing places, peopled by depressed individuals, both staff and patients. It is easy to see how one could become sick after living for a while in such an environment. Glasser[16] is talking about the reversing of this sort of thing when he says *"It is the whole ward attitude, where everyone is involved, but where mental illness is not accepted, that brings the understanding home to them."* Glasser, in effect, is talking about making at least a part of the hospital a learning center, staffed with concerned, compassionate and competent professional workers, who are there to help individuals who are not sick to learn how to become more effective and more responsible members of a community. But he still refers to doctors and patients and hospitals and medicine. Why not go the whole way? Why wait until people become classified as mentally ill and are sent to a hospital for treatment, even if the treatment is that described by Glasser? Why not start where we should start, with an institution known as a school, albeit an expanded one, housing learning and growth services rather than mental health services, since they are for people who are well rather than sick. There would be available, in the pupil personnel services department of the school, the services of a variety of specialists, and the entire school program would be geared to the prevention of excessive personal difficulties rather than to the development of them. This would obviously mean the involvement of all school personnel, including teachers and administrators. Attached to the school would be an adult unit, which would gradually decrease in size as the number of adults coming into it would decrease, because of the earlier attention they had received. A third unit to the complex would be a hospital which would correctly be for those individuals for whom there was at least some question as to the likelihood of their suffering from a disease, although even here, of course, these individuals would be treated as *humans* suffering from a disease. Switzer talks along the same line when he says:[17]

> The model would be an enlightened, considerate, action-oriented program of prevention, of joint and positive impingement on the child by parent, classroom teacher, guidance and counseling personnel, and school administrator, within a group-oriented, broad program that would keep a school building buzzing until long after dark.

Thus, we may hope that the vast amounts of monies that are coming from federal and state sources are not going to deepen the

---

[16] W. Glasser, *op. cit.*, p. 113.
[17] Switzer, *op. cit.*

mental health rut in which we are encased, a rut which is based on the concept of sickness and treatment. Let us rather think in terms of health and learning and schools. The future does not lie in treating as sick people those who are not sick, it lies in helping people to learn how to live the life they can live, with pleasure and with pain, with fear and with happiness, with ecstasy and with sorrow.

What is needed is the more intelligent expenditure of public funds for the expansion of the school, particularly the expansion of that part of it known as pupil personnel services, and at the same time, concentrated effort to help teachers and school administrators to come to a greater understanding of their role in the development of tension and disturbance in children, and the means by which they may help prevent it. There do exist, currently, a few mental health centers which operate almost as auxiliary units of the school, rather than as an extension of the hospital, and it is in this direction that public funds should be directed. The many professional individuals who are now in the field, particularly the psychologists and the psychiatrists, may have to redirect their thinking, in a somewhat more humanistic fashion, toward a helping relationship with troubled individuals, rather than the medical or psychological treatment of a disease or a problem.

While there is much in the way of literature telling us how the counselor should be educated, the actual process of that education remains complicated and difficult.[18] One of the human problems of the counselor educator is the clash in his perception of himself as a counselor and a teacher; also, in formal education we have generally placed much stress on *product* (which is not learning), and little stress on the *process* (which is learning). The teacher is traditionally one who is primarily involved with ideas and product, whereas the counselor is primarily involved with people and change and process. This may be why less understanding about learning seems to have come out of centuries of formal education than has come from a relatively few years of the practice of psychotherapy.

If you ask a teacher what he does, a fairly typical immediate reply will be, "I teach algebra." He is, in other words, at worst a teacher of algebra, and at best, a student of algebra, but very rarely would he feel that he is one who is involved in a learning process with another human, using algebra as a tool. It might be fair to say that the learning that occurs as a result of the algebra teacher's efforts is incidental and, generally, unknown. What is usually measured and con-

[18] *See* Dugald S. Arbuckle, "The Learning of Counseling: Process, Not Product," *Journal of Counseling Psychology* 10:163–168 (Summer, 1963).

sidered as "learning" is the student's retention of algebraic knowledge. The teacher has as the end product in mind the understanding of algebra, and it is this that is important.

This may also be a logical reason why one can take a course in psychology of learning, get an "A," supposedly "learn" about the psychology of learning, and yet, actually *learn* nothing, in that he continues to do all the things that he "learned" he shouldn't do! There has been an increase in knowledge about change, but no change.

If you ask a counselor what he does, his reply will very likely at least include something to the effect, "I help a person to . . ." He is concerned with helping *people,* and this, in turn, would appear to put him closer to process than the teacher. Most often, he has only a general idea about the product, since what happens as a result of the learning process in counseling depends on the client more than it does on the counselor.

The counselor may be the expert in the sense that he helps the client to become involved in a unique relationship with another human being, but it is the client who must determine where *he* wants to go and what *he* wants to do. Thus the client may be helped to come to feel that authority is not so threatening after all, but he must determine whether he wants to work under the same boss, seeing him in a different way, or change jobs, so that he works under a possibly different kind of authority.

The client may be helped to accept her hatred of her mother, and she may also need help to determine what she is going to do with this new "I have hated my mother" self rather than the old "I have always loved my mother" person. The counselor is the process expert, and although he helps in the determination, he is not the determiner of the product. Very often both he and the client are unaware of what the ultimate product might be.

It may also be noted that the counselor very often has to help the client in an unlearning process, or at least help him to do something about some of his "learnings" that are now causing him much stress and pain. It is very rarely that these learnings are part of his formal school curricular experience—except, of course, in those situations where the individual is being pressed to retain more knowledge than he is capable of retaining. It may be, too, that he is pressed to retain knowledge in which he has no interest and about which he has no concern. In most cases, however, the learnings that have caused trouble are those he has experienced in a variety of situations that are incidental in that they are not what the individual was supposed to learn. A child's learning from a teacher may be a hatred of authority or an excitement about discovery; a girl may learn from her mother to enjoy the company of boys or she may learn to fear them; from his church a child may learn an appreciation of different ways of living, or he may learn fear of death. There may be a relationship between the degree of negative learning and the extent to which the "other person" (the teacher, the counselor, the clergyman, the parent) is concerned with content and product rather than with person and process.

The astounding acceleration in man's increase in knowledge has not been accompanied by an equal increase of his ability to use this knowledge for the benefit of himself and his neighbors. As the gap increases, the possibility of man's destruction of himself would also seem to increase. With some notable exceptions throughout the centuries, formal education has, on the whole, paid much more attention to *what* is being "learned" than to *who* is involved in the "learning," with the possible result that educators know more about the content to be assimilated and retained than they do about the actual process of learning, and the actual outcomes and changes that occur as a result of this learning.

It is interesting to note that much that would seem to me, at least, to be very pertinent in this question of learning comes from sources other than education or psychology. For example, we may note Eliot commenting, in answer to the question, "To what does it lead, when you help a boy?":[19]

> To finding out
> What you really are. What you really feel.
> What you really are among other people.

Gibran's Prophet, speaking about teaching, says:[20]

> No man can reveal to you aught but that which already lies asleep in the dawning of your own knowledge. . . .
> . . . For the wisdom of one man lends not its wings to another man. . . .

Cicero also had some feelings on this question when he said, "The authority of the teacher is generally prejudicial to those who desire to learn."[21]

[19] T. S. Eliot, *The Cocktail Party*, Act 1, Scene i.
[20] Reprinted from *The Prophet*, by Kahlil Gibran, with the permission of the publisher, Alfred A. Knopf, Inc. Copyright 1923 by Kahlil Gibran: renewal copyright 1951 by Administrators C.T.A. of Kahlil Gibran Estate, and Mary G. Gibran.
[21] Cicero, *De Fisibus* 11,1, quoted by Montaigne in *Essays*, Chapter 26, Vol. 1, Emil Julius Trechmann, Trans. "Of the Education of Boys," letter addressed to Diane de Faix, Comtesse de Gurson (Oxford: Oxford University Press, 1935).

Somerset Maugham, on being asked what advice he gave young people, said:[22]

> Really, you know, there's only one thing to do, and that's follow your own nose and make your own mistakes. By following one's nose one can't go too far astray.

Pasternak was speaking about learning when he said:[23]

> When I hear people speak of reshaping life it makes me lose my self control and I fall into despair. Reshaping life!

> People who can say that have never understood a thing about life— they have never felt its breath, its heartbeat, however much they may have seen or done. They look on it as a lump of raw material that needs to be processed by them, to be ennobled by their touch. But life is never a material, a substance to be molded. . . . Life is constantly renewing and remaking and changing and transfiguring itself. . . .

It may be that the educator has become so involved in teaching *something*, that he has lost sight of the *somebody* who is learning. The poet and the author may be able to talk about learning because they are sensitive to people, but they do not have to become actually involved in a learning relationship with another human being.

The counselor possibly does well, in a "learning" sense, when he is involved in a therapeutic relationship with a client, but what happens when the counselor becomes a "teacher" of student counselors? The major difficulty arises, I think, because some counselor educators have a problem in distinguishing between a client and a student, and they have difficulty in perceiving their function as a teacher as different from their function as a counselor. They may have the same broad general objectives in terms of the development of the human individual, but the student-teacher relationship is quite different from the client-counselor relationship.

I have been greatly impressed over the years by the extreme reluctance and almost inability of graduate students to overcome years of disciplining in the matter of satisfying the instructor, and to arrive at a point where there is a high level of honesty in their expressions both about the instructor and his ideas and about themselves and their

---

[22] Joel Lieber, "Somerset Maugham Talks About Life," *This Week Magazine* (January, 1961).
[23] Quoted by H. Salisbury in "The Triumph of Boris Pasternak," *Saturday Review* (November 8, 1958), p. 22.

ideas. Even when formal evaluation is removed from a course, and the students know that their grades depend solely on what they want to give themselves, they find it difficult to believe that they are working to satisfy only themselves, not the instructor. The extent to which this is so varies greatly with different student counselors, of course, and Kemp describes the situation well when he says:[24]

> The more closed-minded, the greater the possibility that the counselor-in-training will stimulate change in accordance with the expectancies of the situation. This change is likely to be phenotypical, "party-line" change rather than integrated concepts and new directions for action.

As I try to identify some of the thoughts and feelings about the problems of the counselor as an "instructor," three points seem to stand out:[25]

Even a modestly insightful counselor must surely very soon come to question the apparent contradictions between his behavior toward that fellow human being known as a client and his behavior toward the other person known as a student counselor. Research would tend to indicate, and most counselors, overtly, at least, would appear to agree, that client growth and movement is facilitated when the counselor indicates self-congruence, genuineness and honesty; when he feels an unconditional positive regard toward the client; when he is capable of establishing a high level of empathic understanding. Here, it would seem, the counselor as a supervisor finds his first quandary. Can he function as a counselor when he is a supervisor? Is he the same person when he is either a counselor or a supervisor? Must he, basically, being the same human being, be the same person, or can he be the same person, but function in a different way because of the different function and responsibility he may have?

The problem of self-congruence, honesty and genuineness should not prove to be too much of a problem, since this is something that is an entirely personal business, within the control of the counselor or supervisor, although the extent to which his idea of genuineness and honesty will be viewed as genuineness and honesty by another will, of course, vary. Nevertheless, I would think of this as a personal problem; this is my struggle, and the basic question is the degree to which I am honest with *me*. Whether others view honesty as I do is, on this par-

---

[24] C. G. Kemp, "Influence of Dogmatism on the Training of Counselors," *Journal of Counseling Psychology* 9:155–157 (Summer, 1962).
[25] See Dugald S. Arbuckle, "Supervision: Learning, Not Counseling," *Journal of Counseling Psychology* 12:90–94 (Spring, 1965).

ticular issue, of secondary importance. Empathic understanding, however, is something else again, and the door that must be opened *is* opened by both student counselor and supervisor, not just by one of them. This, in turn, is obviously related to the extent to which the supervisor feels toward the student counselor a high level of positive regard, and, even more important, the extent to which the student feels that this is the way the supervisor feels toward him. It is at this point, I would think, that the supervisor begins to be somewhat entrapped in the world of illusion; it is real to him, but illusion to the other people.

The counselor can, with self-congruence, with honesty, and with genuineness, say to the client, "The extent to which I am a threat to you can be determined by you, because in no overt, action-taking manner do I see me posing a threat to you. I will not do anything to you that may be hurtful or damaging." Can any supervisor, with honesty, say the same to the student counselor?

Peters and Hansen[26] comment that "The practicum provides learning situations which can facilitate the optimal growth of the person by freeing his potentialities to be himself." Indeed it does, but unlike a counseling relationship, it has limitations, and these limitations sometimes do not appear to be recognized by some supervisors.

Patterson[27] would appear to be somewhat contradictory when he says, "Supervision, like counseling, must provide a non-threatening, accepting and understanding atmosphere," and then, on the same page, comments, "The supervisor does evaluate, must evaluate, and should evaluate." In attempting to combine these two impossibles, the supervisor may become even more enmeshed in his illusion.

Some counselors feel that another aspect of the relationship which tends to reduce the evaluative element, and therefore the threat, is when the supervisor's reaction is an honest expression of a personal feeling rather than a judgment. In commenting on an article, for example, Rogers says:[28]

> It is stated that the supervisor has said, in effect "You are defensive as indicated by the use of your words." To me a more accurate summary of the supervisor's expression is, "My feeling about this is that you are using words to cover up, to hide behind." This may seem like a small

[26] Herman J. Peters and James C. Hansen, "Counseling Practicum: Bases for Supervision," *Counselor Education and Supervision* 11:82–85 (Winter, 1963).
[27] C. H. Patterson, "Supervising Students in the Counseling Practicum," *Journal of Counseling Psychology* 11:47–53 (Spring, 1964).
[28] Carl R. Rogers, "Comment," *Journal of Counseling Psychology* 2:195 (Fall, 1955).

difference, but the difference between a *judgment* rendered by a person in authority, and a *personal feeling* which is contributed to the interaction as a part of the existing personal reality is, I believe, very great indeed.

I would hope, with Rogers, that the level of self-actualization of all supervisors would be such that their expressions generally would be those of personal feelings, rather than pontifical judgments. The determination of the judgmental level of a statement, however, is often determined more by the degree of self-actualization of the recipient of the statement than by the one who makes the statement. The white racist may say contemptuously, to a black man, "You are nothing but a dirty nigger." One black man may cringe at this "judgment"; another may react with violence and hatred; another may smile with sympathy, and wonder how he might help this unfortunate ignorant and fearful white man. If I am in the position of authority, namely, if I am the supervisor, then even though I may feel, quite deeply, nonjudgmental, my expression of personal feeling with regard to a certain action of the student counselor is viewed, to a greater or lesser degree, as a "judgment." The self-actualization of the student counselor has reached a high level if he can, in effect, expose himself, with risk, without being threatened. This would mean that he would no longer view "risk" as something external, which he could not control, but rather as something internal, which he could control. The risk, of course, might come from either the supervisor or his fellows in the practicum. Many student counselors view their peers as a greater threat than the supervisor. Indeed, if I am to be honest, is not my expression of feeling, to all extents and purposes, a judgment? Later on, a director of guidance may ask for my opinion regarding the effectiveness of a counselor I have had in a practicum, and who is now applying for a job. If I reflect this personal feeling in some way in a statement about the student counselor, then surely I am being judgmental. The extent to which a statement is threatening is probably less dependent on how it is put than it is on the relationship of the one who utters the statement to the other person, and the way in which the other person views the statement. I may say to a driver, "It is my feeling that you were going too fast." Exactly the same statement may be made by a traffic officer, but surely the statement will be regarded in a vastly different manner. When Carl Rogers would say to me, now, "It is my feeling that you are using words to cover up, to hide behind," I do not hear the same thing that I would have heard if he had said exactly the same words to me some years ago in Chicago. I have no question that he was then, as he is now, a warm, compassionate human being, and I may or may not have changed too much regarding my own level of self-congruence, but his relationship to me then, at least as I perceived it, was quite different. I would react in a different way today, not because he is necessarily any different, or because I am necessarily any different, but because *our relationship as I view it* is different, and this has a profound effect on my perception of what is said. This, I think, is the crux of the problem. The supervisor *is* a supervisor, and as such he carries the weight and the responsibility of judgment and evaluation on his shoulders. I have heard supervisors discussing the effectiveness of student counselors who, in turn, appear to believe that their counseling practicum is an unconditional positive acceptance, no-risk sort of human relationship. Is a supervisor being self-congruent when he develops in students the feeling of absolute freedom without risk, and later helps to determine the sorts of position that they will obtain by his statements about their counseling effectiveness, or lack of it?

There is another aspect of this problem of self-congruence and genuineness, which appears when a supervisor feels that a student counselor is ineffective in many ways, and will discuss this ineffectiveness with others, sometimes to the point of being involved in the removal of a student from a program, and yet, in the name of "unconditional positive regard," will never reveal his feelings to the student counselor himself. Is one being congruent if he *feels* "Gosh, I get the feeling that you were scared stiff of the client when he made that statement," and he *says*, "It is your feeling that you were warm and comfortable with the client," because this is what the student counselor has verbalized to the supervisor. Is, possibly, the need to be loved so strong with some supervisors that they cannot risk the loss of approbation and acceptance by the student counselor by expressing their negative feelings about his behavior? Or would some say that the supervisor, who is also a counselor, should never have any negative feelings toward anyone?

Probably no one would take issue with Anderson and Bown[29] when they say that "maximum therapeutic growth occurs within the context of free communication," but when they say that as the second stage of their supervision "the supervisors *evaluate the recording* in terms of the facilitating or inhibiting factors in the communication," they are referring to an inhibiting, but a very real, factor as far as the

---

[29] Robert A. Anderson and Oliver H. Bown, "Tape Recordings and Counselor-Trainee Understandings," *Journal of Counseling Psychology* 2:189–194 (Fall, 1955).

communicative ability and the growth of the student counselor is concerned. I would agree with Rogers that these supervisory comments are predominantly expressions of personal feeling. I would feel, however, that they are regarded as evaluative because the person who is making them is, sooner or later, very likely going to be involved in an evaluation of the student counselor. If one can be totally honest and say, as he can as a counselor, "I cannot see myself ever involved in a judgmental role regarding this other person," then, of course, we have a different story. Are there any supervisors who can say this about student counselors in a counseling practicum, and at the same time be consistent with their concept of their responsibility as supervisors?

A somewhat different method of reducing the evaluative function of the supervisor is reported by Truax, Carkhuff and Douds.[30] They describe how the evaluation of the trainee's behavior would be based upon "research measuring scales which have proven adequately reliable and valid rather than upon the supervisor's subjective reaction." They then go on to say that this "would also tend to remove that barrier to the communication between trainee and supervisor by removing the supervisor from the realm of evaluation." Here, instead of giving their personal feelings about the effectiveness of the student counselor (what does one do, by the way, with these feelings?), they present more objective evidence. But even if it is some instrument that, in effect, says to the student counselor that he is not indicating much ability in providing a warm and acceptant environment for the client, can the supervisor really remove himself from this evaluation? The student counselor would likely wonder, with some justification, if the supervisor agreed with the picture as presented by the evaluation scale. No matter what scales are used, the supervisor, in his human relationship with the student counselor, has an evaluative role. The stress should be on helping the student counselor to learn to be able to live, and to be honest, and to be free, in a human relationship that is therapeutic, but in which there is also an element of risk. The supervisor may be compassionate, and warm, and understanding, but openness and honesty with him *is* more risky. Self-congruence on the part of the supervisor surely demands that he not deliberately lull the student counselor into a comfortable, but false, sense of security.

When we think of the relationship between the counselor and the client, as compared with that between the teacher and the student, in

---

[30] Charles B. Truax, Robert R. Carkhuff, and John Douds, "Toward an Integration of the Didactic and Experiential Approaches to Training in Counseling and Psychotherapy," *Journal of Counseling Psychology* 11:240–247 (January, 1961).

the first case the verb that applies is "counseling," while in the latter case it is "teaching." The more important verb in both relationships, however, is learning, and learning occurs best in a therapeutic milieu that is acceptant and non-threatening. The supervisor, however, like the teacher, has an assessment responsibility, and this tends to lessen the security and increase the potential threat in the relationship, so that the "other person" is seen possibly more like the student than the client. The supervisory relationship should be as non-threatening as possible, but some student counselors may need to experience the less threatening counseling relationship so that they will be able to be genuine, and grow, in the more threatening supervisory relationship.

Actually, the feeling of the threat in evaluation may reflect the uneasiness of the supervisor rather than the student counselor. The results of a study by Kinney[31] on the effects of grading on the supervisory relationship showed no significant differences in student reaction to supervisors who graded them as contrasted with supervisors who did not grade them. Nor were there any significant differences in student reaction to those individuals who functioned only as graders and those who had a supervisory relationship. The supervisors who graded students, however, did have a different perception of their relationship than did those who did not grade the students.

Another major supervisory issue is related to the "cognitive-didactic" approach as contrasted with the "experiencing-feeling" approach. Advocates of both would be likely to agree that they were concerned with growth and learning and self-actualization, but they did not approach it in the same manner. A study by Walz and Roeber[32] indicated that the usual supervisory response was cognitive and information-giving, with negative overtones, and that the supervisors appeared to be more concerned with what the counselor said than with what he did, and more concerned with the content of a counselor's statement than with the relationship to the client. This might be considered as the telling approach, and would fit in rather reasonably with the supervisor who saw himself as an authority-figure teacher rather than as a counselor. For the supervisor who is a counselor, however, the cognitive-didactic-telling approach would appear to be somewhat contradictory, since most counselors, at least at a talking level, see counseling as a warm, human relationship, with the stress on

---

[31] Peter Kinney, *The Effects of Grading on the Supervisory Relationship.* Unpublished doctoral dissertation, Boston University, 1969.
[32] Gary W. Walz and Edward C. Roeber, "Supervisors' Reactions to a Counseling Interview," *Counselor Education and Supervision* 2:2–7 (Fall, 1962).

process and the movement of the client toward freedom and self-actualization. Here again, however, the supervisor gets into some difficulties when he tries to function, in his supervising, as a counselor. Demos,[33] for example, points out the necessity for supervisory stress on process rather than content, and suggests as typical desirable supervisory questions such comments as, "Were you aware of the feelings and attitudes you were experiencing?"; "Were you able to experience positive attitudes toward the client?"; "Were you really listening to what the client was saying?" These questions are certainly more process- and student-counselor-centered than such statements as "Why didn't you question him about his father?" and "You sounded pretty nervous to me," but are they so different, from the viewpoint of the student counselor? One supervisor might say to the student counselor, "Were you permissive?" as above; another supervisor might have said, "I gather you have noticed that the scale tends to indicate that you were not very permissive," and another might have said "I got the feeling as I listened that you were sort of resisting this fellow." These are all process-, student-counselor-centered comments, but to the student counselor the person who is uttering these words has some feelings about the "goodness" and "badness" of his statements. Sooner or later the supervisor is going to make use of his particular set of goods and bads to determine just how good or bad the student counselor might be. This vision, of course, may be dimmed or exaggerated by the person of the supervisor, but it is there. The supervisor, in a way, makes content out of process. The counselor does not, since this is not his function.

The counselor can say, with a high level of honesty, "And your feeling right now is that it is predominantly your wife who is to blame for this difficulty." The emphasis is on the client, and the client's feelings, and this is real, since the frame of reference is that of the client, not that of the counselor. A crucial difference in the supervisory relationship, however, is that in the long run the frame of reference of the supervisor, not that of the student counselor, is going to be used in an evaluative manner. The supervisor may say, with honesty, "And your feeling right now is that it is the anxiety of the client rather than your anxiety that is causing this apparent stiffness between you;" but in the total supervisory relationship, over a period of time, the supervisor is going to evaluate the student counselor on the basis of *his* frame of reference, which possibly sees the basic difficulty as the

[33] George D. Demos, "Suggested Uses of Tape Recordings in Counselor Supervision," *Personnel and Guidance Journal* 42:704–705 (March, 1964).

anxiety of the student counselor rather than the anxiety of the client. A few months ago I saw an example of this where the supervisor in observing a video tape with a student counselor, indicated in a cognitive fashion that it was his impression that the student counselor was still trying to overpower the client rather than be acceptant of him. My impression of the supervisor was that he was warm and compassionate, and concerned, but by being congruent and honest he was also indicating that he did not have the much quoted "total positive regard" for the student counselor, or at least the student counselor almost certainly did not get the impression of total positive regard. When a person feels hurt, he does not usually view the one who inflicts the hurt as one who also provides "total positive regard." The supervisor could have taken the safer, but less congruent, less honest, and basically less acceptant way, by continuing to operate on the student counselor's frame of reference until the end of the year, then failing him in the practicum!

The increasing use of video tapes and movies in counseling supervision adds another dimension to the cognitive-experiencing issue. The supervisor can, like the counselor, operate almost entirely within the client's frame of reference, and it makes little difference whether he is reacting with the client to the client's experience which he has neither seen or heard, which he has seen and heard via a one-way mirror, which he has heard on a tape, or which he has seen and heard on a videotape or movie. However, the moment the supervisor begins to present his frame of reference, evaluative or no, cognitively or experientially, content or process, I would think that it tends to be interpreted by the student counselor in a content, cognitive sense. When the supervisor says, as he and the student counselor watch a movie or a videotape, "I wonder why you frowned at that moment" or "I have the feeling you were resisting the client when he made that comment," this is the supervisor's frame of reference, it is his reality. He is *thinking*, and he is likely thinking more than "I wonder why" and, "I have the feeling." A comment by Pierson[34] has some bearing on this issue. He stated that the supervisor is concerned with *thinking and feeling*, and that, for the supervisor, process is not an end in itself. In this sense, then, what he says *is* content, and it is cognitive. To a much greater degree than the counselor, the supervisor is involved with *his* own frame of reference as he is "experiencing" with the student counselor.

---

[34] George Pierson, in a personal discussion.

A study by Yenawine[35] of the use of audiotape and videotape in the counseling practicum produced some interesting results. While initially more anxious about the prospects of taping, students using videotape ultimately carried out this responsibility with demonstrably more enthusiasm than did their fellow students using audiotape. Self-disclosure and self-evaluation in relation to the analysis of taped interviews was found to be more pronounced, consistent and frank in the video group. In this group the focus of discussion in reviewing tapes typically centered on the counselor, dynamic aspects of the counselor-client relationship, and manifestations of non-verbal communication. In contrast, comparable discussion in the audio group typically focused on the client, his problems, and counselor techniques related to problem solution. Generally, students using videotape perceived these discussions to be more "objective" and "constructive," and depended less on the practicum supervisor for leadership than students using audiotape. The general feeling was that videotape placed more "cards on the table" than audiotape, and as a result, was a more effective stimulant for learning.

A third issue is the personal bias and orientation of the supervisor as a counselor. The study by Walz and Roeber[36] indicated that no two supervisors reacted to the same pattern of counselor/client statements or used similar wording or meaning in their statements. The reviewers' reactions to the cases presented in Evraiff's book[37] made it abundantly clear that "good" counseling was not perceived in the same way by the different reviewers, and that each reviewer had his own perception of both the content and the process of the counseling sessions. This situation does not present too much of a problem if one views counseling in a methodological sense, and sees as the purpose of the student counselor to learn the particular method of the master. One could then agree with Patterson[38] that the student counselor should choose the supervisor whose methodology he wishes to learn, or even with Ekstein and Wallerstein[39] that the experiencing of several different methodologies might be "nihilistic in its effect." If, however,

---

[35] Gardner D. Yenawine, *A Comparison of the Effects of Audiotape and Videotape Playback of Counselor Trainee Counseling Sessions on Individual and Group Experience in the Counseling Practicum.* Unpublished doctoral dissertation, Boston University, 1969.

[36] Walz and Roeber, *op. cit.*

[37] William Evraiff, *Helping Counselors Grow Professionally* (Englewood Cliffs, N.J.: Prentice-Hall, Inc., 1963).

[38] Patterson, *op. cit.*

[39] R. Ekstein and R. S. Wallerstein, *The Teaching and Learning of Psychotherapy* (New York: Basic Books, 1958), p. 64.

one considers counselor self-congruence and genuineness, warm, non-possessive regard, and empathic ability as basic counselor character-istics that transcend any theoretical positions, then it would seem that experience with counselors with different theoretical positions is most crucial. Only in this way could the student counselor be helped to determine just what theoretical position made most sense to him, or, indeed, whether he was able to function effectively as a counselor under any theoretical position. If a student counselor is exposed to only one theoretical position, he is very likely to adopt what is actually a most superficial position, and become quite parochial in his attitude. This has been one of the difficulties in the past in the "training" of the psychiatrist, and there are many psychiatrists who are astonishingly parochial, principally because of the "one-school-of-thought" that they have experienced in their training. I have seen many thoroughly dedicated "Rogerians" begin to wilt under the attack of a more cog-nitively oriented counselor, and they begin, in this way, to become more self-congruent and aware of just where they do stand. Any change is then likely to be more substantial and based more on fact than fancy. One who does not hold to a certain theoretical position, if we assume that he is a rational, reasonable and scholarly individual, is usually a better critic of that position than one who accepts it. Religion is moving somewhat out of its parochial ghetto, and some theologians are actually listening to other theologians of differing religious view-points. If counselors hold to a somewhat scientific point of view they should surely do the same, and the student counselor should experi-ence differing theoretical positions. If a student counselor had the opportunity of a counseling practicum experience with Rogers, Patter-son and Arbuckle, or with Rogers, Ellis and Whitaker, I would certainly recommend the latter. It might result in more confusion and uncertainty, but it would be the uncertainty of growth and movement, and this would appear to be a much better position for a counselor than the certainty of dogmatism and authority.

Again, of course, this would mean that the supervisors, as coun-selors, are individuals who try to help the student counselor to come to a greater understanding of who he is so that he can develop his own theoretical position at a somewhat more visceral level, and become a more genuine person who can thus develop a human relationship in which others can be helped to grow toward freedom. Even though the ultimate assessment may be from the supervisor's frame of reference, there is no reason why the student counselor should not be encouraged in every way to develop his own means of indicating to the supervisor his skills and capacities and understandings. They can hardly be effective if they are only pale carbon copies of the supervisor! Any total evaluation of the student counselor should take into account the varying theoretical positions of supervisors, and supervisors should be mature enough to distinguish between the extent to which the student counselor has internalized the supervisor's particular theoretical position, and the extent to which the student's own self-actualization has helped him to work effectively with other human beings, utilizing those theoretical concepts that are in harmony with his self.

While there is increasing evidence that the effective practice of counseling and psychotherapy is related to such ingredients as congruence and genuineness, non-possessive warmth, and empathic understanding, there is also evidence that at least implies that many programs of counselor education do not consider these as the basic ingredients around which a counselor education program should be built. Studies by Bergin and Solomon,[40] and by Melloh,[41] for example, indicated no relationship between the level of empathic understanding provided in counseling and such measures as grade point average and practicum grades. In fact, the students who were most effective received the lowest grades in their training programs!

Adding to the skepticism about the effectiveness of counselors and counselor education programs is the fact that there is evidence which implies that lay personnel may be just as effective as professionally trained counselors and psychotherapists. Golann and Magoon,[42] for example, describe an experiment from which they conclude that psychotherapeutic services can be provided in a school setting by carefully selected and specially trained individuals who do not need professional degrees. Carkhuff[43] concludes that the evidence available today "indicates that the primary conditions of effective treatment are conditions which minimally trained non-professional persons can provide." In describing their own training program, Carkhuff and Berenson[44] point out that the most potent therapists were individuals who were "either thrown out of their graduate training programs or

---

[40] A. E. Bergin and Sandra Solomon, "Personality and Performance Correlates of Empathic Understanding in Psychotherapy," A.P.A. Convention, Philadelphia, 1963.

[41] R. A. Melloh, *Accurate Empathy and Counselor Effectiveness.* Unpublished doctoral dissertation, University of Florida, 1964.

[42] Stuart E. Golann and Thomas M. Magoon," A Non-traditionally Trained Mental Health Counselor's Work in a School Counseling Service," *The School Counselor* 14:81–85 (November, 1966).

[43] Robert R. Carkhuff, "Training in the Counseling and Therapeutic Practices: Requiem or Reveille," *Journal of Counseling Psychology* 13:360–367 (Fall, 1966).

[44] Robert R. Carkhuff annd Bernard G. Berenson, *Beyond Counseling and Therapy* (New York: Holt, Rinehart and Winston, Inc., 1967), p. 14.

led a very tenuous graduate school existence." Patterson[45] even goes so far as to suggest that psychologists may abandon the practice of counseling and psychotherapy, the reason being "that it is below the professional dignity of a psychologist with a doctorate to engage in something which can be done just as well by someone with a bachelors degree, or perhaps even less."

These studies do not, of course, refer only to the effects of psychotherapy in a clinical or medical setting. They hold just as true for schools and the children in them. Hill and Grieneeks,[46] for example, report a study from which they conclude "If academic counseling is positively affecting performance it is not being reflected when the criterion measure chosen is grade point average." A study by Gonyea[47] indicated that there was a negative relationship between the extent to which counselors developed the "ideal therapeutic relationship" and the degree to which their clients reported themselves to be improved.

The traditional university program of any kind tends to stress the intellectual, the cognitive. The scholar is one who *knows,* more than one who *does,* and the "publish or else" philosophy is generally interpreted to mean that advancement in the ranks in a college or university is more dependent on your ability to write about what you know than it is on your ability to communicate in some meaningful fashion to students—i.e., teach, what you know. Thus it is not unreasonable that the traditional counselor education program tended to stress what one knew about people, and their culture, and behavior and change, and minimized the place of the counselor in effecting change in the behavior of the individual. There was maximum stress on what the student counselor knew about the client, minimum stress on what he knew about himself. There was an imposition on the student counselor of what others felt to be effective means of learning; there was little opportunity for the student counselor to develop what for him might possibly be effective means of learning, and helping others to learn. There was a stress on understanding the theory of counseling, rather than on the ability to practice counseling. There was, in a sense, an experience provided for the student counselor which was quite con-

---

[45] C. H. Patterson, "What is Counseling Psychology?" *Journal of Counseling Psychology* 16:23–29 (January, 1969).

[46] Arthur H. Hill and Laurabeth Grieneeks, "An Evaluation of Academic Counseling of Under- and Over-Achievers," *Journal of Counseling Psychology* 13:325–328 (Fall, 1966).

[47] G. Gonyea, "The Ideal Therapeutic Relationship and Counseling Outcome," *Journal of Clinical Psychology* 19:481–487 (December, 1964).

trary to the experience which the student counselor was supposedly learning to provide for future clients. It was a case of "Learn what we are telling you to do, in terms of a relationship with future clients, even though this is quite contrary to the behavior you are experiencing with us."

It would seem reasonable enough to conclude that a major issue today for counselors and the educators of counselors is the question of whether or not counseling does what it is supposed to do. If some of the evidence is correct, it would at least seem to be possible that counselor educators are educating student counselors in unverified ways so that they may have an unknown effect on misunderstood clients!

ESSENTIAL INGREDIENTS IN COUNSELOR EDUCATION

While school counselors functionally appear to hold, and to wish to continue to hold, to the teaching and educational model, counselor education programs tend generally to stress the clinical and medical model, even though their graduates may be preparing to work in an educational and learning milieu. One of the reasons for the violent reaction, in schools, to the suggestion that the counselor is a psychologist is the simple fact that psychologists have traditionally been rather ineffective in schools, but their rejection has unfortunately helped to produce the equally ineffective guidance and educational model of the school counselor.

Admissions criteria to counselor education programs continue to be based on such things as grade point averages, Graduate Record Examinations, and the Miller Analogies Test, none of which show much of a relationship with effective counseling. While Matulef and Rothenberg were talking about programs in clinical psychology, they could be referring to counselor education when they say:[48]

> Under the guise of objectivity, we use GRE's, Miller Analogies and grade point averages in determining admissions. . . . Although clinicians claim to and do evaluate personalities every day, they dare not apply their own skills to selecting trainees. We are not talking about screening out pathology as much as looking at professional attributes like empathy, positive regard and congruence.

---

[48] Norman J. Matulef and Peter J. Rothenberg, "The Crisis in Clinical Training: Apathy and Action," *Special Bulletin of the National Council on Graduate Education in Psychology* 2:8 (1968).

It is doubtful if most counselor education programs do much to help to humanize their student counselors, and this may tend to reflect the lack of concern in counselor education programs about the level of humanization and self-actualization of their graduates. It may be that they are more concerned with training highly skilled diagnosticians, whose concern and compassion about humanity may be considered to be of minor importance. Indeed, programs of counselor education, like other forms of human conditioning, tend all too frequently to enlarge the student's area of alienation. A student's professional program frequently teaches him that there is a great deal that he must not believe, very little that he can believe. Rather than helping him to open and enlarge his area of potential experiencing, it restricts him even further. Dreyfus expresses this feeling when he says:[49]

> In many ways schools of psychotherapy tend to reinforce man's aliena-tion from man. The therapist, like the physician, keeps his therapeutic armamentarium between himself and the patient, preventing real inter-human contact. . . . Helping would be therapists to be more human with freedom to respond should be the goal.

Clark is thinking along much the same line when he com-ments:[50]

> What is also needed in the literature are some creative ideas on how to implement a self-actualization model in graduate education. Most graduate schools are run on a behavioristic model in that they require much immediate feed-back of reward and punishment and other manipulatory practices.

An excellent example of this restricting of the freedom of the student counselor, and the pressure on the student *not* to experience and *not* to question, but rather to think as he is told to think, is indicated by this comment, written by a counselor-educator of some renown, on the paper of a student:

> Crap . . . your first big problem will be to bury this self concept junk on the high school level particularly in the educational-vocational level. Counselors should be expected to know, offer alternatives based on accurate and current information. They can save the foot-and-mouth game of reflection for those students who need support and can't be hurt too much by ineptness in training and technique.

---

[49] Edward A. Dreyfus, "Humanness: A Therapeutic Variable," *Personnel and Guidance Journal* 46:573–578 (February, 1967).
[50] Donald L. Clark, "The Counseling Educator and His Own Teaching Approach," *Counselor Education and Supervision* 6:166–169 (Spring, 1967).

The attitude behind this comment is very clearly "Do it my way, because my way is the right way." It is little wonder that the students who are the products of such programs are alienated not only from other differing professional ideologies and values, but probably from most of their fellow humans who do not think as they think. They in a sense then become the conditioning agents of the culture, and the repression of the individual, under the guise of a professional relationship, is continued. This was illustrated recently in a videotape of a discussion among a group of students who were involved in clinical practices. One member of the group described herself as holding to a psychological orientation, and spent the whole time defending her position, and appeared to be totally closed to any individual who did not hold to her concept of her orientation. Another student described himself as holding to a physiological orientation, and he was as defensive and as closed as the other student. It is distressing at the professional level, among those who at least wear the garments of the learned, to find this same narrow indoctrination, this "we have the answers," this learned alienation of self from others, and of self from self.

The evidence would at least seem to imply that it is the humanness, the very person of the counselor, that is the critical factor in the counseling relationship. One may wonder if individuals such as Freud and Rogers and Sullivan and Whitaker had had some other profession other than psychotherapy, would they have been significantly less effective, as therapists, than they turned out to be as professional psychotherapists, and if so, why. One may surmise, of course, that what makes one effective in counseling is possibly what leads one eventually into professional counseling, if, that is, one had the luxury of professional choice.

Van Kaam points out a major weakness in the current methods of educating psychologists, counselors, psychotherapists, and social workers, when he asks:[51]

> Do they all take into account the fact that these therapists are being trained for a pluralistic society? How many seminars are dedicated to the understanding of the varied cultural, subcultural, and religious projects of existence which underlie the lives of their patients? Is there a sufficient number of group therapeutic sessions in which the students can work through their own unconscious hostilities and defensive misunderstandings of religions or cultures which are not their own?

[51] Adrian Van Kaam, *The Art of Existential Counseling* (Wilkes-Barre, Pa.: Dimension Books, 1966), p. 125.

Kell and Mueller[52] feel that the simple purpose of good training is to help counselors to be most human. Carkhuff[53] concludes that the programs which have been "constructed primarily around a core of 'cross-cult' dimensions of effective interpersonal functioning have been most impressive, whereas more traditional, highly cognitive programs are of highly questionable and certainly unestablished, efficacy."

The trouble with programs for the education of counselors* may be that they still *train* individuals who already have been trained, rather than helping individuals to develop their humanness so that they might be more effective in a human relationship. We can assume that the traditional criteria for admission to a professional program such as academic qualifications and scores on measures such as the Graduate Record Examination and the Miller Analogies Test have little relationship with future effectiveness as a counselor. If admission to a program must be on this basis, it possibly should be for the purpose of first trying to find out if one can become effective as a counselor. Then, if one passes this hurdle, he can become more involved in his education for counseling effectiveness. Any core of knowledge should be related to, and built around actual clinical practice, in which the major immediate question asked by the counselor is "Who am I?" rather than "Who is he?" The student counselor, and his teachers and supervisors should surely believe that each client is a unique individual who is to be helped to grow and develop his own potential rather than being bludgeoned into someone else's mold. If this is so, then it would seem reasonable that the student counselor should also be helped to develop so that he too, could determine how he could be most effective as a counselor, if indeed, he can be effective as a counselor. This is a question which most student counselors have not as yet answered when they enter a counseling program, unless they have had some previous intimate human experiences which have provided them with some insight as to their potential as a counselor. We might assume that many of the unknown lay therapists who may not possess the proper academic qualifications would be much better candidates for a counselor education program than would many of those in the program.

Those who are concerned with the professional education of counselors should be equally involved in the process of self-develop-

---

[52] Bill L. Kell and William J. Mueller, *Impact and Change: A Study of Counseling Relationships* (New York: Appleton-Century-Crofts, 1966), p. 65.
[53] Carkhuff, *op. cit.*
*See Dugald S. Arbuckle, "Counseling Effectiveness and Related Issues," *Journal of Counseling Psychology* 15:430–436 (September, 1968).

ment, and the "Who am I" question should apply equally to supervisor, to student counselor and to client. We might theoretically assume that the level of self-actualization and humanness should be higher for the student counselor than for the client, and higher for the supervisor than for the student counselor. If the supervisor is not sensitive to, and acceptant of the hostility of the student counselor, then we might wonder if he can help the student counselor to become more acceptant and understanding of the hostility of the client.

Boy and Pine stress the uselessness of any so-called theory which is not practiced when they say:[54]

> When the counselor educator rebukes the school counselor who says that he is unable to implement a particular counseling theory because of the administrative attitudes within his school, and then in turn rejects student-centered teaching because of the limitations he feels are imposed upon him by a university setting, that counselor exhibits a shallowness in his own personal theory. . . . When one achieves a personal relevancy regarding anything, he then develops a commitment to translate that relevancy into a viable modus operandi that is functional within the context of limitations.

Chenault[55] proposes what she sees as a humanistic model for counselor education: it is based on nine value premises. These are: (1) The goal for the education of students in counselor education is growth, as differentiated from learning. (2) Growth is a creative process. (3) A humanistic counselor education program focuses upon the person as an organic entity rather than as a receptacle for learning. (4) The highest form of morality, personal and professional, is the encouragement of the individual's growing in his own values. (5) Counseling effectiveness is not a function of technique. (6) A necessary condition for growth is the subjective involvement of the student. (7) The highest educational goal is the student's search for meaning, his search for himself. (8) The purpose of a humanistic counselor education program is to facilitate growth as a process. (9) The nature of the growth potential is and should be different for each student.

My only disagreement with Chenault would be a semantic one, since I tend to view growth as the very essence of learning, and I cannot see any true learning other than as an inside-out process rather than an outside-in process. The latter, of course, does describe the

---

54 Angelo V. Boy and Gerald P. Pine, *The Counselor in the Schools* (Boston: Houghton Mifflin Co., 1968), pp. 321–322.
55 Joann Chenault, "A Proposed Model for a Humanistic Counselor Education Program," *Counselor Education and Supervision* 8:4–11 (Fall, 1968).

greater part of formal education, which I would tend to view as neither growth nor learning.

Assessment and evaluation are a part of the counselor's education, but the student counselor should be involved in this assessment and evaluation. The purpose of counselor education is to help to develop a genuine, self-actualized empathic individual, and if the counselor is not this sort of person, then as Olsen[56] says, "he can only fall back upon authoritarian behavior or the carrying out of an accepted technique. A sense of *being* someone has not been an outcome of his counselor education program."

The student counselor, however, should be at a point in his own development so that he can be open, rather than highly defensive toward evaluation of himself—by himself, by his peers, and by his supervisor. If he is not, one may question whether or not he belongs in a counselor education program. If the insecurity of the counselor is deeper than that of the client, the outlook for the client is surely not too hopeful!

Various modifications of a form such as that shown in Table 1 have been used by some supervisors as at least one evaluative tool. When supervisors and students all use such an instrument on themselves, and on each other, each person can get at least a part of the perception of the others. I would assume that if, as a supervisor, I got a low rating on these items, I should at least question my effectiveness as a supervisor. I might also have some questions for myself if my rating of different students differed sharply from those of other students, and if their perception of me differed sharply from my perception of me. Some supervisors I have found become almost traumatized when it is suggested that students might react to them via such a form!

Thus the education, and the learning and the personal development of the counselor should be geared in very much the same direction, although by possibly different means, as is the development of the client. The goal of counselor education is not a more knowledgeable and skilled technician, but a more human and self-actualized individual, capable of working effectively to help others to realize more fully the potential of their true self. And in the long run, the measure of success of the individual counselor is the extent to which he has helped others to become free and responsible members of the human species.

[56] LeRoy C. Olsen, "Success for New Counselors," *Journal of Counseling Psychology* 10:350–355 (Winter, 1963).

TABLE 1

1. **Empathy**—The ability to be "close" to the other—to be intimate without emotional involvement with the other—to experience the other's feeling, but not to have that feeling.
   Don't know _____
   Minimal   High level
   Empathy   Empathy
   1_____2_____3_____4_____5

2. **Non-conditional acceptance**—The ability to accept without judgment, moralizing, the giving of advice—acceptance of the other as he is.
   Don't know _____
   Low level   Unconditional
   Acceptance   Acceptance
   1_____2_____3_____4_____5

3. **Congruence and genuineness**—A high level of openness and honesty—a lack of devious and manipulative behavior—the ability to be oneself with ease and comfort and security.
   Don't know _____
   Low level   High level
   Minimal Congruence   Congruence
   1_____2_____3_____4_____5

4. **Ability to communicate understanding**—Ability to help the other to understand his acceptance of the other—a lack of cognitive confusion—the other feels that he understands.
   Don't know _____
   Little ability   High ability
   to communicate   to communicate
   1_____2_____3_____4_____5

5. **Self-awareness and self-security**—A high level of self-security—a feeling of "I know who I am"—certainly without dogmatism—ability to live comfortably without absolute reassurance and certainty.
   Don't know _____
   Little self-security   High level
   or awareness   security and awareness
   1_____2_____3_____4_____5

6. **Acceptance as potential Counselor**—Acceptance as one to whom I would go if in need of personal attention and counseling.
   Now   Would feel absolutely
   Would not go   free to go
   1_____2_____3_____4_____5

   When he no longer has supervisory relationship with you:
   Would not go   Would feel absolutely
                                                free to go
   1_____2_____3_____4_____5

part 3

THE NATURE OF COUNSELING

chapter 7

THEORIES OF COUNSELING

The moment one begins to peruse the literature on the subject of theories of counseling, he is immediately immeshed in a semantic maze, and while visions of sugar plums may not dance in his head, there is a high level of confusion about such ordinary terms as schools, methods, kinds and theories; personality, learning and growth; philosophy and theory. Let us first attempt to pull together some of the conflicting ideas about theories of counseling, and present what might be called a theory on theories.

A THEORY ABOUT THEORIES

Regardless of the differences in viewpoints about counseling and the counseling process, and methodologies and kinds of counseling, and even purpose of counseling, there is general agreement that we are talking about people and their behavior, and the means and the processes by which people change their behavior and their selves. We are also talking, then, about personality and about learning, and any discussions of counseling theories must take into account theories of personality and theories of learning.

Some individuals question the very existence of such a thing as a discrete counseling theory. Chenault, for example, says:[1]

[1] Joann Chenault, "Counseling Theory: The Problem of Definition," *Personnel and Guidance Journal* 47:110–114 (October, 1968).

. . . counseling theory is necessarily more than a relationship of personality theory to counseling practice. Yet these approaches to counseling which are called counseling theory do not fit the existing definitions of theory in the behavioral sciences. With the exception of the Pepinskys' contribution, there is really no such thing as counseling theory.

Landsman[2] feels that "the uses of theory in the orderly world of science as it is generally known seem to bear little relationship to the uses of personality theory as known in counseling and guidance broadly considered." Wolberg[3] sounds equally skeptical when he says " 'Theories' proposed for these many hundreds of types of procedures have all been based on speculation, and speculation is a self-serving business." Carkhuff[4] would probably agree with all of these criticisms, but he proposes what he would consider to be a more valid way of developing a theory of counseling. He says:

We are suggesting then, a central core of dimensions shared by all counseling and therapeutic processes, complemented by a variety of potential "preferred modes of treatment," given a relevant interaction of counselor, client, and contextual variables.

A "theory" is a somewhat intellectualized term for a concept or an idea that has gradually been worked out by an individual on the basis of work and experimentation and reading and meditation. If it is to be considered to be scientific, it has followed the precepts of observe, predict, test. It is tentative, and it may be disproved. It is an intelligent working frame of reference that can be used until something better comes along. Unfortunately, however, most counselors, if they hold to a theory at all, follow one developed by someone else, and few individual counselors follow the "observe, predict, test" concept in the development of their own personal theory.

Everyone pays homage, of course, to the idea that each counselor should develop his own theory of counseling. Indeed, there would be general agreement with Shoben[5] who talks about counseling theory as

---

[2] Ted Landsman "Personality Theory and Counseling," in Dugald S. Arbuckle (Ed.), *Counseling and Psychotherapy: An Overview* (New York: McGraw-Hill Book Co., 1967), pp. 166–170.
[3] Lewis R. Wolberg, *Short-Term Psychotherapy* (New York: Grune and Stratton, 1965), p. 68.
[4] Robert R. Carkhuff, "Counseling Research, Theory and Practice—1965," *Journal of Counseling Psychology* 13:467–480 (Winter, 1966).
[5] E. J. Shoben, Jr., "The Counselor's Theory as Personality Trait," *Personnel and Guidance Journal* 40:617–621 (March, 1962).

a "personal trait" and Boy and Pine[6] who say that "the role that a counselor assumes is basically an extension of his essence as a person." Peters and Bathory[7] are also referring to a self theory when they say "Theory will only evolve out of working at the problem of conceptualizing and identifying school counseling approaches."

Hipple[8] describes the structural factors to be considered in constructing a personal philosophy and theory of counseling as being: the nature of man, learning theory, behavorial change, goals of counseling role of the counselor, and responsibilities to society.

The development of a so-called "theory for me," however, while it is highly commendable, is also fraught with danger. The development of a theory to defend one's practice is as questionable as the development of a practice on the strength of a theory developed by someone else. Van Kaam[9] is correct when he says that "Theories of personality and psychotherapy should supplement rather than supplant my understanding," but this assumes, of course, a high level of "understanding." Landsman offers a word of caution to those who develop their own theory of counseling:[10]

> The counselor notes a phenomenon of behavior in his practice, creates a theory, and then proceeds to govern his counseling practices entirely by the untested theory. The bright-eyed devotions of the early orthodox psychoanalysts and the militant nondirective therapists both illustrate this sinful temptation.

As does Brammer:[11]

> There are also what I call the "lazy" eclectics. In their state of inertia they pick and choose among the theories largely what their whimsey dictates is attractive at the moment without regard to depth, consistency, or system.

---

[6] Angelo V. Boy and Gerald J. Pine, *The Counselor in the Schools* (Boston: Houghton Mifflin Co., 1968), p. 44.

[7] Herman J. Peters and Michael J. Bathory (Eds.), *School Counseling Perspectives and Procedures* (Itasca, Ill.: F. E. Peacock Publishers, Inc., 1968), p. 80.

[8] John Hipple, "Development of a Personal Philosophy and Theory of Counseling," *The School Counselor* 16:86–89 (November, 1968).

[9] Adrian Van Kaam, *The Art of Existential Counseling* (Wilkes-Barre, Pa.: Dimension Books, 1966), p. 157.

[10] Landsman, *op. cit.*, pp. 166–170.

[11] Lawrence M. Brammer, "Teaching Counseling Theory: Some Issues and Points of View," *Counselor Education and Supervision* 5:120–131 (Spring, 1966).

The acceptance of a theory, in this case a self-determined learning theory, to determine the actions of the counselor is illustrated by O'Hara[12] when he says, "If we teach the student to make increasingly more adequate vocational differentiations and integrations, then our theory says that the result will be more adequate vocational responses." This would seem to put theory as the determiner of the actions of client and counselor rather than their moment-by-moment experiencing of each other. Much the same "trapped by the theory" attitude seems to be evinced by Miller[13] when he says, "A learning theory approach, as described here, clearly leads to the types of controlling procedures that are practical for the teacher and parent." These two latter quotes illustrate perfectly what Corlis and Rabe[14] were talking about when, in describing the counseling encounter, they said, ". . . its occurrence will be instantly altered, if not limited by the introduction of a prearranged focus which in this case is supplied by a personality theory." The fact that they are referring to a personality theory instead of a learning theory should not make any difference, unless we believe that personality refers to humans and learning refers to non-humans!

A number of practicing counselors and therapists were asked to react to two brief questions about counseling theories, and, as would be expected, their replies vary greatly. The following is a summation of their reactions to the first question, which was: do you have a counseling theory?[15]

Albert Ellis: "Yes, I do have a theory of counseling. It simply states that human individuals are not upset by the events that occur to them (whether these occur in the past or the present) but by their cognitive evaluations of these events." Ellis feels, for example, that failing at a certain task is not the problem, but the problem arises when the individual then calls himself "a Failure with a capital F; a pretty worthless person." Such feelings, says Ellis, "are dogmas and categorical imperatives that cannot be substantiated; that cause enormous harm in terms of feelings of worthlessness, anger, grandiosity,

[12] Robert P. O'Hara, "A Theoretical Foundation for the Use of Occupational Information in Guidance," *Personnel and Guidance Journal* 46:636–640 (March, 1968).

[13] Adam W. Miller, Jr., "Learning Theory and Vocational Decisions," *Personnel and Guidance Journal* 47:18–23 (September, 1968).

[14] Rahe B. Corlis and Peter Rabe, *Psychotherapy From the Center* (Scranton, Penn.: International Textbook Co., 1969), p. 2.

[15] These comments resulted from personal communications from Albert Ellis, Dana Farnsworth, John Krumboltz, John Warkentin, Angelo Boy, and C. H. Patterson.

and low frustration tolerance; that result in self-fulfilling negative prophesies; and that would better be changed or minimized if the individual is to lose his disturbed symptoms. They can quickly be revealed to the client by the therapist; the client can be clearly taught how to challenge and question them; he can be shown how to work against them in actual practice in his real life; and he can be persuaded to relinquish them."

Dana Farnsworth did not react directly to the question, but enclosed several publications which, he felt, would describe his basic ideas about counseling. My assumption from reading these materials (and from personal knowledge) is that Farnsworth, like many other therapists, thinks more in terms of the philosophy of his operation and the way in which he operates, rather than holding to any particular theory.

C. H. Patterson: "I believe that every counselor's practice is related to his theory of counseling. However, a counselor's practice may not be related to his verbalized theory; that is, the counselor may not be aware of or have verbalized the actual theory upon which he operates. . . . This matter of style, it seems to me, is the source of confusion about theoretical differences, and probably of the idea that every counselor should develop his own individual theory. I have always considered this as an illustration of a lot of the nonsense which many writers and counselor educators propagate. It is logically inconsistent to believe that there are as many different and equally effective theories as there are counselors. . . . In fact, apparently different theories are effective not because of their unique elements, but because in practice they include the basic common elements of all theories."

John Krumboltz: "I don't know whether I have a theory of counseling or not. I'll let you decide." After reading some of Krumboltz' materials (and from personal knowledge), my decision would be that Krumboltz does not have a theory, but he has, rather, a rationale for operating the way he does as a counselor. He has found something, through experimentation, that makes sense to him, and appears to be effective, but he is not bound to anything. I realize, of course, that Krumboltz is often described as one of *the* behavioral counselors, just as I am described as a client-centered counselor. I am not sure, however, that Krumboltz is any less "client-centered" than I am, or that I am any less "behavorial" than he is!

John Warkentin: "I was rather taken aback that you seemed to assume that 'everyone has a theory of counseling.' If you mean by this term a general attitude or life style within the therapist, that I certainly do have. If you mean by a theory of counseling some philosophical principle, which brings my thinking and feelings into a coherent systematic unit, I do not have such a theory at all. In fact, when I hear people lecture on such a coherent 'theory of counseling' I sometimes wonder if they could be having delusions of grandeur. Whatever my life style is, it is continually changing. A high compliment I recently got from a 'patient' with whom I worked for three years was to the effect that I had improved more than she had. In other words, a 'theory of counseling' seems worthless to me as a philosophical concept unless it is one which is revised every few weeks."

Angelo Boy: "I've reached a conclusion that I do not possess a theory of counseling. What others may call a theory of counseling I prefer to call a process model of the counseling relationship. I cannot theorize how man does, or should, adequately interact with man—I just go ahead and do it in the moment of the interaction. Therefore, counseling is the active extension of a theory; but this theory is not of counseling, but of the self and the nature of man. I begin with my theory regarding myself and the nature of man, and counseling becomes the process whereby I express my theory regarding myself and the nature of man. How a counselor counsels is but an extension of the self, and the self of Angelo Boy is his theory; and Angelo Boy contemplates himself, his nature, and the nature of man, and what he is becomes his theory. What he does in counseling is a process extension of the theory which he himself is. But I cannot call this a theory of counseling—it is a theory of the self which finds expression in the interactive process called counseling.

"When I counsel, then, I am but a process extension of what I am internally. Therefore, there is no theory of counseling (for me); counseling is a process by which I express me, and my attitude toward man."

These reactions are, I think, fairly representative of experienced practicing counselors and therapists, and as much as anything else they seem to demonstrate the personal aspect of counseling. Ellis says he has a theory and Boy says he does not, but Ellis just as much as Boy is indicating his personal belief and his personal mode of operation. In a way, whether one "has a theory" or not seems to be more a matter of semantics than of practice. Some would probably say that Warkentin had an eclectic theory of counseling! It may be noted too, that in terms of the theories that are discussed in the next section, two of these contributors would be described as psychoanalytic, one would be a behaviorist, one a rational-emotive counselor, and two would be client-centered counselors!

I had also asked a second, more pragmatic question, as to what the counselors did and did not do, what they said and did not say, that reflected their personal adherence to a theory. None of the contributors really answered this question, and it was not until I was reading their reactions that it struck me as to why they possibly could not answer the question. It may be that loving and counseling share a great deal in common. If one were to ask, "What did you do when you were in the process of loving that person?" the description of a physical act or a few spoken words would really tell nothing at all about the real depth of the loving that was taking place. So it is in counseling: what one says tells little or nothing about what is really happening, and the depth of the counseling process has to be measured in terms of the mingling and the mixing of the two human beings involved in a relationship with each other.

What then, can one say in attempting to develop, at least a concept, if not a theory, about counseling theories:

1. There would appear to be little or no evidence to indicate that a conscious and intellectual awareness and understanding of a counseling theory is necessary for effective counseling. Indeed, one might wonder if the possession of a theory, personal or borrowed, is a hindrance more than a help. Possibly one of the reasons for the effectiveness of many lay therapists is that their minds and their emotions are not cluttered up with theories which tell them what they must do! Since they do not have any "our theory tells us" attitude, they do not expect anything, and they might thus fit the description of the phenomenological therapist given by Corlis and Rabe when they say:[16]

> He must allow himself to receive what he might not expect, what he might not understand. He must allow the patient to unfold what no theory can predict with individual accuracy: the unique self.

On the other hand, one might assume that for the secure person, for the whole person, a theory would be no more than a guide, and it would not take precedence over one's knowledge and understanding, it would not take precedence over what one's sense and one's sensitivity indicates is the reality of the situation. A theory should not bind the therapist the way religious dogma all too often controls the intellect of the individual. Possibly the crucial difference is that between

---

[16] Corlis and Rabe, *op. cit.*, p. 2.

the understanding of theories, and the way they may relate to one's human involvement, and the dogmatic adherence to a theory, come what may. Thus Wrenn's[17] conclusion that "theoretical orientation is of little influence in determining the manner in which experienced counselors respond," might be considered as a positive indication of the security of the counselors who were involved in his study. They were likely to be more concerned with being effective counselors than keeping the faith with some theory!

2. One may develop a theory on the basis of long years of practice, marked by observation and prediction and testing. This was the route of Freud and Rogers, and one might say it is for the select few who blaze the unknown pathways. It may be noted too, that Freud was not, and Rogers is not, the slave of his theory. They made it, it did not make them. Far too many counselors, however, at least among those who have a theory, base their practice on their theory, or rather on someone else's theory which they have adopted. It is interesting, too, to note that most of the better known vocational counseling theorists are not practicing counselors, but the theories they develop are intended for practicing counselors. We thus have theoreticians without a practice, and practitioners without a theory. It may be that the former will be potentially more damaging than the latter.

3. A theory of counseling cannot be isolated from either theories of learning or theories of personality. While there is somewhat of a tendency to relate personality theory more in the direction of the emotive, and learning theory move in the direction of the rational and the cognitive, this need not be so. Indeed, it should not be so, since personality theory and learning theory are both centered in the human individual, and man is a creature of both mind and emotion. It is difficult to see how one can become involved in personality theory, and ignore learning theory, and the opposite is equally true. Thus a counseling theory, in a sense, cannot avoid being the child of personality theories and learning theories.

4. One cannot separate a viable counseling theory, at least as it applies to the individual counselor, from the person of the counselor, for the very simple reason that it is the person of the counselor that is involved with the client, not his theory. Thus it is absurd to talk about a counselor "following" a certain counseling theory, unless this theory is deeply reflective of his total person. A counseling theory which is

[17] Robert L. Wrenn, "Counselor Orientation: Theoretical or Situational," *Journal of Counseling Psychology* 7:40–45 (Spring, 1960).

functionally meaningful must be reflective of the philosophical base of the counselor.

An exception to this would be those theorists and counselors who view humans in a non-human sense. Certainly one might argue that the above does not apply to a counselor who can adequately be replaced by a teaching or learning machine, or to a client who is a predictable set of behaviors. A consistent operational theory could be developed about such a counselor and about such a client. In my experience, however, I have for some reason been unable to find such a client or such a counselor. In fact, the clients and counselors who come closest to being such creatures are those who are most in need of counseling and psychotherapy. They are the ones who are perilously close to having been destroyed by their society. They are not the whole people; they are not the free people. Their humanity has *almost* (but never more than almost) been destroyed. They have become the victims rather than the creators of their culture.

But basically the stuff of which counseling theory is made must surely be people, and no person is ever any more the total victim of his culture than he is the total creator of his culture. It is interesting to wonder, for example, what might have happened to at least two theories of counseling if Carl Rogers had happened to be born in Freud's Austria, and Sigmund Freud had happened to be born in Rogers' America! But the client and the counselor are two human beings, and it is a human being that one sees and hears and smells and touches as each reacts with the other. This is the paramount fact in any consideration of counseling theory.

5. Any counseling theory must be open to experimentation, modification, and possible proof of error. One of the saddest of sights is to see a supposedly secure, professionally competent counselor vehemently defending a theory. A theory should need no defense. The proof, surely, should be in the pudding. The question is the pragmatic one: for you, does it make functional sense, does it work? This sort of thing is reminiscent of the ancient theologians telling Galileo that they couldn't see what they could see because they weren't supposed to see it. By the time an idea becomes a theory, there should have been a great deal of experimentation, which is why most ideas do not get to the theory stage, but continuing experimentation should be part and parcel of any theory. A theory should be considered as the best we have at the moment, but it should never be taken to mean that it will be the best for all of the tomorrows that follow today.

THEORIES OF COUNSELING

Regardless of how one may theorize, however, there are currently a vast array of theories of counseling, and certainly anyone involved in, or planning to be involved in counseling, should have some awareness of these theories. While this awareness may or may not have any effect on his actual counseling, he should, as an intelligent practitioner, know something about current thinking.

It should be noted too, that generally speaking, in the literature, "schools" and "approaches" and "theories" are, for all practical purposes, synonymous words. Discussions of the psychology of personality or personality theories usually also end up describing theories of counseling and psychotherapy, and the names which are related with them. As one would expect, the same names and the same descriptions turn up again and again, but some authors tend to take a somewhat different, rather than traditional look, at these names and systems. It is interesting to note the relationship between the different counseling theories when they are described in the more traditional manner by different authors. Table 2 illustrates systems of counseling and psychotherapy as described by six authors, and I have attempted to show the relationship that each one of these descriptions bears to the other. I am referring here to the name of the theory or system or school, and the names of the individuals who are associated with it.

Patterson[18] has referred to five basic theories of counseling and psychotherapy:

1. Psychoanalytic. (Patterson, like other authors, tends to distinguish between Freud and "the others" who may be known as psychoanalysts. He refers to Bordin and Alexander, and Adler, Fromm, Horney, Jung, Rank, Sullivan and French.)
2. Existential Psychotherapy. (Major attention is paid to Frankl and his logotherapy, and reference is made to May and Van Kaam.)
3. Rational approaches to counseling. (The major theorists referred to are Williamson, Thorne and Ellis.)
4. Perceptual-Phenomenological approaches to counseling. (Discussed here is Kelly's psychology of personal constructs and counseling, Grinker's Transactional approach, and Rogers' Client-Centered Therapy.)

---

[18] C. H. Patterson, *Theories of Counseling and Psychotherapy* (New York: Harper and Row, Publishers, 1966), pp. 13–487.

5. Learning Theory approaches to counseling. (Here Patterson discusses the conditioned reflex therapy of Salter, psychotherapy by reciprocal inhibition of Wolpe, the reinforcement theory and counseling of Dollard and Miller, the reinforcement theory and counseling of the Pepinskys, Rotter's social learning approach and the inference theory approach of Phillips.)

Carkhuff and Berenson[19] also mention five theories of counseling, which they refer to as potential preferred modes of treatment. It is interesting to note how these compare with Patterson's theories:

1. Psychoanalytic, which they describe by the term "the illusive suicide." (Here they discuss Freud, and mention as neo-Freudians, Alder, Fromm, Horney, Jung, Rank, and Sullivan.)
2. The Existential approach, which they describe by the term "man for each other." (The major name mentioned here is May.)
3. The Trait-and-Factor approach, to which they affix the term, "chance, not choice or change." (This is their major departure from Patterson, but I have placed it in the same column as Patterson's "rational," since it is the rational and cognitive approach of the vocational counseling theorists. The names mentioned, too, are those of vocational counseling theorists—Super, Ginzberg, Tiedeman, Roe, Holland, Tyler, and Hoppock.
4. The Client-Centered approach, described as "apparency in search of a person." (The counselor discussed here is Rogers.)
5. The Behavior Modification approaches, or "to act or not to act." (Four of the contributors are those mentioned by Patterson—Dollard and Miller, Wolpe, and Salter, and others are Eysenck, Bandura, and Krasner and Ullmann. Thus it may be noted that four of the "behavior modification" theorists of Carkhuff and Berenson are the "learning" theorists of Patterson.)

Ford and Urban[20] describe ten systems of psychotherapy, but six of these are what others have referred to as psychoanalytic, one is existential, one is client-centered, and two are either learning theory or behavior modification. Thus the ten systems may be described as:

1. Psychoanalytic. (The six systems described here are the psychoanalysis of Freud, the ego analysis, Alder's subjectivistic system of

19 Robert R. Carkhuff and Bernard G. Berenson, *Beyond Counseling and Therapy* (New York: Holt, Rinehart and Winston, Inc., 1967), pp. 63–131.
20 Donald H. Ford and Hugh B. Urban, *Systems of Psychotherapy* (New York: John Wiley and Sons, Inc., 1963), p. 712.

TABLE 2: KINDS OF PSYCHOTHERAPY

1. Patterson	2. Carkhuff and Berenson	3. Ford and Urban	4. Blocher	5. Sahakian	6. Holland
1. Psychoanalytic— Bordin, Alexander and Adler, Fromm, Horney, Jung, Rank, Sullivan, French	1. Psychoanalytic— Freud Neo-Freudian— Adler, Fromm, Horney, Rank, Sullivan	1. Psychoanalysis— Freud 2. Ego-Analysts 3. Subjective— Adler 4. Will therapy— Rank 5. Character analysis— Horney 6. Inter-personal relations— Sullivan	1. Psychoanalytic— Bordin 2. Social- psychological— Adler, Fromm, Horney, Sullivan	1. Psychoanalytic— Freud 2. Analytic psychology— Jung 3. Individual psychology— Adler 4. Humanistic psychoanalysis— Fromm 5. Neo-Freudianism: The Sociological School— Horney 6. Interpersonal theory— Sullivan	1. Freudian 2. Neo-Freudian— Rank, Adler, Jung, Horney, Sullivan, Fromm, Alexander, Klein, Reich, Rosen, Szasz
2. Existential— Frankl, May, Van Kaam	2. Existential— May	7. Existential analysis		7. Self-actualiza- tionism— Maslow 8. Organismic psychology— Goldstein 9. Personalistic psychology— Allport	

176

Column 1	Column 2	Column 3	Column 4	Column 5
3. *Rational—* Williamson, Thorne, Ellis	3. *Trait-and-factor—* Super, Ginzberg, Tiedeman, Roe, Holland, Tyler, Hoppock	3. *Rational-emotive—* Ellis	10. *Factor theory psychology—* Cattell	3. *Psychological psycho-therapies—* Ellis
4. *Perceptual phenomenological—* Kelly, Grinker Rogers	4. *Client-centered—* Rogers	4. *Client-centered—* Rogers	11. *Phenomenological—* Rogers	Rogers
5. *Learning theory—* Dollard and Miller, Wolpe, Rotter, Salter, Phillips, Pepinskys, Krasner and Ullmann, Skinner, Michael and Meyerson	5. *Behavior modification—* Dollard and Miller, Wolpe, Eysenck, Salter, Bandura, Krasner and Ullmann, Reyna	5. *Teacher Learner*	12. *Stimulus-response psychology—* Dollard and Miller	Dollard and Miller, Wolpe, Rotter, Salter, Thorne, Bach, Moreno, Johnson, Wolberg, Brammer and Shostrom
	8. *Client-centered—* Rogers	6. *Behavioral counseling—* Skinner, Krumboltz, Michael and Meyerson	13. *Factor theory psychology—* Eysenck	
	9. *Learning theory—* Dollard and Miller		14. *The Sociometric approach—* Moreno	
	10. *Reciprocal inhibition—* Wolpe		15. *Stimulus-response psychology—* Mowrer	

individual psychology, the will therapy of Rank, the character analysis of Horney, and Sullivan's theory of interpersonal relations.)
2. Existential analysis.
3. Rogers' client-centered psychotherapy.
4. The learning theory psychotherapy of Dollard and Miller and the reciprocal inhibitor psychotherapy (behavior modification) of Wolpe.

It may be noted that there is no equivalent here of the rational approach of Patterson and the trait-and-factor approach of Carkhuff and Berenson.

Blocher[21] describes six models of counseling theory, and these can be fitted into four of Patterson's theories:

1. Psychoanalytic. (While Bordin is used as the author to illustrate this approach, it can be taken without saying that Freud would rank as *the* person. A second model which would fit in this category, according to other authors, is described as the social psychological model, and the theorists referred to are Adler, Fromm, Horney and Sullivan.)
2. The rational-emotive model of Ellis.
3. The client-centered model of Rogers.
4. The behavorial counseling model of Skinner, Meyerson and Michael, and Krumboltz, and the teacher-learner model.

It may be noted here that the major missing theory is the existential.

Holland[22] refers simply to three theories of psychotherapy, but his three, again, can be fitted into four of the five described by Patterson:

1. Psychoanalytic. (Holland divides psychoanalytic theory into two: Freudian and neo-Freudian, the latter being used to incorporate Rank, Adler, Jung, Horney, Sullivan, Fromm, Alexander, Klein, Rosen, Reich, and Szasz.)
2. Holland's third theory he refers to as psychological psychotherapies. (This includes, from Patterson's categories 3, 4, and 5, the rational-emotive theory of Ellis, the client-centered theory of Rogers, and the learning theory or behavior modification theories of Dollard

---

[21] Donald H. Blocher, *Developmental Counseling* (New York: The Ronald Press Co., 1966), pp. 25–44.
[22] Glen A. Holland, *Fundamentals of Psychotherapy* (New York: Holt, Rinehart and Winston, 1965), pp. 3–34.

and Miller, Rotter, Wolpe, and Salter, plus the work of Thorne, Bach, Moreno, Johnson, Wolberg, and Brammer and Shostrom.)

Again, it may be noted here that the major missing theory is existentialism.

Sahakian[23] has edited a book which contains twenty theories on the psychology of personality. Fifteen of these would appear to fit the five theories of counseling and psychotherapy as described by Patterson. Another author, of course, might obviously make a different selection:

1. Psychoanalytic. (Six theories which would appear to fit this category are described. These are the psychoanalysis of Freud, the analytic psychology of Jung, the individual psychology of Adler, the humanistic psychoanalysis of Fromm, the neo-Freudian sociological school of Horney, and the interpersonal theory of Sullivan.)
2. Existential. (Fitting into this category would appear to be the self-actualization theory of Maslow, the organismic psychology of Goldstein, and the personalistic psychology of Allport.)
3. The factor theory psychology of Cattell would appear to be closely related to the rational or trait-factor theories of counseling.
4. The phenomenological theory of personality of Rogers is another name for the client-centered theory of counseling.
5. The learning theory or behavioral modification theory is represented by the learning theory of personality of Dollard and Miller, the two-factor learning theory of personality of Mowrer, the factor theory psychology of Eysenck, and the sociometric approach to personality of Moreno.

Let us now examine, very briefly, what would appear to be the salient points about these five theories of counseling:

1. Psychoanalytic. We can assume, of course, that the psychoanalysis of today is not the psychoanalysis of Freud, but there would be certain basic assumptions which appear to characterize the psychoanalytic point of view:

(a) Man would appear to be basically an unhappy, unfree and evil creature, governed by aggressive instincts.

(b) The goal of the therapist is to maintain a balance between internal instincts and impulses (the id, which is amoral and unconscious) and social restrictions (the superego, which is the moral voice

[23] William S. Sahakian (Ed.), *Psychology of Personality: Readings in Theory* (Chicago: Rand, McNally and Co., 1965).

of society, imposed upon the individual from the moment he is born). The ego attempts to maintain a balance between the two, and man thus spends his life trying to reduce his tensions. It is assumed that the therapist has done a better job of this on himself than has the patient.

(c) In the more traditional psychoanalysis, the developing sexuality of the individual, from infancy onward, was considered to be the central factor of his developing personality. The developmental history of the individual was considered to be psychosexual in nature, and pathology was related to the blocking and thwarting of the sexual instinct in the early years. Currently, more stress is placed on the total developmental history of the individual, with less on the psychosexual.

(d) The therapist uncovers, interprets and integrates the unconscious repressed material which dominates the individual's life and living. Traditionally, this was done primarily through free association, but currently there is more direct involvement of the therapist. The relationship is stressed more, and some therapists even feel comfortable facing a patient who is sitting up instead of lying on a couch!

(e) The approach of the therapist tends to be rational and cognitive rather than affective and emotive, even though Freud, in stressing the irrationality of man, took sharp issue with the scientific thinking of his day.

Thus the psychoanalytic approach would basically appear to be pessimistic. Man is doomed to live out his life struggling to maintain a balance between forces which are not of his making. He is the victim rather than the creator of his culture. It has been said that Galileo struck the first hammer blow against the smug security of man when he pointed out that the earth we lived on was not the center of the universe, Darwin continued it when he raised the suggestion that, rather than being the superior creatures of God's creation, man had evolved out of some much more lowly forms of life, and Freud hammered the nails in the coffin of man's self-esteem when he made him a creature of his psychosexual instincts!

2. Existentialism. As has been pointed out, existentialism is philosophic in background and philosophic in nature, and thus one would expect a minimal stress on how-to-do-it. The European existentialists, such as Kierkegaard,[24] Jaspers,[25] Heidegger,[26] and Sartre,[27]

[24] S. A. Kierkegaard, *The Sickness Unto Death* (Garden City, New York: Doubleday, 1954).
[25] K. Jaspers, *Reason and Existence* (New York: Noonday, 1955).
[26] M. Heidegger, *Being and Time* (London: SCM Press, 1962).
[27] J. P. Sartre, *Existential Psychoanalysis* (New York: Philosophical Library, 1953).

were concerned with a philosophy and a way of life, and the two major American figures who have looked at existentialism in terms of psychotherapy are May[28] and Van Kaam.[29] While there are probably even more variations in existential psychotherapy than there are in psychoanalysis, there are certain basic characteristics which appear to be common to all existentially oriented psychotherapies:

(a) Man is free—he is what he makes of himself. The outside limits and restricts, but it does not determine one's way of life. Existence precedes essence. Other forces impinge upon and affect the existence of an individual, but he alone determines the meaning of his existence.

(b) Man is alone, in that he must accept ultimate responsibility for his life and living. The ultimate choice must be his, and in this sense he must be alone.

(c) Man is not static, but he is rather in a constant state of growing, evolving, becoming. He is in a state of being, but also non-being. His existence implies nonexistence. His life only has meaning because of the certainty of his death.

(d) Existentialism sees counseling and psychotherapy as primarily a human encounter—a participating in the life of the other. The therapeutic goal is to help the individual to achieve a state of acceptance of responsibility for self, and thus to be free. It is an experiencing with the client. While critics of existential therapy will say that what actually happens is a verbal and philosophic discussion about, rather than an experiencing with, the existentialist would probably feel that this reflects the low level of achievement of individual freedom on the part of the therapist.

(e) The stress in existential therapy is on today rather than yesterday or tomorrow. A real human encounter must be in terms of now, and life and living are in terms of what is, not what was or what might be.

3. **Rational psychotherapy.** The rational and emotive psychotherapy of Ellis is generally reflective of the rational point of view in counseling and psychotherapy. Several points describe this theory of counseling:

(a) What we feel depends on what we think; thus thinking should take precedence over feeling. Our security is measured by our ability to think our way out of our negative and harmful feelings.

[28] Rollo May, *Existence* (New York: Basic Books, Inc., Publishers, 1958).
[29] Adrian Van Kaam, *The Art of Existential Counseling* (Wilkes-Barre, Pa.: Dimension Books, 1966).

(b) It is not the event, but our cognitive evaluation of the event that causes our troubles and stresses and strains.

(c) The major function of the therapist is to teach the client (to persuade, to challenge, to prod) to change his irrational views. The client is taught to view scientifically his irrationality.

(d) It is the present situation that is important, not the past. Ideas about events, past and present, are more important than the events themselves.

(e) The client-counselor relationship, the experiencing—these are not considered to be important aspects in rational-emotive counseling.

(f) It is assumed that the client has the ability, with the assistance of the counselor, to look rationally at his irrationality. It is assumed that he can think about his feelings.

4. Client-centered counseling. The basic characteristics of this theory of counseling are as follows:

(a) The crucial factor in counseling is the establishment of a human relationship which might be characterized by such terms as warm, acceptant, empathic, and congruent. This is possible only if the counselor can reflect these attitudes as a part of his person, rather than as a learned technique or procedure.

(b) The establishment of this relationship is the primary responsibility of the counselor. He is not responsible for the actions of the client.

(c) A person's behavior is directly related to his perceptions of the moment; it is his "perceptual field" which surrounds him to which he reacts. Reality for the client is what is perceived by the client about the client, not what is perceived by the counselor or by any other person. This is a phenomenological point of view—my self *is* the self of which *I* am aware.

(d) An individual has the capacity to modify and change his perceptions, and this can occur if a threat-free relationship can be established with another person. Every human individual has the potential for self-growth, self-development and self-actualization. The counselor helps the client to be who he can be.

(e) Total attention is centered on the whole person of the client, with minimal attention on the whole person of the counselor. The client-centered counselor is not nondirective (which is obviously impossible if there is any form of a human relationship) but he is less overtly directive than other counselors. The client does not get from the counselor the counselor's perception of the counselor, but the stress is on his development of his perception of the counselor, just as it is on his perception of himself.

(f) Since the attention is on the inner self of the client, there is little place for advice or even for information. Reflection is considered to be more important than interpretation, since interpretation is the counselor's perception of the client's reality.

5. Behavioral counseling. It should be noted that while behavorial counselors are learning theorists, not all learning theory counselors would view themselves as behaviorists. Several points may be noted in behavioral counseling:

(a) The behavioral approach is basically that of the traditional stimulus-response psychology, and the individual is viewed more as a set of behaviors than as a gestalt human being.

(b) The behavorial counselor is primarily a manipulator. Both in and out of the counseling hour he manipulates conditions, and thus provides a variety of different experiences which will effect change in the behavior of the client.

(c) While the client is involved in the determination of the direction of change, it is the counselor who accepts responsibility for the kind of manipulation which is used to produce a modification in behavior. The client is the recipient of the manipulation, and he has as little to say about it as has the patient whose disease is being cured by the knowledge and the skills of the medical doctor. The counselor is in control of the operation, and reality is as he perceives it, not as the client perceives it.

(d) The humanness of the counselor is minimized in behavorial counseling, which is predominantly the provision of a series of conditioning or counter-conditioning experiences. A counselor smile is not the spontaneous reflection of the inner feeling of the counselor, but rather a learned counselor response which has, let us say, been experimentally shown to reduce tension in the client. The counselor, in a way, becomes a conditioning machine, which, in turn, has been conditioned to do what research has indicated is effective.

While they are not referred to as basic theories of counseling, attention should also be paid to developmental counseling as enunciated by Blocher,[30] and the reality therapy of Glasser.[31]

While Blocher sees a distinct difference between developmental counseling and psychotherapy, most of the characteristics he uses to

---

[30] Blocher, *op. cit.*
[31] William Glasser, *Reality Therapy* (New York: Harper and Row, Publishers, 1965).

describe developmental counseling would be quite acceptable to many psychotherapists. For example, he does not see clients as being mentally ill but rather sees them as being capable of assuming responsibility for their own behavior and future development; he stresses the present and the future, rather than the past; the client is a client, not a patient, and the counselor is a teacher and partner of the client, rather than an omnipotent medical doctor; the counselor is neither morally neutral or amoral, but has his own values and standards, which he does not attempt to impose on the client. With the possible exception of the more traditional psychoanalysis, all of these characteristics could describe the various theories discussed here, at least as they would be practiced by some counselors and psychotherapists. Blocher's final point is that developmental counseling focuses upon changing behavior, and the developmental counselor uses a wide variety of techniques both within and outside of the counseling session. In this sense, developmental counseling would obviously appear to fit the behavioral modification theory of counseling.

Glasser, while he is a psychiatrist, tends to view the people with whom he works not as being sick, but rather as having not learned, or having lost the ability they did have, to be responsible for their own behavior. Inmates in institutions are irresponsible rather than mentally ill. Thus Glasser's "patients" sound very much like Blocher's "clients." Glasser sees the therapist as first having to become so involved with the patient that the patient can face reality and see how his behavior is unrealistic; the therapist must then reject the behavior which is unrealistic but still accept the patient and his involvement with him; and finally, the therapist must teach the patient better ways of fulfilling his needs within the confines of reality, and thus accept responsibility for his own behavior. All of this sounds very much like Ellis' rational-emotive psychotherapy, the major difference being that Glasser tends to stress a deeper counselor-client relationship than does Ellis.

These various theories are, I think, fairly representative of the current concepts regarding theories of counseling and psychotherapy. Several points of interest may be noted in examining the picture that they present:

1. There would appear to be five basic theories of counseling and psychotherapy, with the psychoanalytic holding its place as the oldest and the most dominant. The existential theory of counseling is the newest on the scene, and it is distinctive in that it is often considered to be more of a philosophical than a psychological theory. While

behavior theories are considered to be somewhat new, actually the learning theories and/or behavior modification theories have been with us for some time. The rational theory of counseling and the client-centered phenomenological theory have also by now been around for some time.

2. Learning theories and behavior modification theories overlap to the extent that they are almost synonymous. Nor should this be surprising, since learning produces behavior modification, or looking at it the other way, behavior modification results from learning. Four names that fairly consistently appear as learning theorists or behavior modification theorists are Dollard and Miller, Wolpe, and Salter.

3. While the existential and client-centered phenomenological theories have much in common, they are usually described as two different theories. It may be noted that Rogers is very frequently considered to be much the same, both as a person and in his thinking, as Maslow, May and Van Kaam.

4. The trait-and-factor theory is predominantly the product of vocational counseling theorists, and it tends to appear most frequently in the vocational counseling literature. It is the rational and cognitive approach which tends to be descriptive of vocational counseling.

5. There is obvious disagreement as to just who, with of course, the exception of Freud, belongs in the psychoanalytic camp. Adler, for example, is described as holding to a theory of neo-Freudian psychoanalysis, of individual psychology, and of social psychology. Ansbacher and Ansbacher[32] suggest that since the position of "neo-Freudians" (that is, stressing social relations rather than biological factors, the self rather than the id and the superego, self-actualization rather than the sex instinct, the present rather than early experiences) is much closer to Adler than to Freud, they should be called neo-Adlerians rather than neo-Freudians. Such individuals would be Alexander, French, Fromm, Fromm-Reichmann, Horney, Kardiner, Mullahy, Sullivan and Thompson. Adler himself says:[33]

> But I never attended one of his lectures, and when this group was to be sworn in to support the Freudian views I was the first to leave it. No one can deny that I, much more than Freud, have drawn the line sharply between Individual Psychology and psycho-analysis. . . .

[32] Heinz L. Ansbacher and Rowena R. Ansbacher, *The Individual Psychology of Alfred Adler* (New York: Harper and Row, Publishers, 1956), pp. 16–17.
[33] Alfred Adler, *Social Interest: A Challenge to Mankind* (New York: Capricorn Books, 1964), p. 254.

6. It is interesting to note that Blocher refers briefly to existential-ism as a philosophical base for counseling, but not as a theory of counseling. The word does not even appear in the index of Holland's book.

7. Over the years, at least five theorists have become irrevocably linked to the theories they have created. To most students of counsel-ing and psychotherapy Freud *is* psychoanalysis, Ellis *is* rational-emotive psychotherapy, Rogers *is* client-centered counseling, and Dollard and Miller *are* learning theory. There are many others, of course, but these would seem to stand out, and few would argue that their prominence is not justified.

Theories of counseling may also be referred to in more descrip-tive terms rather than by traditional names. Corlis and Rabe[34] for example, refer to the two major directions which are basic to person-ality theories in psychotherapy as the reductionistic approach and the holistic approach. They see reductionism as being represented by the psychoanalytic approach and consider its deterministic context as leaving no room for the potential of man's self-directed growth. It operates at the periphery. Holism, on the other hand, sees the indi-vidual as a functional whole, it is phenomenological, and it operates at the center. In more traditional terms, reductionism would probably be descriptive of psychoanalysis and learning theory and/or behavior modification, whereas holism would be descriptive of existentialism and the client-centered phenomenological approach.

A book edited by Parker[35] presents what is described as four theories of counseling, but they read more as four descriptions of how four individuals would operate, or think other people should operate, as counselors. One approach is described as the spontaneous-intuitive, which stresses the direct encounter and confrontation and the role free status of the counselor. This would probably come closest to the existential and client-centered phenomenological theories. Another ap-proach is the cognitive-conceptual, which sees problems in terms of the client's conception of facts or events, and thus if the counselor is to be of any help, he must see the world in a quite different way than it is seen by the client. This bears an obvious relationship to the rational-emotive theory of counseling. A third approach is the pragmatic-empirical, which is seen as the scientific approach to counseling. It would appear to come closest to the learning theories or behavior

---

[34] Corlis and Rabe, *op. cit.*, pp. 2–5.
[35] Clyde A. Parker (Ed.), *Counseling Theories and Counselor Education* (Boston: Houghton Mifflin Co., 1968).

modification theories of counseling. A final approach is the new eclecticism, which would appear to be a combination of whatever appears to be good for the person and the place and the time. This could be viewed as an approach, but hardly as a theory of counseling.

Thus most of the theories of counseling to be found in the literature can eventually be described by certain aspects of some of the five somewhat traditional terms with which we started this section. It is not the purpose of this book to describe the various theories of counseling in detail, but in the next chapter an examination will be made of the more pragmatic and functional *kinds* of counseling, which I would consider as the operational issue on the question of theories.

chapter 8

THE COUNSELING PROCESS

As has been indicated in the previous chapter, there is no paucity of theories about counseling, but there is some question of the relationship, if any, of these theories to the practice of counseling, to the counseling process itself. In this chapter let us examine the rationale, the "why" of counseling, then consider the question of kinds of counseling (if any), and finally look at the effectiveness of the counseling process in terms of human development.

THE PURPOSES OF COUNSELING

Most counselors would see the broad aim of counseling as change, change in attitudes and change in behavior. The counselor might see himself as involved with the client in a cognitive, information sharing sort of relationship, or in a more therapeutically centered relationship, but in both cases the goal would be change in the client. Krumboltz[1] sees the three behavorial goals of counseling as altering maladaptive behavior, learning the decision-making process, and preventing problems. Blocher[2] refers to behavioral changes being assumed in terms of

---

[1] John D. Krumboltz, "Behavioral Goals for Counseling," *Journal of Counseling Psychology* 13:153–159 (Summer, 1966).
[2] Donald H. Blocher, *Developmental Counseling* (New York: The Ronald Press, 1966), p. 232.

new coping behaviors acquired within constructs such as commitment, competence, consistency, and control. In a report of a fairly typical study on the effects of vocational counseling Hewer[3] refers to ultimate employment in a chosen vocation as the goal in the study being reported. Holland[4] simply says, "The ultimate reason for seeking psychotherapeutic assistance is an unfavorable balance between unpleasant and pleasant feelings. . . . It becomes the responsibility of the psychotherapist to recognize, interpret, and attempt to change the nature of emotional experience." Thus, regardless of the argument over counseling being synonymous with or different from psychotherapy, or counseling as a rational and cognitive, rather than an emotional therapeutic experience, there is general agreement that the counselor is one who is involved in helping the client to change his attitudes and his behavior, and thus, in a sense, become a different kind of person.

It would seem that the preliminary basic responsibility of any professional worker is to come to some understanding of the basic purpose of the professional activity that he plans to enter, since there would seem to be no point in going further with one's professional education if this is not understood and accepted. Professionally, however, one can hardly be satisfied with the individual who is able to give no better reason for his professional activities than "just because." Far too many counselors, supposedly professional workers, can give little in the way of valid and scientifically defensible reasons for their actions. Somewhat biting comments have been made by some authorities in the field of human behavior regarding the activities of counselors. Lecky, for example, stated:[5]

> Thus the psychoanalytic pursuit of unconscious complexes with no stated goal except to destroy them, suggests the superstitious fervor of the witch burner, and psychiatry in general may be thought of as engaged in a moral crusade against the demon Neurosis.

When one pauses to wonder just what the objectives of counseling *are*, he is struck by the fact that his list of answers is usually smaller and more difficult to arrive at than when he wonders what his objectives *are not*. Such a circumstance is understandable, since a good deal of the professional education of the counselor has to do with

---

[3] Vivian H. Hewer, "Evaluation of a Criterion: Realism of Vocational Choice," *Journal of Counseling Psychology* 13:289–294 (Fall, 1966).
[4] Glen A. Holland, *Fundamentals of Psychotherapy* (New York: Holt, Rinehart and Winston, Inc., 1965), p. 202.
[5] Prescott Lecky, *Self Consistency* (New York: Island Press, 1951), p. 186.

unlearning rather than learning. Much of what he has learned as a citizen of his community will not make him effective as a counselor, and much of what he has learned professionally, whether he be a theologian, a medical doctor, or a teacher, will help him even less. White, for example, states that:[6]

> when a person acts in the capacity of therapist, his goal is not to dominate or persuade, but simply to restore a state of good health. . . . A therapist has nothing to sell and nothing to prescribe.

It is likely that the goals and objectives expressed by individuals for other people are reflective rather of the needs of the person who expresses the goals than of the people for whom we supposedly have the goals. Often when parents talk about goals for their children, there is no question that the children and their needs have little to do with these goals. They are an expression of the needs of the parents, which may, of course, also be the needs of the children. When the teacher talks about objectives for her pupils, these again are the objectives of the teacher for someone else; often they make little sense to individual children, since they ignore the child completely.

The professional counselor, however, when thinking about goals must be thinking in terms of client satisfaction, not counselor satisfaction. The important question is not whether the counselor will feel better if the client decides to get a divorce, but rather whether this is what is best for the client. Similarly, the teacher may feel happy if the child decides not to run away from home, but leaving home could be the better answer to the problems of the child. We might, therefore, seriously question the objectives of counseling if they are the objectives of the counselor rather than the objectives of the counseling experience as it will apply to a certain individual. Indeed, one may raise the rather intriguing question of whether or not the counselor should have any specific objectives for the client; whether, rather, he should hold to broad general objectives of counseling, which may become more specific as the counselor helps the client to become more realistically oriented in the search for his own goals.

There will be little agreement on the objectives of counseling as long as such objectives are those of the counselor, although evidence tends to indicate that there is more agreement on objectives among counselors who have a high level of professional preparation (such as

---

[6] Robert W. White, *The Abnormal Personality* (New York: The Ronald Press Company, 1948), p. 314.

indicated, say, by having a doctorate in the field and being a Fellow of the American Psychological Association, or a Diplomate of the American Board of Examiners in Professional Psychology) than there is among counselors who have little in the way of professional preparation. Even with professional counselors, however, one has to step carefully before making any blanket statements about the objectives of counseling. This has been brought out most effectively in an article by Walker and Peiffer.[7] They point out, most logically, that we can hardly think in terms of self-adjustment, since a psychotic patient might well have reached a stage of adjustment in purely private terms; nor can we accept client contentment, since we cannot defend the position that all schizophrenics are unhappy or that all sexual psychopaths are sad.

Each person must speak from his own personal frame of reference, no matter how sensitive he may be to the other person's frame of reference. Each person's verbalizations will also tend to be at least somewhat indicative of his own particular professional background, and one of the difficulties of communication in counseling may be owing to the many different professional groups involved in it. Thus when we discuss the "why" of counseling, our differences may not be as great as they appear, and even when we talk about what we do, the discrepancies may not be as large as they would seem to be. The student of counseling is continually faced with the danger of superficially "accepting" some goal or objective of counseling, and only by examining himself in operation can he come close to determining whether or not this goal is even remotely related to his total person. Our basic goals of living, and our basic attitudes toward others, are revealed by what we do, not by what we say. Goals, too, are human, so we should talk in terms of the goals of the counselor, not of counseling.

Rogers, the original "client-centered" counselor, or at least the original Rogerian, shows his intensive involvement with the "other" in all his writings. More than most counselors, he tends to speak through his clients, and one of his books,[8] a compilation of articles written over a ten-year period, illustrates the extent to which he is centered on the client. When he says that the outcome of therapy is "a more broadly based structure of self, an inclusion of greater proportion of experience as a part of self, and a more comfortable and realistic adjustment to

---

[7] Donald E. Walker and Herbert C. Peiffer, Jr., "The Goals of Counseling," *Journal of Counseling Psychology* 4:204–209 (Fall, 1957).

[8] Carl R. Rogers, *On Becoming a Person* (Boston: Houghton Mifflin Company, 1961).

life,"[9] he is describing a very personal operational objective, which he illustrates in his counseling.

Some counselors, in talking about objectives, would at least appear to stress more doing something *with* the client than *for* him; experiencing and living with him, rather than discussing and explaining to him, thus stressing the affective rather than the cognitive; a concern with the total existential being, today, rather than parts of him, yesterday; a high level of confidence in the self-actualizing ability of the individual; a non-deterministic view of man as the maker of his culture.

When Boy and Pine describe the goal of client-centered counseling, they are talking about *their* goal as counselors:[10]

> . . . to help the student become more mature and more self-actuated, to help the student move forward in a positive and constructive way, to help the student grow toward socialization by utilizing his own resources and potential. . . . The counselee's perceptions change, and as the result of newly acquired insights there is a positive re-orientation of personality and living for the counselee. The counselor's focus is more on the affective than on the cognitive components of behavior.

When they describe the goals of the clinical counselor, however, they are on less certain, less personal ground. We might say that they are being less affective, but more cognitive, in the sense that they are using descriptions of the counseling activities of others who have been called, by some, "clinical counselors":[11]

> . . . to help the counselee "feel better," i.e., to help the counselee accept himself, to diminish the disparity between real self and ideal self; and "to help persons *think* more clearly in solving their own personal problems." The counselor must be concerned with feelings and affect as prerequisite to clear thinking. The objective is to help the counselee arrive at the point where he understands himself not only affectively but also rationally or intelligently. At this point he needs external information to understand himself in terms of other persons around him. Man is essentially striving to become a rational, problem-solving organism.

---

[9] *Client-Centered Therapy* (Boston: Houghton Mifflin Company, 1951), p. 195.
[10] Angelo V. Boy and Gerald J. Pine, *Client-Centered Counseling in the Secondary School* (Boston: Houghton Mifflin Company, 1963), p. 43.
[11] *Ibid.*

Byrne discusses goals in an existential sense, with possibly one notable exception:[12]

> The counselor's goal, firmly based on the human worth of the individual, regardless of education, intelligence, color, or background, is to use his technical skills (a) to help each counselee attain and maintain an awareness of self so that he can be responsible for himself, (b) to help each counselee confront threats to his being, and thus to open further the way for the counselee to increase his concern for others' well being, (c) to help each counselee to bring into full operation his unique potential in compatibility with his own life style and within the ethical limits of society.

The somewhat clashing aspect of this description is Byrne's reference to the counselor's using his "technical skills." Existentially, it is rather difficult to think of a close and intimate human involvement, such as that between counselor and client, in which the counselor *uses* technical skills. The counselor gives of himself, and part of that self may be a technical skill.

Hora also talks in an existential sense, with the stress on self realization:[13]

> . . . health is being what one really is . . . the psychotherapeutic process aims at bringing about this authenticity in a human being. . . . It consists of a realization of the attainment of the open mind. . . . The open mind . . . is attained by the realization of the closed mind.

Others also indicate their own personal concept of man and his nature, as viewed from their particular frames of reference, when they write about the goals and objectives of counseling. Tyler,[14] for example, feels that ". . . the psychological purpose of counseling is to facilitate development," while Shoben[15] thinks of values as he writes, "At any rate, perhaps the crucial learning that occurs in psychotherapy is the acquisition of a functional, critically held, and personally relevant system of human values."

---

[12] Richard Hill Byrne, *The School Counselor* (Boston: Houghton Mifflin Company, 1963), pp. 19–20.
[13] Thomas Hora, "Psychotherapy: Healing or Growth," *Annals of Psychotherapy* 4:9; Monograph Number 5 (1963).
[14] Leona Tyler, *The Work of the Counselor* (New York: Appleton-Century-Crofts, 1961), p. 17.
[15] Edward J. Shoben, "The Therapeutic Object: Men or Machines," *Journal of Counseling Psychology* 10:264–268 (Fall, 1963).

Thorne[16] feels that, from the viewpoint of the counselor, the main objective of personality counseling is to protect and secure mental health by preventing or modifying pathogenic etiologic factors productive of maladjustment or mental disorder. The prime obligation of the counselor, he feels, is to help people to live happier and healthier lives by psychological methods of healing and re-education.

Sullivan states his position as follows:[17]

> The interviewer must discover who the client is. . . . And, on the basis of who the person is, the interviewer must learn what this person conceives of in his living as problematic, and what he feels to be difficult. . . . [That] the person will leave with some measure of increased clarity about himself and his living with other people is an essential goal of the psychiatric interview.

Williamson describes the objectives of counseling by stating that "the counselor assists the student to choose goals which will yield maximum satisfaction within the limits of those compromises necessitated by uncontrolled and uncontrollable factors in the individuals and in society itself."[18] He also feels that the counselor "should be prepared to assist the student to solve, choose, master, learn and deal with situations and problems of a wide variety."[19]

Hadley feels that "the most essential goal [of psychological counseling] is to aid the individual in his efforts to achieve an effective relationship with his environment,"[20] while Alexander maintains that the aim of psychoanalysis "is to effect permanent changes in the personality by increasing the ego's integrative power . . . to change the ego by exposing it to conflictful repressed material."[21]

The Committee on Definition of Division 17 of the American Psychological Association describes the objectives of counseling by stating that the counseling psychologist contributes to the following:[22]

---

[16] F. C. Thorne, "Principles of Personality Counseling," *Journal of Clinical Psychology,* Brandon, Vt.: 1950, p. 89.

[17] Harry S. Sullivan, *The Psychiatric Interview* (New York: Norton, 1954), p. 18.

[18] E. C. Williamson, *Counseling Adolescents* (New York: McGraw-Hill, 1950), p. 221.

[19] *Ibid.,* p. 219.

[20] John M. Hadley, *Clinical and Counseling Psychology* (New York: Alfred A. Knopf, 1958), p. 26.

[21] F. Alexander, *Fundamentals of Psychoanalysis* (New York: Norton, 1948), pp. 275–276.

[22] Reported by C. Gilbert Wrenn, "Status and Role of the School Counselor," *Personnel and Guidance Journal* 36:175–183 (November, 1957).

(a) the client's realistic acceptance of his own capacities, motivations, and self-attitudes, (b) the client's achievement of a reasonable harmony with his social, economic and vocational environment, and (c) society's acceptance of individual differences and their implications for community, employment, and marriage relations.

Although these authorities may use different terms such as counseling, therapy, and psychiatry, and although they may use different methods of description, they are all likely describing the same basic process, and their differences reflect a personal difference rather than the differences, say, between those who might be called counselors or psychologists or psychiatrists.

There are human and personal differences as counselors and therapists talk about their objectives of counseling, and there are the same differences when they discuss those things that *should not* be considered as goals or objectives. These differences, however, tend to be reduced when the primary professional function of the individual is counseling or psychotherapy. If, for example, we talk with school counselors rather than school teachers, counseling psychologists rather than clinical psychologists, psychiatrists rather than medical doctors, existential therapists rather than existential philosophers, the level of agreement rises markedly. I can probably safely say that a number of counselors share with me the feeling that the following might be considered some of the "should not's" among counselor objectives:

1. Considering the multi-disciplined background of counseling, it is not surprising that many counselors still talk of the "solution of the client's problems" as one of their objectives. After all, teachers have solved problems for children, medical doctors have told patients what their trouble was, and what they, the doctors, would do to alleviate that problem, and psychologists have probed the psyche to help us to determine how the conscious might better guide the unconscious! Humphries, Traxler, and North make what would still be, for many school counselors, a perfectly acceptable statement when they say that ". . . in counseling, the immediate goal of the counselor and counselee is to arrive at the most satisfying solution as quickly as possible."[23] Still, many counselors would also feel that most individuals become clients because they have not learned to solve their own problems; while assistance in the solution of a problem may afford temporary

---

[23] J. A. Humphries, A. E. Traxler, and R. D. North, *Guidance Services* (Chicago: Science Research Associates, 1960), p. 345.

relief, it does not help the individual to do something about changing the causes of his problems. Thus the assistance that might be given to an individual toward learning how to solve his own problems would seem to be a more valid objective than the actual solution of a specific problem. In most cases, of course, the personal problems of a human being cannot be *solved* by another person, even if the latter is aware of the real problem. Since the client himself is quite frequently unaware of his basic problem, it is unlikely that the counselor would have this awareness, although this in itself would not usually mean too much. It would be unlikely that any professional counselor would feel that he could solve for the client problems which might be expressed by such statements as, "I feel so lonely and worthless, I don't know what to do, and you've just got to tell me what to do to get rid of this awful feeling . . . ," or "I just hate him . . . I hate his guts, and I know I shouldn't feel this way because he is my father; but I do, and I don't know what to do about it . . . ," or, "sure it's time that I burst loose— I'm sick and tired of being tied down by my wife, but I need your advice on just what I can do about it . . . ," or, "I shouldn't have to compete and excel and be better than my husband, but it seems that I just have to, and I wonder why . . . ," or, "My sister's whining and crying is driving me crazy, and I can't see how I can stay in that house until I graduate, but what can I do . . . ?"

These are a few statements made over the space of a short time to one counselor by several of his clients. They are not unusual, certainly, but would any reader of these words feel that he could solve even the immediate problems of these clients, as they have expressed them?

2. We may also question the idea that a primary goal in counseling is to make the client happy and satisfied, although this depends on how one views happiness and satisfaction. A human being may be helped, through counseling, to take a risk and make a choice that may result in pain and failure; another may decline a well paying position because he now realizes that, although he could have easily satisfied his employer, he would not have satisfied himself. Thus while counseling may, in the long run, help the client to develop in himself a deep and personal satisfaction with self, any sort of overt and immediate happiness and satisfaction is a by-product, rather than a primary objective. Indeed, as a result of counseling the client may become less smug, less self-centered, and more concerned with the world around him. He may be helped to move toward such a stage of security that he does not have to be happy all the time to feel that all is well. He

may become secure and solid enough so that he can accept a certain degree of unhappiness and sorrow and despair as a normal part of living, rather than something to be avoided at all costs. It might even be safe to say that the one who pursues happiness—his own happiness, that is, as a major objective of his life—is not revealing a high degree of security and stability.

3. Making society happy and satisfied with the client is an even more unacceptable goal. Indeed, it could hardly be called an objective of either counseling or mental health, although it is true that increasingly in our culture adjustment seems to be measured by the extent to which an individual gets along with the group, is acceptable to the group, and is eventually absorbed by the group. While adjustment may have to be related to the culture, since the individual does not live alone, it might be that real security is something that is a good deal deeper, more internalized, and thus independent of the whims and the likes or dislikes of the passing crowd. The secure individual will not be independent just to be independent. He will not stand up, alone, just because standing up alone gives him a special thrill and a feeling of independence. If it must be, however, that in order to be true to himself he must stand up and be counted, he will do so; and in such a case, whether he stands alone or has the entire group with him will be of little consequence.

A goal of counseling might be to help the individual attain a stage of development at which he can look honestly at himself, and eventually a point where he can derive some element of satisfaction in what he sees. He might, indeed, be able to say to himself, deeply, and with meaning, "I can certainly be a lot better than I am, but all in all, I am not too bad. I can afford to hold my head high, even though others may think I am nothing." This is the sort of person who will be less dependent on the group. He will draw his strengths from his inner self. This is the man who may make society very unhappy with him. He is no organization man, and he may utter truths that others would rather ignore. He will accept the fact that he has to live within the mores of his society, but he will not feel that his very life depends on the adulation and approval of that society. The goals of counseling, at least as I see them, do not include the concept that the counselor must somehow help the client to become a passive, acceptant, agreeable fellow who resembles a vegetable much more than an independent human being.

If, on the other hand, one accepts the concept of a completely determined state of being, then it would seem that we have no choice, and each man must become a simple pawn, the victim of his culture, to do as it demands. The counselor in such a world would also, of course, be the inanimate voice of the state. Any concept of the existential being, of the self-actualization of the individual, of the inner integrity of the person, of the potential for human growth—all of these would be naive illusions. While we may hope that this would not be the view of the counselor, there is no doubt that it is the view of many individuals. A statement, for example, that smacks remarkably of *1984*[24] and *Walden Two*,[25] or the writings in journals like *Pravda*, is seen in a booklet written for school counselors by the Orientation Group, USAF, Wright-Patterson Air Force Base, Ohio, entitled *The Struggle for Men's Minds*. There appears in the introduction a quotation from Samuel Johnson. It reads as follows:

> Every society has a right to preserve public peace and order, and therefore has a good right to prohibit the propagation of opinions which have a dangerous tendency. . . . Every man has a physical right to think as he pleases; for it cannot be discovered how he thinks. He has not a moral right, for he ought to inform himself, and think justly. But, Sir, no member of society has a right to teach any doctrine contrary to what the society holds to be true.

This is not a statement that one would expect to find in a document published by a service that is dedicated to defend the freedom and integrity of every individual American.

4. Another common but questionable idea is that an objective of counseling should be to persuade the client to change certain decisions and choices in favor of those that are "right." The professional counselor approaches the client, not with a bag of answers, but rather with an open and understanding mind that respects the integrity of his client to the extent of believing that he has the right to make his own decisions and choices; and whether or not these would be the decisions and choices of the counselor is of no importance. The professional counselor cannot have preconceived notions and ideas regarding choices and decisions to be made by the client. Many teachers, for example, find it extremely difficult to accept the idea that a student has the right to say nasty things about a faculty member to a counselor, if the student feels secure enough, or harried enough, to make such a statement. The preconceived notion here is that all children are sup-

---

[24] George Orwell, *1984* (New York: Harcourt, Brace & World, Inc., 1949).
[25] B. F. Skinner, *Walden Two* (New York: The Macmillan Co., 1948).

posed to be respectful toward adults, no matter how miserable these adults may be, just as all nurses are supposed to respect all medical doctors, all students to respect all teachers, all privates all officers, and so on. But respect is obviously an attitude that one person develops toward another person because of his feelings toward that person, and people cannot be "told" to feel a certain way. Thus the counselor does not plan and decide for the client, since he honestly does not know what is best for him. His function is to help the client to decide what is best for *him*, not for the counselor, or society, or anyone else, although there will very often be a close relationship among all of these.

It is difficult to talk about the specifics of goals or objectives of counselors who are involved in the counseling process, since the more specific one becomes, the more personal he is. There would seem, however, to be several general points on which counselors and therapists tend to agree when talking about objectives:

1. Any "objective" is affected by the humanistic feeling that man is, basically, a capable, self-determining creature. This is not determined by any particular title that the counselor may give to his counseling, and it applies equally well to those who may call themselves Adlerians or Freudians or Rogerians, or clinical counselors, or eclectic counselors, or client-centered counselors, or rational counselors. The methods or procedures of the individual counselor may differ, but their views of man tend to be somewhat alike. They are optimistic, and although some might scoff, they would appear to have some degree of faith in the fellow man. Certainly they trust him far more than do most of his fellows.

2. Most counselors would probably feel that another somewhat general objective is that of working with the client to help him to move toward a greater level of self-acceptance and self-understanding. He learns, one might say, to be. An individual cannot change himself if he refuses to recognize and accept himself as he is. Such a person spends his life in a futile attempt to convince himself that he is what he is not. Understanding, for the counselor, is a good deal more than just an intellectual statement. True understanding implies self-acceptance, and this understanding will likely come through a re-living, an experiencing, a feeling, rather than through an intellectual step-by-step process.

Much of one's behavior, for example, such as aggressiveness, hostility, promiscuous sexuality, may be part of a vain attempt to convince oneself of one's maleness, an attempt to flee from the latent homosexual tendencies that the individual has learned. The sneering and contemptuous remarks that may be directed at higher education generally, at a college degree, or toward a particular university may indicate the individual's struggle to avoid the acceptance of his own unimpressive intellectual competence. As children grow, they soon learn that they should not be what they are, they should not think what they think. The growing adolescent girl will find it difficult to accept calmly and securely her six feet of height; in another culture, it might not be a problem, but in America it is. A child may soon learn, from his parents and from his teachers, that lack of intellectual competence is not good; since he can do nothing directly about it, he will almost certainly, if he is to survive, find ways to compensate. He may learn too, that he cannot be "poor," and that he must have the ambition to be better than his parents. Sometimes changes are possible, but since the individual is not changing because he wants to, the psychological and physical price that he has to pay is too high. More often than not, however, an actual direct change is not possible, and the individual is placed in the impossible position of having to be what he cannot be. It is unfortunate that the school does not do more to help the child to accept what he is, and work with what he has, rather than pretend that he can do what he cannot, or that he has what he has not. Such a pretense tends to drive him even deeper into the rut of unacceptance, and to set the pattern for years of frustrated striving and avoidance of his real self.

A move toward greater self-acceptance also means that the individual tends to decrease the discrepancy between his real self and his ideal self. Seeing himself as he really is, he is more likely to think in terms of realistic goals rather than fantastic fantasies. Yet some people do become adept at satisfying the cultural demand without any real personal change. A good example is the way in which some school people get around the need for a higher degree. They do not want to become more educated; in some cases they are not capable intellectually of doing any legitimate graduate work. But since they must have a degree, they in effect buy one.

Generally, however, a person who has moved to a greater stability will not try to be a college professor if he is of low intellectual capacity; if he has a small physique, he will not strive vainly to be a football hero; if he lacks an understanding of music, and has no real interest in it, he will cease trying to pretend that he is lover of the opera and all things cultural; if his income is modest, he will not try to convince himself that somehow his fairy godmother will appear and help him to maintain the standard of living that he feels he must pretend he can afford. He will, in effect, come fairly close to accepting himself as he is. In this frenzied culture most children will need assistance if they are to develop into this very stable sort of fellow.

3. A somewhat related goal has to do with the development of a greater level of honesty, particularly honesty toward self, in the client. An essential quality of the counselor is his congruence and his honesty, both toward the client and toward himself. In a human relationship with such an individual, the client may come to have less need to pretend that he is what he is not. The counselor does not buoy the client up with false support, and indeed, if he tries, the client is usually quite aware that such support is false. What man who has lost a hand believes that "things will be just as they were before"? What child who has been forced to repeat a grade believes that "this will really be much better than it was last year"? What girl who has been jilted by her one and only love believes that "you'll soon get over this and forget that it ever happened"? What child who has to go back and live with a brutal parent believes that "things will be much better now"? People have a habit of giving support that is not really honest, although they do not do so deliberately with malice in mind.

On the whole, we live in a culture where we do not call a spade a spade, particularly if the spade happens to be an unpleasant one. We like to pretend that what should be is. Although everyone must live to some degree in the realm of fantasy, such a practice can get to a point where it begins to make living somewhat difficult. It is nice—and it may sometimes be good—to feel that if we believe long enough, what we believe will come true. But we are on psychologically dangerous ground if we assume that we can wish things away, since this very attitude usually indicates that we are carefully avoiding the real basis for our problems. The counselor should not help the Jewish student to believe that it is just as easy for him to get into an American college as it would be if he were a Catholic or a Protestant; it is not. The counselor should not increase the unreality of the black student's dreaming by giving him the idea that it is just as easy for a black student to get a job as it is for a white one; it is not. Acceptance of the reality—and including here an acceptance of the reality of all of the factors involved (a Jewish student may not get into a certain college simply because his grades are too low; a black applicant may not get a job because he does not have the required education and skill)—is not passivity and hopelessness, or bitterness, but it is the first step toward doing something about reality.

It is important to note, too, that the counselor *can* be honest because of his own high level of self-actualization, because of his own level of being. He feels no personal pressure to take sides, to agree or disagree, to tell the client what is right and what is wrong, to encourage or discourage. He can be easily acceptant of the fact that in most human differences what is right for one may be wrong for another. He is aware that the husband who talks about his wife's negative qualities and his plans for a divorce *may* be right about her and about his plans; he *may* be. The student who talks about his miserable teachers and parents *may* also be right on all counts. But the counselor is not the judge, he is not the chooser of sides; by remaining impartial he is more likely to be able to help the client to achieve a realistic outlook on his life and on the lives of others.

4. Objectives should be based on client need, not counselor need. Although any professional worker, including a counselor, should like what he is doing, an even more basic question for those people whose work is with other human beings has to do with the effect of what he does on the recipient of his efforts. Counseling cannot be justified on the basis of satisfactions that accrue to the counselor; it can only be justified on the basis of its effect on the client. More often than not, when the counselor feels, "That was a very good session," it doubtless was a good session; but ultimately the only true measure of the effectiveness of the session is found in what happens to the client. Since every person exhibits himself in what he does and what he says, the counselor must be sure that he is not functioning in a certain manner simply to satisfy some of his own frustrations and unmet needs, rather than to benefit the client. Too frequently the defense of a supposed method or technique is a defense of the self. The rigid type of counselor, who cannot accept the idea that there are "other ways," unconsciously indicates that what he does is very much for his own satisfaction rather than that of the client. There is a marked resemblance between the father who says "I don't want to beat you, but I'm doing it for your own good," the teacher who says, "The only way to gain the respect of the child is to bear down on him so that he'll know who's boss," and the counselor who says, "This client-centered stuff is a lot of nonsense. I've tried it and it never works for me." The father, the teacher, and the counselor are all giving a display of self, rather than showing their professional and learned skills and understandings. The father who beats his child, the teacher who happily bears down, the counselor who dismisses any contradictory point of view—their actions must be taken to bolster self. If the results are positive for the client, it is a fortunate accident rather than the result of any professional action.

Thus there is a very real point to the argument that counselor preparation should include experience in counseling under supervision, and indeed personal counseling of the student counselor himself, so that he may become more aware of the extent to which he is becoming a counselor to satisfy his own needs regardless of the effects on the client. When the counselor can benefit the client as well as satisfy his own needs, all is well, but certainly every counselor should have an awareness of the extent to which he is possibly harming the client in his attempts to satisfy his own needs. The low level of professional competence required of school counselors at the present time almost surely means that many school counselors are working almost entirely for self-satisfaction, with very little in the way of professional evidence to back up their actions and their deeds. "I like my work" is not always a valid criterion to use in measuring one's effectiveness.

KINDS OF COUNSELING[26]

It would probably be correct to say that, up until the time of Rogers, psychotherapy was considered to be something that psychiatrists did to sick people after the fashion of Freud, or some of his followers, and counseling was the offering of counsel, advice, and suggestion to not-too-seriously bothered individuals, usually about difficulties relating to jobs or schooling. In the last quarter of a century, however, there has been extensive reference in the literature to various "kinds" of counseling and psychotherapy, which are to be distinguished from theories of counseling which were discussed in the last chapter. (Purely for purposes of discussion I would think of "kinds" in a more pragmatic, functional sense, whereas "theories" refer to the more theoretical base upon which the counselor is *supposed* to develop his method of operation.) This section will examine some of the better known kinds of counseling, and question the extent to which there are kinds of counseling as distinguished from kinds of counselors.

1. One of the first kinds of counseling is that which might be described as involving basically "well" people, as contrasted to the opposite kind which involves "sick" people. A general point stressed in the literature in any discussion of developmental counseling, for example, is that it concerns well rather than sick people, and is the opposite of what is referred to as crisis counseling. Those who support

---

[26] *See* Dugald S. Arbuckle, "Kinds of Counseling: Meaningful or Meaningless," *Journal of Counseling Psychology* 14:219–225 (May, 1967).

this point of view, however, are not always consistent. Shertzer and Peters,[27] for example, refer to developmental counseling as the "enhancement of an already adequately functioning person," but almost immediately add that it is also concerned with those who have problems that interfere with classroom learning. In a similar manner, Zaccaria[28] refers to the preventive and positive approach of developmental guidance, but then, in describing the modern concerns of education, he sees the future as bringing an intensification of "these problems."

Thus it would appear that the developmental counselor, like other counselors, is going to talk with individuals who have problems and concerns and difficulties, even though these individuals are not sick. This would then mean that most of the people who are described as "mentally ill" would fit into this category, since they are not sick in a disease or injury sense, they do not need a hospital in a medical sense, nor do they need medical treatment. They do need help in learning how to be different, in learning how to become the person they want to become. This is a concept being accepted not only by school counselors, but as has been indicated, by both the M.D. and the Ph.D. psychotherapists.

Glasser,[29] for example, in what he describes as Reality Therapy, refuses to accept the concept of mental illness, and he feels that the whole development of mental hygiene is stalled because the psychiatric approach stresses mental illness rather than responsibility. English,[30] a psychoanalyst, assumes that: getting well means taking responsibility for self, and refusing as far as possible to be abused by persons or fate.

Van Kaam's[31] version of psychotherapy from an existential point of view is very similar. He views therapeutic care as being fertile only when the person who has to grow chooses and for this reason the approach to psychotherapy must be entirely different from that of medicine.

---

27 B. Shertzer and H. J. Peters, *Guidance: Techniques for Individual Appraisal and Development* (New York: Macmillan Book Co., 1965), pp. 38–49.

28 J. S. Zaccaria, "Developmental Guidance: A Concept in Transition," *The School Counselor* 13: 226–229 (May, 1966).

29 W. Glasser, *Reality Therapy* (New York: Harper and Row, 1965), p. 155.

30 O. S. English, "Changing Techniques in Psychotherapy," *Voices* 2:91–98 (Fall, 1966).

31 Adrian Van Kaam, "Counseling and Psychotherapy from the Viewpoint of Existential Psychology" in Dugald S. Arbuckle (Ed.), *Counseling and Psychotherapy: An Overview* (New York: McGraw-Hill Book Co., 1967), pp. 45–46.

Few would question the overt directiveness of Ellis'[32] rational psychotherapy, but he too, departs from the medical model. Hummel[33] has some difficulty in defining what might be called another "kind" of counseling, namely, "ego counseling," but he does see it as being with persons who are relatively free of crippling neurotic defenses.

Thus while medically-oriented psychotherapists such as English and Glasser still use the terms "patient" and "hospital" as do psychologically-oriented psychotherapists such as Ellis, they, like Van Kaam and Hummel, are all generally talking about well human beings and the learning process. They are not talking about sick people and medical treatment.

2. The word "cognitive" also appears frequently as a means of describing a kind of counseling. Williamson,[34] in discussing the trait-factor theory in counseling, sees counseling as a highly personalized and individualized assistance to the individual in his effort, cognitively, to discover his capabilities and the opportunities which exist in school and in vocations. O'Hara[35] sees vocational counseling in much the same way, when he talks about counseling as a dialogue between relatively well adjusted people, which presumes enough openness to warrant a dialogue.

On the other hand, in describing the "cognitively flexible" counselor, Sprinthall, Whitely and Mosher[36] say, "Counseling in this framework is concerned with both the thoughts and the feelings of the clients," while from a behaviorist point of view, Michael and Meyerson[37] say that "Behaviorally oriented counselors agree that telling people what is wrong and what they 'should' do is an ineffective procedure."

---

[32] A. Ellis, "Rational-Emotive Psychotherapy" in Dugald S. Arbuckle (Ed.), *Counseling and Psychotherapy: An Overview* (New York: McGraw-Hill Book Co., 1967), pp. 78–95.

[33] R. C. Hummel, "Ego Counseling in Guidance: Concept and Method," *Harvard Educational Review* 32:463–482 (Fall, 1962).

[34] E. G. Williamson, "Vocational Counseling: Trait-Factor Theory," in B. Stefflre (Ed.), *Theories of Counseling* (New York: McGraw-Hill Book Co., 1965), p. 212.

[35] Robert P. O'Hara, "Counseling and Vocational Psychology" in Dugald S. Arbuckle (Ed.), *Counseling and Psychotherapy: An Overview* (New York: McGraw-Hill Book Co., 1967), p. 112.

[36] N. H. Sprinthall, J. M. Whitely, and R. L. Mosher, "Cognitive Flexibility; A Focus for Research on Counselor Education," *Counselor Education and Supervision* 5:188–197 (Summer, 1966).

[37] J. Michael and L. Meyerson, "A Behavorial Approach to Counseling and Guidance" *Harvard Educational Review* 32:382–403 (Fall, 1962).

Thinking and feeling, of course, go together, and all counseling has a place for the cognitive. Surely the counselor who in answer to the client's squirming question, "Where is the men's room," says "You feel you would like to go to the men's room," is as guilty of questionable behavior as the counselor who says "You should go out with John because he's more suited for you," when the client asks "Which guy should I go out with?" If a client can absorb a rational statement there would seem to be no reason why the counselor or anyone else, assuming that he has a rational answer, should withhold it from him. On the other hand, wisdom is a good deal more than the mere accumulation of knowledge. Wisdom is in and of the human system, whereas knowledge may have little or no relationship to one's day-by-day living. As Kierkegaard[38] put it, "To exist and to know are two very different things."

3. The degree of humanness in counseling would appear to be another measure of the kind of counseling that one might practice. While developmental counseling and behavioral counseling appear to be pretty much the same thing, the behavioral "counselor" would appear to be one who sets up the experiences which will affect the behavior of the individual rather than the one whose own personal involvement with the individual is the principle factor affecting behavior. The developmental counselor, it would appear, retains somewhat more of his humanness than does the behavioral counselor! Blocher,[39] for example, sees the goal of counseling as the formation of an integrated structure of values and ideas, together with a repertory of coping behaviors. Shoben[40] elaborates on what would appear to be a somewhat similar description when he refers to counseling as "a developmental experience in which attempts to solve problems and arrive at decisions are the events out of which, through reflection and the process of 'working through,' personal growth takes place."

Krumboltz[41] uses the term "behavioral counseling" only as a reminder that all counseling is designed to affect the behavior of the client, but he puts minimal stress on the counselor as a gestalt human being, and on counseling as the human relationship between two

---

[38] S. Kierkegaard, *Concluding Unscientific Postscript,* translated by D. F. Swenson and W. Lowrie. (Princeton, N.J.: Princeton University Press, 1941), p. 18.
[39] Blocher, *op. cit.,* p. 9.
[40] E. J. Shoben, Jr., "The Counseling Experience as Personal Development" *Personnel and Guidance Journal* 44:224–230 (November, 1965).
[41] John D. Krumboltz, "Behaviorial Counseling: Rationale and Research," *Personnel and Guidance Journal* 44:383–387 (January, 1965).

humans, when he says, "As we learn more about what activities can be used to bring about the types of behavior changes that clients request, then we as counselors will be better able to fulfill our professional responsibilities." The same minimal stress of the humanness of man and the human relationship in counseling is seen when Michael and Meyerson[42] state that "The heart of the behavioral approach in counseling is that the environment must be manipulated so as to allow strong reinforcing consequences to become attached to the behavior that is desired." Similarly, while Sprinthall, Whitely and Mosher[43] agree that the counselor himself is an important dimension in the counseling process, they also state that "While human qualities may indeed be relevant to counseling, the authors' view is that particular counselor behaviors are a more relevant criterion of counselor effectiveness."

Truax,[44] on the other hand, while acceptant of the evidence of the effectiveness of behavior therapies on human behavior, holds that ". . . man is both a whole being and also a collection of habits and behaviors; that his total being can be seen as a product of the interplay between the molar self and the specific acts and habits that fill in the mosaic of daily living."

Thus one could say that as a developmental or behavioral counselor one is interested in and involved in the development of change in the client, who is viewed as a person who is capable of changing, or of being changed by certain experiences. These experiences might, or might not, involve the counselor in a human relationship with the client. Some behaviorists would likely see the counselor as one who might devise a machine which would produce the experience which would in turn create change in the client. In this sense, Skinner and Pavlov could both be called counselors, as could any behavorial scientist who is interested in creating change in the human being, even though he might never have any human contact with the person who is being changed.

4. The "kinds" of counseling that have probably been with us the longest are those described as "vocational counseling" and "educational counseling." The immediate question, of course, is the extent to which these are discrete kinds of counseling, or should be considered as basically counseling with a vocational or educational bent. In de-

---

[42] J. Michael and L. Meyerson, *op. cit.*
[43] N. H. Sprinthall, J. M. Whitely and R. L. Mosher, *op. cit.*
[44] C. B. Truax, "Some Implications of Behavior Therapy for Psychotherapy," *Journal of Counseling Psychology* 13:160–170 (Summer, 1966).

scribing what the counselor does in one kind of counseling, Ohlsen[45] says the counselor should listen to the client, help her to look at herself, help her to explore what else she needs to know about herself, help her to make a decision, help her to identify what appeals to her the most. In describing another kind of counseling Lair[46] states that it centers around the one-to-one relationship, is concerned with change in the individual who wishes to alter behavior which is unsatisfactory to him, and with specific change in the overt behavior of the student in a particular direction. Ohlsen is referring to occupations and jobs and colleges, while Lair is referring to academic and intellectual performance. It seems that they could be just as easily switched so that Ohlsen could be describing academic counseling instead of vocational counseling, while Lair could be describing vocational counseling instead of academic counseling. Actually, they are both primarily describing counseling, and the vocational counselor described by Ohlsen is an individual who possesses more in the way of knowledge and information about jobs and colleges than other counselors. Educational counseling, on the other hand, at least as described by Lair, is very much counseling, since the problems of the underachieving student are overwhelmingly psychological, and can hardly be solved by the counselor's possession of academic information. As a counselor, I could see where I might have to refer a student who came in seeking specific information about jobs and colleges, since I do not have this information, but I would see no such problem with the student who came in because of his unsatisfactory academic and intellectual performance.

5. In the last few years a rash of books, scores of papers and articles,[47] and a professional journal[48] have appeared on the subject of elementary school counseling, and one might at least assume that

---

[45] Merle M. Ohlsen, "Vocational Counseling for Girls and Women," *The Vocational Guidance Quarterly* 17:124–127 (December, 1968).

[46] George Scott Lair, "Educational Counseling: Concern of the School Counselor," *Personnel and Guidance Journal* 46:858–863 (May, 1968).

[47] For example: Verne Faust, *The Counselor-Consultant in the Elementary School* (Boston: Houghton Mifflin Co., 1968); Verne Faust, *History of Elementary School Counseling* (Boston: Houghton Mifflin Co., 1968); Don C. Dinkmeyer, *Guidance and Counseling in the Elementary School* (New York: Holt, Rinehart and Winston, Inc., 1968); George E. Hill and Eleanore Braun Luckey, *Guidance for Children in Elementary Schools* (New York: Appleton-Century-Crofts, 1968); Herman J. Peters, Bruce Shertzer, and William H. Van Hoose, *Guidance in Elementary Schools* (Chicago: Rand McNally and Co., 1968); William H. Van Hoose, *Counseling in the Elementary School* (Itasca, Ill.: F. E. Peacock Publishers, Inc., 1968).

[48] *Elementary School Guidance and Counseling* (Washington, D.C.: American Personnel and Guidance Association).

this would imply that elementary school conseling was a different kind of counseling from secondary school counseling. This, however, is anything but the case, and one could easily substitute "secondary" for "elementary" in nearly everything that is written on the subject. The primary difference, of course, is that the counselor would be working with younger children rather than older children, and he would be working in a school setting with teachers who differed somewhat from those in a secondary school. Other than this, however, it is fairly clear that the counselor is involved in very much the same professional activity regardless of whether he is operating in an elementary school, a secondary school, or a college.

The preliminary statement, for example, of a joint ACES-ASCA committee on the elementary school counselor[49] came up with the not very revolutionary statement that a counselor should be a member of the staff of each elementary school, and that the three major responsibilities of this counselor should be counseling, consultation, and co-ordination. Numerous papers come forth with what would appear to be rather glaringly obvious statements. Mayer[50] concludes that counseling can and should be the central role of the elementary school counselor. Mayer (in another journal, with Munger)[51] reinforces his earlier conclusion by again concluding that counseling "can and should be the central role of the elementary school counselor." Foster[52] found that five types of educators—elementary school teachers, elementary school administrators, elementary and secondary school counselors, and counselor educators all perceived counseling type activities as the most important function of the elementary school counselor. Nelson[53] concluded that the elementary school counselor is first a counselor with children, and second, a consultant to the adults who affect children. Dinkmeyer[54] comes to similar conclusions when he describes the elementary school counselor's primary functions as counseling, con-

---

[49] "The Elementary School Counselor," *Personnel and Guidance Journal* 44:658–661 (February, 1966).
[50] G. Roy Mayer, "An Approach for the Elementary School Counselor: Consultant or Counselor," *The School Counselor* 14:210–214 (March, 1967).
[51] G. Roy Mayer and Paul F. Munger, "A Plea for Letting the Elementary School Counselor Counsel," *Counselor Education and Supervision* 6:341–346 (Summer, 1967).
[52] Car M. Foster, "The Elementary School Counselor: How Perceived," *Counselor Education and Supervision* 6:102–107 (Winter, 1967).
[53] Richard C. Nelson, "The Preparation of Elementary School Counselors: A Model," *Counselor Education and Supervision* 6:197–200 (Spring, 1967).
[54] Don Dinkmeyer, "Elementary School Guidance: Principles and Functions," *The School Counselor* 16:11–16 (September, 1968).

sultation, coordination, and the development of in-service training in guidance for classroom teachers. Thus, other than the differences in the specifics of one's occupational task, there would appear to be general agreement that one cannot describe elementary and secondary school counseling as two discrete kinds of counseling. This is reinforced by a study by Danielson[55] from which he concludes that "there was nothing to indicate a distinct elementary school counselor personality."

Thus, in a functional sense at least, I would feel that counseling *is* of a different kind if one tends to stress the "well" concept of clients rather than the "sick" concept of patients, if one operates in a basically cognitive fashion rather than in an affective and emotive manner, and if one stresses the humanness of people rather than the behaviors of individuals. On the other hand, it is difficult to distinguish as discrete kinds of counseling the educational versus the vocational and the elementary versus the secondary.

The satire that is most near the truth is the one that bites hardest. Dunlop has analyzed, tongue in cheek, different types of counseling (as well as the techniques commonly used by each type) and has divided the field into nine categories.[56] Unfortunately, even the most hilarious of his examples are only too familiar. Indeed, some counselors (but not, I hope, many!) may actually get the feeling that they are looking in a mirror when they read them.

Here is his description of the nine categories:

Category I: The Empathic Trap Response.

Form A. The Sharer. The counselor is compelled to share, and forgets who is in focus.

> Co.: Gee, you really have a problem. I had a second cousin who had a problem just like yours, and . . .

or

> Co.: I know just how you feel, because this happened to me, and . . .

[55] Harry A. Danielson, "Personality of Prospective Elementary School Counselors: Implications for Preparation," *Counselor Education and Supervision* 8:99–103 (Winter, 1969).
[56] Richard S. Dunlop, "Letter and Comments," *Personnel and Guidance Journal* 47:71–77 (September, 1968).

Form B. The Conversationalist. The counselor does not understand the differences between counseling and conversation.

> Cl.: I just bought a new dress at the Schwartz Store.
> Co.: Oh? I saw some very attractive skirts there.
> Cl.: You can usually get good bargains.
> Co.: But their jewelry is awful.
> Cl.: I know. Junk.
> Co.: What do you think of Macy's?

Category II: The Non-Directive Obsessive Response.

Form A. General Type. The counselor has only one technique at his command.

> Cl.: I feel awfully warm, can't you open the window?
> Co.: You feel warm.

or

> Cl.: Can you tell me how to find the restroom?
> Co.: You want to find the restroom.

Form B. Perseverating Parrot Type. The counselor confuses reflection and repetition.

> Cl.: I'm sorry I'm a little late today, but it's so beautiful out-side that I stopped to look at the flowers, and the birds, and the trees, and the bushes.
> Co.: You're sorry you're a little late today, but it's so beau-tiful outside that you stopped to look at the flowers, and the birds, and the trees, and the bushes.

Category III: The Inquisitorial Response.

Form A. True or False Type. The counselor demands a "yes" or "no" response.

> Co.: Do you like school?

or

> Co.: You're not going to fail again, are you?

Form B. Loaded Option Type. The counselor tells his client how to respond.

> Co.: Don't you think you ought to get a good education so that you can amount to something. You're not really going to marry that clod!

or

> Co.: Why are you talking about your mother like this? Everyone loves his mother; don't you love yours?

or

> Co.: A big guy like you shouldn't be having trouble in gym, should he?

Form C. Multiple-Choice Type. The counselor delimits response options available to his client.

> Co.: How did you feel? Did you feel good or bad?

or

> Co.: How do you feel when your father hits you? Do you hate him or don't you feel anything?

Form D. Declaration of War Type. The counselor challenges his client to defend himself.

> Co.: Why do you feel this way?

or

> Co.: Where'd you ever get an idea like that?

Form E. Der Gestapointerrogationisch Type. The counselor wears jack boots and walks funny.

> Co.: Have a seat. Name?
> Cl.: Jones. John Jones. I feel . . .
> Co.: Address?
> Cl.: Hm? Oh, I live in the dorm. It's no use . . .
> Co.: Your problem?
> Cl.: I had a date with this girl . . .
> Co.: When was that? When was the date with the girl?
> Cl.: Friday or Saturday. Saturday, I think. I never had a date before . . .
> Co.: Don't you like girls?

Cl.: Hm? Sure, but I never felt . . .

Co.: M-hm. You never felt a girl.

Cl.: No! No! I never felt comfortable, I . . .

Co.: How old are you?

Cl.: Nineteen last month. No one even sent me a birthday card.

Co.: Then actually you're a little over 19, aren't you?

Cl.: Well, about a month over. I need help . . .

Co.: Where is your home? Don't you have a father? What's wrong with your mother? Why is your shoe untied?

Cl.: I . . .

Co.: Tell me what you did to the girl.

Cl.: Please, can't you turn off that light? It's in my eyes.

Co.: The girl. Tell me about it. Come on, tell me your sordid little story. I'm here to help you.

Form F. Focus on Minutiae Type. The counselor has strong needs to gather data.

Cl.: (*Sniffling.*) I'm going to have to get an abortion.

Co.: I didn't get the spelling of your last name. Would you repeat that, please?

Cl.: Fox. F-O-X. Like the furry little animal (*weeping*) in the woods, with its c-c-c-cubs. (*Weeps copiously.*) My friend, June, had an abortion. (*Bawling.*)

Co.: (*Writing.*) F-O-X. June Fox.

Cl.: No. I'm Mary Fox. June is my friend. She damn near died. (*Cries heavily.*)

Co.: How old are you?

Cl.: Hm? Twenty-two. I've already made the arrangements with that terrible little man and his ghastly nurse, but I just don't know if it's right. (*Nearly hysterical.*)

Co.: And June?

Cl.: (*Wailing.*) Huh?

Co.: How old is June?

Category IV: The Safety Dodge Response.

Form A. General Type. The counselor is frightened by his client's material, and withdraws to high ground.

> Co.: So your homosexual problem really bothers you. What kind of grades did you make last year?

or

> Co.: . . . and you're very concerned about your relationship with God. Well, a great number of people are. Are you interested in athletics?

Form B. Diversionary Trap Type. The counselor responds to inappropriate material.

> Cl.: Ever since Mother died I've been pretty depressed. I just don't think it's any use. What point is there in going on? And my sister feels awful, too.
> Co.: Your sister is upset.
> Cl.: When my fiance and I broke up I was so angry and distraught that I went out and raced my car through the streets and screamed and screamed. I wrecked the car, and Daddy was furious.
> Co.: Your father has a nasty temper.

Form C. Estranged Type. The counselor is a fool.

> Cl.: Mother and Dad were fighting, and he was pounding on her and knocking her down, so I beat hell out of him and went out and had a steak.
> Co.: How do you like your steak cooked?

Form D. Aborted Reflection Type. The counselor wants, properly, to communicate his understanding, but is afraid to stick his neck out. So he uses a question mark when a period is indicated.

> Cl.: I'm going to run away from home.
> Co.: You're going to run away from home?
> Cl.: I'm going somewhere else to live.
> Co.: You're going somewhere else to live?
> Cl.: No one loves me.
> Co.: No one loves you?
> Cl.: I'm all alone.
> Co.: You're all alone?
> Cl.: Lonely.
> Co.: Lonely?

Form E. Missing-the-Concealed-Inference Ploy. The counselor doesn't know what's going on.

> Cl.: We have no money at all; my husband's an awful drunk and he spends the Welfare check on beer and wine. My daughter's a prostitute, and my son's on dope. I can't go home to my folks because Ma throws knives around, and Pa chases me through the house. My brothers are in jail. My sister's a Lesbian. The cops are always coming around and the windows are broken out and the roof leaks and they've cut off the gas and lights. But I'm really a very lucky person and I don't have no right to complain. I'm really very, very happy. I really am. Really.
>
> Co.: Life is a bowl of cherries.

Form F. The "Aw Shucks" Type. The counselor lacks confidence in his profession and in his skills.

> Cl.: I get nervous before tests.
> Co.: Oh dear. You'd better see your physician about that. I'm only a counselor.

or

> Cl.: I'm having a problem with my mother . . .
> Co.: I should caution you that I'm not a real psychologist, and . . .

or

> Cl.: I'm wondering if I should quit going to church . . .
> Co.: It's best that you consult your spiritual adviser about that.

Form G. Reassurance Type. The counselor insists that his client be strong.

> Co.: Hell, everyone's had that problem. Don't let a little thing like that bother you. Stop crying.

Category V: The Buffalo Stampede. The counselor is not only incompetent but rude.

Cl.: I'm not sure if I should stay in school.

Co.: You're thinking you should do something else.

Cl.: Yes, that's right, I . . .

Co.: You might stay in school, or you might . . .

Cl.: I could . . .

Co.: . . . drop out and . . .

Cl.: I . . .

Co.: . . . get a job, or grow a beard, or join the circus . . .

Cl.: I . . .

Co.: . . . or draw Welfare or something, but you're feeling guilty because everyone tells you to finish school . . .

Cl.: No, I . . .

Co.: . . . but you . . .

Cl.: I . . .

Co.: . . . don't want to stay in school.

Cl.: M-hm.

Co.: And you're about to say, "The hell with it," but you really can't . . .

Cl.: M-hm. I . . .

Co.: So that's the problem as you see it.

Cl.: M-hm.

Co.: Don't interrupt. I notice that you interrupt a good deal. I'm trying to understand your problem so that I can help you.

Category VI: The Leapfrog Interpretation Response. The counselor gets far, far ahead of his client and shows off his psychological know-how.

Cl.: I was up late last night studying, and I'm pretty tired this morning.

Co.: I make you uncomfortable, and you're excusing this by blaming your masochistic study pattern.

or

Cl.: I wish my Dad would lose some weight.

Co.: You're suffering typical penis envy, complicated by Oedipal conflict and castration anxiety.

Category VII: The Inverted Relation Response. The counselor allows his own interests or needs to dominate the interview or influence it significantly.

Cl.: I divorced my husband several years ago, and now that the kids are out of college and on their own I need to find something to occupy my time. I thought perhaps teaching . . .

Co.: Tell me about your husband.

Cl.: Fred? Oh, I'm well rid of him. Better all around. But you see, I had an art major, and I thought perhaps I could . . .

Co.: You feel the divorce was best for everyone.

Cl.: That's ancient history. What would I have to do to get licensed as a teacher in this state?

Co.: Fred is unimportant to you.

Cl.: Also, I need to know if I'd be better in an elementary school or at senior high.

Co.: You've just about forgotten your husband.

Cl.: I suppose I'd have to get a master's degree, but am I too old to learn?

Co.: Your divorce is very painful to you and you resist talking about it.

Cl.: I could go to school full time.

Co.: How do you see yourself as a woman, having lost your husband and all?

Cl.: What?

or

Cl.: I've been majoring in psychology, but those mazes are getting to me.

Co.: M-hm.

Cl.: I've thought about changing to counseling. Work with people, you know.

Co.: You prefer people to pigeons.

Cl.: Yeah. Fewer feathers.

Co.: Psych's a pretty rough course, isn't it?

Cl.: They have their own language.

Co.: Tough to learn?

Cl.: Oh, I don't know. Pretty tough. "Reinforcement schedule," "Rorschach," "Bimodal distribution," funny words like that.

Co.: What are the profs like?

Cl.: They mumble a lot. You thinking to changing to psych?

Co.: I don't know. These damn people are getting to me.

Cl.: M-hm.

Co.: The profs mumble, and they have these curious words —almost their own language.

Cl.: M-hm.

Co.: Like "Curvilinear relationship," and "Z-scores," and "Drumboltz." Words like that.

Cl.: M-hm.

Co.: Do you think I could make it in psych?

Cl.: You're concerned about your adequacy.

Category VIII: The Defensive Response. The counselor is protective of himself.

Cl.: Why won't you school people let me wear a beard?

Co.: Surely you don't blame me; that's the fault of those wicked administrators.

or

Cl.: That's an awful tie you're wearing.

Co.: I happen to like this tie very much. It's been my favorite tie for 20 years. Lots of people like nudes on their ties.

Category IX: The Friendly Adviser Response. The counselor has lots of good advice to offer.

Cl.: I'm really having trouble in History.

Co.: You should get to class on time, and pay attention, and take good notes, and ask intelligent questions.

or

Cl.: Tom keeps making passes at me.

Co.: Slap the s.o.b.

The critical question, then, may not be the somewhat meaningless "What kind of counseling do you practice?" but rather, "What sort of person are you?" If the goal of the intelligent counselor is to effect change in the client so that the counselor, or the state, or the church, may more easily control and direct and manipulate him, then the counselor's actual practice of counseling may be somewhat different than if his goals are viewed as helping the individual to move toward self-determination and individual freedom. If the intelligent counselor could, with honesty, say to the client, "I have no goals for you, but I hope you will let me be with you so that I may be of some help as you try to formulate and do something about your goals," he would likely function as a counselor in a different manner than if he had a precise goal in mind for the client. On this point, Dreyfus[57] wonders whether therapists are not reinforcing the self-as-object views of man, and whether the personality characteristics of behavior therapists are different than those of the more relationship-centered therapists. The evidence indicates that school administrators are different kinds of people than school counselors, and we could assume that it is likely that counselors who are the I-like-to-do-things-to-people type are different from those who are the I-like-to-help-people-to-grow-on-their-own-terms variety. If individual freedoms were suddenly to be drastically reduced in this country, it is interesting to wonder which psychologists and therapists would become the most effective manipulators and controllers working in the service of the new state. It is unlikely that the answer would lie in the kinds of counseling practiced, but rather in the kinds of humans represented by various counselors and therapists.

On the other hand, some counselors might be ineffective in achieving their goals, whatever they might be, because as individuals they are the significant variable, rather than the various techniques or methods which they might be using. Truax[58] hypothesizes that the "high condition" therapists are more effective because they are more potent positive reinforcers, and because they elicit a high degree of positive effect in the patient, while "low condition" therapists are ineffective and produce deteriorative change in patients because they are noxious stimuli who serve primarily as aversive reinforcers.

There would thus seem to be two points of difference which stand out in the discussion of kinds of counseling and kinds of counselors, and both of these have been brought into sharp focus by the increasing stress on behavior therapies.

1. Is the crucial element in counseling the human relationship between the counselor and the client, or does counseling also include anything that might be done to the client to induce change, including certain actions in which the counselor might have no personal involvement with the client? If the latter, it would seem that counseling then becomes meaningless as a term and almost anyone who might be described as a change engineer would be a counselor. As a medical doctor, I might know that anxiety can be lessened by the use of a certain drug, which may be purchased at a drug store, and I tell this to

---

[57] Edward A. Dreyfus, "Humanness: A Therapeutic Variable," *Personnel and Guidance Journal* 45:573–579 (February, 1967).
[58] C. B. Truax, *op. cit.*

a patient. As a teacher, I find out that the attention span of children is maintained at a higher level if every hour at least five minutes is given to relaxation and movement. As a war-minded autocrat, I find that people can become more acceptant of war and violence by having it continually portrayed on all the communication media as necessary and desirable. Anyone could obviously add endlessly to this list, but surely such individuals could not be called counselors or psychotherapists. Thus, because the counselor is involved in change, I hope we do not muddy the waters either by insisting he is not involved in change at all, or by saying that everyone who is involved in the development of change in others is a counselor. Most "behavior therapies" I would not see as therapies, but rather as means and methods, primarily those of conditioning and reconditioning, of changing behavior. This could be in the direction desired by either the individual concerned, or by others who feel they are more capable, and who also feel that it is ethically more desirable that they determine for the other what his better behavior might be. They are means by which someone does something to another person, or for another person. The human relationship between the doer and those who are the recipients of the action is a minimal factor, and may not even be a factor at all. Dreyfus[59] has classified behavior therapies with medical model therapies because they all stress the importance of techniques and the ministration of some form of specific treatment with but minimal attention to the role of the relationship to the treatment process. It is the particular ministration, it is felt, that produces the change.

2. If then, we could limit counseling to that experience in which the human relationship between counselor and client is the major aspect of the experience, then the kind of counseling might be more generically described by the degree of humanness of the counselor and the client is the major factor in the relationship. What the counselor does—his techniques, his methods, his various procedures, would be important only in the sense that they are reflective of the person of the counselor, and of his objectives. The kind of counseling would then be described through the description of the counselor, and the basic question determining the kind of counseling he practices would be his degree of humanness. On the one hand the counselor might see his function, and the purpose of his relationship, in much the same way as the behavioral engineer would, only the significant variable would be the human relationship. His purpose would be to change the individual into some predetermined "better" pattern, and this would likely

---

[59] Edward A. Dreyfus, *op. cit.*

be in terms of someone else's decision as to what a member of a society should be like. It might be to help to condition a number of individuals to become more interested in being nurses, because society is lacking in qualified nurses; it might be to help individuals to become happier with eating a new kind of food developed from algae from the sea. Its purpose, in effect, would be the dehumanization of the human race, so the humans would become more literally things and objects, and patterns of behavior, with no particular individual rights or individual freedoms or individual choices. Life would become comfortable, but empty. Anxiety, unhappiness, loneliness, hostility—all would be reduced or removed. We would, in other words, no longer be living as *human* beings, but rather as conditioned sets of behaviors.

On the other hand, the counselor might see the purpose of his human relationship as the enhancement of the individual, the development and the flowering of the individual as a free human being, one who is able to live the life of the human; one who does not need certainty, one who does not have to have guarantees of happiness and joy. Man would be the determiner of his direction, and the counselor would be one who would help the client, as a free individual, to accept the responsibility for his own determination of the direction his life might take. It would be a life with risk and with tension, but it would be living. It would be a life of uncertainty, but it would be the life of the free man, responsible in his humanness to himself, and for himself. Such a free man would be capable of caring, and being concerned for the other. Such a counselor and such a client could never become the victims of the culture, because they would have accepted their responsibility as makers of the culture. Thus, the degrees of the counselor's humanness, the extent of his dedication to the individual freedom of man, to the dignity and the worth of man—these are possibly the crucial questions which will determine the kind of counselor, and automatically, the kind of counseling, in which we are involved.

THE EFFECTIVENESS OF COUNSELING*

In attempting to look at the effectiveness of counseling, it would seem reasonable to first question the research methodology itself, which has pretty much tended to imitate the time-honored scientific practices followed in the physical sciences and in medicine. Most counselors

---

* *See* Dugald S. Arbuckle, "Counseling Effectiveness and Related Issues," *Journal of Counseling Psychology* 15:430–436 (September, 1968).

tend to follow this scientific model, if any at all, when attempting to discover the results of their work. There have been scores, probably hundreds of studies, for example, on the effects of various "kinds" of counseling, on the questionable assumption that one could actually isolate, as a precise measurable variable, such a thing as "client-centered counseling," or "rational counseling," or "vocational counseling," or "trait-and-factor theory approach," and so on. Even more questionable, of course, is the related assumption that we can isolate the human beings, client and counselor, who are involved in the counseling process. Thus we might debate the accuracy of the evidence on the results of a certain "kind" of counseling, in which a number of "counselors" are involved with a number of "clients." In a somewhat curious contradiction, we insist as counselors on the uniqueness of the human individual, and yet, in our research, we seem to find no difficulty in lumping him as one of many faceless members of a group. In actuality, could we not say that there is only one "Rogerian," one "Freudian," and one "Adlerian"? Even then, however, all we could say would be that thus and so appears to have happened to an individual *after* a human relationship with Rogers, but we still would not necessarily know if this was *because* of the relationship with Rogers. The unfortunate difficulty with "controls" in most of our research is that they are viable human beings, and even if we found six humans who appeared to be exactly the same, had three of them had a series of contacts with Rogers while three others did what they would usually do, we still would not *know* that the reason for the greater change in the three individuals who experienced counseling with Rogers was that contact with him.

When we have been involved in research with human beings, and their behavior, we have generally followed a pattern which was set up for things and objects, and if the assumption of the behavioral scientist that man is a set of behaviors is correct, then this pattern is reasonable enough. If the assumption is not correct, however, and many *believe* (do not know) that this is the case, then perhaps we should try to devise some means of research which will operate on the assumption of the uniqueness of man as a human being, with humanness as his unique quality. On this point, Bergin[60] suggests:

> The best way to capitalize on the ferment and promise in this area is to foster clinical innovation, evaluation of practice, and a continuing

[60] Allen E. Bergin, "An Empirical Analysis of Therapeutic Issues," in Dugald S. Arbuckle (Ed.), *Counseling and Psychotherapy: An Overview* (New York: McGraw-Hill Book Co., 1967), p. 208.

ability to move toward the new and the valuable. If this means recasting the scientist-practitioner model in new terms of innovating practice and naturalistic inquiry rather than an integration of traditional practice and physics-style research, so be it. The old model has done its job and now holds back the development of a more viable psychological profession.

Thus it may be that the individual counselor must become involved in research in which he at least controls the variable of himself, in that he will generally be consistent in his inconsistencies. One will not say, "I follow the trait factor theory in my vocational counseling because it gets results" because this doesn't really mean anything. Rather one might say, "I must try to find out the results of my involvement with certain students, in what I describe as vocational counseling geared to the trait factor theory." Counselors should, as Sanborn[61] suggests, ask themselves what behavioral characteristics they are looking for in students who go through their school, although it might be better to try to help students to develop the behavioral characteristics that they consider to be desirable rather than those set up by the counselor. There might, at least, in this way be some degree of research accuracy, but whether certain characteristics of students, years after they have left school, could be credited to the effect of the school, let alone the effect of an individual counselor, might be held in some doubt.

Different researchers, too, very frequently disagree with the validity of each others' research. The periodic publication of such criticism represents only a small part of the actual disagreement. Representative of this conflict is a statement by Mills and Mencke,[62] who, in referring to a previously published paper, stated, "On the basis of the above noted methodological errors, the findings of the Demos and Zuwaylif article seem to be in serious question, and cannot be accepted as representing differences between effective and non-effective counselors."

It is interesting to note, too, that the major criterion of change is often what the client feels rather than what the client does. While there is an obvious relationship between what I feel and what I do, the more pragmatic and realistic measure of positive growth is my action rather than my thought. I may come to feel more certain about my bias

---

[61] Marshal P. Sanborn, "Following My Nose Toward a Concept of a Creative Counselor," *The School Counselor* 14:66–73 (May, 1966).
[62] David H. Mills and Reed Mencke, "Characteristics of Effective Counselors: A Re-evaluation," *Counselor Education and Supervision* 6:332–335 (Summer, 1967).

toward certain individuals, or my anxiety about my cheating on my income tax may be reduced greatly, or I may come to lose my feeling of uneasiness about lying over certain matters. In all of these cases I feel better, but in the meantime my level of prejudice, my cheating, and my lying continue to increase. Thus it would seem that behavior is a more valid criterion of the effectiveness of counseling, at least if we are to think of counseling effectiveness as being related to our behavior with others.

At any rate, as a profession ages, one could presume that it develops more precise answers to the question, "What is the result of what you do?" In the case of counseling, however, we might wonder if we have more evidence now questioning the effects of counseling than we have supporting the positive effects of counseling!

In many ways Rogers was one of the first to challenge and question the effectiveness of at least traditional psychotherapy, and those who attacked him indicated rather clearly that they had little in the way of empirical evidence to back up their statements about the effects of their particular brand of psychotherapy. It is likely that at least part of the violence of the reaction against Rogers was because he was presenting at least some evidence as to what happened to clients with whom he was involved, whereas his opponents could give little other than their opinion.

Probably the major gadfly in the side of all counselors and psychotherapists, however, was Eysenck. In an article published some years ago,[63] he presented evidence which resulted in his flat statement that "the figures fail to support the hypothesis that psychotherapy facilitates recovery from neurotic disorder." A few years later Levitt[64] presented evidence which caused him to come to a similar conclusion regarding children. He said, "It is concluded that the results of the present study fail to support the view that psychotherapy with 'neurotic' children is effective."

In more recent years Bergin[65] presented compelling evidence questioning the efficacy of psychotherapy, and in a statement which sums up much of what he presents, he says, "Most controlled studies of psychotherapy reveal no significant effect of treatment." Carkhuff does much the same thing in several chapters in a book edited by

---

[63] H. J. Eysenck, "The Effects of Psychotherapy: An Evaluation," *Journal of Consulting Psychology* 16:319–324 (August, 1952).
[64] E. E. Levitt, "The Results of Psychotherapy With Children," *Journal of Consulting Psychology* 21:189–196 (June, 1957).
[65] A. E. Bergin, *op. cit.*, p. 177.

Berenson and himself,[66] and their statement is that ". . . there are no professional training programs which demonstrated their efficacy in terms of a translation to constructive behavioral gains in clients."

Another research problem is that any measures of the effectiveness of counseling must be related to the purposes of counseling as they are perceived by the counselor. On this point Boy and Pine comment that:[67]

> Measuring the outcomes of counseling is basically a matter of measuring human behavior and personality, for if counseling has been successful, then positive behavioral changes have taken place. But objectively measuring behavioral changes is extremely complex and involves first selecting objective evaluative criteria.

There is no question that determining, with some degree of scientific exactness, the specific outcomes of the counseling of *a* counselor with *a* client is fraught with much difficulty. If we hold to the concept that each human being is unique, obviously the complexity of the human relationship varies with each counselor and each client, and the existentialist would feel that the total examination of man, piece by piece, is impossible. The behaviorist would not agree with this, and Eysenck[68] would appear to be fairly well satisfied that counseling and psychotherapy have no effect whatsoever on human behavior.

In many of the current journals, the research being reported has taken place in an educational milieu, and the criteria that are used are usually the achievement of the individual in this educational setting, or some modification in his attitudes, concepts and general behavior. For example, Spielberger, Weitz and Denny[69] report, as a result of a study, that anxious college freshmen who regularly attended group counseling sessions showed more improvement in their academic performance than students who were not counseled or did not regularly attend counseling. Ivey[70] reports that "there is some indication in

---

[66] B. G. Berenson and R. Carkhuff, *Sources of Gain in Counseling and Psychotherapy* (New York: Holt, Rinehart, and Winston, Inc., 1967), p. 7.

[67] Angelo Boy and Gerald J. Pine, *Client Centered Counseling in the Secondary School* (Boston: Houghton Mifflin Co., 1963), p. 234.

[68] H. J. Eysenck (Ed.), *Handbook of Abnormal Psychology* (New York: Basic Books, 1960), pp. 697–725.

[69] Charles D. Spielberger, Henry Weitz, and J. Peter Denny, "Group Counseling and the Academic Performance of Anxious College Freshmen," *Journal of Counseling Psychology* 9:195–204 (Fall, 1962).

[70] Allen E. Ivey, "The Academic Performance of Students Counseled at a University Counseling Service," *Journal of Counseling Psychology* 9:347–352 (Winter, 1962).

this study that students who receive more intensive and long-term counseling are more likely to improve their marks than those who receive short-term counseling." Baymur and Patterson,[71] referring to an underachieving high school population, state that "a comparison of the two counseled groups with the two noncounseled groups indicated that they differed significantly in Q-sort adjustment score change . . . and in increase in grade point average."

Similar positive growth of a group of high school children with behavior problems, who had experienced counseling, as compared with the lack of growth of those who had not, was indicated in a study reported by Arbuckle and Boy.[72]

In somewhat different words, Broedal, Ohlsen, Proff and Southard[73] reported the same thing with a population of gifted underachieving high school students.

On the other hand, Searles[74] reports as a result of his study that three-interview counseling does not appear to have any significant effect on the first semester academic achievement of superior freshmen in a small liberal arts college, while Goodstein and Crites[75] state that there was no evidence, from their study, that vocational educational counseling, as it is usually conducted, leads to greater academic achievement by low ability college students.

One might safely assume that a change in academic achievement is the result of some behavioral change or modification in the individual, and this, of course, might occur because of some modification of the environmental milieu. Braaten,[76] for example, concludes that in "successful" client-centered therapy there is a highly significant movement in the verbal communications of the client from nonself to self.

[71] Feriha B. Baymur and C. H. Patterson, "A Comparison of Three Methods of Assisting Underachieving High School Students," *Journal of Counseling Psychology* 7:83–90 (Summer, 1960).
[72] Dugald S. Arbuckle and Angelo Boy, "An Experimental Study of the Effectiveness of Client-centered Therapy in Counseling Students with Behavior Problems," *Journal of Counseling Psychology* 8:136–139 (Summer, 1961).
[73] John Broedal, Merle Ohlsen, Fred Proff, and Charles Southard, "The Effects of Group Counseling on Gifted Underachieving Adolescents," *Journal of Counseling Psychology* 7:163–170 (Fall, 1960).
[74] Aysel Searles, Jr., "The Effectiveness of Limited Counseling in Improving the Academic Achievement of Superior College Freshmen," *Personnel and Guidance Journal* 40:630–633 (March, 1962).
[75] Leonard D. Goodstein and John O. Crites, "Brief Counseling with Poor College Risks," *Journal of Counseling Psychology* 8:318–321 (Winter, 1961).
[76] Leif J. Braaten, "Non-Self to Self in Client-Centered Psychotherapy," *Journal of Counseling Psychology* 8:20–24 (Spring, 1961).

In another study, Williams[77] concludes that educational-vocational counseling restores a normal level of adjustment and degree of congruence among the client's perceptions of himself, his ideal self, and other persons. After a long-range "eight years after" follow-up study, Merenda and Rothney[78] appeared satisfied that intensive counseling with high school students resulted in more favorable attitudes and behaviors. The conclusion of a study reported by Sorensen[79] is that a few counselor-initiated interviews do not produce sufficient change in the classroom behavior of low ability high school students to result in grade improvement. Gonyea[80] reports that vocational counseling with college students does not appear to be a factor in significant change in the appropriateness of vocational choice.

These studies, which are probably fairly representative of the research being conducted on the effectiveness of counseling, are all, to a greater or lesser degree, vulnerable. Since the object of investigation is the human being, they operate with a multiplicity of unknowns, and every study is subject to a series of "ifs" and "buts." This in no way detracts from their value, but all results should be taken as highly tentative, subject to possible drastic change at any time.

It has already been pointed out that what one feels about what has happened does not necessarily indicate what one will do, but client feelings about counseling do at least give an immediate perception. Here are some examples of what clients say about counseling and psychotherapy. An adult male client says:

> I think I learned, for one thing—I learned to trust someone with information. It gives me a good feeling to trust, and to allow myself to experience the feelings that go along with the verbalization. It's one thing to be able to speak in a detached and specific manner about some specific subject—some particular problem. But it's another thing entirely to be able to allow yourself the luxury of indulging in all the same feelings that should go along, that are natural concomitants of this particular problem, or whatever it is.

---

[77] John E. Williams, "Changes in Self and Other Perceptions," *Journal of Counseling Psychology* 9:18–30 (Spring, 1962).

[78] Peter F. Merenda and John W. M. Rothney, "Evaluating the Effects of Counseling—Eight Years After," *Journal of Counseling Psychology* 5:163–168 (Fall, 1958).

[79] Mourits A. Sorensen, "Counseling Marginal Students on Classroom Behavior," *Personnel and Guidance Journal* 40:811–812 (May, 1962).

[80] George G. Gonyea, "Appropriateness of Vocational Choices of College Students," *Journal of Counseling Psychology* 10:269–275 (Fall, 1963).

Another adult male client:

And it was quite clear, Dr. San, that I couldn't accept myself as I was, so I had to construct someone that I could like and accept. I introjected how others felt about me, and God knows how much of this is left. All I know is—and it's kind of amazing—I remember clearly the feeling—I don't know why I couldn't tell you—but it—was a kind of good-bye. I realize that one of my characters, one of my favorite characters, was leaving—and I felt sad and resentful.

A number of junior high school boys and girls comment in this way about the effects of counseling:

"It's made me confident—sort of better able to do things."
"It's made me less afraid—I don't fear new people or new things."
"It has enabled me to face the issue of being dominated."
"It made me realize that I'm not sick."
"It enabled me to stop fighting things in my life which were, really, now that I look at them, pretty unimportant."
"It enabled me to realize that my progress depends more on me than on the teacher."
"It has helped me to become more clear about my future."
"It has made me realize that I don't have to always be in a state of anger—always suspicious of people."
"It has helped me be less nervous and tense when I'm in school."
"It has helped me to improve my school work because—well— I'm not fighting school anymore."

When asked "How do you feel about the effects of counseling," a number of clients replied in the following manner.
A female said:

How Do I Feel? Through the help given me in these sessions of therapy, I have been able to get on an even keel again. The permissive atmosphere which was established allowed for an outpouring of feelings and emotions from the past and present such as I had never experienced before. This left me free to concentrate on regaining control of myself, and I learned how to help myself over any bad spots which come along. I don't know what the future will bring, but in the past three weeks I have succeeded in throwing off a life which I had grown to hate but had allowed to become a habit which could not be shaken. I know I have many more problems to face and temptations to resist, but somehow I feel I have gained the strength to face life squarely and accept what it has to offer.
All this I was not able to do with medical and spiritual help, so I feel client-centered counseling was most successful in my particular

case. I also feel I can return again if necessary. It's wonderful to feel like a human being again and to be able to face people again.

A male client said:

How Do I Feel? Although I do not feel that we have fully worked through the problems at the present time, several positive things have happened. The anxiety about my school work has been reduced to the point where I could at least do some studying—although it has been neither adequate nor very efficient. Secondly, the recurring thoughts have receded to the point where I have them only occasionally and for not very long and where I can inhibit them. This has resulted in a very great drop in my anxiety, because, although intellectually I know that this is sheer nonsense, emotionally I have been very afraid of becoming mentally ill, and of losing control of my thought proccesses. Just a few meetings were enough to reduce this fear very markedly. With that, my irritability at home decreased.

A female client said, simply:

Did I gain anything yet—honestly—No—just more analyzing myself and more confusion.

Another, feeling more growth, said:

I have gained a greater understanding of myself, and, indirectly, others. I think I know myself better—can understand my reactions to situations in a better light. I surely feel more at ease—at peace even.

Comments of other clients were:

As a client now, I see myself as a person who has a much greater understanding of himself . . . why he has the need to behave in a particular fashion; however, there still is this need in some areas which, though understood, has not been fully accepted as to its origin; appearingly the acceptance of the why, at the moment, is too threatening to me. Intellectual understanding is one thing, acceptance of this understanding on the emotional level is something else. I feel now that, though I still have feelings of inadequacy, I have become free in part from much of the painful life that has little or no purpose and thus lacks the solid satisfaction that endures . . . the needs which are insatiable and lending to a circular form of existence can only supply one with a moment or two of satisfaction which then dies in the wake of the insatiable need itself; satisfaction that endures is derived from living which implies growth, not existing. At the moment I have great hopes or better said, "Great Expectations" which have been formed by a realistic understanding and partial acceptance of me; the "Great

Expectations," however, in my case, are somewhat different from Pip's in that mine are associated with a greater understanding and acceptance of myself, and thus the freedom to grow in the direction of man's potential goodness . . . to approximate as closely as possible my potential, which is living.

and:

I really don't know. I do know that I am trying to accept myself and others. I still have many fears and superstitions. My problems on sex and religion are being solved.

Some other client reactions to psychotherapy:[81]

". . . it has meant the beginning of the most dynamic experience —being alive."
"For the first time in my life it seems that I'm not locked into some predetermined series of actions."
"I do not now feel that I am utterly committed to a bad choice."
". . . it opened me to life."
"I have found the way to give without sense of depletion."

Possibly a comment of Axline is as good as any to describe how counseling can be effective. In talking about Dibs, one of her young clients, she says:[82]

Yes, Dibs had changed. He had learned how to be himself, to believe in himself, to free himself. Now he was relaxed and happy. He was able to be a child.

Still, the nagging question must remain. Was this the effect of a procedure known as psychotherapy and counseling, or was it the result of an intense human experience between a small boy and a woman named Virginia Axline? Or is this, after all, the real description of counseling and psychotherapy.

---

[81] Rahe B. Corlis and Peter Rabe, *Psychotherapy from the Center* (Scranton, Pa.: International Text Book Co., 1969), pp. 128–130.
[82] Virginia M. Axline, *Dibs: In Search of Self* (Boston: Houghton Mifflin Co., 1964), p. 181.

chapter 9

OPERATIONAL ISSUES: I

All counselors doubtless have in their minds certain issues or difficulties. Some would probably see the day-to-day operational issues as paramount, while others would think of the more theoretical and philosophic issues as basic. It is unfortunate, but probably true, that a man must have some food in his belly before he can afford the luxury of pondering about why he is bothering to put food into his belly. Practical existence comes first, and counselors are no different in this respect than the rest of mankind. As they become more experienced and skilled and capable in what they are doing, the "what" and "how" begin to pose less of a problem than the "why." It is difficult, too, to sharply distinguish operational from theoretical, and a rather common method of operational escape from responsibility is to describe some suggested procedure as being "too theoretical"! In any case, several of the chapters that follow will attempt to describe what appear to be some of the more immediate on-the-job operational issues, as well as some of the more basic theoretical and philosophical issues that confront the counselor as he works with the changing person in the even more rapidly changing culture.

It will be noted that there are few answers, since each counselor must devise for himself the answers that will make the most sense for him today, but quite possibly no sense whatsoever tomorrow.

WHOM TO COUNSEL

One of the most immediate operational issues has to do with the question of who is to be counseled, and this is obviously directly related to the question of counselor function. It would seem reasonable to say that any child who is well enough to be in school should have counseling services available for him *if he needs them.* As long as the counselor's office is seen as a place where information which is unavailable from other sources may be attained, it may be assumed that many students who come to see a counselor will have a primary interest in, and a need for, information. There will be other students who will have problems and tensions of a developmental nature which may or may not be alleviated by the use of information, and there will be still other students whose problems are deep enough and complex enough to warrant intensive counseling and psychotherapy even though they remain as students in the school, and others who may have to be referred for institutional attention. The student is, above all, a gestalt human being, but when he goes to see a counselor he is not a student going to see a teacher, nor is he a patient going to see a medical doctor.

In some schools, on the other hand, a real attempt is made to help all children who need help, but the counselor is rendered somewhat ineffective because he has to do everything, and thus does nothing very well. Too frequently the school takes literally the idea that if a counselor "has" 500 students, then he must see 500 students; or when school people read about an ideal situation with a counselor responsible for about 200 children, they visualize the counselor spending an equal amount of time with all 200 of those children. The counselor should *know* all of his children, and they should know him, or at least know who he is and what he does, but some children he will see very often, and others he will see not at all. I cannot go along with the idea of the counselor's seeing all of the children for compulsory interviews so that they can get to know him, since very frequently they have no real reason to see him, nor do they want to see him. From the point of view of the counselor, there is no evidence to indicate that a brief interview can give a very valid picture of the client to the interviewer. Testing would surely be much more economical of both time and money as a means of helping the counselor at least to know *about* the children.

Ryan and Gaier[1] stress this point in discussing a study which indicated that the socioeconomic status of the student was a significant factor for both the frequency with which he was referred to the counselor and the problem areas discussed. They suggest that, counter to the usual we-see-every-student-once-a-year philosophy, unequal attention possibly should be paid to certain social classes. This would simply seem to be another way of saying that the children who need the most attention should get the most attention.

In many schools most of the counseling will be of a cognitive, information-providing nature for those students who are college bound. In other schools most of the counseling will be of a cognitive, information-providing nature for those students who are seeking a job. Too frequently, however, more time is spent on the college bound youth, even though those seeking a job are in greater numbers and have greater needs. In all schools, too, there will be some students whose difficulties are such that they will not be alleviated by the simple presentation of information, educational, vocational or personal. If there is only one counselor in the school, all he can do is allocate his time the best way he can so that the most children possible will benefit from his services. If there are two or more counselors, a division of labor would result in more efficiency. In any school with three counselors, for example, it does seem a bit ridiculous for all three to be doing everything, when there could be a very natural division of labor.

While all counseling is, in a sense, of course, personal, one counselor could take the major responsibility for those students who are college bound. The odds are that this counselor would often be functioning in a "guidance" role, having rational discussions with individual students or with groups of students who are going to college. It is likely, too, that most such students would benefit from contact with a counselor, although there will be many who are quite capable, on their own or with the help of their parents, of making perfectly good decisions without any help from a counselor. Needless to say, the counselor should not go running down the halls pursuing these students. There will, of course, be students who are in need of therapeutic counseling who will come to see such a counselor supposedly to talk about college plans. When such students get into real difficulties, it would depend on the counselor's capacities and interests

---

[1] Doris W. Ryan and Eugene L. Gaier, "Student Socio-Economic Status and Counselor Contact in Junior High School," *Personnel and Guidance Journal* 46:466–472 (January, 1968).

whether or not he continued with them or referred them to another colleague spending all his time with such counseling.

A second counselor could take the major responsibility for those who will seek jobs after graduation, or those who will leave school for jobs before graduation. Such a counselor might spend a good deal of time in the field, getting acquainted with employers, and keeping up to date with the rapidly changing opportunities in the community and the surrounding area. Despite the increasing mobility of the American worker, a student who leaves school will most likely find his employment in the same general area. Often too, this counselor might function in a guidance role in an intellectual discussion with stable students who are thinking logically and reasonably about their job futures. Here, too, most of the students who are seeking jobs would probably benefit from conversation with the counselor, although, as before, there would be many perfectly capable youngsters with no particular need for the services of a counselor. Some students, too, who come for a discussion about employment would be in need of counseling, and, as before, it would be a question of referral to a colleague, or continuing with the student as a client.

A third counselor might take as his primary responsibility therapeutic counseling as it is viewed in this book; and just as some of his colleagues would refer some of their students to him, so he would refer some of his clients to them. This counselor would probably see the smallest proportion of the student body, but he would spend a good deal more time with individual clients. One or two discussions about colleges or job possibilities might well suffice for the majority of the students who are so concerned, but the number of sessions with students whose problems are of an emotional nature will be much greater. It is the responsibility of the school to provide such a service, and it can be effective as long as the school staff, the children, the community, and the counselor know just who the counselor is and just what he is supposed to do.

All of these counselors would, of course, coordinate their efforts, and all would work closely with the teaching staff. The relationship of the therapeutic counselor to the teacher might pose something of a problem, however, since his effectiveness as a counselor with the children depends, as has been mentioned, to some extent at least on their concept of his relationship with the administration and the teaching staff. He must be seen by the children as one who will work *for them* rather than for the teachers or the administration. On the other hand, it is essential that the teachers particularly do not feel that in working for the children the counselor is working *against them*. Some teachers may feel that the counselor spends too much of his time with the children, and not enough with them. If there were a division of labor, however, as described above, the "college" and the "job" counselors could spend a good deal of time with the teachers without particularly damaging their relationship with the children. It is the "personal problems" counselor who will find this dual relationship more of a problem.

Most counselors have little or no choice as to who is going to see them, at least for the initial session. In the school situation, it is desirable for word to get around that the counseling office is a place where anyone can go and receive a friendly reception regardless of who he is or what his problem may be. Better to have the problem of wondering what to do with the large number of clients who wish to avail themselves of the services of the counseling center than to wonder why it is that everybody stays away from the counseling center as if it were contaminated.

In many schools, however, there is a lack of communication between counselors and students as to counselor function. Many students would never consider coming to see a counselor about a personal problem because they view them as being concerned with the provision of academic and vocational information. In fact, many students see the counselor as a teacher whose subject area is academic and vocational information. A study by Bigelow and Humphreys[2] could have been duplicated in many schools. They found the major discrepancy in student and counselor perceptions was that counselors felt responsible for personal problems while students felt they were concerned primarily with vocational and school-related problems.

At the same time, many of the counselors who feel they are capable of working with individuals with personal problems do have a preferred kind of client. In a study by Thompson,[3] for example, it was found that counselors indicated a preference for clients having characteristics pointing to higher school success as related to achievement, future aspirations, problem types, and problem causes. The nonpreferred client was found to be experiencing more emotional problems largely stemming from conflict with others such as parents, school authorities, and peers, and he was usually not achieving up to par.

[2] Gordon S. Bigelow and Ray A. Humphreys, "What Kinds of Problems Do They Bring? Student, Counselor Perceptions Vary," *The School Counselor* 14:157–160 (January, 1967).
[3] Charles L. Thompson, "The Secondary School Counselor's Ideal Client," *Journal of Counseling Psychology* 16:69–74 (January, 1969).

Thus the student who would most likely to be referred for counseling would have the misfortune to be the least preferred by the counselor!

Many students who need counseling, of course, do not come to the counseling office, while other students who do not appear to have as much need for counseling want to spend most of the school day there. If counseling is effective, the client who wants to while away his time in the counselor's office can be helped to see why he does so; and he might then leave the counselor's office, or he might enter into counseling in a more beneficial way. In any counseling situation where the client seems to be actually doing nothing but wasting his own time and that of the counselor, we must, among other things, question the effectiveness of what has gone on in the counselor's office.

The client who does not come in, however, poses a different and a more difficult problem. Although it may not be the responsibility of the individual counselor, it is the responsibility of the counseling or guidance office at least to see if something can be done. The office certainly cannot pursue the client, but neither can it shrug its shoulders and watch an individual disintegrate without trying in some way to help him. Certainly the counseling office, and the individual counselors, and the teachers, can all do an effective job of helping children to feel that they are always welcome; but even so, there will always be children who will be wary of anything that smacks of authority or control, or who may be unable or unwilling to face up to their problems, or who may have learned from their parents and their culture that when you are in trouble, you keep quiet so that you won't get into more trouble. Understanding and educated teachers can often help a child to reach the point of going to see a counselor; and sometimes the teacher or principal might even make himself the "fall guy" by telling the child that he has to see a counselor—while being very careful in no way to implicate the counselor in the "you have to" deal. Thus the child may arrive at the counselor's office full of hostility toward the teacher and the school, and, possibly, the counselor. Although this is not the best situation, at least the child is in the counselor's office, and then there is a possibility that something positive might happen. The counselor may help the child to dissociate him from the authority that has commanded, "You have to see the counselor," but he cannot hold an unwilling client, and the prognosis will not be good if the client continues to feel that he is with the counselor only because he has to be there.

On the other hand, counseling with the unwilling client may not be quite so impossible as some believe it to be. I was involved in a study where junior high school boys who were disciplinary cases were involved in an experiment where they were put into three groups. One group received the usual disciplinary action, one group had nothing at all happen to them, and the third group was required to appear before a counselor for a minimum number of counseling sessions. Various measures were used before and after to determine differences. One of the conclusions of the study was that even when students are forced to appear for counseling, *some* of them benefit with *certain counselors.*[4]

A study by Grosz[5] also indicated that positive client expectations for counseling did not have to be present before an effective counseling relationship could be established between the client and the counselor.

Another example of the effectiveness of a nontherapeutic method of getting individuals into what eventually develops into a therapeutic relationship is seen in a research study in which delinquent children were paid to come to see a counselor. Practically all came with the feeling that this was a good deal, and that the counselors were really a prime lot of suckers to be taken advantage of. Yet, after a while, at least some of the children became voluntary clients in a real counseling relationship.[6]

In the long run, the crucial question regarding the unwilling client is whether or not the counselor can, with total honesty, say to the client, if need be, "I am not the one who said you *had* to be here, and you may leave here at any time if you feel that that is what you really want to do." No counselor should be placed in a position where he must, in effect, say to the client, "I am sorry that I cannot allow you to leave even though this is your wish." At the very least, every counselor should be able to say, with total honesty, "*I* had nothing to do with your having to come down here to see me. . . ." We can assume that he might also add, "but I'm glad to see you, and if there is anything that I might be able to do. . . ."

---

[4] Dugald S. Arbuckle and Angelo Boy, "An Experimental Study of the Effectiveness of Client-centered Therapy in Counseling Students with Behavior Problems," *Journal of Counseling Psychology* 8:136–139 (Summer, 1961).

[5] Richard D. Grosz, "Effect of Client Expectations on the Counseling Relationship," *Personnel and Guidance Journal* 46:797–800 (April, 1968).

[6] Charles W. Slack, "Experimental Subject Psychotherapy: A New Method of Introducing Intense Office Treatment for Unreachable Cases," *Mental Hygiene* 44:238–256 (April, 1960).

THE CLIENT

It is fairly clear from the preceding comments that the client is not always viewed in the same way by the counselor, or by the individual who may go, as a client, to see the counselor. Who, then, is this fellow who comes in to see the counselor? Let us look first at some theoretical and clinical versions of the client, both from school and nonschool personnel, and then go on to see how this client views himself. Some counselors would likely feel that the client is a different person if we are talking about a student who goes in to see a school counselor, as contrasted with a client, young or old, who goes in to see a counselor or a psychotherapist. Others, including myself, would feel that the differences are minimal, and practically all of the descriptions in the following pages are applicable to any individuals, young or old, in school or out, who might be called clients.

Tyler[7] states that an individual becomes a client because "he must deal with a situation, or situations, for which there is some doubt as to the appropriateness of his response." Bordin[8] states that clients are likely to be looking for help, and for reassuring signs that help will be forthcoming. He also points out that almost all clients consider coming to the counselor a reflection upon their adequacy as individuals.

Whitaker and Malone,[9] on the other hand, look at this question in a somewhat different light. They point out, for example, that in seeking therapy the client tacitly blames his culture for its failure to provide him with adequate "growth nutritional," i.e., with therapy. Thus the very act of coming to the therapist points up many of the deficiencies of the community in which the patient lives. More particularly, it implicates those members of the community who live in close relationship with him.

Sheen[10] states a theological point of view that might be unacceptable to some theologians:

---

[7] Leona Tyler, *The Work of the Counselor* (New York: Appleton-Century-Crofts, 1953), p. 69.
[8] Edward Bordin, *Psychological Counseling* (New York: Appleton-Century-Crofts, 1955), pp. 186–187.
[9] Carl A. Whitaker and Thomas P. Malone, *The Roots of Psychotherapy* (New York: The Blakiston Co., 1953), p. 71.
[10] Fulton Sheen, *Peace of Soul* (New York: McGraw-Hill Book Co., Inc., 1959), pp. 147–148.

The person who seeks help with the psychiatrist considers himself "ill." He wants a cure and not a sermon. His doing of what he ought not to have done he regards as a symptom. Hence there is no sense in telling him that he sins; either he knows this, and "cannot help it," or he does not admit it and is scared away because he came to seek out the physician and not the moralist.

Rogers gives an excellent picture of the expectancies of the client:[11]

> The client may have expected the counselor to be a parental figure who will shield him from harm and who will take over the guidance of his life. He may have expected the therapist to be a psychic surgeon who will probe to the roots of his difficulties, causing him great pain and making him over against his will. He may have expected him to be an advice-giver, and this advice may be genuinely and dependently desired, or it may be desired in order that the client can prove the advice wrong. He may, due to unfortunate previous experiences with psychiatric or psychological counselors, look upon this new experience as one where he will be labeled, looked upon as abnormal, hurt, treated with little respect, and thus may deeply dread the relationship. He may look upon the counselor as an extension of the authority which referred him for help—the dean, the Veterans Administration, the court. He may, if he has some knowledge of client-centered therapy, view the counseling interview as a place where he will have to solve his own problem, and this may seem to him a positive or a very threatening possibility.

In a later article, in discussing the necessary conditions for personality change, Rogers describes the client when he says, "The first [of two persons] whom we shall term the client, is in a state of incongruence, being vulnerable or anxious."[12] Rogers thinks of incongruence as referring to a discrepancy between the actual experience of the organism and the self picture of the individual, insofar as it represents that experience.

Another description of the client is given by Ellis.[13] In a symposium on marriage counseling, he referred to the neuroticising ideas to be found in the client as:

---

[11] Carl R. Rogers, *Client-Centered Therapy* (Boston: Houghton Mifflin Company, 1951), p. 66.
[12] Carl R. Rogers, "The Necessary and Sufficient Conditions of Therapeutic Personality Change," *Journal of Consulting Psychology* 21:95–103 (April, 1957).
[13] Albert Ellis, "Symposium on Neurotic Interaction in Marriage Counseling: Neurotic Interaction between Marital Partners," *Journal of Counseling Psychology* 5:24–26 (Spring, 1958).

1. The notion that it is a dire necessity for an adult human being to be approved or loved by almost everyone for almost everything he does.
2. The notion that a human being should be, or must be perfectly competent, adequate, talented, and intelligent in all possible respects; and that he is utterly worthless if he is incompetent in any way.
3. The notion that one should severely blame oneself and others for mistakes and wrongdoings; and that punishing oneself or others for errors will help prevent future mistakes.
4. The notion that it is terrible, horrible, and catastrophic when things are not the way one would like them to be; that others should make things easier for one, help with life's difficulties; and that one should not have to put off present pleasures for future gains.
5. The notion that most human unhappiness is externally caused or forced on one by outside people and events, and that, since one has virtually no control over one's emotions, one cannot help feeling bad on many occasions.

There are those counselors too, of course, who apparently never see the client as a total living person. Some of them see the client as a set of behaviors or a combination of problems. Some do not even see the client as a "problem," but only as a symbol of a problem! Weitz,[14] for example, points out that:

> It is important to note that (except in unusual circumstances) the counselor can never participate in or deal directly with the client's problem, or the events which initiated it, or the client's anxiety. He can deal only with the symbols abstracted from these events.

Esper[15] investigated the differences between junior high school students of three categories—those referred to counselors, those who were self-referrals, and those who had no contact with counselors. He found that the self-referral counselees tended to reflect a higher frequency of problems; the non-contact group seems to get the better grades, while the referral group got the poorest grades; the self-referred group were the most intelligent, the referred group the least; both referral groups displayed a higher incidence of problems in counseling regarding school; adolescent girls were more apt to be self-referred and boys were more likely to be referred for counseling.

[14] Henry Weitz, "Counseling as a Function of the Counselor's Personality," *Personnel and Guidance Journal* 35:276–280 (January, 1957).
[15] George Esper, "Characteristics of Junior High School Students Who Seek Counseling," *Personnel and Guidance Journal* 42:468–472 (January, 1964).

In comparing college freshmen who utilized counseling facilities with those who did not, Mendelsohn and Kirk[16] found that the students who seek counseling score less toward the judging side, more toward the intuitive side, less toward the feeling side and more toward the introversion side. It was suggested that the customary attention to subjective experiences characteristic of the intuitive type and the greater tolerance for or enjoyment of ambiguity characteristic of the perception type predisposes such individuals to make use of the counseling approach.

There is evidence too, that certain kinds of students take up a larger share of the counselor's time. Barnard, Clarke and Gelatt,[17] for example, found in their study that the clients were mostly boys, they were typical of the community with regard to socioeconomic level, appeared to come from fairly stable homes, and were above the school average in academic aptitude. They also had adjustment problems, the major manifestations of which were poor academic achievement and overt nonconformity to classroom behavior and school rules. It is interesting to note that in this paper, as in so many others, the proposed solution for these difficulties is more counseling. Some consideration might be given to the modification of the school experience which causes the problems, rather than an intensification of the attempts to "adjust" the students to an unrealistic and oppressive environment.

Goetz and Leach[18] reported some interesting evidence in a study of the attitudes of withdrawees and continuers in college. They found no difference in attitudes toward facilities, teachers, and counselors. While one might assume that students who dropped out would be more in need of counseling than those who stayed in college, this study indicated that the few differences that did exist showed that continuers had more negative feelings than withdrawees.

Class structure is also a determiner of clients. Tseng and Thompson,[19] for example, found that counseling tends to attract clients who are more affluent, more ambitious, and more success oriented, and that

---

[16] Gerald A. Mendelsohn and Barbara A. Kirk, "Personality Differences Between Students Who Do and Do Not Use a Counseling Facility," *Journal of Counseling Psychology* 9:341–352 (Winter, 1962).

[17] Marjorie L. Barnard, Robert Clarke and H. B. Gelatt, "Students Who See Counselors Most," *The School Counselor* 16:185–190 (January, 1969).

[18] Walter Goetz and Donald Leach, "The Disappearing Student," *Personnel and Guidance Journal* 45:883–887 (May, 1967).

[19] Michael Tseng and Donald L. Thompson, "Differences Between Adolescents Who Seek Counseling and Those Who Do Not," *Personnel and Guidance Journal* 47:333–336 (December, 1968).

counseled students more nearly reflect the middle class ideals and value structure. Students who did not seek counseling were less certain about their occupational plans than those who did seek counseling.

Occupational goals also have some relationship to the potential clientele of counselors. Thus Holland,[20] for example, found that arts and sciences students in college were more amenable than business students to long-term counseling. Segal[21] found that writers were freer, more willing to express emotion, and more willing to deal with ambiguity than were accountants, and they were thus a better bet as clients.

Critics of school counseling, the "the kids are in school to study" type, do not always appear to realize that the personal problems that may become the business of the counselor are very much related to academic achievement in school. Taylor,[22] for example, after a survey of the literature, came to the following conclusions:

1. The degree to which a student is able to handle his anxiety is directly related to his level of achievement.
2. The value the student places upon his own worth affects his academic achievement.
3. The ability to conform and/or accept authority demands will determine the amount of academic success.
4. Students who are accepted and have positive relationships with peers are better able to accept themselves.
5. The less conflict over independence-dependence relationships a student copes with, the more effort he places on achievement.
6. Activities which are centered around academic interests are more likely to produce successful achievement.
7. The more realistic the goal the more chance there is of successful completion of that goal.

In a somewhat more psychological vein, Gowan[23] states that:

. . . achievement is an indication that the individual has successfully transferred a large enough portion of his libidinal drives to areas of cultural accomplishment so that he derives a significant portion of his gratifications from them. We need always to consider how an individual is to receive psychological pay for tasks accomplished.

---

[20] J. L. Holland, "A Theory of Vocational Choice," *Journal of Counseling Psychology* 6:35–45 (Spring, 1959).

[21] S. J. Segal, "A Psychoanalytic Analysis of Personality Factors in Vocational Choice," *Journal of Counseling Psychology* 8:202–210 (Fall, 1961).

[22] Ronald G. Taylor, "Personality Traits and Discrepant Achievement: A Review," *Journal of Counseling Psychology* 11:76–82 (Spring, 1964).

[23] J. C. Gowan, "Factors of Achievement in High School and College," *Journal of Counseling Psychology* 7:91–95 (Summer, 1960).

The reasons why one must become a "client" have been discussed, one might presume, since man has existed. Jung comments that "a psycho-neurosis must be understood as the suffering of a human being who has not discovered what life means for him."[24]

In an interesting discussion of Freud and Marx, Fromm[25] points out that alienation was, for Marx, *the* sickness of man. Man is independent only when he is free *to* as well as free *from*, and Freud saw the independent man as one who had emancipated himself from the dependence on mother, while Marx saw the independent man as one who had emancipated himself from dependence on nature.[26]

Mowrer, who feels that it is somewhat sinful not to be acceptant of the reality of sin, asks, "Is it any wonder that we are suffering from what Frankl calls an 'existential vacuum,' that is, *meaninglessness?*"[27]

Levitsky contrasts the two sets of forces that, he believes, exist within all of us, "as growth forces which motivate us to face anxiety and learn new ways of handling it to our satisfaction, and non-growth forces which motivate us to avoid anxiety, not to grow, or to make compromise solutions."[28]

The violence of the debate over terminology describing various kinds of human problems and difficulties has always seemed to be somewhat of a tempest in a teapot since they are all, surely, from the same basic human tree. The descriptions in the previous pages apply to all of us—the difference is merely one of degree. Clients do not have a disease that the counselor does not have; the counselor has simply learned to live more effectively with what he has and with who he is. Even for those who are called mad or crazy or insane or psychotic, the human relationship still remains. In talking about insane people, Krim, who had been considered as one of them, says, "the majority had lost confidence in their own ability to survive in the world outside . . . but positively no serious effort was being made to equip them to become free and independent adults."[29] Percival, another "mad" person, in an article which first appeared in 1848, writes, "The lunatic

---

[24] C. G. Jung, *Modern Man in Search of a Soul* (New York: Harcourt, Brace & World, Inc., 1933), p. 225.
[25] Erich Fromm, *Beyond the Chains of Illusion* (New York: Pocket Books, Inc., 1962), p. 50.
[26] *Ibid.*, pp. 70–72.
[27] O. Hobart Mowrer, "Science, Sex and Values," *Personnel and Guidance Journal* 42:746–753 (April, 1964).
[28] A. Levitsky, "An Approach to a Theory of Psychotherapy," *Journal of Existential Psychiatry* 4:134 (Fall, 1963).
[29] Bert Kaplan, *The Inner World of Mental Illness* (New York: Harper & Row, Publishers, 1964), p. 67.

doctors appear to think that patients do not feel their position; now I know that many lunatics are extremely sensible [sic] to ridicule; this sensitiveness is, indeed, one of the phenomena of an unsound mind."[30] Another patient, Mary MacLane, says, "Badness, compared to nothingness is beautiful."[31]

Self-descriptions such as the following have been used by clients, child and adult, in school and out. Positive self-statements would be:

> I am a responsible person.
> I usually like people.
> I express my emotions freely.
> My hardest battles are with myself.
> I am optimistic.
> I am sexually attractive.
> I can usually make up my mind and stick to it.
> I am satisfied with myself.
> I am relaxed, and nothing really bothers me.

Self-statements on the negative side would be:

> I put on a false front.
> I often feel humiliated.
> I doubt my sexual powers.
> I usually feel driven.
> I feel helpless.
> I don't trust my emotions.
> I have a feeling that I am just not facing things.
> I am no one. Nothing seems to be me.
> I just don't respect myself.
> I am confused.
> All you have to do is just insist with me, and I give in.

These are descriptions that most of us could likely say are "pretty much like me" or "not very much like me." Probably few of us could say to any of them, "No—never—absolutely not!"

High school and junior high school counselors describe the client in the following ways:

> "He is a person who is unloved and has retaliated by involving himself in norm-violating behavior."
> "He is a person whose viewpoints have not been taken seriously because people have not taken the time to be interested enough in him to listen."

---

[30] *Ibid.*, p. 248.
[31] *Ibid.*, p. 279.

"He is a person whose functional effectiveness is impaired because of a lack of congruence between what he is and what he would like to be."

"He is a person who has become a victim of our societal institutions, which do not take the time to be sensitive to his needs."

"He is a person whose emotional development has been unattended because of increasingly automated human relations."

"He is a person whose individuality is usually in conflict with the demands of the group."

"He is a person who has bottled up his feelings because he feels that people will not be perceptive or understanding of his views of life."

"He is a person whose needs have been sacrificed because of the larger needs that the group has imposed on him."

"He is a person who would like to be emotionally free but has not acquired the inner conviction that he should be free."

It cannot be stressed too much that the children who are being described here, and in the pages that follow, are basically "normal," "ordinary" school children. They are not "queer" or "strange" or "deviate." They are the school children with whom the counselor works, and they are representative of the children with whom the teacher works, in a somewhat different way, with somewhat different objectives. Some self-referred junior high school children speak in this manner about themselves:

"I thought I'd explode if I didn't talk to you."
"Keeping things inside prevented me from doing my best work in school."
"I don't like to be singled out for ridicule and sarcasm."
"Nobody seems to respect me or my opinions."
"I feel discriminated against."
"I don't have any friends—none at all."
"I get nervous during a test—I go blank."
"My parents favor my younger sister."
"My parents are separated—and their separation just rips me inside."
"I'm a pawn for people who use me."
"I want to be a plumber . . . but when I mentioned it at home, all hell broke loose."
"I'm fed up with the double standards that surround me."
"I'm angry about the rumors that have been spread about me."
"Everytime I try to express an opinion, he just cuts me off."
"I wanted to develop an inner strength . . . something that would sustain me in life—and not be washed away in the first rainstorm."

In somewhat more detail, here are some reactions of other clients to the question, "Why are you a client?":

In thinking back on why I entered counseling as a client, it is difficult for me to actually point to a particular factor or any one reason. Generally speaking, it appears that the main over-all reason for entering the counseling relationship was that I was becoming continually less able to cope with the problems encountered in everyday living; this seemingly was brought about as I began to take stock of myself, trying to find meaning and purpose in living. Actually, it seems as if a course in Mental Hygiene and a course in English Literature were the things that helped me to see the type of life I was living and the neurotic trend that seemed to be associated with it. In looking around me I could, and still can see a society that has lost sight of its end and has become painfully entangled in its means; I felt that there must be more to life than this hopeless entanglement of means, and that in reality the fulfillment of means utilized as ends are insatiable needs that form the vicious circle which is so characteristic of neurosis.
. . . . . .

I'm a client because I could no longer control my actions or emotions. This was leading to excessive use of alcohol accompanied by hysteria and no knowledge of what had happened the following day. I became very depressed, because my sense of morals and a strict upbringing made me aware things had gone far beyond any sense of decency I might still have. . . . . . .

I felt that I was becoming excessively concerned with myself and my troubles and withdrawing further and further into myself and away from society. It became absolutely necessary to seek immediately some means of finding out what was wrong and to take necessary steps, at all costs, to remedy the situation. . . . . . .

I am a client because my anxieties about my work in my academic program were becoming so intense that they were interfering with my work. The study materials—books, etc.—were becoming the stimuli for so much anxiety—being, of course, a constant reminder of the subject matter that I could hardly sit down to read, or to write papers, but would become tense and fidgety—to the point of not being able to study at all. Also, my experience with some of my diagnostic tests courses was stirring up a great deal of anxiety, so that I was beset by recurring thoughts of a sexual, and at times abnormal nature, which I could not inhibit. I concluded that some of my defenses were crumpling, and that the time had come to get some help. I was particularly concerned that my difficulties might affect my wife and my children, because I was also becoming irritable at home. . . . . .

One of the main reasons I sought help was that I was (and still am, to a degree) very sensitive; had many fears and superstitions, problems with religion, and sex. I have tried to help myself with the help of Dr. Del and tried to analyze my behavior. . . . . . .

Because in recent years I have become a very miserable, despondent person within myself—*very* despondent, envious, lonely, inefficient and feel that I don't have a mind of my own any more. Always looking at everyone else and always thinking what I need, what I should do, being very unhappy generally. Everything I attempt to do is a chore and I am completely dissatisfied with life in general. I feel that I make mistakes in everything I shop for, plan for and just cannot feel at *ease* any more. I feel that making decisions has become a task—a real one. Knowing that having an interest, other than being the mother, wife, daughter, and homemaker has become one of my greatest thoughts. And from that I just flounder and flounder around —what do I want to do, what will keep me "occupied in thought" as well as time. . . . . . .

I felt that at this time, when there are a *few* things about me that are disturbing, that now would be a good time to try to do something about it. This in contrast to waiting several years, when such disturbances might grow into something really serious. I also felt this to be the best opportunity—at the University, while I'm studying, early in my life and early in marriage. . . . . . .

I thought I would find a magic formula that would enable me to sleep. Since I was eighteen years old, it has been difficult to relax, and six nights out of seven I would get three to five hours a night. Basically I felt uneasy about myself—thought I was a fake and did not form relationships with people easily, although I was friendly (I thought). . . . . . .

I'm a client because I know my emotional immaturity is creating many problems for me that I wouldn't have if I could find a way to grow up. I hope that in therapy I will gain a better understanding of myself. . . . . . .

As a client I have undergone approximately twenty sessions. I feel very fortunate in having matriculated at the University, for I feel that I might not have had the opportunity to undergo counseling therapy. I spent a rather difficult first semester debating whether or not I should expose myself to therapy. After all, wasn't this admitting I was sick and unable to help myself? As I think back on this hectic period, my problems mounted increasingly; the tensions and anxieties of daily living became extremely difficult to cope with. Defense mechanisms were structured; yet nothing seemed to alleviate the fears and the tensions. One crutch after another failed; each exit became a dead end. There seemed but one unopened door—my religion. This became the only answer, this had to be it! Unfortunately, or perhaps fortunately, I twisted this excellent means to a desperate end. Consequently, more anxieties were being produced, till in complete frustration I chose to enter psychotherapy. . . . . . .

It would seem, then, that the client who comes in to see another person called the counselor about his personal difficulties, is quite often characterized by at least some of the following traits, none of which will be really modified or altered by the use of "medicine," since he is not organically sick:

1. The client is often anxious. He is anxious about failing in his courses, anxious about doing well on his job, anxious about his lack of

capacity as a husband, anxious about being able to live in a new environment, anxious about deviations that he does not want to modify but that are unacceptable to society. Although anxiety, of course, is common to all human beings, the relationship between the anxiety and the object or event producing it may often be a measure of one's disturbance. Thus anxiety prior to a championship tennis match might be expected, but an equal state of anxiety before playing a friendly match with a friend might be considered unusual. A mother might be considered to be reasonably anxious about a child who is failing in all of his school work, but a similar degree of anxiety because her son received one B instead of all A's would be a somewhat different story. Then, too, the event or situation producing the anxiety may be something that will change, and so reduce the anxiety, whereas an event or situation that will remain means that the individual's reaction to it must be changed. Thus a man who is somewhat fearful for his life during a hurricane has anxiety of a short duration, but the homosexual who is anxious over the reaction of the culture to him is either going to have to adjust to such a culture if his anxiety is to decrease, or to change himself so that the reaction of the culture to him will change. Neither of these choices will be easy.

Then, too, having no anxiety might be considered more abnormal than having some anxiety. I remember an episode from Air Force days when I shared some anxiety with Air Force personnel because it appeared that the aircraft on which we were passengers was going to explode; and I can remember the irritation I shared with the others at another passenger, a fighter pilot who actually went to sleep on the floor of the plane, with the philosophical comment, "We can't do anything about it anyway, so why worry. . . ."

Clients are often extremely anxious, too, about what others would call very little or trivial things. "Will I look right?" "What will I do if I can't answer that question?" "What if it snows and I don't have my rubbers?" "What will I do if Joe doesn't meet me?" "What will I buy for Don's dinner?" Although such anxiety is out of proportion as far as the rest of the world is concerned, it is not out of proportion as far as the client is concerned. Far too often we hear such a comment as "Oh, I wouldn't worry about a little thing like that." The trouble with this statement is that "it" is little only to the person who makes the comment, not to the anxious one. It is surely, at best, a doubtful procedure to reject a client's feelings that something is big enough and important enough to cause anxiety with an airy, "Why, that isn't anything to worry about at all." The most likely reaction to this sort of comment would be a resigned, "Oh, well, I guess you can't blame him. He's just like the rest of them—just doesn't understand me."

The anxiety and fearfulness of the client are very real. The fact that what is not a threat to nearly everyone else is a threat to him means that there has to be a modification and change in the client. The dark room remains dark, but to the child who has grown, that same darkness is no longer a threat. Two of my children were once given a basement room as a bedroom when relatives were visiting, but the night was not far along before they were squeezing into bed with father and mother. The new room was too "spooky," they felt, and the fact that it was the same room where they played all day did not alter the fact that it was spooky. Their fear might even have been contagious, since neither father nor mother took their place, but all four spent the night in the one bed!

Whatever the anxiety may appear, overtly, to be about, any continuing stage of anxiety usually reflects an anxiety about one's self. This anxiety may also be shown by an "I cannot understand you" or "I cannot hear you." What these very often mean is that the person does not want to understand or to hear because of the implications of what might be being said, and the easiest way to avoid anxiety about doing something is to avoid understanding or hearing, for then one can hardly be expected to do anything.

2. The client is often hostile, and his hostility may be shown in a variety of ways. He may be overtly aggressive and contemptuous, unable to accept any ideas or suggestions that might contradict his own, or that might imply that someone else knows more than he does. This is a difficult person to work with, particularly if one is in a supervisory position, since he will react with sensitivity to any sort of criticism, no matter how gentle (if criticism can be gentle) or constructive. As a member of a class, he will often feel that the instructor's comments are personalized, that a criticism of some idea of his is a personal attack upon him. Similarly, he makes a difficult "boss" or teacher, since he can brook no opposition or suggestions that a job might be done in a different or better way than that suggested by him. No matter what his position or role might be, he will find it difficult to relate closely with almost anyone—other than a counselor. Other people seldom have the patience or the understanding to attempt to relate with such a person, a fact which in turn accentuates the difficulties, since these hostile individuals are often correct in their feeling that people do not agree with them. As with other clients, it is usually only in a therapeutic relationship that the client begins to feel there is

no need for the elaborate defenses he has built up. He finds, for the first time, someone who is acceptant—in a secure manner, not in a weak and passive way—of him and his hostilities.

There are many ways, of course, in which a man may express his hostility in a more socially acceptable manner; often an individual may be consciously unaware of the fact that what he is expressing is really a deeply rooted hatred or hostility toward someone. Because a woman soon learns that a mother who hates her child is an awful person, she may show her hatred by being one who loves and loves and loves her child, and indicates to all her great love for her dear darling. The philanthropist, of either the 25 cents or the million dollar variety, may be sneering at people by his donation. The comic may show his veiled contempt for his audience by getting it to laugh at him and to pay him for the privilege of laughing.

Overt or not, our hostility is usually related to our own anxiety about ourselves. Even the little child, when he says, "I hate you," to his mother, is also probably feeling, "And I hate me too." It is generally easier to assert our disdain and contempt for others than for ourselves, and perhaps to express a feeling of "I hate me" by saying, "I hate you."

Much of man's prejudice, indeed, is self-rejection rather than rejection of others. When someone else is doing something that is obviously bigger and better and superior, it is only the solid and stable individual who can say, without any twinges or negative feelings, "He is a better person than I," or "He won because he was better." Minority groups are often tolerated when they are small and pose no threat to the majority; only when they become more potent in strength and numbers, and begin to challenge the status of the majority, do they become a threat. At the same time the members of the minority group cannot afford to show their hostility, and may develop a passive aggressiveness, so that their hatreds are expressed by their meekness and humility.

3. The client often feels guilty; the more the socioreligious pressures upon him, the greater the likelihood of feelings of guilt. Much of our cultural behavior would appear to be controlled by the guilt concept, and even advertisements stress the fact that the potential purchaser would not want to be guilty of various things. The more one learns that he "should not" do and feel, the more likely it is that he will have many feelings of guilt, since he will continue to do and feel, and it is the feelings about what has been done that cause the trouble and tension rather than the actual doing. Thus a client may feel guilty

about wanting to marry someone of a different religion; he may feel guilty about speaking and acting harshly toward his children; he may feel guilty because he does not think kindly of his parents; he may feel guilty about masturbation; he may feel guilty about cheating; he may feel guilty about having sexual relations with a girl; and so on. Some would say that this is the voice of one's conscience, and that if we did not have any control by guilt we would have no social order. The trouble is that the guilt feeling itself is a contagious sort of thing that seldom changes one for the better. If an individual felt guilty only about some act that most people would agree was questionable—such as brutal treatment of one's children—and then moved ahead to a more stable attitude, and thus more positive behavior toward the children, this would be fine. That, however, is not usually what happens. If an individual is restrained from striking his children only because he feels guilty about it, then there is every likelihood that this same attitude toward his children will be expressed in an equally questionable, but possibly not equally guilt-producing manner. Thus, although guilt may repress or change or modify the act or the behavior, it does not change the attitude that produces the behavior.

4. Low self-esteem is another overt characteristic of many clients. Such a lack of respect for oneself may show itself in statements to this effect, or by depression or general unhappiness, or it may be shown by the contempt or ridicule that the client directs toward others. Low self-esteem is also shown by a discrepancy between the individual's ideal self-concept and his actual self-concept. This discrepancy has been brought sharply into focus in research studies by Rogers and Dymond,[32] where the ideal self-concept was described as the organized conceptual pattern of characteristics and emotional states that the individual consciously holds as desirable (and undesirable) for himself. The greater the discrepancy, the more poorly he feels about himself.

5. All of these items are, of course, related, although the inability to make a choice might be thought of as another characteristic of some clients. Of course, making a choice is a problem for all individuals, but a disturbed person may be completely unable to accept the responsibility for making a choice—and thereby a decision—which would then leave him subject to question and criticism. If one never makes a decision, one will never get into trouble or be blamed or criticized for making a choice. The inability of one client to make a choice of break-

---

[32] Carl R. Rogers and Rosalind F. Dymond, *Psychotherapy and Personality Change* (Chicago: The University of Chicago Press, 1954).

fast cereal might seem amusing to some, but to the person involved this choice was a major decision that she simply could not venture.

Today, much more than a decade ago, all of these traits might be considered as a part of the search for identity, particularly among the young. More and more of the young want to change the "system," often drastically, and fewer and fewer want to join it as it is. In their hostility toward the system, they demand instant change, and when a rigid structure makes even minimal change difficult, their idealism often turns to a harsh cynicism. Their anxiety is more about the condition of the world than it is about their self, and many try to develop their self-esteem by battling the wrongs, real or imagined, of the establishment. The young today are probably less guilty in the sense of their own freeness and openness about their feelings and their bodies, but they, especially the affluent ones, are more guilty about their inability to do much about the milieu surrounding them. Choice, too, has become a different kind of problem, since for many it is the excess of choices, rather than the lack of choices which poses the dilemma. The eternal and youthful cry, "I want to be free," does not mean the same today as it did even a decade ago.

RESTRICTIONS AFFECTING COUNSELORS

The counselor, particularly the counselor in the school, faces many real restrictions, but without doubt the major restriction facing any counselor is the counselor himself. Like everyone else, he is subject to the disease of parochialism, and he may tend to close his eyes and ears to evidence and ideas which may contradict some of his more cherished concepts. A few years ago, in a famous psychiatric clinic, I heard a fine and respected elder psychiatrist say, "No, I don't know anything about Rogers and I don't want to. . . ." He almost certainly did not mean the remark as it sounded, but it was a good example of the "I don't want to hear anything that implies something I have been doing is wrong" attitude. It takes a person of high calibre—particularly a person who has been asked for the answers for years—to accept such a notion, and, of course, such notions are often presented as evidence when they are actually little more than notions.

It is probably not unfair to say that in many high schools the level of the counselor's professional education is low, and hence he operates mostly by ear. Many of the things he does he may do because of a kind heart, and he may do them almost intuitively, and the result may often be very good. But if this is true, the reverse is equally true. Many disturbed students are not receiving adequate help simply because their counselors do not know what to do. Thus when some counselors and teachers say, "I don't believe in the Freudian stuff" (or that client-centered business or that psychological nonsense), what they are really saying is simply, "I don't know anything about it, and I'm more comfortable not knowing anything about it."

In the case of the medical therapist versus the psychological counselor, there is no question about the high level of the professional education of both; but it may be that they have come through different doors into the same room, have worked happily for a while, then suddenly discovered that another person was in the room, doing the same work, and neither one can see how the other fellow got there. Professional workers are subject to the disease of provincialism just like anyone else. We all have an unfortunate tendency to read, for example, in our own narrow sphere, with no realization that other people are involved in much the same work, using different techniques and methods and procedures, and often arriving at results that are much superior to those that we have achieved. Every professional counselor must continually check himself, to see if perchance he happens to be rejecting an idea or a procedure primarily because his own ignorance in the particular area threatens him, or because of his own provincialism, which may, of course, be the educated word for ignorance. There are different methods, and different counselors do use different methods; surely it is ironic if, of all people, the counselor—supposedly the most acceptant of individuals—rejects in scorn another counselor because he is not of the true orientation or school or methodology. If counselors are professional workers, then in the long run the competence of the counselor must be determined by pragmatic evidence.

The school counselor may also find himself an "issue" because of a negative identification that may have developed in the eyes of the students in the school. He can, of course, take some steps to at least reduce the likelihood of negative identification; he need not be seen as too friendly with the teachers, as having an office adjacent to the principal's, and so on. No matter what he does, however, the counselor will frequently discover that the client's picture of him may be the cause of some difficulty. The school counselor can reduce his identification with the school administration, but he will continue to be viewed by some children as the agent of the principal. He may frequently also be considered a teacher, and his clients may be somewhat disturbed when he does not "teach" them. Almost any good counselor, regardless of methodology, is going to cause some client unhappiness by not giving him the immediate answers and reassurances that are wanted. The counselor who causes all of his clients to leave his office singing his praises might be looked upon with as much skepticism as the counselor who is roundly condemned by all his clients.

The title of "Doctor" may also be a problem, although in a school it will be somewhat different from in a clinic. Not too many schools have counselors who are "Doctors," and most children know only one kind of doctor. Thus they may frequently expect that Dr. Brown, counselor, will use certain instruments in his little bag and prescribe certain medication. They may be passive, and expect the doctor somehow to examine them, tell them what is wrong, and tell them what to do. They may well be somewhat frustrated and confused when Dr. Brown does none of these things. On the other hand, in a counseling center or a psychiatric clinic the non-doctor therapist, such as a social worker, may be considered by some patients, and by some members of the staff, to be something of a second-class citizen. The Ph.D. "doctor," on the other hand, will frequently be considered by the patients as a psychiatrist, and the prescribing of medication as one of his functions.

The actual verbal approach of the counselor is often, of course, a very limiting factor. Some counselors apparently feel that they must answer every question the client asks, and while rarely is a direct answer needed for a personal question, counselors could at least say "I don't know" if they don't know the answer. Instead, some try to answer such questions as, "Why am I always so fascinated by automobiles?" or, "Why must I always procrastinate so much?" or, "What does it mean when I dream of my mother with a series of breasts instead of two?" or, "Why can't I make up my mind to do something, and then go ahead and do it?" or, "Tell me why I am always afraid of these ridiculous things that I know are just superstitions?" Even the boldest of interpreters would be somewhat careful about saying what any of these questions might mean, or just what the client could do about them; and the counselor who actually tries to answer such questions is almost certainly doing so because of his own uneasiness or ignorance, or both. The basic counseling problem, after all, is not solved by answers from the counselor. Much more basic is the understanding by the client of just why he must ask such questions, and just what sort of answers he might be able to find for himself.

At the other extreme are those counselors who feel that they have committed a grave sin if they answer any question, and some clients no doubt wonder who is most in need of counseling—the counselor or themselves!

The confusion of functions in the school is often a very real restriction, and probably the most common issue in the school setting is the impossible combination of jobs, as with the principal-counselor or the teacher-counselor. In many respects the major blame for this situation lies at the door of the counselor himself, since if he does not know what he can and what he cannot professionally do, then he can hardly blame someone else for being somewhat confused on this matter. Certainly most will agree that the school principal simply cannot be a counselor. He may be an adviser, and a sage friend, and a kind person, but he cannot be the counselor, since as the principal he is primarily responsible for the welfare of all of the children and the staff. He is the person who must take disciplinary action when it is necessary. He is the top authority who can decide what will happen to any child in the school—a role that is quite contradictory to any concept of the counselor as the individual who helps the person to work out a decision for himself.

The teacher-counselor combination, is, unfortunately, still a common sight in American schools. I may be one of the culprits in this situation, since some years ago I was, I believe, the first person to write a book dealing specifically with this question, using the term "teacher-counselor."[33] Since then, however, it has become abundantly clear, to me, at least, that the two simply do not go together. This does not mean, of course, that the teacher is not a very important member of a personnel services team; but he is a member as a teacher, not as a counselor. The teacher is no more a counselor than he is a social worker, a psychologist or a psychiatrist. Since there still are so many "teacher-counselors," however, it is well to look at some of the reasons why the person who is a teacher cannot function as an effective counselor at the same time.[34] As indicated earlier, it is also highly questionable that teaching should be considered as a prerequisite experience to involvement as a school counselor.

1. There is a specific area of knowledge that the counselor must have; knowledge that must continually be added to and modified and thrown out, and this knowledge is simply not possessed by the teacher unless he is willing to sacrifice the knowledge that, as a mathematics

---

[33] Dugald S. Arbuckle, *Teacher Counseling* (Cambridge: Addison-Wesley Publishing Company, Inc., 1950).

[34] Dugald S. Arbuckle, "The Conflicting Functions of the School Counselor," *Counselor Education and Supervision* 1:54–59 (Winter, 1961).

teacher, he must continually pursue. Contrary to what some teachers think, one cannot be an effective school counselor by only being nice to children and nodding the head at the appropriate moment. There is a vast body of knowledge that he must *know*. This knowledge is not possessed by the teacher, nor will it be, unless he abandons the mathematics or history or whatever it may be that used to be his particular body of knowledge. At this point, of course, he is no longer effective as a teacher of mathematics or history.

2. There are certain skills that must be possessed by the counselor, and these are not possessed by the teacher, other than by chance, since he has no need for them. While the line between a skill and an aptitude or a personal trait may sometimes be very thin, we can distinguish skills that are related to the area of occupational information and testing, and there is at least an element of skill related to the problem of a deep and understanding communication with another person. Thus on this count, although there may be no conflict between these skills and those involved in teaching, the time factor is such that one person is going to find it difficult to be effective in both.

3. There are also a number of required functions from which the teacher can never completely divorce himself, and this, more than any other reason, is why teacher-counselors are, at least in my observation, primarily and overwhelmingly teachers, not counselors. As teachers they manipulate and direct and control, and as "counselors" they do the same thing. As teachers they think in terms of the welfare of society as taking precedence over the welfare of the individual, and as "counselors" they feel the same way. As teachers they measure, evaluate, grade, and separate the "bad's" from the "good's" and as "counselors" they do the same thing. As teachers they know and they feel that they are the authority figure in control and they are thus the ones who determine the curricular experience and practically everything else that happens to the child. There is little or no self-determination, and this person as a "counselor" shows the same level of acceptance of any concept of self-determination or freedom of choice. Finally, we might say that they are teachers, and as such are involved in the overt process of teaching something to someone; they are involved hardly at all in the learning process with another learner. As the "counselor" they are still the teacher, teaching something to someone.

Some will say that many of these functions do not have to be performed by the teacher, but that they are functioning in this way because of the sort of people they are rather than because this is something that is required of them. This is very often correct, and many of these conflicting functions can be minimized, but this often results in the teacher's being considered "not so good" by the school administrator. This raises the intriguing thought that possibly the teacher who will make a good counselor is one who is unhappy with this role as teacher, and who is not doing very well as a teacher—at least in terms of some of the traditional measures of the "good" teacher!

Thus it would appear that every individual who has a part-time counseling function, with some other job title attached to the word "counselor," should check carefully to determine the degree to which he is being rendered ineffective as a counselor because of his other conflicting functions. He might exert every effort to see that he becomes either a full-time teacher or a full-time counselor, and we may hope that the day is not too far off when every school counselor is a fully qualified professional worker. This he can never be if he is satisfied to accept a dual role, a part-time status, which makes him an ineffective fish and an equally ineffective fowl.

There are, of course, many other contradictions that face all school counselors. "Rules and regulations" may often clash with sound professional procedures, and it is unfortunately all too rare that a counselor, or a group of counselors, takes some action about such a situation. The "counselor" who does not attempt to do something about the fact that he has to act as a hall warden, or as a reporter to the administration on the behavior of children, or as an evaluator of which children are "good" and which children are "bad," has no reason to complain, since he is probably doing what he wants to do anyway. Nor can the rehabilitation or employment counselor complain about the fact that he has to see a certain minimum number of clients, that he has to get through with them and decide what they should do, if he has not done his utmost to change such a situation. Some counselors are all too prone to say, at conventions and meetings, "Well, I certainly know that we shouldn't be doing this, but you know how it is . . ." when actually they appear to be quite satisfied to take actions that are professionally unsound.

A counselor working in a clinical or medical setting may sometimes find too that rules and regulations cause him certain difficulties. Frequently, for example, in writing a report on his "case," he may have to provide a diagnosis of the ailment at the end of each counseling session. This requirement may prove somewhat difficult to fulfill, if not impossible, particularly if he must use a prescribed set of categories. Again, however, a counselor working in such a situation should take steps toward its modification if he really feels he is doing something that is counter to his professional concept of his position.

Another very obvious contradiction of roles is the decision, by the counselor, on whether the client is "well enough" to go back to college, to take a certain type of job, and so on. The counselor is placed in a conflicting situation when an administrative officer says to him, "You have had Dil in counseling for the past few months. We have a letter here from him saying that he feels he is well enough to come back to college. What do you think?" It might be that the counselor could, without revealing any particular confidential information, and with the consent of the client, give to the administrator a picture of the state of health of the client, but leave any decision on whether this is "well enough" or "not well enough" up to someone else. There should be complete frankness between the counselor and the client on this matter, so that the client knows exactly what the counselor is going to say.

A much worse situation is one where the client is coming to the counselor with the knowledge that here is the fellow who is going to evaluate his state of health, and then pass that evaluation, which will determine his acceptance to college, on to someone else. This is surely anything but a therapeutic role. The counselor is not the one to decide, for someone else, what the cleint can do and what he cannot do. His function is to help the client to achieve a state of health so that he can decide for himself, and there are others in the culture who can determine whether or not this state of health is good enough for the client to do what they want him to do.

chapter 10

OPERATIONAL ISSUES: II

This chapter continues the discussion of operational issues, and one of the thorniest of all has to do with the meaning of words.

THE SEMANTIC PROBLEM

Many of the apparent differences among counselors are simply a lack of understanding of just exactly what one means when he uses a certain word or a descriptive phrase. Two words that still cause confusion are "counseling" and "psychotherapy," and neither really has any meaning until an individual counselor or therapist indicates what *he* means by each term. Thus we find individuals who call themselves psychotherapists doing what others would call counseling, and we find individuals who call themselves counselors doing what others would call psychotherapy. There are many differentiations between the two. One of the most common refers to counseling as dealing with a generally normal individual, and psychotherapy as dealing with an abnormal person; or some would say that counseling does not get to the same depth as psychotherapy; or some would say that counseling is concerned with the conscious, whereas psychotherapy deals with the unconscious materials. Bordin, for example, states that the counseling relationship is characterized by less intensity of emotional expression, and relatively more emphasis on cognitive and rational factors than is the case in psychotherapy.[1] Mowrer refers to counseling as a process of giving help "to persons suffering from fully-conscious conflicts which are accompanied by so-called normal anxiety."[2]

Tyler[3] thinks of the aim of therapy as some sort of personality change, while she feels that we should use "counseling" to refer to a helping process whose aim is not to change the person but to enable him to utilize the resources he now has for coping with life.

Buchheimer and Balogh[4] see the approach in therapy as historic and symbolic, relying heavily on the reactivation and consideration of unconscious materials. The content of conversation is the consideration of past experiences and the reconstruction of that which has happened and has been repressed, thus causing distortions of the present. Through the counseling conversation, on the other hand, the individual will revise his distortions and thereby alter his behavior. The emphasis is on the present, and on verbal material that is within the individual's immediate awareness or that he can easily be made aware of.

Byrne[5] sees counseling and psychotherapy as having much in common, and considers the major difference to be the degree to which psychotherapists uncover and work with hidden psychological dynamics because the individual seeking help reports a long-standing dissatisfaction with life, accompanied by long-standing ineffective or unwanted behaviors. He points out that the school counselor is not usually called upon to function as a psychotherapist, the reason lying in the relationship between function and clientele.

Then, too, some medically oriented psychotherapists would tend to feel that the practice of psychotherapy is limited to the realm of those who possess a medical degree, while what the others do is counseling. However, there are many nonmedical psychotherapists who work in certain institutions with their medical colleagues; all do practically identically the same thing, and they call it psychotherapy.

While there may be a logical difference between intellectual

[1] Edward S. Bordin, *Psychological Counseling* (New York: Appleton-Century-Crofts, 1955), p. 15.
[2] O. Hobart Mowrer, "Anxiety Theory as a Basis for Distinguishing Between Counseling and Psychotherapy," in Ralph F. Berdie (Ed.), *Concepts of Programs of Counseling* (Minneapolis: University of Minnesota Press, 1951), p. 23.
[3] Leona E. Tyler, *The Work of the Counselor* (New York: Appleton-Century-Crofts, 1961), p. 12.
[4] Arnold Buchheimer and Sarah Carter Balogh, *The Counseling Relationship* (Chicago: Science Research Associates, 1961), p. x.
[5] Richard Hill Byrne, *The School Counselor* (Boston: Houghton Mifflin Company, 1963), pp. 37–38.

guidance with a person whose stresses and strains do not control his actions, and counseling with an individual whose actions are dominated by and subject to his emotional stresses, there is no such differentiation between counseling and psychotherapy. There is not always, for example, a clear and distinct line between the conscious and the subconscious. When a person is swimming, he is partly in the water and partly out, rarely completely submerged or completely out of the water. Most professional school counselors are well acquainted with students who are pushed by subconscious pressures as causes of their difficulties; and the purpose of the counseling is to help the student to work out these parts of his totality that are only dimly, if at all, understood and accepted. Sometimes, of course, the distinction is quite clear. Nevertheless, anyone who works with people who are under stress is going to have a difficult time cataloguing what he is doing as either counseling or psychotherapy on the basis of the conscious or the subconscious.

Similarly, with regard to the depth of the process, it is probably correct to say that, traditionally, most counselors in schools have not worked with people who are completely divorced from our reality, and might thus be called psychotic, but have worked rather with those who would possibly like to be divorced from our reality, but know they are not, and might thus be called neurotic. One of the obvious reasons is that most of the former individuals are to be found in hospitals or similar institutions, whereas, until recently, counselors were to be found in hospitals only as patients.

In the last decade, however, with the advent of a high level of preparation at the doctorate and post-doctorate level for such professional workers as school counselors, counseling psychologists, rehabilitation counselors, and psychiatric nurses, it is obvious that people who may be called counselors are working with psychotic patients as are psychotherapists. On the other hand, a psychiatrist who has a private practice, or one who works in a University Clinic or a Counseling Center, most likely spends the bulk of his time with individuals who are neurotic rather than psychotic; and thus he is, if we must have a difference, a counselor rather than a therapist.

There are not only different levels of education for those who are involved in counseling and psychotherapy, there are different kinds of education as well. If we accept the definition of counseling given in this book, then it follows that those professional workers, whether called psychotherapists or counselors, are performing the same basic task, although they may be performing it in different ways because of their different educations and their different personalities. It might even be better to think in terms of psychotherapies, rather than psychotherapy. Then, possibly, psychotherapists who do different things would be more acceptable to each other, and would not threaten each other to the extent that they appear to today.

When one refers to the "practice of psychiatry," one usually means the practice of psychotherapy. Hence a psychiatrist might be described as a medical doctor who practices psychotherapy, while a psychologist is a Ph.D. who practices psychotherapy—though not all psychologists do. Psychoanalysis is generally considered by medical doctors to be a more intensive psychotherapy, although some differentiate between the two. Fromm-Reichmann comments that there is no valid *intensive* psychotherapy other than that which is psychoanalytic or psychoanalytically oriented, a statement that would obviously be challenged by many psychotherapists who, though working intensively with extremely disturbed individuals, do not think of themselves as psychoanalysts.[6] On the other hand, although most medical personnel assume that only a psychiatrist can practice psychoanalysis (Freud was one medical doctor who did not see this), it is difficult for some to see just why a medical background is necessary to operate in an area that is overwhelmingly psychological in nature.

Tyler's reference to "no change" would seem to be rather pointless, since it would be impossible for one to utilize to a greater degree what he now has without undergoing any change! Nor can I see Buchheimer and Balogh's point of differentiation between the past and the present, since most individuals, when talking about themselves, mingle the past with the present. Even the school child under modest stress will be likely periodically to bring in the past as he talks about the present.

It would seem to me that the competent, professionally educated school counselor, as he goes about his daily professional tasks, is going to become involved in practically all of the human relationships that have been described by various individuals as either counseling or psychotherapy. Not in one day, or with one person, but over a period of time, with many different children, many of whom could not even be described as clients. He will work with some children almost entirely at a cognitive rational level, and with others he will spend much time in the area of feelings and emotions; with some children he may

---

[6] Frieda Fromm-Reichmann, *Principles of Intensive Psychotherapy* (Chicago: University of Chicago Press, 1950), p. x.

provide simple answers, which will affect their futures but create no drastic change; some children will bring much subconscious material to the surface, others practically none at all; some children will spend much time on the past, which has taught them to be as they are, and others will be concerned mostly with the present. The counselor should be able to function effectively with these children, and as long as he can, it matters little whether he describes what he is doing as counseling or psychotherapy. If the term "psychotherapy" is bothersome to certain school administrators or medical personnel, the counselor might just as well refer to his function as counseling, and continue to do what he is doing anyway!

After all, the most "client-centered" of counselors is not going to "reflect feelings" when the cheery new student asks if English 3 has as its teacher Mr. Brown or Mr. Smith. If the counselor knows, he will likely say, "Mr. Brown." On the other hand, if a grim and tense student says to the same counselor, "Well, I guess you should know—which of these miserable courses in English has Smith as the teacher . . ," the counselor will most likely react to the feeling behind the student's question, because obviously the student is not asking an intellectual question. He is expressing a feeling. Similarly, the counselor would feel that when a man quietly says, "I will kill myself tonight," the counselor reaction will not be, "Oh, you mustn't do a thing like that," because again the individual is expressing deep, intense feelings. Such a cliché as the one above would be little better than a rejection of the individual, who has possibly already been rejected by all whom he has known.

It is surely idiotic for any counselor to defend any of his actions on the basis of his supposed methodology. One does not do something, or not do something because he is a this or a that, but rather because the evidence has tended to indicate that this is the way that *he* can be most helpful with the other person, and it matters little whether he is functioning as a "vocational counselor," an "educational counselor," a "personal counselor," or a "psychotherapist." Right now I could think of several school counselors who could be described by any of these names if one happened to look through their windows at the right time!

Part of the semantic difficulty may reside in the very terms that have been used supposedly to describe different methodologies in counseling. Thus the terms "directive" and "nondirective" are unfortunate, since no counselor could avoid being directive. The very act of extreme acceptance of the client by the counselor is a means of direction of the client. Thus the question actually is, "How directive are you?" rather than "Are you directive or nondirective?"

Another term causing trouble is "client-centered," although it is much better than "nondirective." It is hard to conceive of any counselor, professional or not, denying that he is client-centered. What else could he be—counselor-centered, culture-centered, or what? Yet again, there are differences. When one has listened to many counselors in action, it is obvious that they vary a good deal in the degree to which they are client-centered. The question is not, "Are you client-centered?" but rather, "Just how client-centered are you?" If the answer is "Not at all," it is difficult to see how such a person could be a successful counselor. Nor is the degree of "client-centeredness" necessarily related to what the counselor says.

INTERPRETATION AND/OR REFLECTION OF FEELING

"Interpretation" and "reflection" are two words that have often been used to distinguish two different kinds of counseling, and yet it would appear that the difference is only one of degree. Before one can reflect a feeling, after all, he has to be interpretive about just what that feeling might be. He may be reflecting a feeling by saying "You are worried about this," but this is the counselor's interpretation. If, of course, the counselor did nothing but repeat words, which alas, is exactly the extent of what some counselors do, then he would not be interpretive. The reply "You are worried" to the statement "I am worried," is a repetition of words, and if this is the best the counselor can do, it is not likely that he is very effective.

McKinney thinks of interpretation as the assistance that the counselor gives to the client in seeing relationships between present behavior and underlying causes or motivations. He goes on:[7]

> It is well established that an effective counselor does not interpret behavior until the client is *ready to grasp it and assimilate it effectively in living.* Interpretation runs the gamut. The counselor may merely repeat in an integrated manner many of the statements the client has made during the interview so that he may see their implications; or he may point out underlying repressed motives. Probably the

---

[7] Fred McKinney, *Counseling for Personal Adjustment* (Boston: Houghton Mifflin Company, 1958), p. 277.

most effective kind of interpretation consists of helping the client go just a little farther—just a little beyond where he was planning to stop.

Buchheimer and Balogh,[8] on the other hand, think of "surface" interpretation as a counseling lead, "depth" interpretation being that aspect of psychotherapy which seeks out the fundamental reasons for past and present behaviors.

One might generally describe the reflection of feeling as the attempt by the counselor to understand from the client's point of view and to communicate that understanding to him. One might say that there is less likelihood of counselor involvement in such a reflection than in an interpretation, and yet even here it is the counselor who is, in effect, saying, "This is the way I understand and feel you. . . ." Some would say that this differs little from skillful interpretation, since the effective counselor will never interpret too far ahead of the client. This is probably why, many years ago, Rogers had ceased talking about reflection and clarifying, and was saying instead:[9]

> [I]t is the counselor's function to assume, in so far as he is able, the internal frame of reference of the client, to perceive the world as the client sees it, to perceive the client himself as he is seen by himself, to lay aside all perceptions from the external frame of reference while doing so, and to communicate something of this empathic understanding to the client.

Hora questions the value of interpretation for another reason:[10]

> That which is, speaks for itself. That which speaks for itself is understood. What is understood needs no interpretation. What is interpreted is seldom understood.

Jung[11] gives a word of warning to dream interpreters when he says, "Do anything you like, only don't try to understand."

Even the interpretation of the analytical counselor, as he inter-

---

[8] Buchheimer and Balogh, *op. cit.*, p. 54.

[9] Carl R. Rogers, *Client-Centered Therapy* (Boston: Houghton Mifflin Company, 1951), p. 29.

[10] Thomas Hora, "Healing or Growth," *Annals of Psychotherapy* 1:32 (Monograph 5, 1963).

[11] C. G. Jung, *Modern Man in Search of a Soul* (New York: Harcourt, Brace & World, Inc., 1933), p. 12.

prets the meaning of the transference relationship to the client, might be described as a reflection of subconscious feeling. This would also apply when he was interpreting to the client the possible meaning of various resistances that he might be expressing.

Thus probably all counselors, to some extent, reflect the feelings of the client—shallow and deep, conscious and subconscious, verbal and nonverbal—and what some call reflection, others will call interpretation. Far too many counselors, however, in the name of "client-centered," merely repeat over and over again what the client has said, until both become fearfully bored!

Some might say that Ellis (Co = Counselor, Cl = Client), for example, is reflecting feeling in the following example.[12]

> Cl.: I don't know. I think it's natural being bothered by having people being disturbed and not understanding why they're disturbed. I mean, I can see why they might object, but I don't see why they don't want me to talk the whole thing out and find out why they're disturbed because I'm upset.
>
> Co.: Well, if I'm hearing you correctly you're sort of saying that—ah—that you are not objecting to their getting upset, but you at least would like them to talk it out with you.

While Rogers (Co) might appear to be "interpreting":[13]

> Co.: Yeah, yeah. But you felt he didn't quite understand you on that really.
>
> Cl.: I thought that he felt that I was being blunt, and that I just meant that I didn't want to talk to him any more.
>
> Co.: And I, if I sense some of your feeling now, it is, uh, a little tenseness that, that maybe he didn't really get that, he felt you were shutting him off on something.
>
> Cl.: Yes, that's what, and that isn't what I meant.

But Rogers is *the* "client-centered" counselor, and Ellis is *the* "rational" psychotherapist!

Most beginning counselors who take some pride in their "analy-

---

[12] From the tape *Loretta*, American Academy of Psychotherapists.
[13] *Ibid.*

tic" or "diagnostic" title question or probe the client to death, while most beginning counselors who fly "client-centered" at their masthead "reflect" the client to distraction. Carl's counselor, for example, is reflecting feelings and statements:[14]

> Co.: You feel they happen more often than they should just to be nightmares.
> Cl.: Yes. Seems like I never dream . . . (etc.).
> Co.: You feel you're somewhere you really don't belong.
> Cl.: Yes . . . (etc.).
> Co.: No matter how you think about it or feel about it, or try and talk about it, it seems to still be there.
> Cl.: Yes, it still . . . (etc.).
> Co.: For a short period of time you feel that you are acceptable. People are not noticing you.
> Cl.: Yes. I feel . . . (etc.).
> Co.: So, even being accepted now and getting away from this feeling of being alone is a problem.

Much of the superficial reflection is to ease the tension of the counselor, and there would be less direction if the counselor were merely to keep quiet, or to make understanding sounds. Jane's counselor, for example, by his "reflection," may encourage her to keep talking about what might be trivia:[15]

> Co.: You're worried about the cause of the drop.
> Cl.: . . . . . .
> Co.: You're wondering if you worry more about these things than other people do.
> Cl.: . . . . . .
> Co.: You feel possibly if you stopped worrying about it they might straighten themselves out.
> Cl.: . . . . . .
> Co.: You feel you should do things about this, do something for it instead of worrying about it all the time.
> Cl.: . . . . . .
> Co.: You feel you should be working now.

[14] William Evraiff, *Helping Counselors Grow Professionally* (Englewood Cliffs, N.J.: Prentice-Hall, Inc., 1963), pp. 46–47, dialogue entries C80–C88.
[15] *Ibid.*, p. 95, dialogue entries C164–C172.

Nonetheless, the reflecting and interpreting of the counselor, at least of the experienced counselor, does tend to be more with the client than does questioning and probing. In the following, for example, the therapist (D = Doctor) is being more diagnostic, more directive, and is trying to find out something about the client (P = Patient) much as would a medical doctor during a medical examination. At the same time, of course, he is interpreting what the client is saying to him:[16]

> D.: Tell me how you are feeling and when it started, can you?
>
> P.: I think so. I feel, I don't know, I feel at ease with certain people and with others I don't feel at ease. Like I'd say it started when my father got sick. I . . . I sort of took it on myself. I thought maybe it was my fault when my father got sick. I know that things have not been going too smoothly at home. I was out of work all summer, and there were many arguments, so when my father got sick I thought maybe it was my fault, but that feeling went away, of course. But my nerves haven't been the same since that.
>
> D.: Since he got sick?
>
> P.: That's right—I just seem to be ill at ease—now I mean I am talking to you—I feel natural now. With certain people I do, but at home I don't. I don't understand it.
>
> D.: You spoke before about feeling disappointed.
>
> P.: I have a depressed feeling. I—it's so hard to explain— I feel like I am waiting for something to happen, and it's never going to happen—and I feel like I gotta run away and I go out of the house and—well, I want to go right back home again. I know there's nothing out of the house. I don't have too many friends. I was going with a buddy but he's down south now and I have a feeling—and I have a lonesome feeling, to tell you the truth. (Sighs.) I don't know—I don't know what I'm looking for—forward to something that's not going to happen.
>
> D.: Is it dreadful do you think, what might happen, or is it pleasant?

[16] Ruben R. Pottash, "A Psychotherapeutic Interview with an Adolescent," in Benjamin Harries Balster (Ed.), *Psychotherapy of the Adolescent* (New York: International Universities Press, Inc., 1957), pp. 160–164.

P.: Well, that's just it, I don't know. (Pause.) I've been going out very seldom now. I stay around the house all the time—I'm working in the store all the time, and well, I go to the movies, and that's all. We close now Thursday night and Sunday night, but I go to the movies or I go to a friend's house or relatives. But Saturday night was the first time for a long time that I went out since my father's been sick. That happened so suddenly. On a couple minutes' notice I went out. But when I got up Sunday morning I felt all right until I started to get a depressed feeling. I couldn't understand what it was, and I thought maybe I was sick or something—because I have had pains in my stomach all the time and my mother kept saying, "Why don't you go to the doctor," and I thought maybe I'll put it off until tomorrow and it will go away.

D.: Do you have any idea what you might be depressed about?

P.: I dunno. I thought it might be that I'm lonesome. You know, I feel like I'm alone. Even when I'm with a lot of people I feel like I'm alone.

D.: Hasn't it always been that way?

This example (in which Co = Counselor and Cl = Client) is more reflective:[17]

Cl.: Um-hm. So I don't know what I'll do. (Slight pause.) I usually do wait till the last possible moment, and then make a quick decision. (Laughs.) One way or the other.

Co.: You're kind of saying you won't handle it very well.

Cl.: No, I won't; that's right. I'll do it the way I usually do it. Slipshod. (Pause; sighs.) Could I use a cigarette now. Oh! (Trembling.)

Co.: Right this minute, that is just what you would want.

Cl.: (Sighs; tears; pause.) I guess I'm upset now. (Sighs; pause.) Having state visitors come and visit our school tomorrow and they put up such a big show. And

---

[17] John M. Shlien, "Time-limited, Client-centered Psychotherapy: Two Cases," in Arthur Burton (Ed.), *Case Studies in Counseling and Psychotherapy* (Englewood Cliffs, N.J.: Prentice-Hall, Inc., 1959), pp. 316–317, dialogue entries C33–T41.

everyone gets very excited and . . . big fuss. (Pained, stricken look.)

Co.: What—what's hitting you now?

Cl.: I don't know.

Co.: Something upsetting, something that makes you feel like crying?

Cl.: (Pause; crying softly; words lost.) And I don't know why either. I just got very upset. (Still crying.)

Co.: Uh-hm. Something just came over you, and you really don't know what started it.

Cl.: (Long pause; still crying.) I must have been getting a little too close to something—I didn't want to talk about, or something.

Co.: You really don't know what made this happen. (Client looks for clock.) You've still got about fifteen minutes.

Cl.: (Pause; still crying.) Something hit me. (Laughs.)

Co.: Hm?

Cl.: Something hit me.

Co.: Something hurts.

Or, we may compare the personal involvement of this counselor:[18]

Co.: You were starting to say I—I did something?

Cl.: I—sort of have a feeling that you forced some of it.

Co.: Oh. By what I did or by what I am as a person?

Cl.: By, in a sense . . . uh . . . you're telling me, "Listen, you're just going around and about, now let's get to the point." And then I felt (pause) this—if I went on going around, I'd never get to the point and I'd never get well. Or—and that you would not continue therapy.

Co.: The fear of losing me?

Cl.: That—that was pretty strong.

Co.: But I never threatened you.

Cl.: No, I know. I don't know what it was. But I know I had that feeling.

Co.: Maybe you had another feeling too (pause), a feeling of a relationship with me.

---

[18] Arthur Burton, "Paradox and Choice in Schizophrenia," in Arthur Burton (Ed.), *op. cit.*, pp. 268–269.

Cl.: Yes, I did—very strongly I remember until . . . uh . . . at one point when—remember when I felt you were accusing me of terrible crimes and . . .

Co.: Hm-mm.

Cl.: At this point . . . uh . . . it sort of went around and I (buzzer), you became in a sense the opposite—an enemy, not as a friend.

Co.: At that time I was an enemy.

Cl.: Yes, I felt very strongly that you . . . now stop wandering around and come to the point. (Laughs.)

Co.: Hm-m.

Cl.: And—(pause).

Co.: But you wanted to be a child then. (Pause.) Your psychosis represented that, (pause). And remember I put it to you that you either take your psychosis or you take reality. It was up to you, remember?

with this reflective and less involved counselor:[19]

Cl.: Yeah. I'm afraid of being ordinary. Yet I'm afraid this is what is asked of me.

Co.: You want to be different and you want to—

Cl.: (Breaking in) I want to live a life I can enjoy. And the kind of life that seems to be offered to the average man is not to me enjoyable. Sitting and watching television five nights a week. Alternating television with movies.

Co.: You're not contented with the lot that most people have.

Cl.: No! I hate it!

Co.: Something better, something more exciting—

Cl.: That's right. But I don't know how to get it. That's the trouble. I feel bound—by something or other—it must be me! (Laughs.) There's nothing else that seems to be doing it. I can't blame it on anything else. But there's this knot—somewhere inside of me.

Co.: Feel tied up by something in you that's kind of a mystery to you.

Cl.: Yeah! Makes me want to get mad—and cry—and run away.

[19] Madge K. Lewis, "Time-limited, Client-centered Psychotherapy: Two Cases," in Arthur Burton (Ed.), *op. cit.*, pp. 334–335.

272 : *The Nature of Counseling*

Co.: Lots of mixed up feelings about it.

Cl.: Yeah. Also feels I can never get at it the way I've been trying to get at it. . . . It's as if I can't put my attention on it.

Co.: Like a blind spot.

Cl.: Yeah. I can see effects in my life I don't like; yet I can't see their cause. I must be deliberately blinding myself because it would be painful to know. But what could it be?

Co.: What could it be that might cause me so much hurt?

Cl.: Yeah. Do I think I'm a failure—a ruined human being —or something of the sort? It must be something like that. That I don't feel worthy—of anything.

Co.: Am I flop—completely unworthy of any kind of good life?

And finally, we might compare this questioner (Co), also known as a counselor:[20]

Co.: Can you tell me a little more about how you seem to be held back?

Cl.: Well, mathematics mostly.

Co.: Mm-huh. How does that affect you?

Cl.: Well, I haven't done very good on the tests in taking them.

Co.: Mm-huh (pause). Could you tell me a little bit about your background, where you are from, what you plan to do, and so forth?

Cl.: Well, I'm from (name of town).

Co.: Yes.

Cl.: Have you ever been there?

Co.: No, but I know where it is.

Cl.: I'm in pre-vet school. I'd like to take up veterinary medicine if I can make the grade.

Co.: Mm-huh.

Cl.: That's my only trouble.

Co.: When did you decide on veterinary medicine?

Cl.: Well, I've been kind of interested for some time. I live on a farm and I work with a lot of livestock.

---

[20] Robert Callis, Paul C. Polmantier and Edward C. Roeber, *A Casebook of Counseling* (New York: Appleton-Century-Crofts, 1955), pp. 105–106, dialogue entries C1–C13.

Co.: Do you know any veterinarians?

Cl.: Well, yes, our local veterinarian.

Co.: Mm-huh. And you'd like to be doing the work he seems to be doing at the present time?

Cl.: Yes.

Co.: You haven't worked with him, though, while he is working with animals, or anything like that?

Cl.: Well, yes, I've worked some.

Co.: Have you?

Cl.: Mm-huh.

Co.: What made you choose veterinary medicine as the field you wanted to go into?

Cl.: Well—

Co.: (Counselor interrupts) Was it any one person or just working on the farm?

with this counselor:[21]

Cl.: (Smiling) No. No. I was thinking, ah . . . that . . . sometimes . . . well, I mean I, then, ah, late, you know in the last ten years I've been . . . more tired than the average person that . . . people get tired, but, ah . . . I don't know, in fact lately it . . . seems as though I could keep on going with much less . . . sleep than I have . . . when I've felt all right . . . (smiles) . . . since I don't have very restful sleep I . . . I think I'm awake now more than I'm asleep.

Co.: You mean you've always needed a lot of rest.

Cl.: I've always needed a lot of rest.

Co.: And you mean that you feel that you need less now than before.

Cl.: Yes, I used to . . . require a good night's sleep and if I didn't have a good night's sleep I'd be . . . tired and . . .

Co.: You'd have a generally tired feeling.

Cl.: Yeah . . . Although when I used to take, ah, you know, those drugs . . . and . . . different things like that to get over the tired . . . feeling, but, ah, at my age . . . and I don't think, and for the little I did do, I don't think I should have been tired, as I always was.

---

[21] Dugald S. Arbuckle, *Guidance and Counseling in the Classroom* (Boston: Allyn and Bacon, Inc., 1957), pp. 240–241.

Co.: You mean you weren't particularly exerting yourself.

Cl.: Well—I, just a little bit but nothing . . . to tire me the way I . . . did get tired. And then it was probably always . . . like . . . I said in . . . my mind, and my mind was on the go a lot.

Co.: Yeah. Maybe not so much the physical effort, you mean, as the . . .

Cl.: Mental.

Co.: As the mental thinking . . . or worrying . . . or wondering.

Cl.: Yes.

Co.: And that wore you out more than your physical effort.

Cl.: Yeah. Uh hummm- (pause—31 seconds).

Co.: And you mean you . . . don't have as much of that feeling now as you . . . used to have, ah?

Cl.: No. Lately I haven't had, have had . . . have had half as much sleep as I . . . used to think that I required.

Co.: And you don't feel any worse.

Cl.: Oh, I feel tired, but . . . not as . . . tired . . . well, I suppose a different tired feeling.

Co.: A different sort of tiredness, you mean?

Experienced counselors vary tremendously in their degree of reflection of feeling and what would appear to be out-and-out interpretation. There would appear to be a high level of reflection of feeling, for example, in this excerpt of a session with an adult client:

Cl.: . . . and if I could, I'd be more secure. . . .

Co.: And this was tied in with resentment toward me. . . .

Cl.: Yes . . . I was resentful of the fact that I couldn't . . . (long pause). . . .

Co.: You were feeling close to me, but there was both threat and reassurance in that you could feel close to me without this sexual relationship. . . .

Cl.: Yes . . . it is . . . you see . . . I've never had a relationship like this . . .

and in this one with an adult client:

Cl.: Yeh—I still do—it hits me, and is gone—but why don't I remember the pleasant things . . . why . . .

Co.: A sort of a feeling . . . there *must* have been some nice things . . .

Cl.: Yeh—yeh. . . .

Co.: It couldn't always have been. . . .

Cl.: No—no—it wasn't—it wasn't. . . .

Co.: You mean it not only couldn't, it wasn't. . . .

Cl.: No—it definitely wasn't . . .

There is more of a combination of reflection of feeling and interpretation between these counselors and these junior high school clients (Cl):

Cl.: Dances, clothes, boys, parties . . . that's all they think of. . . . It's so stupid and foolish. . . . I'm glad I'm not like them.

Co.: I feel all these interests are ridiculous, but sometimes I feel, deep down, that I'd like to go to parties and dances and be popular like other girls. . . .

. . . .

Cl.: I love animals. . . . I want to get some kind of a job later on working with animals . . . particularly horses. . . .

Co.: Animals aren't like people . . . animals are friends— they're affectionate . . . they'll return your love . . . they're loyal . . . I can trust them. . . .

. . . .

Cl.: I'm not afraid of anyone or anything. . . .

Co.: It helps me to say I'm not afraid of anyone or anything when I'm really afraid.

. . . .

And what would appear to be out-and-out interpretation is being given by these counselors *to* these junior high school clients:

Cl.: These women teachers bug me. . . . I get the feeling that they don't like boys because some time in their life some man jilted them.

Co.: Maybe your attitude toward them is conditioned by your attitude toward your mother. There seems to be a relationship.

. . . .

Cl.: Becoming a veterinarian is important. . . . I think

that I'd be happy at it because . . . well, for a long time I've loved animals . . . I've loved caring for them . . . sort of makes me feel good inside . . . kind of important.

Co.: Sometimes loving animals is a lot easier than loving people.

. . . .

Cl.: I'm sort of cold toward him—it's hard to explain but . . . well, I sort of enjoy being distant . . . sort of testing him . . . trying to see just how much of my coldness he'll take.

Co.: The same sort of coldness that you told me exists between your father and mother.

. . . .

Cl.: I find myself sort of wanting to lose my books. . . . I doodle in book pages . . . blot out paragraphs . . . even destroy even numbered pages.

Co.: Maybe books represent infringements on your leisure time.

. . . .

Cl.: Everybody tells me I can do the work. . . . I don't know why I'm doing so lousy . . . I . . . I just can't seem to get myself to take an interest in school . . . my folks are disappointed. . . . I know they're burned and hurt and yet it doesn't make any difference . . . I just can't get going even though I *know* I can do the work.

Co.: It seems everybody says I've got the potential . . . and I know I can do well in school . . . but maybe I fail because it's a good way to get back at people.

And yet, in all of these examples there is obviously interpretation by the counselor of just what the client is communicating. Thus it would seem that any *involved* counselor must be interpretive in order to communicate to and with the client, even though his interpretation could be accurately described as a reflection of feeling.

DIAGNOSIS

Diagnosis may be considered as the analysis of one's difficulties and the causes that have produced them. More clinically, it may be thought of as the determination of the nature, origin, and maintenance of ineffective abnormal modes of behavior. More simply, it might be considered as the development, by the counselor, of a deeper and more accurate understanding and appreciation of the client. Blocher sees diagnosis in counseling as:[22]

> the process through which the counselor comes to understand the client, the client's world, and the meaning that his interaction with that world has for him.

Diagnosis of the more clinical sort has had a long and honorable medical history, and it is directly related to prognosis and treatment. Psychologists have generally accepted without question the need for diagnosis, and many counselors apparently operate on the assumption that effective counseling without diagnosis is impossible. Many student counselors tend to take diagnosis for granted without, possibly, asking enough questions as to just what diagnosis is, why it is needed, how accurate it may be, and what one does with a diagnosis once one has it. The diagnosis of some counselors assumes that the problems of the mind and the heart are the same as the problems of the physical body, even though it is rather difficult to see how those procedures that are successful in the treatment of a diseased kidney would be equally satisfactory in the treatment of fears developed in a child by insecure and frightened parents. Because the medical profession has generally taken for granted the concept that emotional disturbances are diseases, a person is frequently assumed to be a skilled practitioner in "mental health" if he possesses a medical degree, even though his psychological knowledge of personality disorders may be a good deal less than that of a student who has just been granted an undergraduate degree in psychology.

The diagnosis of a leg as inoperative because of a fracture of the tibia, caused by a sudden contact with a solid object, necessitating the setting and immobilization of the leg in a cast for several weeks may not be as complicated as the diagnosis of a pain in the belly as an inflammation of the appendix, caused by unknown factors, necessitating immediate operative procedures for its removal; but neither of these can be compared with the complexity of the diagnosis of a relatively frequent psychological problem such as that of the very intelligent boy who consistently does very poor academic work, or that of

---

[22] Donald H. Blocher, *Developmental Counseling* (New York: The Ronald Press Co., 1966), p. 130.

the overly aggressive child who insists on pushing other children around.

It can be assumed that the purpose of diagnosis is to develop such a picture that intelligent action can be taken on the basis of it. The easier it is to arrive at the picture, the more likely it is to be accurate, and the action taken to be appropriate. Thus a broken leg may be such that the diagnosis is quite simple, or it may be a complicated break requiring an equally difficult diagnosis. But in any case, the problem, the injury, the ailment is something that, we might say, "is there." The task of the medical doctor is, nearly always, to do something about a difficulty that "is there." When the medical doctor gets into the treatment of certain physical diseases, however, a diagnosis of, say, cancer, does not do much good, because no one knows yet what causes cancer, and thus no one knows the treatment for it. In the majority of physiological ailments and organic ailments, however, the cause is known; and once this happens, a remedy is speedily found.

With emotional disturbances, however, knowing the cause is often a rather minor matter, and not too much can be done, just as the dentist cannot do much for the rotting and decaying teeth of his patient that he knows were caused by foolish diet when she was a child. He can, however, remove her teeth and put in a false set, not as good as the originals, but still not too bad. Like the dentist, I knew with a high degree of certainty the causes of the fears of one of my clients, and in time she knew the causes too, but this did not remove the fears. Probably the basic point here is that the dentist could remove the decayed teeth and put others in their place, just as the medical doctor could skillfully set the broken bone and initiate procedures to speed its healing; but in both cases the patient was outside of this activity. Others were doing something to parts of his body. The counselor, however, cannot remove the fears of the client, and any diagnosis by the counselor *must assume that somewhere, sometime, the client is going to be able to make use of that diagnosis;* otherwise, why make it? Thus the psychoanalyst's interpretation to the client of his transference and his resistance is part of the therapist's diagnosis, being given, when the therapist feels that it is appropriate, to the client, so that he may make use of it for further development.

Some counselors tend to be more skeptical than others about both the virtues and the necessity for diagnosis in counseling. Many patients can vouch for the variety of ailments that they appear to have had on the basis of diagnoses by several different medical doctors who have had no contact with each other. An interesting comment on the validity of diagnosis has been made by Wittenborn:[23]

> If psychiatrists believe consistently that certain symptoms go together, the ratings which they make for their patients may reveal their belief concerning symptom-clustering. Accordingly, if syndromes are revealed among the symptoms, the possibility remains that the syndromes are more descriptive of consistencies which exist in the behavior of psychiatrists than they are descriptive of consistencies which exist in the behavior of patients.

Some counselors, too, feel that in an understanding and acceptant atmosphere the client will come to see the "why" of his behavior, and any action that is taken will be *by him* on the basis of *his diagnosis* rather than that of the counselor. But, one might say, if the counselor is a student of psychology, he must have certain diagnostic understandings, and how can he avoid being diagnostic, at least in his own mind, even though he may not verbalize his conclusions to the client? There is little doubt that every effective counselor must see an enlarging picture of the client as the counseling proceeds, although this picture may be primarily one that is being developed by the client for himself and for the counselor.

On the other hand, while the goal is to help the client to develop an accurate picture of his life and living, it is obvious that the picture that he presents to himself, and to the counselor, may be totally inaccurate. As a matter of fact, this is why he is a candidate for counseling. As Corlis and Rabe put it:[24]

> A diagnosis formulates how the patient is currently functioning. The diagnostic description contains his motivations and his customary patterns of responding.
>
> Whereas the descriptions come from the patient, the diagnosis comes obviously from the therapist. Frequently, the "presenting problem," the patient's complaint, is not the patient's real problem at all.

Nonetheless, the only real "real problem" is the problem that is perceived by the client. A clinically accurate diagnosis makes little or no sense, counseling-wise, if it is not acceptable to the client. Probably

---

[23] J. R. Wittenborn, "Symptom Patterns in a Group of Mental Hospital Patients," *Journal of Consulting Psychology* 15:290–302 (August, 1951).
[24] Rahe B. Corlis and Peter Rabe, *Psychotherapy from the Center* (Scranton, Penn.: International Textbook Co., 1969), p. 21.

the question for the counselor is: is the self-diagnosis of the client one that *he* has developed, with the counselor's help, or is it one that has been imposed upon him?

Diagnosis, in a way, implies the possibility of "pigeonholing" the client as belonging to a certain category or a certain type; and the implication that follows is that for a certain type there is a certain treatment. One of the most frequently quoted studies is one by Pepinsky in which he evolved a group of diagnostic categories describing various client ailments.[25] Pepinsky himself, however, never intended that these be actually used in counseling in a rigid manner, and he stated:[26]

> We are not arguing here for the use of diagnostic categories in reconstructing the learning of a client prior to his initial contacts in counseling. On the contrary, we believe that our present notions about relevant and irrelevant drives, and their associated stimulus and response events, furnish a more parsimonious and helpful account of client learning.

Nevertheless, categories are handy things to seize upon, and too frequently we see counselors who seem to operate on such concepts as: "John Smith—problem: lack of information"; "Mary Brown—problem: lack of assurance"; "Jim Bowie—problem: self-conflict." And indeed the poor client is often categorized long before the counseling begins. The process of counselor direction has thus begun even before the client has had a chance to express himself to the counselor. On the other hand, some counselors would say that this does not necessarily apply, and that as long as the counselor is a professional and skilled therapist he will detect an incorrect or inappropriate diagnosis, and no harm will be done to the client. But counselors are human beings, and it would be a rare counselor indeed whose personal relationship with another individual would not be affected by the fact that he had already determined in his mind that there was a problem of a certain type that could best be treated in a certain manner. At best, it would seem that the open mind becomes somewhat clouded by prior diagnosis, and that a more appropriate procedure is to take the client where he is, as he is.

---

[25] Harold B. Pepinsky, "The Selection and Use of Diagnostic Categories in Clinical Counseling," *Applied Psychology Monograph*, No. 15, 1958.
[26] Harold B. Pepinsky and Pauline N. Pepinsky, *Counseling: Theory and Practice* (New York: The Ronald Press Company, 1954), p. 114.

While Bijou[27] was referring to behavorial counseling, he could have been talking about counseling generally when he stated that "diagnostic information would be sought only if it could be shown that such data would serve to advance some specific aspect of the counseling process." Carkhuff and Berenson, however, are highly skeptical of diagnosis:[28]

> . . . we have long felt that traditional diagnostic categories are not only often intellectually repugnant but usually meaningless for purposes of dictating differential treatment. Most frequently, the diagnostic constructs are not relevant to the lives, particularly the therapeutic lives of the clients.

What happens, however, if a diagnosis is not established and the counselor starts off on the wrong foot? Knight expresses this danger when he says:[29]

> This case clearly illustrates the importance of establishing a dynamic diagnosis before embarking on treatment. If diagnosis is bypassed, as in this case, much time may be lost and treatment may not be used to best advantage. Fortunately for the patient in this case, the supervisor's request to discontinue the contact precipitated enough "distress" on the part of the patient that the therapist was encouraged to carry out more active diagnostic efforts. Had a dynamic diagnosis been sought for earlier in the course of the contact with the therapist, more time would have been available for a more thorough working through of the patient's guilt, and for a more comprehensive consolidation of therapeutic gains.

Some counselors, however, would not start off with any previous diagnostic concepts, but rather would help the client to develop these for himself as the counseling proceeded. In the above example, the reason for the inappropriate therapy, if such was the case, seems to have been that the therapist *had* established a diagnosis that was incorrect or unacceptable to the client.

In a way, the question of diagnosis brings up the earlier question of the role of the counselor as either a service individual or a re-

---

[27] Sidney W. Bijou, "Implications of Behavorial Science for Counseling and Guidance," in John D. Krumboltz (Ed.) *Revolution in Counseling* (Boston: Houghton Mifflin Co., 1966), p. 45.

[28] Robert R. Carkhuff and Bernard G. Berenson, *Beyond Counseling and Therapy* (New York: Holt, Rinehart and Winston, Inc., 1967), p. 234.

[29] Aldrich C. Knight, in Stanley W. Standal and Raymond Corsini, Jr., *Critical Incidents in Psychotherapy* (Englewood Cliffs, N.J.: Prentice-Hall, Inc., 1959), p. 148.

searcher. The latter is primarily a diagnostician. He tries to determine causes. He tries to answer the question "Why?" Although certainly no one would deny his crucial role in the study of the process of counseling and psychotherapy, one may question the capacity of the person who is primarily a diagnostician to relate in a meaningful way with a client. Students will attest to the dreadful teaching that takes place when the teacher is a researcher whose specialty is, say, the human heart, but not the means by which one relates with a group of individuals so that they can learn something about the human heart.

The "What" instead of the "Why" is stressed by Glasser:[30]

> Our usual question is *What? What* are you doing—not, *why* are you doing it? Why implies that the reasons for the patient's behavior make a difference in therapy, but they do not. The patient will himself search for reasons; but until he has become more responsible he will not be able to act differently, even when he knows why.

Some counselors are not concerned with any previous diagnosis, and they will say, "I don't want any data on the client. We'll both start together when he comes in to see me." While such an attitude may seem far-fetched and even shocking to some, I have been impressed by the number of counselors of varying hues who are advocates of diagnosis, but who disregard the diagnosis of others regarding a client, and operate on the basis of their own diagnosis after they have seen him.

The individuality of counselors, and their disagreement even among themselves with regard to professional questions, is shown in a most interesting fashion by the reactions of fifteen therapists to the question, "Do you make a diagnosis before therapy begins?" Typical of the atypicalness of the reactions are those quoted below. Ackerman writes:[31]

> My answer to this question is emphatically in the affirmative. I consider it of the utmost importance to achieve a clear diagnostic definition of the patient's disorder before making any final commitment about accepting a patient for treatment. This does not mean, however, that the diagnostic study is pursued in any routine or ritualized manner. It is not a question and answer interview. The interview itself is a dynamic, open-ended process. Its flow is determined by the perception of significant cues as to foci of pathogenic conflict and anxiety. The early interview contact, while primarily diagnostic, is simultaneously oriented to the patient's therapeutic needs. Nevertheless, a final

---

30 William Glasser, *Reality Therapy* (New York: Harper and Row, 1965), p. 32.
31 Nathan W. Ackerman, in Arthur Burton, *op. cit.*, p. 70.

decision as to the acceptance of a particular patient for treatment rests on a clear picture of the patient's disorder. In order to apply therapy in a psychologically specific manner, one must know exactly what is wrong with the patient. The diagnostic study includes clinical psychiatrist evaluation and, wherever other examinational procedures may be indicated, psychological studies, a home visit, a medical examination, and so forth.

Szasz comments as follows: [32]

> I cannot answer this question without commenting on the word "diagnosis," which I consider to be seriously misleading if used in connection with psychotherapeutic considerations. In other words, if "diagnosis" refers to ascertaining the kind of "psychiatric disease"— such as hysteria, obsessive-compulsive neurosis, schizophrenia, and so forth—the patient "has"—then my answer would be that *I do not make a "diagnosis"* before beginning psychotherapy. If, however, "diagnosis" refers to gaining an impression of the sort of person the patient is, how he grew up, the nature of his personal relationships and his work, the degree of his freedom in the conduct of his life, and so on . . . then I would answer emphatically "Yes. *I do make a diagnosis.*"

Jacobi says: [33]

> I never venture a diagnosis before working with the patient for a certain time. Even if the patient brings with him a diagnosis formulated by another analyst, I question it and wait until it is proven correct by the passage of time. If a case reveals characteristic symptoms, it can, of course, happen that I cannot avoid a diagnosis; but I always look upon it as a hypothesis as long as I am not completely certain.

Arthur Burton's own answer is: [34]

> I do not give much credence to formal diagnosis before psychotherapy begins. This does not mean that I do not consider the diagnosis at all. I believe every psychotherapist mulls this over in the course of psychotherapy and revises his formulation as he goes along. Formal diagnosis, as, for example, psychiatric hospital diagnosis, catches the patient at a cross-sectional period which may be not at all representative of his psyche and his functioning. These formulations then tend to become solidified and interfere with psychotherapy because of implications of a poor prognosis. The history of long-term psychoanalysis or psycho-

[32] *Ibid.*, p. 107.
[33] *Ibid.*, p. 139.
[34] *Ibid.*, p. 279.

therapy is that the patient may experience phobic, schizoid, obsessive, depressed, paranoid, manic, compulsive and similar manifestations at one or another stage in the course of treatment, and of course has alternating psychotic and neurotic phases, however mild. I tend to agree with Whitaker and his school that, in treating schizophrenics at any rate, we more properly speak of a transference psychosis rather than a transference neurosis. Formal diagnosis seems at times to be somewhat a function of the training, psychiatric milieu, and unconscious needs of the one making the diagnosis rather than something indigenous to the life history of the patient. In the case presented here a diagnosis of psychoneurosis, character disorder and schizophrenia could have been made at several cross-sectional points in her illness career. All of these were correct and all were incorrect if interpreted as intellectual abstractions of some hypothetically median patient.

And John Shlien's:[35]

No. Diagnostic techniques are not sufficiently valid, for one thing. Also, they do not help; if anything, they have an adverse influence on the relationship, since they tend to categorize the client in the counselor's eyes, and give the counselor an intimidating and unwarranted "expert" status (he should be an expert, in fact, but not on that basis), and in general focus attention on artificial and impersonal issues. Finally, there is no specific treatment to be applied, so of what use would specific diagnosis be if it were accomplished? Psychotherapy is not medicine. Human misery is not an organic disease.

To clarify, diagnosis as discussed here does not mean the *judgment* exercised by the counselor at almost every step. Neither is it *prognosis,* which assesses the constructive resources and estimates the probability of achieving health. Diagnosis is the classic psychiatric classification and description which is static, and focused wholly on pathology. Therapy, in contradistinction, has a fluid tone, and anticipates change. It will encounter the pathology ("what is wrong") but can rely only on "what is right" with the organism.

We do indeed use measures of change in therapy, but these are for research to discover the facts about change in groups of clients, and these measures are not yet so keen as to be satisfactory for that purpose, much less for individual diagnosis.

Some of the more analytically oriented counselors feel that diagnosis is essential, and that our current major problem is the inaccuracy of diagnosis. They would probably agree with Mahan when he says:[36]

---

[35] *Ibid.,* p. 349.
[36] Thomas W. Mahan, Jr., "Diagnostic Consistency and Prediction: A Note on Graduate Student Skills," *Personnel and Guidance Journal* 42:364–367 (December, 1963).

But the most striking result is the confirmation once again of the difficulty of predicting overt behavior from psychological test data. Prediction unfortunately does not follow directly from diagnosis; the "over-determination" of human behavior makes extremely hazardous the effort to isolate variables when it is the interaction of variables that is paramount. Perhaps the time has come when the training programs in school psychological services must integrate into their emphasis on individual understanding the psychological study of social situations, roles, institutional pressures, and . . . "treatments."

The answer to more accurate and empirical diagnosis, of course, is the replacement of the human being by the machine, and if diagnosis is seen as the primary function of the counselor, there would seem to be no good reason why he should not also be replaced by the machine. Meehl and Dahlstrom describe the problem of using the "too human" clinician in diagnosis:[37]

> While it would not be too surprising to find that the "clinical eye" has trained itself to recognize configurations not readily identified by conventional linear methods of statistical analysis, it might be presumed that the clinician's subjective judgment, however experienced, assigns less than optimal weights. In addition to this systematic bias, the human judge throws in some more or less random error variance due to his unreliability.

There is plenty of evidence to indicate that the electronic digital computer can carry out complex processes that are much the same as processes that may be observed in human beings who are thinking. Kleinmuntz,[38] for example, has demonstrated how the tape-recorded verbalizations of an MMPI profile analyst could be approximated by programmed instructions. It is likely that an increasing number of functions that have been considered to be part of the professional responsibility of the counselor may be taken over by the machine. Robinson,[39] for example, would almost seem to be describing a day that will soon be past when he says, "A counselor attempting to analyze a client's characteristics so as to have a basis for selecting the most relevant counseling methods needs to use at least four 'diag-

---

[37] P. E. Meehl and W. G. Dahlstrom, "Objective Configural Rules for Discriminating Psychotic from Neurotic MMPI Profiles," *Journal of Consulting Psychology* 24:375–387 (October, 1960).

[38] Benjamin Kleinmuntz, "Profile Analysis Revisited: A Heuristic Approach," *Journal of Counseling Psychology* 10:315–324 (Winter, 1963).

[39] Francis P. Robinson, "Modern Approaches to Counseling 'Diagnosis,'" *Journal of Counseling Psychology* 10:325–333 (Winter, 1963).

nostic' approaches." This is exactly what the machine will be likely to do more effectively, and this may all be to the good. The hard fact is that if a machine can do better what a certain counselor is doing, then the machine should take over. But the machine cannot establish the human relationship that is the crucial factor in counseling, and it may be that the client of the future will come to the counselor with his machine-established diagnosis and prognosis in hand. The most logical rational choice may have been presented to him by the machine, but, as a somewhat irrational human being, he will still want to see the counselor to talk about what he should do with this logical rational choice that has been handed to him!

ECLECTICISM

Some differences still exist among counselors as to the place of "eclecticism" in counseling, although, like other terms, much depends on just how one interprets it. It is interesting to note too that eclecticism is much less of an issue in current books and articles than it was in the past, and this may be some indication that counseling is outgrowing its "technique" stage. It has not outgrown it yet, however, and it is for this reason that eclecticism is still included in this book as an issue. If one thinks of the counseling process as consisting of a series of techniques, isolated from the personality of the counselor, to be used according to the client and the type of problem that he presents, then one can readily see how the counselor can be eclectic in his approach. He is eclectic in that he uses those techniques and methods that seem most appropriate for a certain client at a certain time. If, on the other hand, what are called methodologies are actually qualities of the individual counselor, it is difficult to see how the counselor could be eclectic. The counselor's sense of values, the counselor's deep feelings regarding the worth of the client, the counselor's feelings regarding his capacity and moral right to measure and evaluate, the counselor's feelings toward his basic function as a counselor—these are part of the counselor's self, and there must, surely, be a consistency of counselor self. The lack of support by some counselors for the practice of eclecticism in counseling arises basically because they equate it with counselor self-inconsistency.

This was probably part of the thinking of Rogers over two

decades ago when he challenged the generally accepted concept of eclecticism:[40]

> These schools of thought will not be abolished by wishful thinking. The person who attempts to reconcile them by compromise will find himself left with a superficial eclecticism which does not increase objectivity, and leads nowhere. Truth is not arrived at by concessions from different schools of thought.

If one is to think of eclecticism in terms of superficial techniques, then every counselor must, surely, be eclectic. If the counselor who asks a question sometimes instead of never asking a question, if the counselor who sometimes gives information instead of never giving information, if the counselor who sometimes gives direction instead of never giving direction is thereby eclectic, then it is difficult to see how any counselor could possibly avoid being eclectic.

Perry and Estes have discussed this issue in an interesting manner:[41]

> Somehow recent professional literature gives the impression that if a therapist is to follow a school, be it psychoanalytic or non-directive, he must faithfully apply the same procedure to all comers, assuming his theory to be all-embracing. If he is to be an eclectic, it seems that he must apply the "appropriate" procedures to all comers, perhaps assuming *himself* to be all-embracing. Members of a school, it is true, can pretend to a certain humility, because it is to a theory, not to themselves, that omnipotence is attributable. To be an eclectic, on the other hand, apparently requires utter insouciance; as one put it, in print: "The therapist must be all things to all men;" and another: "We have no hesitancy in shifting from one approach to another if the first does not produce the mutually desired results. . . ."
>
> It is our notion, on the other hand, that a clinician's proper task is to construct a small-scale system as a rationale for what he sees. At the present state of knowledge it has seemed to us that the clinician does well to make use of various concepts, principles, and laws, however unrelated they have claimed to be, provided only that he make a reasonable coherent synthesis. But if his rationale is to be clinically useful, he should neither claim it to be applicable to all clients nor limit it as uniquely "appropriate" to an individual. It is his responsibility to do thinking which is to a degree *ad hoc,* but the *hoc* must be

---

[40] Carl R. Rogers, *Client-Centered Therapy* (Boston: Houghton Mifflin Company, 1951), p. 8.

[41] William G. Perry, Jr. and Stanley G. Estes, "The Collaboration of Client and Counselor," in O. Hobart Mowrer (Ed.), *Psychotherapy: Theory and Research* (New York: The Ronald Press Company, 1953), p. 118.

general enough to include a range of cases and also specific enough to provide coherent data; it must offer a mean between the normative and the idiosyncratic. . . .

One can hardly disagree with these delightful words, and Perry himself would be one of the first to agree that the counselor cannot be eclectic in his display of self, unless he is exhibiting a remarkable degree of self-inconsistency.

Williamson gives what would generally be considered a good description of eclecticism in counseling when he writes:[42]

> Counseling . . . may be thought of as embracing a wide variety of techniques, from which repertoire the effective counselor selects . . . those which are relevant and appropriate to the nature of the client's problem and to other features of the situation. . . . Each technique is applicable only to particular problems and particular students. . . . Rather, the counselor adapts his specific techniques to the individuality and problem pattern of the student, making the necessary modifications to produce the desired result for a particular student.

McKinney sees no clash in the counselor's being eclectic in that he uses various methods. He describes the counselor in this way:[43]

> In view of the client's maturity and emotional balance he may be directive or non-directive. He may try to prevent certain conditions from arising, or he may correct an existing condition. He may put an emphasis on immediate relief or palliation, or direct his attention to a long term attempt at enabling the individual to achieve a reorganization of his personality. He may, on the other hand, see that the client requires treatment that is beyond his training and may seek consultation or make a referral to some specialist.

Thorne has written a chapter that he entitles "Directive and Eclectic Personality Counseling," implying that there is an eclectic "method."[44] But in the first paragraph of the chapter he writes ". . . to make a definitive statement concerning the eclectic orientation that is basic for the proposed system of practice. . . ." There is a vast difference, however, between an eclectic *orientation*, which surely every professional counselor should have, and without which there will

---

[42] E. G. Williamson, *Counseling Adolescents* (New York: McGraw-Hill Book Co., Inc., 1950), pp. 219–220.

[43] McKinney, *op. cit.*, p. 32.

[44] Frederick Thorne, "Directive and Eclectic Personality Counseling," in James L. McCrary and Daniel E. Sheer (Eds.), *Six Approaches to Psychotherapy* (New York: The Dryden Press, 1955), p. 235.

be provincialism or even downright ignorance of counseling, and an eclectic *method* of counseling.

Thus Marzolf states that:[45]

> . . . the eclectic in counseling is one who is willing to utilize any procedure which holds promise even though their theoretical bases differ markedly. . . . In contrast with the eclectic, the doctrinaire counselor resists all temptation to use any procedure, which, in his view at least, is incompatible with his theory. To do so would be intellectually disconcerting. . . .

One could certainly agree with Marzolf that any counselor who operated on the basis of allegiance to a theory, *per se,* would be worse than doctrinaire—he would be plain stupid. On the other hand, the consistency of a counselor may be the consistency of a basic personal approach to a human relationship.

Eclecticism in the professional educational and development of the counselor is essential, since without it the counselor can hardly arrive at any learned conclusions based on a great variety of evidence. Without such breadth we have the unhappy situation where Christians assume that religion means only Christianity, capitalists that democracy means only capitalism, Americans that good living means only America, and counselors that counseling means only Freudian, or client-centered, or psychoanalytic, or Adlerian. These are the individuals who, when they go to heaven, will have to live in restricted areas, surrounded by high walls, so that they may continue to live under the illusion that they are the only people there!

Although eclecticism may appeal to the student counselor as the democratic and broad-minded approach to counseling, if we are to speak of it as an actual method of counseling, then there are several serious questions as to its efficacy:

1. It carries with it the implication that counseling is a somewhat superficial bag-of-tricks technique. The counselor, as the technician who pulls out the appropriate treatment for the particular problem or individual, thus becomes one whose professional preparation should be a *training* rather than an *education.*

2. The view assumes too, generally without evidence, that there are certain techniques and procedures that for a certain individual in a certain situation are more effective and better than others. If anything, the evidence, some of which has been referred to earlier, points the

---

[45] Stanley S. Marzolf, *Psychological Diagnosis and Counseling in Schools* (New York: Henry Holt & Co., 1956), pp. 327–328.

other way. There certainly is serious question whether or not a student counselor should learn that this particular technique is the right thing to do, under these circumstances, with this client. Because clients are not inanimate objects, or even organs, they have a habit of contradicting the counselor who has arrived at a set concept of just what to do at a certain time with a certain type of person.

3. It would not, surely, be doctinaire to say that an individual must arrive at some degree of consistency with himself if he is to be honest and sincere, and thereby at least have some hope of being successful in working with other individuals. If the counselor, for example, cannot completely accept a client's attacks on the counselor's religion, then in the long run he might be better off to be honest with the client and admit that this does irritate him, rather than trying to pretend that he is acceptant and understanding about something to which he is actually reacting in an emotional manner. The client, too, is going to find it difficult to relate, and to get close to an individual who appears to fluctuate and change. Probably everyone can think of some people he has known who have posed a difficulty for him; although they have been nice and pleasant, he could never feel that this was the real person speaking. The real person was never revealed, most likely because the individual could not bear to reveal the real person to himself. Teachers, too, who know the frustration and difficulty children have with authoritarian parents, know the even more difficult time the children have if their parents lack even consistency in a vice. It is easier for a child to understand, and react to, and defend himself from a brutal father, than it is to react to a father who beats his child one day, then the next day cries and gives him a dollar to make up for his miserable behavior the day before.

Eclecticism, too, gives the counselor an easy avenue of escape at all times. It is much easier for the counselor to say to himself, "I am breaking this long silence because the client seems to be blocked, and I will use a new approach . . . ," than it is for him to say, "Why am I feeling pressured to break this client silence? What is it that makes me uneasy? Am I really acceptant of this client's right to be silent, or am I breaking the silence because it is beginning to threaten me?" It is easier for the counselor to say to himself, "I have answered the client's plea for support and help by telling him that he will be all right, because this is a technique that is sometimes useful," than it is for him to say, "I have answered the client's plea for help in this way because this sort of response reassures me, although it may be worse in the long run for the client." When the client says, "Okay, so maybe I am biased, maybe I am just white trash, but damn it, don't you think that evidence shows that Negroes in the South do know less than the whites?" the counselor may find it easier to say to himself, "Well, the reason I agreed that there might be one or two studies that implied this was so was because I felt that I needed to use a technique of agreement to give him some support . . . ," than to say, "The reason I made this statement was that I share his bias. . . ."

These examples could obviously be multiplied many times. If the counselor has arrived at some level of consistency of operation, then he must give himself a close scrutiny when he departs from it, and attempt to determine the why of his departure. When he has no consistency, there is little or no need for a check on himself, since he has accepted the concept that he does what he does for professional reasons only.

Thus in the long run, it would seem that the effective counselor is one who has worked out for himself, through the experience of experimentation, the means by which he can most effectively use himself in a human interaction known as counseling. His orientation has been eclectic, rather than parochial, and while his own life is in a constant state of movement and change, he has learned that there are certain modes of operation which are most effective for him, thus there is a degree of consistency in his operation as a counselor. While he is open to consider any means that will work with the client, he is aware that his own human limitations are such that he cannot be all things for all people. He is acceptant of the thought that there is no model, no method, no technique which will be consistently successful for him with any other human individual who may come to him as a client.

COUNSELOR DIRECTION AND COUNSELOR CONTROL

Traditionally, counselor direction and counselor control over the client was pretty much taken for granted, and both the medical model and the educational model generally reflected a "we know what's best for you philosophy." Both the student and the patient have generally been considered as individuals to whom something is done by somebody who knows more about it than they do.

Notes that were used some ten years ago in teaching residents and fellows in psychiatry in a Boston hospital are still probably fairly typical:[46]

---

[46] Unpublished material.

The course of the therapy, and the management, is directed and controlled by the doctor. The direction is determined by an appraisal of the patient's material, but once a working hypothesis in this respect is elaborated, the doctor follows this direction until the matieral is exhausted or until the doctor is blocked.

In the same material, under the heading of suggested procedures for using minimal activity (sic), we note the following:

(1) Begin by a general question which cannot be answered by yes or no. Avoid leading questions. Avoid questions which suggest the answer. Use such questions as, "How are things going?" "How do you feel?" "What's been happening?" "What are you thinking about?" "What's going on in your head?"

(2) When the patient begins to talk, don't interrupt: allow him to go on. If he hesitates or stops talking, pause for a few seconds or longer and give him a chance to continue. If the silence continues, introduce another general, non-leading question as mentioned above.

(3) If the patient talks about topics which do not further your goal, allow him to continue for several minutes, while waiting for him to bring up the topic in which you are interested. If he persists in talking about irrelevant topics, show no interest in the material, take no leads, ask no questions. If necessary introduce another general question.

(4) As soon as the patient mentions a word or topic that you want to hear more about, hold him by one or more of the following devices in the order presented. Proceed to the use of more active techniques (d,e,f,g,h) if simpler techniques (a,b,c) do not succeed. You are trying to indicate "Go ahead, we're interested."

  (a) Non-verbal activity on the part of the doctor: look up, show interest by postural change, facial expression, nodding gestures. If a glance will do, say nothing.

  (b) Use sounds, conversational grunts, syllables, and ejaculations such as *ah, uh uh, hmm, so, well, really, but, and.* If a simple syllable will do, say no more. Reinforce the inflection with an encouraging look; let your voice carry along. Avoid an air of finality.

  (c) If the patient stops or heads away from the significant topic, repeat the patient's last word or phrase bearing on the topic. Say it with a rising inflection as though you were asking a question: "Upset?" "Blue?" "Your heart?"

  (d) If this fails, elaborate this last word or phrase with an incomplete statement: "you said . . ."; "you said you were . . ."; "you mentioned pain. . . ."

  (e) If a patient persists in avoiding a topic, ask a *general* question about this topic which cannot be answered by a simple yes or no. If a general question suffices, do not make it specific. "What did you say about your headache?" "What do you mean?" "What did you mean by nervous?"

(f) In some cases, if these indirect procedures fail, you may have to resort to a direct question aimed at the pertinent topic, such as, "In what part of your head do you feel pain?" "What was the feeling in the dream?"

(g) If the patient shows overwhelming affect, you may drop the topic for the time being, and introduce another non-leading question as under (1) above, keeping alert for the charged topic later in the same interview or in a subsequent interview.

These suggestions, it may be noted, are exactly the same sort of suggestions that would be given to the medical doctor who is being told how to treat a damaged kidney. There is no question here about who is in control, and any "nondirectiveness," as indicated above, is quite obviously a technique or method being deliberately used by the therapist to get the patient where he wants him to be. The patient here would appear to be very much the same patient who lies in the bed, passively waiting for the doctors to do with him what they will.

The typical psychiatric interview usually reinforces the patient's original feeling that the doctor is the one who is in control, and that he is the one who will determine what is to happen in the future.

In discussing such an interview, Fromm-Reichmann states:[47]

> The first interview should begin with the patient being asked about his complaints, and about the nature of his problems and his suffering, which made him or his relatives and friends decide to have the patient ask for the advice of a psychiatrist. Coupled with this, the acute distress which has precipitated the patient's decision to see a psychiatrist should be investigated. After that, the psychiatrist wishes to clarify, as early as possible in his contact with his prospective patient, whether the patient has come on his own volition, whether he has been advised to come by friends or relatives, or whether he has been prodded into doing so against his own wishes.

Let us note the first few minutes of two such psychiatric interviews (Co indicates the therapist):[48]

---

[47] Frieda Fromm-Reichmann, *Principles of Intensive Psychotherapy* (Chicago: The University of Chicago Press, 1950), p. 45.

[48] These excerpts are taken from two records, "The Initial Interview in Psychiatry Practice," Yale University, Department of Psychiatry (New York: International Universities Press, Inc., 1954).

Interview 1

Co.: Will you sit there. What brings you here?

Cl.: Everything's wrong, I guess. Irritable, tense, depressed. Just, just everything and everybody gets on my nerves.

Co.: Yeah.

Cl.: I don't feel like talking right now.

Co.: You don't? Do you sometimes?

Cl.: That's the trouble. I get too wound up. If I get started, I'm all right.

Co.: Yeah? Well, perhaps you will.

Cl.: May I smoke?

Co.: Sure. What do you do?

Cl.: I'm a nurse, but my husband won't let me work.

Co.: How old are you?

Cl.: Thirty-one this December.

Co.: What do you mean, he won't let you work?

Cl.: Well, for instance I, ah, I'm supposed to do some relief duty two weeks, this month, next month, September, and he makes it so miserable for me that I'm in a constant stew. And he says that my place is home with the children. I agree, but I wa . . . I need a rest. I need to get away from them. I need to be with, oh with people. I can't stay closeted up in the house all the time.

Co.: How many kids are there?

Cl.: Two.

Co.: How old are they?

Cl.: Three, five months.

Co.: Mmm.

Cl.: Oh, it isn't only that. It's a million things.

Co.: Tell me some of them.

Cl.: Well to begin with, there are a lot of things I didn't know about him before we got married that I should have known—at least I feel I should have.

Co.: You've been married about four or five years?

Cl.: Four years.

Co.: Mmm.

Cl.: In November. And, I think he's a chronic alcoholic. He drinks every day, and he just can't seem to let the stuff alone. He says he can, but he can't. He never has been able to except, the one time the doctor had him on a diet. And then he ate candy bars. Candy bars, I suppose he had to have sugar. But it's just, I feel that it's, it's, either going to ruin me or the kids or all of us. It . . .

Co.: What does he do?

Cl.: He's a truck driver.

Co.: One of these long-distance hauls or what?

CI.: No. He used to do it. He doesn't now. They just do, ah, hauling within the state. And about, mm, five or six months ago he went on trailers. Well, I know it's hard, but he comes home and he starts taking it out on all of us. He starts nagging the minute he gets in the house.

Co.: Is he away a good deal?

Cl.: He eats and he sleeps in the house, and that's all there is to it. And it's an insult to me naturally.

Co.: Mmm.

Cl.: Once in a while he's decent. I keep thinking of divorce, but that's another emotional death. And I don't want to do it with the kids right now. They're too young.

Co.: Divorce is an emotional death?

Cl.: I think so.

Interview 2

Co.: Please sit down. You just came down here?

Cl.: Yes.

Co.: From the hospital?

Cl.: Yes.

Co.: Ah, when did you—

Cl.: Oh, I went there about two weeks ago.

Co.: Oh, two weeks ago.

Cl.: Yes.

Co.: Yeah, and, ah, do you know what the reason is you've come down here?

Cl.: No, I don't.

Co.: Mmm. Well, I've been asked to see you to help the doctors with—

Cl.: My case. That is . . .

Co.: That's right. Yes. Why, ah, what happened that you went to—?

Cl.: Oh, I, I was very nervous and I didn't seem to have the desire to go anyplace. And I'd argue with my mother, and there wasn't any reason to argue with her because, ah, I don't know. Ah, I'd wake up and find my head being smashed in and everything.

Co.: Your head, ah, being—

Cl.: I was being molested at home. And I thought perhaps if I went some place else, I would at least be safe.

Co.: Mmm. Molested? How is that?

Cl.: In every way. In, in, ah, I don't know—kicking my face in and everything.

Co.: Tell me about that.

Cl.: Well, I can't tell you too much. I feel very ridiculous speaking about it, a little bit ashamed, I guess. But, ah, I don't know and I'd be asleep all through it. And then, as the day progressed, I'd remember that I was. And I'd actually feel the bangs and everything in my sleep. And, ah, I find it so all the time with me. And I don't know how to explain it or why.

Co.: Not . . . not—

Cl.: And I'm sure there's a reason. I'm sure those people know me. And . . . ah . . . they seem familiar in a sense, but I can't replace them.

Co.: The ones . . . the ones—

Cl.: That are molesting.

Co.: Who molest you?

Cl.: Yes.

Co.: Mmm.

Cl.: And my memory, I don't believe it lies what little is there. And, ah, there seems to be a reason for it, but, ah, I can't remember enough as I talk to tell you. I mean, it's, it's more like stupidity and ignorance on their part. That's all—the impression I get.

Co.: They do it because they're stupid, ah, not, they have no particular reason?

Cl.: Well, it's theirs, no. I, I, I, it's their own, ah, ideas, I suppose. I don't know how to explain it to you. I mean it just isn't fair. I mean I haven't done anything to deserve them.

Co.: It's sort of unfair . . .

Cl.: And anyway, I mean, even if you are guilty.

Co.: Sure.

Cl.: Of something, I don't know, ah.

Co.: You sometimes think you might be guilty of something?

Cl.: No, I don't think I'm guilty of anything. No, I wouldn't even lie if I were. I mean, I mean if you are, you seem to deserve it, and it doesn't hurt you half as much.

Co.: But so, you are innocent, and yet you get all this punishment.

Cl.: Yes, I do. Whatever the reason is, I don't know.

Co.: That's quite real—these—

Cl.: Yes.

The concept of doctor control over patient in the clinical situation differs very little from the concept of teacher control over student in the school situation. Just as the domination of the medical doctor over the patient had been pretty well accepted in psychotherapy, and still is, so the domination of the authority figure in the school, the teacher, and, too often, the counselor, over the child is taken for granted. The variation in therapist domination and control in the preceding clinical examples is no different from the variation in counselor (Co) control in the following school examples:[49]

Co.: (pause) You've been working for your father for some time, is that right?

Cl.: Mm-huh.

Co.: How do you like working on the farm?

Cl.: Pretty well.

Co.: Do you . . . (pause) . . . Are you planning to work with your father this coming summer?

Cl.: Yes, if I don't continue school.

Co.: There is a possibility that you might stay in school this summer?

Cl.: Yes, sir. (pause)

Co.: Well, can you tell me a little bit more about your background? Tell me something about your home life.

[49] Robert Callis, Paul C. Polmantier and Edward C. Roeber, *A Casebook of Counseling* (New York: Appleton-Century-Crofts, 1955), p. 121, dialogue entries C17–C25.

You've lived with your parents until you came down here, is that right?

Cl.: Yes, sir, besides the two years I put in the service.

Co.: Mm-huh.

Cl.: Of course, my mother—ah—deceased here a year ago.

Co.: . . . (pause) . . . Was that somewhat unexpected?

Cl.: Well, not too much.

Co.: . . . (pause) . . . How would you describe your mother? . . . (pause) . . . What was she like? (pause).

Cl.: Well, she liked farming and she liked associations— one thing and another.

Co.: Did she have many church activities?

And another counselor with thirteen-year-old Beth (Cl):[50]

Co.: Tell me more about you. Where did you come from today?

Cl.: Um. . . . You mean from home?

Co.: Well, did you have time to go home before you came today?

Cl.: Yes.

Co.: Oh. What time do you come home from school usually?

Cl.: Well, I got out about three o'clock.

Co.: Oh, I see. That's just about a regular hour. Are you on a nine-to-three session?

Cl.: Yes.

Co.: Oh. And what school do you attend?

Cl.: Umm. . . . Nathaniel Hawthorne.

Co.: Oh. And does it have a number? Is it a junior high?

Cl.: Yes, it's 196. Junior High School 196.

Co.: Oh, I see. What grade are you in at the junior high?

Cl.: Ninth.

Co.: The ninth grade. Were you there in the seventh and eighth?

Cl.: Yes.

Co.: Oh, I see. So you really know your way around in that place by now. You are an experienced ninth grader, aren't you?

Cl.: (Laughs) Yes.

Co.: Oh. Well, I was just wondering had you always lived

---

[50] Buchheimer and Balogh, *op. cit.*, pp. 192–193, dialogue entries Cl–C12.

there in that neighborhood, that you know many people there, too?

Cl.: Yes, I lived there ever since I was born.

Co.: Oh, really? That's just fine. That's your home town to you.

Cl.: M-hm. . . .

Co.: How are you doing in the ninth grade?

And another counselor with Jane, a high school student (Cl):[51]

Co.: You feel you'll take it to a point, and then. . . .

Cl.: Mm-hmm. Like those clothes. I know even Betty, my best girl friend now, says that, yeah, she's looking forward to college and the few weeks before, because her mother's going to want to go out and buy her clothes, too, and she would rather just skip it.

Co.: So your friend has the same problems about clothes, and her mother wanting to buy, as you do.

Cl.: Yeah, although she says that she likes her mother's taste, and she usually likes the things her mother gets her, but she doesn't like the bother of going out either. I don't like to buy a whole bunch of clothes at once because I—like when I bought this, I fell in love with it, and so I bought it, but I'd rather. . . . I like to buy underwear too. Why I don't know. Then there's no choice. You just buy some and wear it, but going out and looking for something when I have no idea what I want is too frustrating. I'd rather not do it. I don't like to be in crowds either, elbowing through Hudson's, anything like that.

Co.: You find it pretty uncomfortable, going through big crowds when there seems to be no point. You're not certain what you want. You'd rather wait when you have a specific object in mind, and then go and pick it out.

Cl.: I suppose quite a few people feel like that. I'm not alone.

Co.: You feel other people feel this way too.

[51] William Evraiff, *Helping Counselors Grow Professionally* (Englewood Cliffs, N.J.: Prentice-Hall, Inc., 1963), pp. 117–118, dialogue entries C120–C128.

Cl.: Sure, some must. But then there's my mother. She feels that I've got to go out and get those clothes. I'll go with her.

Co.: You'll go to satisfy her.

And finally, this school counselor (Co) with an adolescent girl:[52]

Co.: Have a seat. How are things going?

Cl.: Well, they're better than they were before, I've started thinking sort of positive, instead of thinking I couldn't do things. I've started thinking that I *could* do them, and it's worked. In math I got a D last time but I said I was going to fix it, that I was going to do better, and I did it.

Co.: I decided to improve myself and make up my mind that I could do a lot better than I have.

Cl.: And it's happening in other subjects too. Like in tests —I don't know—it just seems all of a sudden I'm starting to think I can do it. Like in science—you take notes and everything, and I didn't think I was going to do well at first because there was going to be a hard test, but I studied for it, and I said I was going to pass it, and I did, and got an A.

Co.: I used to look down on myself, but now I don't look down on myself. I just think more positively and things begin to happen and things seem to improve.

Cl.: And even at home, I find that I know more things, and I can talk about more things, and it's much better. And I'm more confident in myself, too, and the teachers have noticed it. All of a sudden something hits you, and you suddenly come out of the dark.

Co.: Suddenly you become, in a way, a new person.

One may contrast these last two examples with the counselor domination and control expressed in these words:[53]

---

[52] Angelo V. Boy and Gerald J. Pine, *Client-Centered Counseling in the Secondary School* (Boston: Houghton Mifflin Company, 1963), pp. 172–173.
[53] Albert Ellis, "Rationalism and Its Therapeutic Implications," *Annals of Psychotherapy* 1:55–64 (September, 1959).

In the course of rational psychotherapy, the patient is not merely shown that he has such irrational ideas as these, but the therapist persistently keeps attacking, undermining, and annihilating these idiocies. Even more to the point: the therapist teaches the patient how to observe, infer, and ferret out his own illogical thinking; how to trace this thinking back to its main ideological sources; and how to question, challenge, and uproot these asinine ideologies and to replace them with realistic, flexible, more effective beliefs.

. . . the therapist often actively and unequivocally forces, persuades, cajoles, or practically pushes the patient into various kinds of actions which, in many instances, serve as the very best kind of counter-propagandizing influences.

In the following excerpts from the tape *Loretta,* already mentioned, there seems more counselor direction on the part of therapists Ellis and Felder than is the case with Rogers.

Ellis (Co).

> Co.: This group of visiting psychologists and psychiatrists from . . . have been having a workshop here, and we are seeing a few of the people like you at this hospital to see if we can understand a little about the problems and perhaps help you somewhat with them, even though we're just going to see you. I'm just going to be talking with you for this hour or so and not any longer. Now do you mind telling me what it is that bothers you most?
>
> Cl.: Well, it doesn't bother me but it does seem to bother everyone else and that is that I talk too much.
>
> Co.: All right—now what is it that bothers other people— that you talk too much?
>
> Cl.: That's what I understand.
>
> Co.: And it doesn't bother you?
>
> Cl.: Not particularly.
>
> Co.: And why do you think they may be bothered by it?
>
> Cl.: It might be the way I talk.
>
> Co.: The way you talk? What way would that be?
>
> Cl.: I seem to have a way of aggravating the situation.
>
> Co.: Yeah. Could you be a little more specific? Do you know how you aggravate the situation?
>
> Cl.: Well, I apparently—when things get a little too rough

and they want to drop the subject right away, and I'm not quite ready to do that—I like to talk them out.

Co.: Ah—can you remember a recent incident—such as one that might have happened today—where the situation had a . . . ?

Cl.: Nothing happened today.

Co.: Well, yesterday, or the day before—recent, actual incidents where somebody got upset because you presumably aggravated the situation.

Cl.: Well, I can think of one that had to do with meetings.

Co.: All right—fine.

Cl.: I can't think of . . .

Co.: All right. I'm sure that one will come to you as we talk. But anyway, you are not disturbed by this normally, but other people are. Now, are you disturbed when they get upset?

Cl.: It bothers me when they become upset.

Co.: Now why does it bother you when they become upset? Over what?

Cl.: I don't know. I think it's natural being bothered by having people being disturbed and not understanding why they're disturbed. I mean, I can see why they might object, but I don't see why they don't want me to talk the whole thing out and find out why they're disturbed because I'm upset.

Co.: Well, if I'm hearing you correctly you're sort of saying that—ah—that you are not objecting to their getting upset, but you at least would like them to talk it out with you.

Cl.: Yes, I would like to know what it is that disturbs them.

Co.: Then if you did know it, do you think that you'd be able to change your behavior—change their behavior—or what?

Cl.: I don't know.

Co.: But you think it would be helpful at least to know the answers?

Felder (Co).

Co.: Do you want to sit over here? Did you know we were going to see you again today?

Cl.: No, I just thought it was going to be one doctor.

Co.: Do you want him back?

Cl.: Why, I don't care; it's immaterial to me.

Co.: O.K. Ah, you knew you were coming back today, but you thought it would be the same doctor?

Cl.: I thought it was just going to be one doctor.

Co.: Just one time—yesterday.

Cl.: I didn't know about today, no; I mean I knew I was going to talk to a doctor, but I didn't know the whole group would be there.

Co.: Well, I was in the group yesterday.

Cl.: I didn't have a chance to notice everyone.

Co.: And I wanted to start today by telling you my feelings about yesterday. Ah, I came away from it with a headache.

Cl.: I had a headache today, so I think—I tried to read a book and I couldn't.

Co.: And I had two, two main feelings about yesterday. Ah, one of them is a little bit complicated. I felt you entertained us and we enjoyed it, but that, that it was kind of a dirty trick on you, for us to enjoy your entertaining us.

Cl.: I'm glad you were entertained.

Co.: The second feeling I had, and I would like to find some more about that today, is that you have been helped some place along the line.

Cl.: I don't know. I had shock treatment. I know I have had insulin, some insulin, and deep insulin.

Co.: I don't mean help in that kind of way. I meant, I had the feeling you were helped by some person, rather than some, something artificial.

Cl.: I don't know.

Co.: Ah, then there is something else I wanted to tell you. After they told me they wanted me to talk to you today, as I was going to sleep last night, I thought about you, and—ah—I was sort of half asleep. This was half a dream—when you're half asleep and half awake —ah, you and I were there in this place wherever it was, and I was offering you a mushroom.

Cl.: Oh, dear.

Co.: And I got the feeling that you were afraid to take it because so many mushrooms were poison, and then immediately you changed into a goose.
(Loretta laughs)

Co.: A goose or a duck, I'm not sure which—which had two heads and two necks. And one pointed in each direction—opposite directions.

Cl.: I wouldn't know what to think about that.

Co.: Well, I wasn't asking you what you thought about it, I just—

Cl.: I beg your pardon.

Co.: Wanted to tell you about it. To sort of bring you up to date where I am with you.

Cl.: Well, that's nothing. I had a dream that I was in the . . . hospital and I did. (Pause)

Co.: I don't know what you're asking me. But I'd like to tell you I think you are capable of anything you, you dream.

Cl.: Well, I dreamed that, ah, I had a tooth that needed to be extracted, and I didn't want it taken out, and they said: You can have it taken out of your own free will, or we'll give you shock treatment and take it out; and I said, No, I don't want shock treatment; and they said, I don't care, you're going to get it anyway. You're going to have that tooth taken out.

Co.: I felt kind of mad when you were saying that.

Rogers (Co).

Co.: This must seem confusing and odd and so on, but I felt really sorry that the interview had been kind of cut short, because I felt sort of, there were other things you wanted to say.

Cl.: I don't know, but I am being moved right off, transferred, and I just wondered if I am quite ready for a transfer. I mentioned it was annoying that the woman talked, has been yelling like that, but I really rather liked the ward—

Co.: Uh huh.

Cl.: I have been helping with the . . . I had thought I could go home from there. I know being transferred means I'll probably be put to work in the laundry all day, and I don't feel quite up to that.

Co.: Uh huh. So that is one immediate thing for concern, am I ready to face everything that is involved in moving away from a spot where—

Cl.: You feel kind of oriented to a place when you are here—

Co.: Uh huh. You get sort of used to it and . . .

Cl.: Well, I meant to correct one thing. When I said "No" before, I didn't mean I was tired of talking to that doctor; I just meant "No" that I was ready—that I wondered why I couldn't go home.

Co.: Yeah, yeah. But you felt he didn't quite understand you on that really.

Cl.: I thought that he felt I was being blunt, and that I just meant I didn't want to talk to him any more.

Co.: And if I, if I sense some of your feeling now it is, uh, a little tenseness that, that maybe he really didn't get that, he felt you were shutting him off on something.

Cl.: Yes, that's what, and that isn't what I meant.

Co.: Yes.

Cl.: Uh, I don't know. I am wondering if the transfer is a good thing. I mean they make you feel so important around here, and still you aren't, but then when I go over to "Two" I know that's an open ward—that's a dormitory, and I have been wearing not so many of my own clothes because I didn't like to launder them. It's just—if I'm quite ready for that change.

Co.: Uh huh, and—

Cl.: But my father and the others don't come to visit me, or anything, and I don't get out at all on weekends, or anything.

Co.: Uh huh, and that . . . in the ward where you are now that you feel they seem to make you so important, but then really you are not, is that . . . ?

Cl.: That's really it. I am important and I'm really not.

Co.: I see. So—

Cl.: I know that you are not very important when you move to that ward.

Co.: So if you are not very important in the ward where you are right now, if you were transferred . . . ?

Cl.: I would be even less important.

Co.: So that it is something that concerns you . . .

Cl.: I think it means working all day in the laundry too, and I'm not quite ready for that. I mentioned earlier that I had this tickling sensation in my knees when I was on 6C, when I was getting reserpine.

Co.: Uh huh.

Cl.: . . . and (not intelligible) . . . I think it was, and I asked the doctor at that time if he would move me so that I could go to work and work in the laundry, and the transfer came today. I didn't ask to be transferred this time.

Co.: But it troubles you whether you are really ready to face some of the things that would be involved . . .

Cl.: I don't know. There isn't much to face. It's kind of confusing. I think . . .

Co.: I see. It is more a question of facing the uncertainties, is that what you mean?

Cl.: I don't know what I mean. I just know that . . .

Co.: Now you feel kind of mixed up.

And yet, the contrast is not as simple as it may seem. The brash noisy counselor *may* basically be more acceptant and compassionate than the quiet, verbally "client-centered" individual. The student counselor can only answer this question by trying his utmost, possibly with some help, to reach some stage of self-actualization and genuineness so that he can accept himself, at whatever level he may be. He may then be able to evolve some methodology of counseling that will be best for him and best for those clients who relate with him, or he may, of course, also come to the conclusion that counseling is not for him. Certainly the student counselor should be wary of the counselor education program in which all the staff speak the same line—it is most unlikely that a number of genuine counselor educators who are free enough to be who they are will all be the same, smiling the same smile, frowning at the same insult, but mostly beaming brotherhood at each other and at everyone else!

One of the good things that has happened in the counseling profession in the last few years is that the words "directive" and "nondirective" are mercifully beginning to leave our vocabulary, and if there is another revision of this book it is likely that they will not appear at all! It is also being realized that the extent of counselor domination and control depends far more on the person than it does on the words he uses, and the words are important only to the extent to which they reflect the real person of the counselor.

Corlis and Rabe[54] answer their question, "Who is the boss?" by saying, "Nobody. Nevertheless, the problem raised by the question is not a straw man. Both patient and therapist will encounter their own problem of wanting to put down the other, or to raise him unnaturally." They also go on to say, "The therapeutic relationship is not an equal one in the sense of what each partner needs, but it is equal in the requirement that each must give all he can." A criticism of Carkhuff and Berenson[55] of client-centered counseling, namely, that "it has neglected the whole person of the therapist and the two way flow of communication," might be considered as a valid criticism of any counseling. While Blocher[56] is talking about a teacher-learner model of counseling, he could be talking about any counseling when he describes the counselor as one who "can exercise responsibility in much of the counseling process while recognizing the individual's right to reach self-determined decisions or even to make no decision at all."

Thus it would seem that there must be some degree of counselor direction, at least as long as the counselor is viewed as one who is involved in a human relationship with the client, and although the verbalizations of a counselor are to some degree reflections of his attitudes as a person, they themselves are less important than the attitude that causes the verbalizations—which may, after all, not always be what they seem. Some counselors believe deeply not only that the client can be, but that it is his right to be the determiner of his future; that he, the counselor, is secondary in the counseling relationship; and that the direction should therefore come from the client, not the counselor. One might well debate the empirical reality of such a belief. Some will say that this is all right with neurotic individuals, but that it can hardly be correct with psychotic individuals who are completely divorced from reality. One can well understand, too, how a therapist whose education has been in hospitals with severely psychologically maladjusted individuals might be less certain about the capacity of all people for self-direction than would the therapist whose professional education has been in a counseling center or a guidance clinic, where the majority of the clients have had emotional dis-

---

[54] Corlis and Rabe, *op. cit.*, pp. 48–49.
[55] Carkhuff and Berenson, *op. cit.*, p. 68.
[56] Blocher, *op. cit.*, p. 31.

turbances of a less serious nature. Yet, in some ways, this is a point that cannot really be argued. The counselor may in some respects be like the clergyman whose parish is in an area where filth and corruption are rampant, where good deeds are few, yet who continues to see people as basically fine rather than rotten, strong rather than weak. Is he being naive? Is he being foolish? Is he being unrealistic? Or is he, possibly, by being who he is, having a subtle and marked effect, is he really communicating in a devious manner with some, even though he will not communicate with many? Whatever may happen, this is the way he is, and this belief is reflected in his consistency of purpose and action. Such a counselor is similarly consistent in his feeling that the client must ultimately *accept responsibility* for the direction in which he will go, if he is ever to become a free individual.

ADVICE AND INFORMATION

One of the most general means by which a counselor may show that he is the controlling and directing force is by the giving of advice. In fact, this is probably why the giving of advice is so ego-supporting; it implies that the one who asks for the advice is on a lower level than the one who gives it. The probable satisfaction of some school counselors with their job comes from the fact that they are frequently asked, "What do you advise me to do?" The resulting counselor response may be more supportive for the counselor than it is for the client.

The school counselor, traditionally, has been an individual anything but reticent in the offering of advice. Thus the general lay concept of counseling is that it is the giving of counsel, which in turn is usually considered to be advice. Williamson probably offered as direct a statement as anyone in the field with regard to the use of advice when he said:[57]

> . . . the counselor is ready to advise *with* the student as to a program of action consistent with, and growing out of, the diagnosis. For convenience, we may summarize methods of advising under the headings, *direct, persuasive,* and *explanatory.*

Even here, however, it should be remembered that many counselors, when talking about the place of advice, are thinking in terms of teaching rather than counseling. There would obviously be much more

---

[57] Williamson, *op. cit.*, p. 233.

of an argument for the offering of advice to a rational individual under no stress or strain, than for giving advice to a highly disturbed individual who might clutch it as a complete answer to his difficulties, or reject it and the counselor completely.

The psychiatric and psychological literature has generally accepted the use of advice by the therapist as part of his function, but at the same time considered it as something that should be used with care and discretion. Sullivan, for example, says:[58]

> . . . Thus the advice comes in at the very end to round out the obvious. As a psychiatrist, you see, I sometimes have to round out the obvious, because there are some people, notoriously obsessionals, who are very unwilling indeed to draw a conclusion—and therefore the psychiatrist gives them the conclusion. Actually, the "advice" is for the most part an overwhelming display of the factors relevant to the problem plus a clear statement by the psychiatrist of what he firmly believes can be done about them.

Another psychiatrist, Colby, comments as follows on this issue:[59]

> One type of interposition common in the beginning, as well as at other stages of the therapy, consists of advice. At times the therapist must offer practical suggestions to the patient whose reality judgment is so impaired as to jeopardize his best interests. For example, a patient whose concept of his body is distorted may be advised not to undergo the plastic surgery he has planned. Or it may be suggested that a patient change his living quarters where he is under the constant unnerving pressure of homo-sexual feeling toward a roommate. As with all advice-giving on the part of the therapist, it should be done cautiously, and in small doses. The therapist must be prepared for the prospect that often his advice will not be taken, or, even worse, that it will be followed but have bad results.

Hadley, too, accepts the use of advice as legitimate, but suggests caution:[60]

> Suggestion and the giving of direct advice are techniques similar to reassurance and should be used with the greatest of caution. In nearly all counseling relationships the counselor is a figure of authority to his

---

[58] Harry S. Sullivan, *The Psychiatric Interview* (New York: W. W. Norton & Company, Inc., 1954), p. 213.
[59] Kenneth Mark Colby, *A Primer for Psychotherapists* (New York: The Ronald Press Company, 1951), p. 150.
[60] John M. Hadley, *Clinical and Counseling Psychology* (New York: Alfred A. Knopf, Inc., 1958), pp. 156–157.

client. Consequently, even offhand suggestions of alternative behavior patterns or remarks not intended as suggestions may do great harm to the client if they are not carefully thought out.

Marzolf also suggests the use of advice, with caution, although he does not actually use the term:[61]

> At certain times and under certain circumstances, suggestions may be made to the client without arousing resistance, a possible result of the counselor's intervention in the thinking of the client. A young client may not consider a particular course of action merely because he has never known about it or thought about it. One may also suggest sources of information, ways of approach to teachers about situations that have confused the client, courses of study to consider, occupations to investigate, or ways to improve social effectiveness. Such suggestions should not, however, be made so freely so as to deprive the youth of all opportunity to do his own problem-solving and thus make him dependent.

All of these statements are from experienced professional counselors whose comments are to be valued. There seems to be no question in the minds of the authorities above that counselors can and should give advice, although, like certain drugs, it is something that should be given with caution.

However, paraphrasing a comment made by Thorne, referred to earlier, I would feel that the more a client asks for advice, the less likely it is that advice will be of any benefit to him. The measure of the stability of an individual is the extent to which he is free to reject, or accept advice, without rancor or hostility or tension.

Ingham and Love express a somewhat similar point of view on the question of advice:[62]

> . . . or he could seek an answer from the counselor about whether to marry, get a divorce, or have children; about extra-marital sex experience, educational or vocational choices, or the continuation of psychotherapy. Almost any important decision that a person must make can be brought to the therapist's office. The therapist should not feel that he is in a position to know what the other should do, let alone decide for him. . . . Furthermore, even if he were right (as of course he often would be), it would ordinarily be undesirable for him to express his opinion so that it could be received by the patient as advice.

[61] Stanley S. Marzolf, *op. cit.*, p. 552.
[62] Harrington V. Ingham and Leonore R. Love, *The Process of Psychotherapy* (New York: McGraw-Hill Book Co., 1954), p. 22.

The counselor should be careful to distinguish between advice and information. The latter may be thought of as objective and untouched by the bias of man; it is pragmatic and empirical. It is fact, or as close to fact as one can get. Probably most counselors would agree that information has at least some place in the counselor's armamentarium, but there is a great divergence as to the degree of importance of this information, the kind of information which is necessary for effective counseling, and the use of this information.* Boy and Pine[63] see information as a relatively unimportant aspect of the counseling process, and they feel that ". . . it will be the individualizing and humanizing element of counseling which will be of significant help to people, and not the information and advice-giving which a well programmed computer will easily handle." Ehrle,[64] in talking about employment counseling, apparently feels somewhat the same way when he says, "Job advice may be given during counseling, but it is only a part of the total counseling process, and incidental to the primary purpose of counseling."

Krueger,[65] on the other hand, presents a dire warning of the disastrous results of the counselor placing stress on such terms as "relationship" and "acceptance," and warns that these do not relate to the "earthy" needs of the student. For him, "the most sensible approach to counseling in secondary schools is still the clinical, somewhat structured approach . . ." and the impression is that this approach would include the generous use of information and advice. Goldman[66] sees the preferred role of the counselor as combining ". . . the functions of assessment and information collection with the function of helping his clients to utilize the resulting information in a broader process that includes exploration, and possibly change, of self-concept and prevalent modes of behavior."

The above comments reflect a difference in a point of view about the use of information by the counselor in his talks with the client, but

---

* See Dugald S. Arbuckle, "Counselors, Admissions Officers, and Information," *The School Counselor* 16:164–170 (January, 1969).

[63] Angelo V. Boy and Gerald J. Pine, "The Counseling Process: A Perspective on Information and Advice," *The Vocational Guidance Quarterly* 14:201–204 (Spring, 1966).

[64] Raymond A. Ehrle, "Employment Counseling and Job Advising," *The Vocational Guidance Quarterly* 14:205–208 (Spring, 1966).

[65] Albert H. Krueger, "Letters and Comments," *Personnel and Guidance Journal* 45:1033–1034 (June, 1967).

[66] Leo Goldman, "Information and Counseling: A Dilemma," *Personnel and Guidance Journal* 46:44–46 (September, 1967).

the much sharper issue, which is definitely ethical in nature, is the question of the dissemination of information gathered about the client by the counselor to people other than counselors, and the use of this information by others in ways which may be damaging and hurtful to the client. The question here is really twofold: there is the question of whether or not the counselor should accept the gathering of information about the client and its transmission to other agencies and individuals as part of his professional function, and there is also the question of the extent to which this is a breach of the ethical obligation of the counselor to retain as confidential much of the personal information which he has about the client. This ethical issue will be examined in the next chapter.

Relevant information may also be of no help. When a high school student who has been driven by compulsive parents to excel academically is provided with information that indicates that his chances of getting into a decent college are most remote, it is unlikely that he will say, "Thank you," and relax. Information may not have quite the personal sting of advice, but when it clashes with one's concept of who he is, its immediate effect is not likely to be very positive.

Information may be traumatic (what is my I.Q.?) or it may be of no particular relevance (do you like hockey?) or it may be supportive (do you have many clients like me?); but in any case it is of little help to the client in his growth toward a better understanding about himself. Several of my psychiatric colleagues feel the same way about the M.D. therapist's functioning as a medical doctor rather than a therapist, and giving medical information or advice to the patient. The medical doctor does certain things for the patient that the therapist does not do, and he gives certain things to the patient that the therapist does not give. It is difficult to be two people whose functions contradict each other.

Many of the clients who come in to see the school counselor, of course, are going to be quite capable of using relevant information, *and if they want it, and if the counselor has it,* there would seem to be little reason for withholding it. Even though in the actual counseling relationship information will play a very minor role, the school counselor will periodically be called upon to supply information. There would seem to be no reason why he could not do so and at the same time maintain his counseling relationship with the client. Generally speaking, however, he should be seen not as the giver of information, but rather as the individual who will help a person to get to the point where he can make sensible use of sensible information. In any case, in the very near future it is likely that the information-giving function of both teacher and counselor will be taken over by the machine, so that all that will remain for the counselor will be his real function—counseling.

QUESTIONS

Being asked questions by a client is a rather routine experience for any counselor, and yet, they may sometimes pose special problems. Let us look at some of the questions about questions:

1. There are questions that are obviously expressions of feeling rather than questions per se. When a client exclaims, "How do you expect me to go on living with her?" or, "What am I supposed to do when she tells me I'm a bum—just sit there and take it?" or, "Who is to blame anyway—me or my husband?" or, "How can you or anyone else expect me to take that job?" and so on, these are not really questions, although some student counselors might actually react to them as if they were questions demanding intellectual answers. Regardless of methodology, most counselors would feel that a proper reaction to the above statements would be either some understanding nod, or "uh-huh," or "Hmmmm . . . ," or a reflection of feeling such as, "It's pretty hard to see just how you could do that," or, "That's asking quite a bit," or, "Is it one, or the other, or maybe both of you?" or, "It's pretty unreasonable for anyone to expect such a thing of you," and so on. Thus the counselor who is alert to, and reacting to, the expressed feelings of the client will not make the mistake of thinking that every statement that sounds as if it had a question mark after it must have an answer by the counselor.

Sometimes such a question may be a desperate request for reassurance. The counselor may feel more impelled to answer such questions as, "Surely *you* don't expect me to go ahead and do that, do you?" or, "Can't anyone help me in this—must I *always* be alone?" But here again it is the feeling to which the counselor should react. The tone should be gentle and understanding, but it would seem better that the words be, possibly, "Surely there is *someone* who does not feel that you have to do this" or, "Isn't there ever *anyone* who seems to be with you?" Note here too that while the counselor may feel compelled to say, "I don't feel that way," or, "But I am with you," the real deep feeling on the part of the client that *this is actually so* will come only when he can say, maybe just to himself, maybe to the counselor too,

"But there is someone—*you* don't expect me to do that" or, "Why . . . I'm not alone, I'm not alone . . . there *is* someone. . . ."

A somewhat similar sort of question may be asked when the client feels threatened by what he thinks might be a negative reaction of the counselor to something that he has said. Thus if the client, who has been talking about the stupidity of all of the people who vote the Democratic ticket, suddenly pauses and says, "By the way, are you a Democrat?" It is fairly clear that he has said to himself, "What if this guy is a Democrat?" Or it could be that this is his way of expressing his contempt for the counselor, assuming that the counselor is a Democrat. If the answer is "No," the counselor might be tempted to take the easier and safer road and say "No." If the answer is "Yes," however, he might feel that he has only a choice of lying, of telling the tension-evoking truth, or of trying to avoid answering the question either by asking some other question, or by detouring around it.

Again here, either a "Yes" or "No" answer, true or false, counselor comfort or no counselor comfort, is not really reacting to what the client is saying. A fairly safe rule of thumb in this matter is "Don't tell lies"; so we could dispense with the lie, if not for moral reasons, then for the empirical reason that when a counselor lies, it will eventually, and probably fairly soon, catch up with him. An honest reaction to the statement might be, "You mean that after all that you've said about the Democrats, you're a bit concerned about what I am. . . ." This might very well get a reaction of, "Well, yes, what are you?" At this point the best reaction might be a simple, truthful answer, something to the effect, "Well, actually, in trying to figure out some of your difficulties here what I am really doesn't make any difference, does it?" Actually, clients rarely press for an answer, but if they do, it would seem rather pointless to endlessly go around in a circle, all in the name of "reflection of feeling."

2. A question which relates to the personal involvement of the counselor, however, may be a somewhat more complicated matter. The client is conceivably after more than just an answer when he asks, "By the way, are you married?" or "How do you get along with children?" or "Did you ever fail any subjects when you were in college?" or "Did you ever get fired?" or "Do you believe in going to church?" and so on. Personal involvement with the client is not the professional task of the counselor; indeed, it is likely that personal involvement will make counseling less effective, if not quite impossible. Unlike the previous type of question, these questions are probably asked by the client as questions to which he wants answers, possibly for reassurance, pos-

sibly to help him feel superior to the counselor, possibly to help him feel closer to the counselor. When a woman client who is having trouble with her children asks the counselor "Are you married?" a very likely next question is, "Do you have any children?" to be followed by, "How do you get along so well with them?" The development of such inquiries brings into question the effectiveness of the counselor; has he in some way given the client the feeling that he is a friendly confidante rather than a warm but professionally competent individual who is working with the client on some of his difficulties?

Whatever the reason for questions of this nature, the counselor may find "reflection of feeling" on such occasions not easy, for the very obvious reason that there is little or nothing in the way of feeling to reflect. Many counselors feel that a brief, noncommittal, nonencouraging answer is as good a response, generally, as any; and if the question is pushed, then there is more in the way of feeling to which the counselor can react. "You really want an answer to a question like that . . . ," and so on. There would be a difference of opinion on counselor reactions to this sort of question, although there would be general agreement that the counseling session is not a question-and-answer period, regardless of who is doing the questioning and who is doing the answering. The student counselor may sometimes find himself bogged down in this sort of situation, waking up suddenly to the fact that he has become an answer man, with the questions more and more personal and his involvement deeper all the time. Even at this point, however, it is better to extricate oneself, even if it means threat to the client and possible disruption of the counseling, since what is happening is not likely to be good for either the counselor or the client. It may be, sometimes, that the best counselor reaction to the probing and pressing question by the client, "Come on now, tell me, how do you get along with your wife?" would be a, "Well, an answer to that question, you know, really wouldn't be of any help to you or to me . . . but it's sort of interesting why you keep pressing me with that question."

3. Another form of question is the one that seeks an interpretation of the client's actions or thoughts or dreams. For example, a client may talk for some time, without any indication of undue stress or strain, about the difficulty of making choices, and then, in a conversational tone, ask, "What does that mean anyway? Do you know any of the possible reasons why I just seem always to shy away from making any decisions?" Or he might say, "And then one of those dreams that I always have, and have had for years, is that I'm standing on a block of

ice that gets smaller and smaller and eventually disappears, and I fall into the water. What does that mean, anyway?"

Again here, there is little in the way of feeling to which the counselor may react; this is a straight question, asked as a question. There may, of course, as with other questions, be many ulterior or subconscious motives, but overtly at least these questions are asked as questions. Whether the counselor does or does not know what the behavior or the dream might mean, he should be wary about passing on to the client his version of its meaning. An intellectual presentation may not mean any more than the intellectual presentation of an intelligence test score of an I.Q. of 115 to a person who considers himself stupid. A person *must be* as he sees himself, and will change only when he can accept change, not when evidence indicating that he is different is presented to him.

Usually the counselor would react to this sort of question. He might say, "Well . . . I gather it's pretty hard for you to see any meaning to this sort of behavior"; or possibly, "It's pretty important for you to find some reason behind this behavior of yours." Some might press the client with "Well, hard to say . . . what do you think it might mean for you?" There might thus be a variety of *reactions* to the question, but most counselors would agree that the counselor would not, at least immediately, answer it. On the other hand, a counselor who was competent in the matter of dream interpretation, might feel that at a certain point, he would present his interpretation of the dream to the client.

4. Then, of course, there are noncommittal questions, in relation to which the most logical procedure is to answer them simply and briefly. A client, finding it difficult to start talking, might say, "This is certainly a cold spell that we are having, isn't it?" Although some counselors might feel that the client's uneasiness should be reflected, this would seem a somewhat cold manner in which to initiate a relationship. Why not just give a pleasant, "Yes, it really is cold weather that we have been having . . .," and the odds are that the client will be reassured that the counselor is human, and continue in a different vein. The counselor should be consistent, and he will almost certainly be different from what the client expects, but he need not be so different as to appear abnormal. Such a result sometimes comes about when the student counselor, trying to be "client-centered," refuses to react to any question, and the client, reasonably enough, feels that the counselor is a very queer fellow indeed!

It is true, of course, that many questions seemingly innocent enough will, if answered, be followed by a more involving type of question; but the counselor has to use his own understanding and skill to differentiate one from the other. A good general principle of operation is that the counselor should react to the *feeling* expressed in the question rather than to the question per se, and if he does react to the question, he should be brief and noncommittal.

Here are two junior high school counselors reacting to questions from self-referred students. It may be noticed that while both react to the feeling expressed in the question, one of them reacts in the first person.

> Cl.: Are you a member of the faculty? Do you know Mr. Jones?
>
> Co.: I'm wondering whether or not I can tell everything to the counselor. . . . I'm wondering whether I can trust him. . . .
>
> . . . .
>
> Cl.: Are you married?
>
> Co.: It makes a difference to me if the counselor is married or not . . . it's important for me to know. . . .
>
> . . . .
>
> Cl.: What do you think of a teacher who blames a kid for something he didn't do? Don't you think it's unfair?
>
> Co.: I'm upset because I feel that I'm being blamed for something I didn't do . . . it really bugs me because I think it's so unfair.
>
> . . . .
>
> Cl.: How important are those tests we took last September? Do they count very much. . . . I mean do teachers use them to put you in different classes?
>
> Co.: I'm kind of concerned about those tests. . . . They worry me a little. . . . I wonder how they'll be used. . . .
>
> . . . .
>
> Cl.: Isn't there some way you could talk to our parents and tell them how we *really* feel?
>
> Co.: We don't think *we* could get anywhere telling our parents how we really see this whole thing. . . . We're afraid to talk to them. . . . We feel they might not listen to us. . . . We want someone else to do it.
>
> . . . .

Cl.: If you're chewing gum at the end of the day . . . after school . . . can they keep you after?

Co.: Someone found me chewing gum after school and kept me after. . . . It doesn't seem fair to me.

. . . .

Cl.: I don't know whether I should try or give up . . . whether to try to improve or just forget the whole thing. What do you think I should do?

Co.: You really can't decide if trying would be worth it.

. . . .

Cl.: He has no right to play favorites . . . to let one kid do something and not allow me to do the very same thing. He has no right. Do you think he has a right?

Co.: You don't feel that he's being very fair.

. . . .

Some counselors would be very critical of some of these re-actions, feeling that they are far overdoing the "reflecting" bit. Some of the questions, for example, may be no more than questions, requiring a direct answer. One boy might simply want to know if you are kept in after school if you are caught chewing gum; another might want to know how important tests are; another might ask "are you married" simply as a get-acquainted comment. The crucial question really is: is the counselor responding to the basic human communication?

SILENCES

Client silences often cause some strain for the student counselor. Many student counselors complain, in fact, that most typescripts and tapes always seem to record clients who are very willing to talk, and all the counselor has to do is grunt every now and then, or decide when or where he should interrupt the client. There are several points that might be noted on this question:

1. The beginning counselor will likely find that client silence poses a threat to him. As the silence lengthens, the pressure on him to do something about it builds up—usually not for the welfare of the client, but rather to ease his own tension. Thus, logically, we might say that the counselor should aim for a degree of personal security such that whatever action he takes on the matter of client silence will be

taken solely for professional reasons. Since most would agree that counselor comfort is important, and that there should be honesty in the client-counselor relationship, it is an interesting question whether or not the counselor who feels this uneasiness should be honest and indicate this feeling to the client. Most counselors would say "No" to this, but some, possibly an increasing number, would say "Yes."

2. Silences, as much as words, are indicative of feelings. The counselor who reacts basically to client feelings might use such comments as "It's pretty difficult to get started talking . . .," or, "This is a real tough thing to talk about . . . it would seem easier maybe just to let it lie . . .," or, "It's a real nice feeling . . .," and so on. The counselor here must be almost intuitive as to what the client is feeling; while his words will sometimes be a fairly obvious reflection of feeling, it may sometimes be that if the counselor is to speak at all, it will be in the form of an interpretation.

Some counselors feel that there should be a reaction from the counselor if the silence appears to become threatening to the client, and thus the counselor might, under certain circumstances, take over the direction of the session. Very often, when a good relationship has been established, the client will indicate that there is no need for counselor verbalization. I once interrupted a long client silence, and was gently chided by the client. She was doing quite all right, and didn't need my talk!

3. Silence can also be therapeutic, and probably this is one of the attractions of a church. It is one of the few places where one can go and meditate quietly, without any interruptions. The counselor's office is another place where the same thing can take place. The client may be having a real therapeutic experience when he is silent, just as much, if not more, than when he is talking. Most counselors have had the experience of sharing a warm and unique silence with a client, where both client and counselor could almost feel the growth that was taking place.

Counselors who feel that they just must talk, and who feel silence difficult, might ponder over the results of a study reported by Cook.[67] He found that the lack of silence (at least 97 percent speech in a number of two-minute segments) characterized the unsuccessful counseling sessions, whereas the lesser percentage of speech tended to characterize the more successful counseling sessions.

---

[67] John J. Cook, "Silence in Psychotherapy," *Journal of Counseling Psychology* 11:42–46 (Spring, 1964).

TESTING AND MEASUREMENT IN COUNSELING

There would probably be general agreement among teachers and counselors that the purpose of testing is to provide more valid and reliable information about the individual who was tested. There may be some question, however, as to the extent to which both teachers and counselors appear to be more interested in knowing more about the student than they are in helping him to know more about himself. Information about the student may be needed for grouping and placement, and, later on, admissions officers and potential employers are also going to want to know about the student. This is a legitimate and reasonable use of information about the student, and the procuring of this information is one of the auxiliary functions of the school. This, however, has little to do with counseling, and any debate over the use and place of testing in counseling should not confuse the use of testing as a part of the total school program with the use of testing in counseling.

Although not all counselors would agree as to the place, if any, of testing in counseling, the majority who do see testing as a part of counseling stress that the information that is garnered as a result of testing must be for the use of the client himself, not for the use of the counselor. In other words, the information derived from testing is for the client, and the determination as to what to do about it is the responsibility of the client. On this point, Tyler comments:[68]

> The most important principle about the use of tests in counseling . . . is that the information to be obtained is *for the use of the client himself*. . . . A test is useful for counseling purposes only if there is a considerable amount of evidence as to just what characteristic it is measuring and if the counselor can state in clear, unambiguous terms what the significance of an individual's score is in relation to various life decisions.

Most counselors operate on the assumption that the more a client *knows* about himself the better he *understands* himself, and knowing is usually viewed in a cognitive sense. Byrne would reflect the feeling of many counselors when he says:[69]

[68] Tyler, *op. cit.*, p. 106.
[69] Byrne, *op. cit.*, p. 129.

. . . the success of counseling depends partly on increasing the student's understanding of himself. In many instances growth of understanding does not require reference to cumulative record data but can be attained solely through interview processes. Usually, however, reference to appraisal data, including those obtained by testing, is fruitful.

However, the extent to which I can change when I see or hear something that clashes with my concept of me must surely be related to my level of self-actualization, to the degree to which I have become a free individual. Thus it would seem reasonable to assume that only those rather solid students with a high level of self-understanding could internalize and make use of critical information about themselves.

Also questionable, of course, is the assumption that the more a counselor knows about the client, the more effective he can be with him. Berdie, Layton, Swanson and Hagenah[70] appear to agree with this statement when they say that "no experimental evidence at present justifies the assumption that *effective counseling depends on the counselor's knowledge about his counselee. . . .*" Yet they operate on the assumption that "*the more information we have about students, the better we can work with them.*"[71] And again, "Our thesis has been that test scores and other counseling information are used to help the counselor and the counselee to originate and study hypotheses concerning the counselee's future behavior."[72]

The most obvious reason why a counselor would use tests would be, as indicated, to gather more information about a client, information that he might feel that he could not obtain as accurately and as quickly in any other way. When counselors of various orientations discuss clients or patients—frequently called, not without some significance, "cases"—they normally have the results of test data, and the psychologist is often considered to be the fellow who provides the counselor with this information. The counselor who feels that he needs this information must need it either to pass on to the client or to help him in his work with the client. In any case, this is a counselor-directed procedure, in which there is no doubt that the counselor has decided that he needs to know more about the client; he determines what

---

[70] Ralph F. Berdie, Wilbur L. Layton, Edward O. Swanson, and Theda Hagenah, *Testing in Guidance and Counseling* (New York: McGraw-Hill Book Co., Inc., 1963), p. 121.
[71] *Ibid.,* p. 11.
[72] *Ibid.,* p. 133.

clients will be tested, when they will be tested, and how they will be tested.

It has already been pointed out that many counselors who see diagnosis as an integral part of the counseling process have little use for anyone else's diagnosis. Thus, even if exhaustive test data are provided by some hard working psychologists, as often as not these data are either politely ignored or thrown out the window by the current counselor. Even diagnostically oriented counselors often tend to put little weight on the results of measurement devices; they are more likely to operate with a client on the basis of their own evaluation of him, with, possibly, suggestions from several of their colleagues. A "psychiatric examination" is more often than not the pooled judgment of several therapists, or sometimes even the judgment of one therapist after a brief interview with the patient. A psychological examination usually refers to the use of standardized instruments of measurement. Whether the more subjective personal interview is any better or any worse than the standardized tests is open to debate, although some counselors would consider both of them unreliable and invalid.

The counselor may find no particular problem on this issue. He has no need for test data, if *he* is not going to *do* something for somebody, but rather help someone to make some decisions for himself, and thus to do something for himself. He does not have to know, from test data, whether a client is an underachiever or an over-achiever. The client who has a problem related to academic achievement will, generally fairly soon in the counseling process, present both to the counselor and to himself his picture of a person who is doing more or less than he probably could do. Although the one who is doing more might be more of a problem for himself, the academic society generally considers only the one who is doing less to be a problem. In most schools today, the guidance department will have provided the child, fairly early in his school career, with some information as to where he stands with regard to achievement tests or measures of general aptitude and intelligence. The counselor may feel that he had no particular need for this information, and that the client would make use of it if and when he wanted to.

One might say, "Well and good, but what happens if a client describes himself as an intelligent student who is doing poorly, whereas he is actually achieving at his level of capacity?" Actually, an I.Q. of 150 means nothing to a person who has come to see himself as a very dull person, with a low intellectual level. Nor does a low I.Q. mean anything to a person who has learned that he must be an intelligent person. The first individual, from an operational and a realistic point of view, has a low level of intelligence, and the second person has a high level of intelligence. The counselor does not have to know, and does not particularly want to know, before he sees the client, that there is an inconsistency between what some evidence says that the client possesses in the way of capacity and what he sees himself as possessing. If the counseling develops as it can, both the counselor and the client will come to feel, "Why must I push myself to do what I know I can't do?" or, "Why do I have to convince myself that I can't do anything, while I really know that I can do a good deal more than I have been doing?"

The counselor operates at the level of the client, and the first individual mentioned above is, for the time, a person of low intellect because *this is what he feels himself to be;* and the second person is a person of high intellect because this is what he feels himself to be. This situation is no different from that of the client who is helped by most teachers, but feels that all teachers are picking on him, or the client who insists that the principal is out to get him, although the principal is sincerely concerned with trying to help him. Most people, however, when the threats and the fears and the pressures are no longer present, will tend to come to a better balance between what they have and what they want. The student with high intelligence may come to have less need not to do well academically, and thus will almost automatically do better. The student with low intelligence will become more secure with himself and with what he has, and will have less need to convince himself that he can do more than he actually can. The student with musical talent will feel the desire to develop and make use of his aptitude when he no longer has to show someone that he cannot do anything that that person wants. The boy who has no liking for athletics will no longer bloody himself in athletic competition, since he will be secure enough to accept the loss of the affection of a neurotic father that is related solely to athletic achievement.

It is true, of course, that the school counselor is concerned with many activities other than counseling. He may be one who makes use of test data for placement and selection, but he should not feel any particular personal need for test data on those students who come to him as clients. One might assume, too, that the professional education of the counselor is such that he knows enough about human beings and human behavior not to need test data to give him a fairly accurate picture of this person who is called the client.

One may then ask, does this fellow who calls himself a counselor, then, ever make use of tests? *Some* counselors would answer, "Yes, if the client wants them," although we might at least wonder here about the extent to which counselor imposition increases as he becomes more involved in the use of tests. It would probably be fair to say that, in most schools and with most counselors, the client has little or no choice in the matter of "test or no," and that the meaning of the test data is the counselor's version, presented to the client.

Patterson[73] feels, reasonably enough, that as long as tests are used to help the client to evaluate himself, they can be a part of counseling, since the evaluative function is absent. Actually, however, this rarely happens (other than in books), and even if the counselor did present test data to the client simply as information, with no personal involvement, and even if the client was the one who determined what tests he would take, it is still the counselor who has decided what tests are available, and thereby been evaluative, since we can assume that there is no school where the client simply puts his hand in a test grab bag containing all tests, and pulls out what he wants; and since he doesn't know much about tests, it would be rather pointless saying, "What would you like to take? You make the decision."

In the school program described by Boy and Pine,[74] the testing program is primarily the function of the teachers, with the counselors acting as advisers and consultants. Certainly achievement and intelligence testing would appear to be a rather logical function of the teacher, and one may well question whether tests of various other kinds have any place in the school, or at least in the domain of the teacher and the counselor.

Again, however, we must distinguish between the perfectly capable and rational student who wants further information about himself in the way of test data, so that he can compare himself with others as to intelligence and interests and aptitudes, and is thus in need of *guidance,* and the student under stress and strain, who sees tests as the answer to his problems. Even in these days, however, when testing, if not counseling, has become socially acceptable, the odds are that most individuals who seek testing are really in need of counseling although they seek testing to supply answers to their problems, tests supply only information, and few individuals under strain have their problems dissolved by the presentation of information, valid or otherwise. Thus when the client says, "Do you think that some testing might do me

---

[73] C. H. Patterson, *Counseling and Guidance in Schools* (New York: Harper & Row, 1962), pp. 149–151.
[74] Boy and Pine, *op. cit.,* pp. 138–139.

good?" a reply that in most cases would be fairly accurate, although maybe not appropriate, would be, "These might . . . ah . . . give you some answers that you don't have now. . . ."

In a somewhat similar situation I had a client who had been referred to me and who indicated during the session, that he felt, generally, that he had things pretty well under control and could operate under his own steam. He raised the question, however, of having interpreted to him the data from tests that had been administered as part of a university experiment with which I had no connection. In this case, after some verbalizing of the client's feelings, I agreed that I would be happy to comply if the client wished. Some counselors would probably question this decision, particularly since the tests had been administered prior to the counseling, and had no relation to it; but my attitude was that my decision represented an acceptance of the feelings of the client, and that it did not involve any overt out-of-the-counseling act by me.

The counseling session might develop into a situation where a good deal of information with regard to test data would be supplied by the counselor to the client. In more cases than not, however, the original request for testing need not actually develop into testing unless the counselor is so unskilled as to miss the feelings being expressed, and blunders ahead with a voluminous discussion of tests and testing without ever giving the client a chance to get closer to what he was trying to say when he tentatively asked the question about testing. Even when the client comes in for the sole purpose of testing, as often occurs in a vocational guidance center, more often than not the client is in need of counseling—possibly vocationally oriented, but still counseling, rather than vocational testing. The client who, after a number of counseling sessions, rather consistently raises the question of testing, may feel secure enough so that he can go to the point of taking a look at some test data; or, of course, he could, becoming more threatened, be looking for an easier way out. The good counselor, however, should be able to help the client to see just why he wants test information. When the client can see this, he may have no further need for testing; or, on the other hand, he may be even more certain, but for possibly different reasons, that it would be good for him to take a battery of tests.

Some counselors would feel, at this point, that the client should be referred elsewhere for testing, and, possibly, for test interpretation, simply because they do not see themselves as skilled in test administration and test interpretation. Others would talk to the psychologist who had administered the tests about their meaning, and then interpret the results to the client. In the majority of the schools of America, however, the counselor will have to do some testing, if any is to be done. In such a situation, it would be rather pointless to ask a client "What sort of tests would you like to have?" since this would be about the same as the medical doctor's asking the patient, "What sort of examination do you think you need?"

On the other hand, some counselors have prepared a little brochure that describes, in simple language, just what tests are available, and just what their purpose is. The counselor should bear in mind that while he may have to supply information to the client, it should be information, written or otherwise, and not advice. Once the client has had a chance to read or to discuss with the counselor just what is available and what might be expected, it is then up to him to make the choice of what he wants to take. The question, "Well, which of these two—the Kuder or the Strong—do you think that I should take?" should pose no problems to the counselor who is operating on the basis of the feelings of the client. We could assume that what the client is expressing here is, "They're about the same, and it's a pretty hard choice for someone who doesn't know anything about tests to decide which one—or maybe I should take both of them. . . ." The client must make the choice, not because the counselor is being coy, or is using technique Number 108, which says, "Thou shalt not answer questions," but very simply because the counselor does not have, for the client, an answer.

Goldman,[75] in supporting the use of tests in counseling, sees tests as providing information such as pre-counseling diagnostic information, information about the counseling process itself, and information relating to the client's post-counseling decisions. He also sees tests as having uses that do not have the element of providing information—the stimulation of interest in areas not previously considered, laying a groundwork for later counseling, and providing a learning experience in decision-making.

In the long run, the counselor must, of course, make his own choice. My own feeling on the matter is that testing certainly has a place in the total educational program of the school, although we appear to be involved now in what might almost be called a testing frenzy, and federal money could possibly be used in more effective ways than in increasing the amount of testing going on in schools. As

---

[75] Leo Goldman, *Using Tests in Counseling* (New York: Appleton-Century-Crofts, 1961), pp. 22–31.

far as counseling is perceived in this book, counselor involvement in testing would appear to be a hindrance rather than a help, a means by which the counselor will become less, rather than more, empathic with the client, and a means by which the client may possibly increase his illusion that increased knowledge about self, divorced from self, is somehow synonymous with self-understanding and growth toward freedom.

MISCELLANEOUS ISSUES

Another reaction that may cause some counselor concern is an unexpected statement by the client, although this should occasion no despair on the part of the student counselor as long as it does not result in his anxiety. It is one thing to be surprised; it is quite another to be frightened. A beginning interview may be progressing in a conversational way when suddenly the client says, quietly, "Did you know that I was a Lesbian?" or, "By the way, I slept with the Dean over the weekend," or, "Are you nervous . . . you look that way?" and so on. As long as the counselor is a secure and acceptant individual, he does not have to worry about the long-range negative effect of his momentary loss of aplomb. Probably every counselor has his list of "bloopers," where he made statements that are obviously ridiculous to even the greenest of student counselors. I have recorded one example where the client says, "Say, you look sort of puzzled . . . ," and the reply that comes back is, "Who . . . me . . . no. . . ." The client's logical reaction to this was a laugh, but the relationship at least appeared to be good, and a few minutes after this exchange the client was deeply involved in his problem. In a discussion of this example, it was suggested that *if* the counselor really was puzzled, a more appropriate answer would simply have been, "Well . . . yes . . . I am sort of puzzled." In this case, however, the reaction would not have been an honest one, since the counselor, at least during the interchange, was not aware of being puzzled; he was just surprised—and of course a counselor should *never* be surprised!

Unexpected and violent oaths, highly colored jokes, unusual or bizarre statements may, for a while, pose problems for the student counselor, but in the long run they will not be a serious issue as long as he is not actually threatened by them. If, however, he is, and if such statements are taken as a challenge, to be reacted to as a challenge, or as the sort of thing about which people simply do not talk, then the counselor is in need of some assistance to solve his own problems. Such situations as these will become counseling problems only if they represent a personal problem for the counselor.

A question that is raised by some students is, "Where do you sit, and do you look at the client all the time?" It would be safe to say that the counselor does not sit with a desk between himself and the client; a general position is one where both client and counselor can look at each other if they want to, or look away from each other without any awkwardness. A counselor has to use his own judgment as to just how consistently he looks at his client; obviously, too, this will vary with clients, and vary with the individual feelings of any one client. A counselor should be able to look steadily at the client if need be, but he should be sensitive enough not to give the impression of staring at him. The counselor's "looking at the client" should be governed by good sense and good taste.

Another possible problem for some counselors occurs when a client who seems very much in need of continued counseling decides that all is well with him, and wants to terminate the counseling sessions. If the evidence seems to hint strongly that the client is only getting to the point of being threatened by the uncovering of some of his basic difficulties, the counselor must sometimes wonder if the termination is in some way due to his ineffectiveness as a counselor. All would agree that when the client says, "Well, it's pretty clear that this is doing me no good, so I don't see any need to return," the counselor would not say, "Very well, let's call it quits."

There might, however, be some debate as to just how the counselor should react and just what he should say. Probably most counselors would react, in varying ways, to the expressed feeling of pointlessness in continuing the counseling relationship. Some more diagnostically oriented counselors might be interpretative and present to the client their feeling of his fearfulness about what might happen if he continued the counseling relationship.

In any case, all professional counselors would probably agree that the client's initial announcement that he has had enough should not result in the immediate termination of the counseling sessions. On the other hand, the reaction of the counselor should leave the client free to decide for himself whether or not he still wants to terminate; and in some cases, he will terminate. Other counselors may feel that this is one reason why the counselor should be more interpretative. But if this procedure results in "holding" the client, he is more likely to be literally held, not because he wants to, but because he feels that the counselor wants him to stay. I was once told that I should have used this procedure to hold a client who wanted to leave; and yet this was exactly what had been done previously by two other therapists, with distressing results. The counselor can do only what he feels and what he believes in, and while his operational techniques will be continually modified, he cannot work against himself. Other counselors may be right in saying, "This is what I would have done," and even right that this is what the counselor should have done. But the counselor has to believe in the action himself, before he does it; otherwise he is little better than a record from which issue the words of someone else.

The complete lack of choice possible to some clients may also pose a problem. This is most obvious in the school situation, where, even though the client may be raging at the mean and miserable behavior of a teacher, he has no choice about leaving the teacher. He has to stay in school, and, more often than not, he has to go back to the same teacher. Such a lack of choice is a basic cause of many of the problems that are presented to the school counselor, and very often the fact is that the child must endure, for another year or two, an unrealistic curriculum, and quite possibly equally unrealistic and unsympathetic teachers. This is enough to test the mettle of a mature adult, and we can assume that an immature but nevertheless basically sound child is going to need some help to come through the experience a strong and stable individual.

Because youth must have practice in making its own decisions, many children would find school a better place if they were able to make the choice to withdraw from it, as they can from college, for a year or so. Their decision might be a poor one, for an unhappy school experience is not always because of a poor curriculum and poor teachers. Nevertheless, the adolescent grows up in a more realistic environment when he knows that he *can* make a choice, and that when he has made it, *he* will be held responsible for it. In our present culture, unfortunately, it almost seems that we are moving to a situation where the age of self-determination may never be reached. We may yet get to the point where, when mother has at last been removed from the picture, after the individual has been "educated" for many, many years, has been married, and has become a father, the state will take over. Then the individual may live in a happy state of irresponsibility for the rest of his days, letting someone else make his decisions for him, and thus never having to blame himself for anything that might go wrong. This state of total determinism never can, of course, be reached, and the counselor can help the child to develop the capacity for independent action, even though he may, for the moment, necessarily live in dependency. When the time comes, the child will then be capable of becoming a truly independent individual, standing on his own feet, and making his own way, and will have no need for counselors.

chapter 11

THEORETICAL ISSUES: ETHICAL

The counselor, like anyone else involved in a close and intimate human relationship, will periodically find himself face to face with ethical issues. And more often than not, the dilemma will be that there will be no easy answer, one way or the other. The counselor will find himself a part of what could be life and death decisions, and as long as he is involved, as indeed he must if he is to be a counselor, then the problems he faces are obviously ethical in nature. The crucial ethical issue is the existence of a human being as a free individual and as a contributing member of the society of which he is a part.*

The professional organizations most concerned with counseling are well aware of the importance to their profession of problems of an ethical nature, as they may affect both the individual member of the organization and the organization itself. The American Psychological Association's Committee on Scientific and Professional Ethics and Conduct and the American Personnel and Guidance Association's Committee on Ethics have a double function in that they protect the counselor from the public (the counselor has no protection in the matter of legal suit) and they protect the public from unethical counselors. They also have a remedial and helpful function, of course, and there are counselors and psychologists today who think of these

---

* See Martha L. Ware (Ed.) *Law of Guidance and Counseling* (Cincinnati: W. H. Anderson Co., 1964) and Wesley Huckins, *Ethical and Legal Considerations in Guidance. Guidance Monograph Series* (Boston: Houghton Mifflin Co., 1968).

committees as professional groups that gave them much assistance during a difficult time.

In 1960 The American Personnel and Guidance Association took its first legal step in defending one of its members. A previous circuit court decision, described below, had been appealed to the state supreme court:[1]

> The Circuit Court of Dunn County (Wis.) recently ruled that a guidance counselor had no legal responsibility for the suicide of a counselee student.
>
> Claiming their daughter was emotionally disturbed, the parents of the student in question charged the guidance counselor with negligence on three counts: failure to notify the parents of her condition; failure to secure psychiatric treatment for her; and failure to provide proper guidance.
>
> The court stated in effect, that the counselor was a teacher not a medical expert. To expect him to recognize the student's condition without benefit of necessary training and experience "would require a duty beyond reason," the court stated.

The Association then filed a brief with the Supreme Court, and it presented a significant argument that had not been raised before, namely, that a counselor cannot be held liable for an event that occurs weeks after counseling, and particularly when a medical question is involved. The result was that the original decision of the circuit court was upheld, and the Association had functioned effectively in protecting the rights of one of its members.

It is extremely difficult, however, to protect the unwary public from the various quacks who call themselves counselors and psychologists—both of these being omnibus terms that can mean almost anything. Such individuals find that the title "Doctor" gives them added authority and more business, and that it is a title easy to acquire, since few clients will ask "What is your doctorate and where did you get it?" As has already been mentioned, there are numerous institutions where one may receive a doctor's degree in wondrous and various fields by going through the motions of taking an extension course and paying a rather substantial sum. To the shame of the professions of education, psychology, and counseling, there are individuals possessing high positions who proudly parade such "degrees."

---

[1] *College and University Bulletin* XII:3 (October 15, 1959) (Washington, D.C.: Association for Higher Education, National Education Association).

Certification at both the professional and state levels is one way to combat this unhappy situation, but the public has also to be educated to distinguish between a professional counselor and a quack.

Any counselor who has worked on a committee concerned with problems of ethical behavior soon realizes that it is a very "sticky" area where, far more often than not, there is no clear-cut indication, with no doubts whatsoever as to whether the behavior of a counselor in question was unethical or not. Any committee making a decision on the ethical behavior of a counselor must at all times be keenly aware of the ethical soundness of its own position. It may place a particular strain on a counselor who flies the "never judge or evaluate" standard, to find himself a member of a group that is determining the ethical fitness of one of its members, possibly on the basis of highly questionable evidence.

The American Psychological Association has done an excellent job in trying to answer this question by posing a whole series of questions and situations, and then giving the reactions of the committee to them.[2] Not all members of the American Psychological Association, however, agree with all of the answers as given by the committee. Every counselor, sooner or later, must face some of these ethical issues as personal problems, which he must answer for himself, to himself.

In discussing unethical practices, Schwebel makes three "assumptions":[3]

1. Self-interest causes both unethical behavior and unethical practice. The personal profit motive may be a cause, the need for self-enhancement may be a cause, and the need to maintain security and status may be a cause.
2. Unsound judgment due to inadequate training and/or unsupervised experience, or due to ineffective selection, causes unethical practice; but since self-interest is not a primary factor, the behavior of the psychologist is not unethical. Unsound judgment may be shown in maintaining confidences in staff relations or in maintaining confidences about anti-social behavior.
3. Ignorance causes unethical practice. Here too, since self-interest is not a primary factor, the behavior of the psychologist is not unethical. Ignorance of technical information may be a cause, or ignorance on the part of the counselor of his own values, especially those that are incompatible with respect for the integrity of the individual, may be a cause.

---

[2] *Ethical Standards of Psychologists* (Washington, D.C.: Committee on Ethical Standards for Psychologists, American Psychological Association, 1953).
[3] Milton Schwebel, "Why Unethical Practice," *Journal of Counseling Psychology* 2:122–128 (Summer, 1955).

Some readers would probably question Schwebel's statement that incorrect behavior caused by ignorance is not unethical; or some might say that while it might not be unethical of the individual, it is unethical for the employer to hire such a person without checking on his credentials; and it is unethical of the graduating institution to graduate a person who is so ignorant. It would seem that somewhere along the line, when injury is done to a patient or a client in a supposed professional relationship, then somebody, somewhere, has committed an unethical act.

Warnath discusses an important point when he refers to the relationship between problems of ethics and goals to be achieved:[4]

> Essentially the problem of ethics is one of frame of reference. When the student personnel staff can agree on basic goals and the methods to be used in achieving the goals toward which they are moving, ethical problems will become solvable. However, so long as there is confusion in goals or discrepancies between goals and methods, the situation will remain controlled by the individuals in their separate offices, and communication will be difficult. The first step for any staff in determining the right or wrong of future activities is to admit that it is uncertain about its over-all goals and procedures. The second step is to agree on some firm philosophy of student personnel work drawing on some of the proposals which have been written up in the field. The third step is to carry on research in the areas of uncertainties about application. And finally, as the fourth step, each personnel staff must act as a group of professional people . . . mature enough to be willing to develop consistency between practices and professed goals.

For school counselors, however, there are several crucial ethical issues which must be faced immediately if they are to function as professional workers. Let us examine some of these issues.[*]

STATE CERTIFICATION AND PROFESSIONAL ACCREDITATION

The legal determination of what is required to educate a counselor continues to be controlled by state departments of education, and thus in the United States there continues to be fifty versions of what is necessary to educate an individual so that he might be "certified" to be

---

[4] Charles F. Warnath, "Ethical Considerations of Student Personnel Work as Viewed by a Counseling Psychologist," *Personnel-O-Gram* 13:8–11 (October, 1958).

[*] *See* Dugald S. Arbuckle, "Current Issues in Counselor Education," *Counselor Education and Supervision,* 7:244–252 (Spring, 1968).

a counselor. It is obvious that one may question the professional status of any occupation when the criteria for certification vary drastically from state to state, and when the determination of professional adequacy is made by state department of education officials, some of whom would have little professional standing in the very field whose workers they certify! Equally distressing, of course, is the fact that certification is generally, not by graduation from an accredited program, but rather by an official determination, usually person by person, as to whether the applicant has satisfied the official's interpretation of state requirements for certification. While the official requirements change with painful slowness, interpretations of these requirements vary as the personnel vary, and when personnel turnover is high, so is the level of confusion.

Thus on the basis of state certification, the position of the school counselor is not a definable position, at least on the national level, and the student who sees counseling in the schools as his future occupation will immediately note a wide divergence as to the criteria for the professional education of the counselor.

Dissatisfaction with this individual, state-by-state pattern of counselor certification was evident well over a decade ago, and various members of the American Personnel and Guidance Association began to press for professional approval or even accreditation of programs of counselor education by the appropriate professional body. A major step came in 1962, with the publication by the American Personnel and Guidance Association of six position papers on standards which should be developed for the selection and professional preparation of secondary school counselors.[5] In the same publication it was indicated that a revised statement would be published by January, 1964, thus "allowing time for further consideration before action is taken by the 1964 Senate."[6] A revised set of standards was voted upon and accepted by the Association for Counselor Education and Supervisions at its 1967 convention in Dallas.

Whether the results of all of this activity are worth the effort is questionable, since the standards suffer from two overwhelming flaws. The first of these is that they are based on opinion, rather than the evidence of empirical research. Scores of grass roots committees over the years have contributed their opinions on various questionnaires,

---

[5] *Counselor Education: A Progress Report on Standards* (Washington, D.C.: American Personnel and Guidance Association, 1962).
[6] "Standards for Counselor Education in the Preparation of Secondary School Counselors," *Personnel and Guidance Journal* 42:535–543 (January, 1964).

and the majority opinion has eventually appeared as a "Standard." This might be considered as the democratic approach to research, and it is somewhat akin to having the teacher determine the "right" answer by having the students vote on what they consider to be the "right" one. The "opinion" procedure would be questionable even though it were the opinion of those individuals in the country who have shown over the years that they have a high level of understanding in the field of counseling and counselor education. This, however, has been anything but the case, so that the second major flaw is that the opinions are not even valid as expert opinion. A U.S. Office of Education directory[7] lists some 325 institutions as having programs of counselor education, and this is to be expected, since the way one gets listed is to say that one has a program of counselor education! Nor does one have to have too much involvement in counseling and counselor education in order to become a member of the Association for Counselor Education and Supervision. Thus an opinion from one who has little or no involvement in counseling and counselor education becomes just as valid in determining a "standard" as does the opinion of one who has spent his life in the field. Hill[8] bemoans the fact that only one third of some two thousand members of ACES bothered to answer a ten-minute check list, and questions their level of professionalism. A more logical answer might be that those who were most professionally involved in counseling and counselor education could see no sense in having standards for a profession determined in this way, and simply refused to play the game.

Thus the standards, whatever they might be, might be questioned from a research point of view, and a perusal of them tends to buttress the fact that they represent opinion rather than evidence. It is not so much that there is anything questionable about the standards as such, but it is rather that the standards do not get at what would appear to be the crucial elements of a counselor education program. Thus it could well be that two programs could be rated as acceptable on the basis of the standards, but one would prove to be quite ineffective, the other quite effective. Much stress is placed on the cognitive aspects of the program, and much of it reads somewhat like a program for the education of chemists. The standard referring to self-understanding and self-evaluation of the student counselor is dealt with

---

[7] *Directory of Counselor Educators* (Washington, D.C.: U.S. Office of Education, December, 1964).
[8] George E. Hill, "The Profession and Standards for Counselor Education," *Counselor Education and Supervision* 6:130–136 (Winter, 1967).

rather casually, the statement being that "opportunities . . . are provided." More important would be the extent to which the opportunities were used, and what was the result of their use. After all, the provision of a gymnasium in a school is not necessarily any indication of top physical condition among the students! The practicum experience, of necessity, is described in a cognitive sense, and a top ranked practicum according to the standards, could very easily prove to be totally meaningless to a group of students. In a similar manner, the qualifications of the "well qualified" staff are described in the usual terms of degrees and experience.

Thus it would seem that the American Personnel and Guidance Association, at the current time, feels that it can go no further than providing sets of standards for a quality program of counselor education.[9] It has, as yet, refused to accept the responsibility of being the accreditating agency of school counselors, as has its two most involved divisions, the Association for Counselor Education and Supervision, and the American School Counselors Association. Thus the certification of school counselors continues to be an issue, but—for at least some time to come—it would appear that state certification, varying from state to state, on a person to person basis, will continue in effect. Thus a program of counselor education which would be considered to be totally inadequate on the basis of professional standards will continue to produce individuals who will be certified as counselors in various states, and a person who could be called a legitimate "counselor" in one state would be considered illegitimate in a neighboring state.

THE INVOLVEMENT OF THE FEDERAL GOVERNMENT

Federal involvement in public education has, of course, been an issue for many decades, but one decade ago it was a minor issue as far as counselor education was concerned. Today, it is, without doubt, a major issue, and it may well become *the* major issue. Money represents power and control, and the more federal money is poured into the education of counselors, the more the federal government can control the direction of counselor education, and thus counseling. The major involvement of the federal government in counselor education began with the passage of the National Defense Education Act of 1958, and

---

[9] *Manual for Self Study by a Counselor Education Staff* (Washington, D.C.: American Personnel and Guidance Association, March, 1967).

today that involvement has increased tremendously, and shows every indication of continuing to increase. It is surely crucial that when federal funds are provided for professional purposes, the direction of the use of those funds be determined by those who are professionally most competent in the field. This, in turn, should be determined by their professional peers, and not by federal bureaucrats, with little or no professional competence in the particular area. While in the last one or two years there has been an increasing criticism of the activities of the United States Office of Education by individual members of the American Personnel and Guidance Association, there has been little indication of action by the APGA against bureaucratic control of federal funds assigned for the purpose of counselor education. If federal funds are provided so that students may attend quality programs of counselor education, it would seem logical that those involved in counseling and in the education of counselors should be the determiners of the criteria for excellence in counselor education, as well as the determination of those institutions which have such programs. How far bureaucratic control has taken over, however, was illustrated when the Director of the Division of Educational Personnel Training made several basic changes in the criteria for the determination of quality in counseling and guidance institutes, counter to the recommendations of the American Personnel and Guidance Association. He also personally selected individuals for panels to determine which institutions should be solicited for NDEA Institutes in counseling and guidance even while the public information was indicating a certain deadline for institute proposals which were welcome from any institution. Institutions which did not receive contracts for Institutes found it extremely difficult to get anything in the way of useful information as to how their particular proposal was less effective than one which was considered adequate. At one stage, one program which had found favor with the Office of Education was being presented as a model, with the very strong implication that this model was to be followed if a proposal was to be seriously considered. The same situation holds true in the granting of NDEA Title VC Fellowships. Thus, a very real credibility gap existed between counselors and counselor educators and various offices of the federal government, particularly the Division of Educational Personnel Training. One or two bureaucrats hold very real power, and until the professional bodies take action, the direction of counselor education is going to be affected by a few such individuals. This determination, as to what constitutes a "good program," is particularly intriguing when one considers the increasing evidence which raises serious questions as to the efficiency of any of the current training programs for counselors.

It would probably be quite safe to say that the proposals for counselor education that have been funded by the US Offices have hardly satisfied a criterion of counselor education effectiveness based on empirical evidence. In a survey of nine of the full year proposals that were funded for the year 1967–68, one may note many similarities. In all, the objectives are broad and human and highly desirable and bookish, but there is serious question as to the extent to which the program was built around the objectives, as contrasted with the objectives being fitted to the program. The programs that are offered are still primarily cognitive in nature, with the stress of knowledge and knowing. The offering is still overwhelmingly via courses, for which semester hours of credit are offered, and in which, we can assume, the student has the usual experience of being evaluated and judged on the basis of someone else's version of what he knows. It would appear that the major stress is on the development of knowledge in the broad area of the social sciences, it is to a lesser degree on knowledge about the client, and it is to a still lesser degree on knowledge about the counselor. In only two institutes is there a planned no-credit experience of self-understanding and self-appraisal. There is minimal evidence of any belief in the concept that the major resource that the counselor brings to counseling is himself, at least in the sense that minimal stress is placed on the self-development and self-understanding of the proposals, but there is no way of telling this from the written proposal. The most important ingredient in any program—the staff—remains generally little more than unknown names to the evaluators. We know little more than that most of the staff have doctorate degrees and a few years of experience in counseling or teaching, which may mean much, or little. Thus, the U.S. Office, is, in a way, playing a game of blind-man's-bluff with the professional education of schools' counselors, as well as with the American taxpayer's dollar. Many of the proposals which are funded might well provide an effective experience in counselor education, but the odds are that many which were not funded might have provided an even more effective experience. On the whole, the proposals which are funded do not appear to be too different or any more effective, than most standard counselor education programs in many institutions around the country, and few, funded or not, would appear to be closely geared to the criteria that have been discussed.

It is of interest, and some concern, to note the recommendations that were made by the Special Subcommittee on Education of the House of Representatives after its investigation of the Division of Educational Personnel Training. The recommendations, three in number, said little or nothing, and no statement was made regarding the control and direction of counselor education programs by the Division of Educational Personnel Training. From this we may reasonably enough assume that the Committee approved of the current degree of control and direction of a professional program by the federal government.

The American Personnel and Guidance Association, too, would appear to be more concerned with the lack of federal funding (in the quotation below, called "diminishing interest") than with the manner in which federal funds are used. An official publication of the Association, for example, states that:[10]

> The American Personnel and Guidance Association and its members have viewed with alarm the diminishing interest, organization and effort of the Office of Education in providing services, information and technical staff for the guidance profession. . . . The Farwell task force is designed to initiate a remedy for the general lack of leadership exerted by the Office of Education.

It might be that if the American Personnel and Guidance Association had shown better leadership on questions dealing with the use of federal funds, they would not now have to be concerned about the decline of federal funding.

THE QUESTION OF CHANGE[11]

There would be little argument that the major function of the counselor is to help the client to, in some way, change. The change may, of course, be very minor, but the very fact that the client comes to the counselor means that he is saying, "I want to know something, or do something, or in some way have something happen to me so that I will be not quite the way I am now." It may be a student simply asking about information on several colleges or it may be an individual caught on drugs, seeing nothing ahead but the choice of slow destruc-

---

[10] *The Guidepost* (Washington, D.C.: American Personnel and Guidance Association, 11:2–3, February, 1969).
[11] *See* Dugald S. Arbuckle, "Values, Ethics and Religion in Counseling," *National Catholic Guidance Conference Journal* 13:5–17 (Fall, 1968).

tion by drugs or more immediate death by suicide. In both cases, the counselor would be involved with the client in the process of change— and both would pose an ethical dilemma, a very minor one in the first case, a major one in the second case. What are some of the facts of this dilemma of change:

1. Tremendous as our powers of change may be today, those who are involved in operant conditioning assure us that they are nothing compared with what lies just around the corner. Some see the counselor of the future as a behavioral engineer, and a rather routine problem brought to the counselor might be the predetermination of the sex of a planned child. Somewhat more complicated but quite within the realm of the reality of the not too distant future would be the request for counseling in the determination of whether or not a planned child will be a genius or a person of low level intelligence, or possibly, one who will be able to withstand unusual environmental stresses and strains. At such a stage, of course, sexual involvement for the purpose of reproduction would be distinctly old-fashioned, and too risky, since one would not know in advance what kind of child was going to be born. Even now scientists can put together a simple form of desoxyribonucleic acid (DNA), the bodily form of every organism on earth, with full biological power. The goal ahead is to rewrite the genetic code, and thus redesign the bodily form of organisms. Man might then take direct command of the evolution of his own body, right from the very creation of life itself.

Thus the power of the control and direction and manipulation of one human by another is, without doubt, going to increase tremendously in the very near future, and Vance[12] puts it modestly when she says, "Certainly man's understanding of technique in the behavioral sciences far surpasses his understanding and commitment to certain goals." If this poses somewhat of an ethical dilemma now, it will soon pose the question of the very survival of the human race, as individual human beings, with individual rights and individual integrity. Even today we all know some "counselors" who are so fascinated by the technology that their mode of operation differs very little from that of the experimental psychologist in his rat laboratory. Who the creature being experimented with is of no particular concern; the fascination of the counselor lies in his ability to change and modify the "other" almost as he wishes. Tillich[13] was certainly correct, at least for some

[12] Barbara Vance, "The Counselor—An Agent of What Change," *Personnel and Guidance Journal* 45:1012–1016 (June, 1967).
[13] Paul Tillich, Report of a speech given at M.I.T. in *Time,* April 21, 1961, p. 57.

counselors, when he said, ". . . technique has become not merely a means to an end, but an end in itself."

May[14] felt this pressure when, in talking about existentialism, he said ". . . it seemed to many observers to be ineffectual against the onmoving lava of conformism, collectivism, and the robot man." But he also voiced the feeling and the faith of the existentialist, as well as those who would distinguish individual man from a random collection of behaviors, when he added, "No matter how great the forces victimizing the human being, man has the capacity to know that he is being victimized, and thus to influence in some way how he will relate to his fate. There is never lost that kernel of the power to take some stand, to make some decision, no matter how minute." But the hard fact of life, neither moral nor immoral, is that the power to change grows daily. This reality must be faced by the counselor, and he must raise for himself the question of where he stands, today and tomorrow, rather than looking wistfully backward at a yesterday that is gone.

2. As the power to change grows, the more serious becomes the simple question, "Who determines who will be changed, and what will be the direction of the change, for what purpose." Our Western civilization has been generally based on the supremacy of man over the state, and this shows in the political concept that the government is our voice, not our master, and when it no longer is our voice, then we change it. While most Americans would still hold to this concept in theory, its practice has often been, at best, rather halfhearted. Counselors, as any student could tell, show a wide variance in their practice of the concept of "individual rights," especially the rights of the young as contrasted with the old. Van Kaam,[15] for example, is very much on the side of the individual when he says:

> . . . when I am acting as an authentic counselor I want the unique personality, the freedom, the spontaneous initiative of my counselee; I want him to grow in his own independent being. . . . Therapeutic care does not want to force, to push, to impose, to seduce. What is more, as soon as the counselor tries to overpower the counselee, if only by suggestion, his activity is no longer therapeutic care.

Williamson,[16] however, shows some doubts about the capacities

---

[14] Rollo May, *Existential Psychology* (New York: Random House, 1961), pp. 41–42.
[15] Adrian Van Kaam, "An Existential View of Psychotherapy," in Dugald S. Arbuckle (Ed.), *Counseling and Psychotherapy: An Overview* (New York: McGraw-Hill Book Co., 1967), p. 36.
[16] E. G. Williamson, "Youth's Dilemma: To Be or To Become," *Personnel and Guidance Journal* 46:173–177 (October, 1967).

of the individual when he says, ". . . does he have the right to become less than he could become . . . unfortunately . . . many of us are inclined to let the individual make his own choice in a simplistic misunderstanding of freedom within democracy." Moser[17] seems to place a somewhat questionable capacity on the shoulders of the clergyman, while giving no credit to the client when he says, "Since God is able to direct the clergyman in other areas, the same power will abide in advice giving." This attitude is apparently ecumenical, since Saalfield,[18] a priest, reflects somewhat similar feelings when he says, "The Catholic counselor should ask the pupil 'How often do you go to Mass and confession?' Catholic counselors must create right attitudes." Many students in schools and colleges will attest to the wide divergence between the supposed acceptance of the theory of individual rights, and the actual practice of this belief. It is unfortunate that counselors are among those who show a high level of distrust of the capacity of the young, or for that matter, of anyone other than themselves, to determine the direction that one might go.

The feeling that "I know better than you what is the best direction for you" is all too common when the young are with the old, when parents are with their children, when teachers are with students, and even, alas, when counselors are with clients. Shoben[19] points to the major flaw in this attitude when he says, ". . . it is equally a mistake to assume that predictive success or the power of behavioral control somehow reveals the normative ends toward which conduct may properly be directed." Van Kaam[20] is speaking to the same issue, when in talking about the teacher, he says, ". . . he should create the ideal conditions in which the child himself can awaken to these values; and the most ideal condition for this awakening of a spontaneous insight and estimation is not to force such ideals upon him. In that case we prepare him only for hypocrisy or an uncreative mechanized life or even neurosis."

But man in a sense is conditioned not to believe in himself, he is conditioned away from himself. He learns all too frequently, from his parents, his teachers, his clergymen, how not to become the authentic

[17] Leslie E. Moser, *Counseling: A Modern Emphasis in Religion* (Englewood Cliffs, N.J.: Prentice Hall, Inc., 1962), p. 116.
[18] L. J. Saalfield, *Guidance and Counseling in Catholic Schools* (Chicago: Loyola University, 1958), p. 80.
[19] Edward J. Shoben, "Personal Worth in Education and Counseling" in John D. Krumboltz (Ed.), *Revolution in Counseling* (Boston: Houghton Mifflin Book Co., 1966), p. 63.
[20] Adrian Van Kaam, *The Art of Existential Counseling* (Wilkes Barre, Pa.: Dimension Books, 1966), p. 70.

person, how never to experience the ecstatic thrill that comes only to those who are free—free to live and free to die, but never to be chained. The respect that one has for his freedom and his rights is usually reflected in the respect that he shows for the rights and the freedoms of others. The autocrat is always the slave, since his continuing lack of trust in others is merely a reflection of his lack of trust in self.

The counselor too, of course, is a conditioned product of his society, but the counselor should be different. He should be the one who has somehow intervened, with help or on his own, and cut into the bland and painless process which is manipulating and modifying and molding him into a faceless image. He is the one who somewhere has said, "Wait. What is this? Must I do this? Must I become this person? Why?" He has assumed control of his own destiny, and he has accepted responsibility for the direction he might go. He is a free man, and he expects neither a kindly God nor a kindly nature to lead him by the hand, and accept responsibility for his life and living. Nor is he fearful of what a vengeful God or a vengeful nature might do to him. He can accept the risks of living the free life of the free man.

CONFIDENTIALITY

Many counselors would agree that the confidentiality of the counseling relationship is the crucial factor without which counseling would be impossible. There are a number of areas in which this confidentiality becomes an issue:[21]

1. Information about the client, and the use of it, is probably the major area where the confidentiality of the counselor is challenged. While counselors might differ with each other about the kind of information which they might need, and the use to which they would put this information, most would likely agree that as long as this is within the context of the counseling relationship, the only purpose of the information is to help the client in his growth and his development and his actualization. If some of this information goes beyond the limits of the counseling relationship, however, it may obviously be quite damaging, and I have the uneasy feeling that a good deal of information which has been gathered as a part of the counseling relationship is transmitted to admissions or employment officers who then use it as

---

[21] *See* Dugald S. Arbuckle, "Counselors, Admission Officers, and Information," *The School Counselor* 3:164–170 (January, 1969).

the reason for their rejection of the student. A counselor might talk to a hospital psychiatrist about the latent homosexuality of one of his high school clients, and certainly no harm or damage would be done to the client, but that same information transmitted to an employment or admissions officer might well blight the student for the rest of his life. A counselor might talk to a doctor about his quandary in trying to help a student who has been using marijuana, but the results would be quite different if he passed this information on to an employment or admissions officer. A counselor might be helping a client to struggle through his concern over a continued record of cheating over a period of time, but this same information conveyed to an employment or admissions officer, as part of the student's school record, would be disastrous. Thus, it would appear to me that there is a very real question concerning the extent to which school counselors are guilty of an immoral and unethical breach of confidentiality in the transmission of information, about students who have been clients, to employment and admissions officers.

The hub of the question, of course, is what information is considered to be "confidential," and just what is meant by the term "confidential." Heayn and Jacobs[22] refer to four levels of openness, with Level 1 being the most open and Level 4 being the most confidential. In Level 3 they include such "matters of judgment" as student descriptions, staff recommendations, psychological reports, psychiatric evaluations, social service reports, medical information, legal information, and agency reports. If to this latter level we were to add the counselor's own reports (if the counselor believed in the writing of such reports), then could we not say that this was information which was for the professional use of the counselor, and came under the description of "highly confidential"? As such, it would not be available to employment or admissions officers, only to those who might be regarded as the counselor's professional colleagues, involved in the counseling process. Even here, of course, there would be safeguards and restrictions, and certainly information given to the counselor directly by the client should be revealed to another professional colleague only with the knowledge and approval of the client.

The information which would be given to employment and admissions officers might be somewhat like that in Level 3 above, but this would be between the school administration, and the teachers, and those seeking the information. This would be considered to be an

---

[22] Maurice H. Heayn and Howard L. Jacobs, "Safeguarding Student Records," *Personnel and Guidance Journal* 46:63–67 (September, 1967).

administrative function, and teachers and administrators are not being incongruent in accepting a function which is evaluative and judgmental of students, since this is part of their professional task. Even here, of course, one might hope that descriptions of students would be objective rather than subjective, but the collection and distribution of such information would be the business of the school administration. One of the sources of information about the student would likely be the teacher who should surely be capable of writing student descriptions if such are necessary. The counselor simply would not be considered to be one from whom the administration could get information about the personality characteristics of the student, to be passed on to others.

In the past few years the impression that I have gathered is that the goodly majority of American school counselors do spend much of their time accumulating information, some of it personal, some of it gathered during counseling sessions, some of it very judgmental. This information is passed on to employment and admissions officers, and again, my impression is that the majority of counselors who are doing this are doing so quite willingly, and do not feel under any particular duress. There are exceptions to this, of course, one such being a group of eight counselors (Craig, Cravens, Handly, McCormick, Pounds, Schere, Wells and Winans in Kirkwood High School, in Kirkwood, Missouri).[23] They have stated that "Undue expectations are being placed on secondary guidance counselors in the college admission process. We wish to reflect our serious doubts upon the type of information requested by numerous colleges and universities in their recommendation forms." They go on to say that "Professional counselors are placed in an unethical position when required to officially recommend that a specific student and a specific college are compatible."

Such comments about students which might be considered to be highly questionable coming from any source are still being supplied by counselors to employment and admissions officers. Fairly recently, for example, I have seen one counselor's report, which is available for admissions officers, which describes a girl as being "very much of the hippie type." In another school, another counselor's report, in describing a boy, uses the word "very effeminate" several times. These descriptions, as is often the case, may describe the writer of the report better than they do the person who is supposedly being described, but

---

[23] Craig, et al., "Reader Reflections," *The School Counselor* 15:148–150 (November, 1967).

it is surely obvious that such comments will hardly be helpful to the student when he is applying for a job or trying to get into a college. We may note that APGA stresses that the "major responsibility (of the counselor) is to assist individuals through the counseling relationship" and ". . . he works with other individuals in the employment environment . . . *for the benefit* of the counselee . . ." Also, they state that "he should not be expected to perform tasks inconsistent with his professional role as a counselor." ASCA stresses that the counselor should "assist *each* pupil," as his major function, but it also adds "assist parents" and "assist other members of the staff." When anyone in the school makes a statement which may be prejudicial to the future of a student, then there should at least be no question about its accuracy and its objectivity, but it is surely not within the realm of the professional function of the counselor to make such a statement.

Entirely apart from the ethical aspects of such statements, the counselor leaves himself legally vulnerable. A 1968 court case involving Bates College in Maine, for example, ruled that a counselor's recommendations and other school records are not privileged information. The case involved the parents of an applicant from Connecticut who wished to see a copy of the transcript of the applicant's high school record which they thought contained some misinformation as well as some derogatory remarks by a counselor. Bates College refused to reveal this information and subsequently their records were subpoenaed. After a number of hearings with the State of Maine Superior Justice, the judge ruled against Bates College on the grounds that the transcript, recommendations, etc., were not privileged information.

The following principles of operation, on this question of the using of information would appear to be feasible, and they should present no insurmountable obstacles, assuming that they make sense to counselors, and that the counselors are not the "Yes, I agree that that would be good, but you know how it is . . ." type of person. If they are, of course, they will simply do whatever seems easiest, or whatever the employer tells them to do!

(a) The school should accept the responsibility for maintaining a close relationship with admissions and employment officers, and it should contribute *certain* information to these individuals. This should be the semi-public kind of information which is to be found in school records regarding the student's academic ability, his intellectual capacities, and the more subjective reaction of teachers or administrators who may be familiar with him. The primary purpose of the university is the intellectual development of the student, and it is highly questionable to refuse a student admission because of some real or fancied moral lack, or to say that one must have a certain level of emotional stability before one is admitted.

(b) The gathering of this information should be a school administrative responsibility—grades, intellectual and academic test scores, and teacher's or administrator's recommendations. Such information would logically be collected by a vice-principal or by a placement officer, if such a position existed. Counselors might periodically use such information to help students, but any contacts from colleges and universities would be with the school administration, not with individual school counselors. Students should clearly understand just what information is available to potential employers, college admissions officers, and others who might have a legitimate use for it.

(c) The personal information the counselor receives from clients, as a part of the counseling relationship *must* be kept confidential. If it isn't, he won't receive very much, and if any counselor in almost any high school is not intimately acquainted with various activities that are going on, it is likely to be so, not because little is happening, but because the students feel that the counselor can't be trusted with certain information. Students who are in schools where the counselor is the major determiner of whether or not they get into a college or get a job have made it clear to me that the information they give to the counselor is carefully guarded, and sometimes downright false.

Nor can a counselor ethically say, "Well, I give good information about students but I never give bad information," since if he does give information he accepts an ethical responsibility for the validity of the information which he conveys. He either gives no information about the individual client, or he gives out information which may be either helpful or damaging to the client. If a school guidance director asked my opinion about one of the counselor-education graduates, I would give my honest opinion, because this is the kind of relationship I have accepted with the student and he knows it and I know it. He knows, as well as I, that I have an ethical responsibility in my relationship with the employer, as I would with an admissions officer in a graduate school. With a person whom I have had as a client, however, I have no information to convey, because I do not see this as my accepted professional responsibility.

This does not mean, of course, that the counselor goes around with sealed lips, totally alienating everyone; nor does it mean that the counselor should not sometimes take overt action to do something about that which is causing stress and trouble for students. A counselor can do something about an impossible curriculum or an impossible teacher without revealing individual confidences, just as he can do something about student behavior which is damaging to certain students. He *is* a part of the school system, but he *is not* an administrator or a teacher, with the authority and the particular responsibilities of the administrator and the teacher.

(d) The counselor will likely have his own personal records, hopefully kept to a minimum, and the information here should be confidential in fact as well as in theory. The purpose of this information is very simple—it is to help the counselor to be more effective in his relationships with his client, and the client should surely have the right to feel secure in his knowledge that this is as far as this information goes. Such information should periodically be destroyed, and a good rule of the thumb for any counselor is that if one has information that might in the future be damaging to a client, then get rid of it.

2. The question of confidentiality has become more of an issue in recent years with the vastly increased use of audio and video tapes in counselor education. While it is generally agreed that a counselor should not record, or make use of a one-way mirror or a closed-circuit television camera without the approval of the client, Marcuse, some years ago, presented an interesting defense for the use of covert recording:[24]

> The whole purpose in covert recording, if such be indicated as required by the data, is to enable one to obtain more information, to facilitate rapport, and in the long run (it is hoped) to be of benefit to the individual therapeutically. . . .
>
> To reiterate, concentrated sulphuric acid, a scalpel, or morphine may certainly be misused, but this does not constitute an argument against their legitimate use. . . .
>
> Whether research is concerned with the nature of the behavior involved in jury decisions or how best to aid a patient requesting therapy, the best method for eliciting such data should be used. Doing this is both proper and needed. Covert recording can respect the patient's confidence and can be constructive.

It is true, of course, that counselors generally would consider it quite ethical to make covert recordings of children or of psychotic patients. When this is the case, one might well ask how the counselor determines whether or not the individual is old enough not to be a

---

[24] F. L. Marcuse, in "Comment," *The American Psychologist* 12:278–279 (May, 1957).

child, or stable enough not to be psychotic, so that he will know when to record covertly! Covert recording carries with it a good deal in the way of invasion of the privacy and rights of the individual, and it would seem that the counselor should not record unless the client gives his approval. It is true, of course, that this means that the counselor will sometimes be unable to record sessions that would have been worthwhile for the education of student counselors, for the education of the counselor himself, and for a greater understanding of the client.

If one is to have a recording of a beginning session, however, it must be covert in that the recorder is on when the client comes in. The counselor should, of course, immediately ask permission of the client, and then, even if he is turned down, he at least has a recording of his being turned down! Many counselors question the wisdom of recording a first session, since the client is under stress anyway, and having to begin the conversation by requesting permission to record is possibly not the best way to establish a feeling of rapport.

Some counselors feel that since one never knows which sessions will be particularly good ones for the purposes of research and teaching, it is best to record all sessions, even though most of them will be erased. It sometimes happens, too, that in a certain session the counselor is faced with an unusual situation, or some challenging and threatening incident; and it is obviously beneficial if he has the session on tape so that he can study his own reactions.

3. A related question is the extent to which audio and video material and other data on clients should be used for teaching and learning. Most counselors would probably agree that one never uses such material unless it is with a professional group for professional purposes. Most would also agree that when audio and video tapes are used they are always edited, since not only the identity of the client is usually revealed in a counseling session, but a good deal of confidential information about other individuals as well. Most would agree, too, that a tape should not be used if the client has explicitly stated that it is not to be listened to by any person other than the counselor. On the other hand, most counselor educators probably have tapes whose use has been accepted by the client because of his trust in the counselor, but which the counselor will not use because of the possibility of identification. In the long run, the counselor must use his own professional understanding, and his sense of decency, being always aware that the client may have given his consent only because he felt a debt of gratitude to the counselor, and that one is never quite sure how professional all members of a professional group may be.

There would seem to be little question that movies and video tapes of actual counseling sessions should be used only with the consent of the client, and that they should be shown only to those individuals whose professional status is assured. This would raise some question as to whether such movies should be shown to large classes of students taking courses in counseling. Tapes and movies of counseling sessions are for the professional improvement of counselors and student counselors, not for recreation and amusement. Respect for the individual implies respect for the confidentiality of what goes on, an attitude required of every member of a group just as much as it is of the individual counselor.

4. Much the same thing applies in any staff discussion of a "case" in which various records are usually referred to. The counselor discussing the client should be very careful that he does not needlessly disclose material that is confidential, although some people would say that this is greatly affected by the personnel at the staff meeting. If, for example, it happens to be a meeting of the counseling staff with certain deans, teachers, and others to discuss the problems of a certain student, it is likely that what the counseling staff will say will be a good deal more restricted than if the people at the meeting were fewer in number and limited to the counseling staff. Names of individuals other than the client should be brought in only when necessary for an intelligent discussion of the problem, and they should certainly never be brought in for "thrill" or to show off. Respect for the client should also include respect for the individuals who are involved with the client. A counselor once, in a staff meeting, elicited comment by disclosing that one of the girls involved with his client was the daughter of the principal—a disclosure showing respect for neither the principal nor his daughter, since there was no need whatsoever for their being identified.

At the university level, the presence at staff meetings of graduate assistants and fellows may also raise a problem, in that the client being discussed may well be a colleague of one of the individuals present. When this happens, it is probably just as well that the graduate student affected should leave the discussion, since he is put in an embarrassing, if not unethical, position. Another problem occurs when graduate students have access to records that are of a confidential, or at least a semiconfidential nature. Such a student always occupies an "in-between" status; the students see him as partially a staff member, whereas the staff people see him as primarily a student, and the poor fellow has to function as both! As much as possible, there should be a clarification of his status—to himself, to the staff, and to the students, but the problem will always remain to some extent.

OTHER ETHICAL ISSUES

Another ethical question concerns the extent to which the counselor should let the counselee know about any overt action that he might take on behalf of the client, if, indeed, he should take any at all without the suggestion by, and certainly the agreement of, the client. Should the counselor take steps to change what he knows to be a very negative home situation when he feels that he has a good chance of being successful, even though he also knows that the client would probably not want him to take any action at all? Should the school counselor talk to a teacher who, because of his lack of understanding of the true situation in which a boy is involved, is making things difficult for him, even though the boy is afraid that he will get into trouble if the counselor talks to the teacher? Should the counselor intervene with school authorities when he knows, from counseling sessions with another student, that a boy is being punished for deeds that were actually committed by someone else? Should a counselor talk with children who are showing a lack of understanding and acceptance of another child because of their possible misconceptions about her?

A somewhat similar problem often occurs when the counselor works in a Health Service, a Psychiatric Clinic, or any other hospital setting. There the clients, or patients, will with increasing frequency ask for various kinds of medication to make them sleep, to keep them awake, to steady their nerves, to reduce their tension, and so on. Whether the counselor is a medical therapist or a nonmedical therapist should have no effect on the procedure in a case such as this, but some counselors do not want to appear as the doer or giver of things, and the client would be referred to medical personnel, who would make the decision whether or not the individual should have medication. In some cases there might be consultation between the medical doctor and the counselor, but it would be the medical doctor, not the counselor, who made the decision, even if the counselor was also a medical doctor. The basic reason is not the somewhat out-dated fact that only the medical doctor has the legal authority to prescribe such medication—since many psychologists and other nonmedical therapists have equal knowledge of such medication and its effects, but simply the fact that the act of prescribing the medication puts the counselor in a position of authority and decision.

Referral may also become a problem of an ethical nature. When the client wishes to be referred elsewhere, normally it raises no problem—unless, of course, the client wishes to be referred to someone who is known professionally as an unethical individual—and this would not often happen. It may happen, however, that the counselor decides that he cannot ethically continue a relationship because of his feeling of lack of capacity to work with the client, but the client refuses to be referred, insists that he is quite satisfied with the present situation, and will cease to have any counseling if the counselor refers him. Another such situation occurs when the counselor with a private practice is being paid for sessions that he feels are doing nothing for the client, and he has the choice of continuing with the client, who will not accept referral, or terminating a client who does not wish to be terminated. Still another problem comes when it is obvious that an individual should be referred, but there is nowhere to refer—although the counselor would feel that it is very rarely that understanding and acceptance are not of some help to any individual. The reverse side of this coin, and one that frequently occurs in schools, is when a person who calls himself a counselor feels that he must refer practically every potential client who reveals anything in the way of a personal problem. When this is the case, surely the individual should be called a referral technician rather than a professional counselor!

The part-time counselor will soon find that the fact that he has several jobs will raise some special ethical problems for him. If he is a teacher and counselor, for example, he will find conflict between his allegiance to a group of children as a teacher and his allegiance to an individual child as a counselor. He may find that, as a teacher, he is expected to be freer with information about a child than he feels, as a counselor, he should be. He may find that parents regard him as a teacher, and he cannot, in effect, say to parents as well as to teachers and school administrators, "But you cannot expect me to do that because I am a counselor," since they will immediately reply, "But you are also a teacher, are you not?" Although this conflict of allegiance raises many difficulties for the teacher-counselor, most of them can be reduced if the teacher feels that he can function better as a teacher if he operates nearly all the time as a counselor.

These difficulties are well-nigh insurmountable, however, for the individual who is a principal. A surprising number of schools still refer blithely to the fact that their counseling is done by their principal, but this surely shows a lack of understanding of counseling and the functions of the counselor. As a principal, one owes allegiance to the teachers, and to a lesser degree to the community; and one cannot function ethically as a counselor if his primary concern is any other than the individual child. Thus, any counselor going into a new position, particularly in a school situation, should know in advance just what is expected of him, or he may find himself saddled with tasks that make his title of counselor nothing but a mockery, and he might well be accused of unethical behavior, or ignorance, or both, if he accepts such conflicting tasks. A school system needs superintendents, and principals, and teachers, and they may be fine and honorable individuals; but they do not, and they cannot, function effectively as counselors.

Another question deals with whether or not the counselor can excuse unprofessional behavior because of ignorance. His behavior might be excused by others, but the question here is whether or not the counselor can look himself in the eye and say, "There was nothing unethical about that; I was just stupid." It surely seems within the realm of ethical behavior to say that any individual is being unethical if he attempts professional tasks that he is incapable of performing because of his lack of skill and knowledge. Certainly a counselor's fellows should not condemn, but rather try to help; yet each individual counselor may wonder if he is functioning in an ethical manner when he becomes involved in a close and possibly crucial human relationship with another person, and at the same time knows that he does not know what he is doing. Any counselor, of course, no matter what his experience, is going to face situations that he cannot understand, and at times be faced with questions for which he has no answer, but this is part of his professional work, rather than an involvement in a situation about which he knows nothing.

A final ethical question concerns the inconsistency of counselors rather than their ignorance. This is a particularly pertinent problem during the education of the counselor, and too frequently the assessed "effectiveness" of the student counselor would appear to depend more than anything else on just whom he happens to have as a supervisor. In Evraiff's book,[25] for example, the following comments were made by the various reviewers regarding the effectiveness of several student counselors:

The counselor of Carl, for example, had the following said about him:

---

[25] William Evraiff, *Helping Counselors Grow Professionally* (Englewood Cliffs, N.J.: Prentice-Hall, Inc., 1963), pp. 366–367.

From Arbuckle: You start off very dominant, but appear to become more acceptant of the client, who seems to make real progress. You tend to be too concerned with techniques and methodology.

From Stefflre: Your third interview was good, but the last was not very good. You were not "close" to the client.

From Roeber: By interview three you were doing pretty well, but you withdrew too much in the last interview—you became a silent partner. You follow the words, but not the melody.

From Dugan and Blocher: You made excellent use of techniques, and created a warm, positive relationship. In the last interview Carl was able to talk more positively about himself. You need to accept more responsibility.

Jack's counselor might have heard the following:

From Arbuckle: You have difficulty accepting Jack, and insist on dominating and controlling him. You tend to be too technique-centered. You are not too aware of "self" as yet, but you show high promise of self-understanding.

From Stefflre: You follow the "party-line," but you are on your way to becoming a competent counselor—and a free person.

From Roeber: You are too "methodology"-centered. You did not establish too much in the way of a positive relationship with Jack.

From Dugan and Blocher: You were too "technique"-centered. There appeared to be little or no communication with Jack. You appear to have no goals.

Jane's counselor might hear:

From Arbuckle: You understand intellectually, but did not appear to get close, and to empathize with Jane. You stressed the intellectual content rather than the feelings, which were more apparent on the tape than in the typescript.

From Stefflre: You did little more than respond with statement of content. You were skilled in omission, and you appeared to avoid areas where you felt uncomfortable. I have respect for your analytic ability.

From Roeber: You appeared to be dedicated to a client-centered methodology. You have more than the ordinary talent for counseling.

This suggests that supervisors of student counselors should be very wary of the validity of their own assessments, and it also raises a question as to the extent to which supervisors are dedicated to helping the student counselor grow toward effectiveness in his own way rather than simply becoming a pale carbon copy of the supervisor in order to receive a positive assessment. Some student counselors may never be able to determine just how effective they can be because their supervisors will never give them a chance to operate as they really are. While it may be expensive, it would seem highly desirable from an ethical point of view for every student counselor to be evaluated by several supervisors so that there might be more chance that their personal bias could be cancelled out!

EXAMPLES OF ETHICAL PROBLEMS

One of the marks of a professional counselor is the way he measures up to various ethical issues that press in upon him. Many of these issues represent, basically, assaults upon the integrity of the counselor. One school counselor, for example, has mentioned the following as examples of ethical issues that involve him:

> The pressure brought on by the insecure and autocratic administrator who wants the counselor to reveal confidences.
> The problem of being aware of environmental imperfections yet not being able to do anything about them because action would demand the revelation of client confidences.
> The prostitution of the counselor's professional role.
> The pressure brought by various people not to involve myself in therapeutic counseling.
> The self-protecting reactions of decision-making groups only willing to see one side of the coin.
> The protection that tenure laws afford the incompetent teacher.
> The badgering of youngsters as part of the educational process.
> The badgering of teachers as part of the educational process.
> The badgering of offspring as an aspect of parenthood.

Another school counselor has experienced the following ethical problems:

> Pressures on the counselor to reveal confidences given in the counseling relationship.
> Parental perception of the counselor as an investigator and enforcer.
> Parental expectation that the counselor will manipulate teachers for the benefit of the client.
> Pressures that the counselor should act as a teacher—i.e., "the counselor should not listen to kids—he should explain and discipline."
> Adult pressures and expectations for the counselor to act as an intermediary on their behalf—as an instrument by which some would like to control youngsters and make them conform.
> The pressure exerted subtly and overtly on the counselor to help the client to adjust, but not necessarily to grow if growth and development are not in harmony with adult standards and goals.

Wrenn presents a few examples of ethical questions:[26]

(a) How can consultation be had with another person about the student without violating the student's confidences? (b) What is ethical for the counselor when the student, within the counseling relationship, relates wrong-doing or crime? (c) When fellow counselors, teachers, or administrators inquire about a counselee, how does the counselor keep their good-will while maintaining the integrity of his relationship with the student? (d) What does the counselor do when the problem is over his head but there is no referral agency available, or the student will not accept referral?

Here are some examples of ethical issues faced by different counselors:

Example 1

John Rose saw the counselor at the beginning of his senior year in high school. He impressed his counselor as a sincere, highly motivated young man, who found in these interviews an opportunity to express himself at least partially. The counseling sessions, however, also revealed a tendency to unrealistic thinking, a strong undercurrent of anxiety, and at times some degree of confusion.

While part of John's problems were immediately connected with school, his deepest concerns were inevitably related to his home situation and background. During his childhood, from the age of about five or seven to his early teens, he had been forced to live apart from his parents as simply another member of the large family of one of his uncles, who resided in Texas. Both parents had come from lower socioeconomic groups and had received but a limited education. The father, a carpenter by training, had worked in mines and factories, but now made little effort to find employment, leaning on the bottle for his chief support. The mother, although still employed, had also fallen into the habit of excessive drinking. Life within the home was one of frequent arguments, discord, and nagging, with very little understanding. Basically, within his family either in the past or the present, John had found little attention, affection, or self-expression.

In the spring of his senior year, John was booked by the police on the charge of exhibitionism in the Townsville Public Library. Released with a warning, he reported his difficulty to the Guidance Office at

---

[26] C. Gilbert Wrenn, "Status and Role of the School Counselor," *Personnel and Guidance Journal* 36:175–183 (November, 1957).

school. Referred to the school psychologist, John's problem was diagnosed as requiring long-term treatment. Since the facilities for such treatment were not available at the time within the school structure, he was given a second referral to the hospital clinic and advised to leave school until such time as he might wish to return and at the same time could be psychiatrically cleared for further study.

In the period of a little over a year since John left school, he has returned several times for talks with his counselor, including one visit to his counselor's home. These sessions have had two main purposes from John's point of view: (1) to enable him to release some of his feelings and obtain some approval for his various efforts at obtaining personal and social adjustment; and (2) to obtain guidance and approval in his search for vocational adjustment.

During interviews John has readily admitted the fact that he has not been wholly successful in combatting the need to exhibit himself, and a number of isolated instances have occurred since his leaving school. However, he was making serious efforts to fight the need, and with some degree of success. Unfortunately, the clinic had found it impossible to admit him immediately because of case load. His counselor urged him to keep applying for early admission, but after a year of delay on the part of the clinic encouraged him to seek admission at another clinic. At this time, it would appear that the clinic at another hospital will be able to give him treatment.

Following his departure from school, he took and held a factory job that offered some security but none-too-high pay and little opportunity for advancement. He is strongly motivated to rise above his present socio-economic level, but is restricted by his lack of higher education or specialized training.

(1) An additional element of his dilemma is represented, however, by the usual necessity of completing the personal history data found on most application forms for any higher level or more interesting occupational outlet. Recently he was seeking a bank job in which he was highly interested. The application form called for previous education, reasons for leaving school, and any police history. He left the form incomplete and came to see his counselor for advice. "Almost any job I really want asks these questions. I'm almost sure to be stymied in getting ahead if I tell the truth. If I don't get a better job, I'm going to be just so much more unhappy . . . and if I'm always under this pressure, I'm going to find it all the harder to keep out of trouble. What should I do?" What should the counselor advise John? To tell the whole truth? Avoid jobs with such searching questionnaires? Conceal his personal history?

(2) Recently, his counselor was contacted by a representative of an agency to obtain information relative to his clearance for employment. What information if any should be released by his counselor? Should he urge the boy not to use his name as a reference? Should he inform the boy in advance as to what he would feel obligated to disclose if used as a reference? These are the specific questions asked by the representative of the agency:

1. Would you recommend John for employment?
2. Do you consider him to be a stable, well-adjusted individual?
3. Do you think that he will get along well with fellow employees?

Example 2

Bill Din is a college freshman. He seemed to have no really valid motivation for attending college other than his father's desire to have him in college. His academic record for the first semester was poor, and he was placed on probation, although all objective evidence seems to indicate that he is a student of superior ability. In working with the student to try to develop some worthwhile motivation, the counselor became involved with a friend of the father.

In time, this friend informed the counselor that the boy's mother is dead, and the father is serving a jail sentence as the consequence of some "sharp" business dealings. Thus the boy has no parental guidance or direction and is left almost entirely to his own devices, being alone at home with a housekeeper while his father is imprisoned. He is well-to-do, has a new Cadillac convertible car of his own, and spends all of his time "living a gay life."

One of Bill's instructors comes to the counselor to get some information regarding Bill. He has discovered that Bill has superior ability which is evident on the few occasions when he does some academic work. But he wonders about the boy's family situation. Why does he seem to be so poorly motivated? Under these circumstances, and with the knowledge that the counselor possesses, how much or how little should he pass on to the faculty member?

Example 3

Mary San is a college sophomore. She is friendly and pleasant in all relationships with other students and faculty. Prior to entering college, she was in Europe for three years working as a secretary. During this period of her life, she developed a keen interest in international affairs. Apparently her group there spent considerable time in the discussion of the world situation and in deciding what should be done to insure the future peace of the world. As a result, she returned to the United States critical of the way our government was handling foreign affairs and with a general feeling that the solution might be a drastic shift in social and political organization.

Although Mary came from a substantial, conservative Middle-West home background, she has always had some tendency toward inward revolt against the conservative point of view. It was interpreted by her family, however, as the "enthusiasm of youth" and since it reached only minor proportions, such as occasional family arguments, the family thought little about it. Later they became quite distressed by her activities. The time spent in Europe seemed to intensify these feelings. After returning, she worked for about a year in a textile factory before entering college. Here she became very much interested in union activities, and the excitement involved in those activities seemed to stimulate her further. She came to a conclusion that labor work would be her chosen vocational field, a decision that led to her desire for further education.

While a student, she has continued her contact with the union movement. By a fellow student with somewhat similar inclinations, she was introduced to a local "progressive" group with members from local colleges. This organization is very active and probably provides further fortification of her "liberal" or extremist tendencies.

Mary is very active in extracurricular affairs, her interests centering mainly in student government and the school newspaper. She is also active in the political organization called Americans for Democratic Action.

About three weeks ago, an F.B.I. agent called on a routine loyalty check on this girl, who is being considered for a position of trust in the government. Since much of the preceding information had been obtained from the counselee and her parents through interviews, what is the counselor's position? What information should be given to the F.B.I. agent?

Example 4

Horace Pen established himself early in college as an unusual student. He was very able, very personable, and impressed one immediately as possessing qualities of leadership. He had had his two-year hitch in the Air Force before coming to college.

When class elections were held shortly before Christmas recess, he was elected freshman president. He quickly demonstrated his abilities both as class president and also as representative of the Student-Faculty Assembly.

A review of his two-year record—or rather of his record up to about Easter of his sophomore year—indicated the extent to which he had won not only student but faculty attention. At about Easter time, one of the departmental chairmen requested that Horace be given a work scholarship and be assigned to him. The request was carried out, and Horace began his duties. Later, by sheer accident, an instructor noticed that a boy who had not turned in a major assignment had suddenly acquired an A grade for it. A check of records indicated that not only had this change been made but that at least two others had occurred. It soon became evident that the records had been left briefly where they were available to Horace and to no other student. When Horace was interrogated about the situation, he admitted that he had made the changes.

In due course, the case came before the school department heads. They were reluctant to give the boy a dishonorable dismissal because of his previous fine record, even though it was felt that such action was indicated. Horace was finally permitted to withdraw with the understanding that application for re-admission at a future date would be denied.

About a year later, Horace applied for admission to a Midwestern university and his counselor received a letter requesting information about his withdrawal.

(1) What is the counselor's ethical obligation in such a situation?

(2) Does the fact that a complete statement of the case would likely lead to rejection have any bearing on it?

Example 5

Henry Dot has completed his sophomore year at college. The victim of a broken home in his early youth, he was raised by three uncles who did what they could for him. However, he was forced to shift for himself and worked at odd jobs from a very early age. He was graduated from high school at the age of nineteen, having missed a full year of schooling because of ill health. He served two years in the Navy following high school and became interested in teaching.

Following his military service, he did various jobs and became manager of two stores. But he wanted to get a college education and train to be a school teacher. As a college student, he maintained a satisfactory record and impressed the faculty as a very conscientious, sincere, and intellectually curious young man. On his own, he visited the Counseling Center and requested assistance for some problems of personal adjustment. The school psychiatrist, feeling that he was a rather disturbed young man, suggested psychotherapy, which Henry has been receiving regularly at the V.A. Mental Hygiene Clinic. His irregular home background has probably contributed to his problems of personal adjustment, and originally there seemed to be a question of needing some help in making a more satisfactory heterosexual adjustment. Henry's counselor has worked closely with him. The psychiatrist at the Mental Hygiene Clinic feels that he has made considerable progress and now has rather good insight regarding his problems of adjustment. Some additional therapy is indicated at this time.

Henry has applied for admission as a junior to several teacher's colleges. The counselor's problem is: (1) Should he recommend such an individual for teacher-training? (2) If so, how much of this information should be passed on to the other institution or school?

Test scores indicate that he is a young man of superior ability. His interest in teaching seems to be strong and genuine. He has had valuable related work experience. But what of his own emotional adjustment at this stage? Also, is the counselor violating the student's confidence if he passes on any of this information?

Example 6

Sally Rin was probably one of the most able students in the college that she attended. All scores on the Ohio State Psychological Examination would place her at, or above, the 95th percentile, liberal arts college freshman norms. She was also one of the most confused and distressed young women ever to come to this counselor's attention.

Her family background was substantial. Her father was a medical doctor. Her mother had graduated from a well known Southern women's college. A brother was preparing for the priesthood in the Roman Catholic Church.

Sally had been sent to school in Italy for two years. While in Rome, she had observed certain things, of which her interpretations had a profound effect upon her. This was evident in her cynical attitude toward life, toward people and religion, and toward the Roman Catholic Church in particular. Her attitude was very distressing to the family.

In discussions with her counselor, the reasons back of this attitude became evident. While in Rome, Sally had seen children starving almost outside the Vatican Walls, while inside everything seemed to go on as usual. As she put it, "I could not understand how the Church could stand for Christian principles and do nothing about these poor impoverished people. I can never again swallow the stuff they put out." It was evident that a terrific conflict had been set up in this counselee's mind. Now she was disturbed by the effect that her attitudes had upon her family. Also the loss of her religious faith had taken away from her the very basis of her former stability, and she realized it. She said that sometimes the only solution seemed to be suicide.

Her parents had suggested that she take her problem to the local priest. This she refused to do, saying "What could he do except urge me to return to the Church? I would rather talk with a Protestant minister, even though I don't think that he could help me."

What should the counselor do in helping the student to solve this difficult re-orientation? With whom should the case be discussed?

The following are hypothetical counseling situations involving a conflict of responsibility:

Ethical Situation 1

On the day set for final examinations for Senior English, Mrs. Weber discovers that some exam sheets are missing from her filing cabinet. She informs the students that their test will have to be postponed until the next morning, graduation day, since she will have to construct a new test. During a counseling conference on the same day, Gary tells the counselor that he had access to the stolen test and knows who took it. Finally he admits it is his friend Bob who was the guilty party. Gary and Bob are college-bound seniors who might not be allowed to graduate if the counselor were to report this. After talking with the counselor, the boys suggested that they would give back the tests if he, the counselor, would return them to the teacher without indicating who had stolen the test sheets. What should the counselor do?

Ethical Situation 2

Jean has come to the counselor for several sessions during the past two months, but it is only at the one yesterday that he learns that she is pregnant. She tells him that she has told only one other person, her best friend, who helped to arrange for an abortion. Jean is planning to go to a nearby city the next day, Saturday, for the abortion. Her parents have been told that she is staying for the week-end with a friend, whom they know well. Jean is obviously upset by the prospect of the abortion, but tells the counselor that she "would rather die" than tell her parents. Jean also refuses to name the father of her expected baby. The counselor urges her to confide in her parents, and when Jean continually refuses, he is puzzled. Should he inform the parents? Or what?

Ethical Situation 3

Ken D., a high school senior, revealed during a counseling relationship that he had engaged in homosexual activities for about a year. He had become increasingly worried that he would be "found out" and this anxiety caused a drop in his school achievement, which was the "reason" he came to see the counselor. He also expressed hope that he might learn to prefer heterosexual relationships, although he had been repeatedly disappointed and continued to be attracted to males. The counselor, who was rather inexperienced, had not encountered such a problem before and did not know whether to refer Ken to a psychiatrist or try to counsel him. He chose the latter alternative, although felt later that he hadn't helped Ken at all. Two years following Ken's graduation from high school, the counselor received a recommendation form from a prospective employer. Ken had applied for a job as a counselor in a boys' summer camp. Should the counselor mention his knowledge of Ken's homosexual tendencies?

Ethical Situation 4

Helen has come to see the counselor at the recommendation of a teacher who is concerned about Helen's failure to keep up in her school work. Usually she is a B student, but for the last three months, she hasn't maintained a C average. Helen is quite negative for the first two counseling sessions. At the third session, however, she tells the counselor that she has been associating with a group of older teenagers who have been taking LSD. The police have been aware of this group for several months but haven't been able to find out who the "ticket agent," or source of the LSD is. Helen eventually tells the counselor the names of all the members of the group, after she feels she can trust him. One day the principal approaches the counselor. He tells him that the police have asked the principal if he has any clues as to possible leads in the case. Should the counselor tell the principal anything?

Ethical Situation 5

An unmarried male counselor, the only counselor in a small school, has been counseling a high school girl who is known by many students and teachers to be sexually promiscuous. The counseling has been somewhat successful, but also of longer duration than usual. A few of the teachers and some of the students have been speculating as to the true nature of the counseling attention. The parents have called the principal to ask him if there were truth to the fact that the counselor was behaving "immorally." Rumors have become strong enough to cause the principal to pressure the counselor to cease counseling this particular girl. The counselor feels, however, that to terminate counseling at this point would destroy all the good that has been accomplished. Also, there are no alternate counseling opportunities presently available for her. He feels a strong professional obligation to the girl, but also to his school. How can he best proceed under these circumstances?

Ethical Situation 6

Mr. Williams, the history teacher, knows much about history but little about teenagers. He displays his ignorance frequently in class, in teacher's meetings, and socially. Many of the students dislike him or feel sorry for him, but few have any respect for him. Recently, he has had a rash of flat tires, garbage deposited on his porch, and broken windows. The counselor learns during his meeting with Tom, a rowdy freshman, that Tom's gang has been responsible for Mr. Williams' calamities. Tom defends his actions, saying that no one likes Mr. Williams and everyone wants him to quit teaching. Tom indicates that the incidences of disturbance will continue. The counselor has a close relationship with Tom and does not want to break his confidences. However, he is also concerned about Mr. Williams. What should he do?

Ethical Situation 7

Mr. X, an elementary school counselor has talked several times with Mary, a fourth grade student who is quite unhappy and has low school achievement. Mary discloses to the counselor that her father is gone much of the time, and when home, is usually drunk. He beats both Mary and her mother occasionally. From other of Mary's comments, the counselor concludes that Mary's mother is of questionable character, too, and has several men friends. One day a representative of the State Department of Children and Family Services comes to Mr. X, asking for information about Mary. He says that neighbors have called the department with complaints that Mary is severely neglected, often left alone all night. They contend she is improperly fed and clothed. The counselor is asked to disclose information gained in counseling so that it may be used as evidence to remove Mary from her home environment. What should the counselor do?

Ethical Situation 8

During a counseling relationship with David, the counselor administered the Mooney Problem Check list and the MMPI. David had indicated that he was worried about his mental health and sometimes "thought he was going crazy." Some months later, the principal asked the counselor for all of David's records, since David was transferring to another school. The principal also said David was transferring because of recurrent problems with other children and teachers. Should the counselor include the MMPI and Mooney Check List Information?

chapter 12

THEORETICAL ISSUES:
PROFESSIONAL

There are numerous theoretical "issues" that become issues for the counselor because of the very nature of his work. The first of these is an every-day aspect of living—namely, reality.

REALITY

Although there is no absolute reality, Murphy may be somewhat optimistic when he says:[1]

> The inner world has become just as real as the outer world; hardly anyone in an odd corner dares anymore to refer to the world of fantasy as "unreal." It may be called a different kind of reality, but even this does not seem coercive or constraining upon us.

It is the search, and the action and the motion that are real, rather than some preconceived "reality" that one must seek out. It is likely that Fromm[2] means this when he says, "All that the human race has achieved, spiritually and materially, it owes to the destroyers of

---

[1] Gardner Murphy, *Freeing Intelligence Through Teaching* (New York: Harper & Row, 1961), p. 38.
[2] Erich Fromm, *Beyond the Chains of Illusion* (New York: Pocket Books, Inc., 1962), p. 173.

illusions and to the seekers of reality." One might reword this slightly, and say that our debt is to those who create the new realities and are unwilling to accept the old as fixed and rigid and immutable. Sartre is looking at the same question when he comments:[3]

> There is no reality except in action . . . man is nothing else than his plan; he exists only to the extent that he fulfills himself; he is there-fore nothing else than the ensemble of his acts, nothing else than his life.

When May[4] says, "There is no such thing as truth or reality for a living human being except as he participates in it, is conscious of it, has some relationship to it," he is expressing the phenomenological concept that reality lies in the individual's experience of the event rather than in the isolated event. One might also say that there is, really, no "event," without the human individual. Hatreds and bogey men and chairs exist only as they appear to the individual as they become a part of his experiencing, his living. Thus, we may say that there *is* a world of reality; but, on the other hand, it cannot be reality apart from the people who are the basic part of it. This is a problem faced by all student counselors, and even many of the more sophisti-cated and experienced counselors and therapists still appear to feel strongly that "reality," for them, must somehow also be reality for their client. Rather than accepting him, and thus his reality, and living through it and experiencing it with him, they sit on the outside, subtly or directly imposing their concepts upon him. They thus impede and make more difficult his growth toward greater freedom and self-actualization. It is difficult to modify or change one's reality if one is never allowed to experience deeply just what that reality might be. The insightful counselor, however, sooner or later becomes involved in asking just what reality is, anyway, or whether there is any such thing as an absolute reality. Is reality what we see, and is a wooden table therefore a hard solid piece of matter, rather than consisting of billions of atoms in wild motion, which is the way a table may be seen by a physicist? Is the "color" that a color-blind person sees not real, and the real color that which is seen by people who are not color-blind? Is the avid skier being unrealistic when he glories in the wonderful two feet of snow that has just fallen, while all his non-skiing friends groan

---

[3] Jean-Paul Sartre, *Existentialism and Human Emotions* (New York: The Wisdom Library, 1957), p. 32.
[4] Rollo May, *Existential Psychology* (New York: Random House, 1961), pp. 17–18.

about the miserable weather? Are the psychosomatic headaches real, or can we say to a person who moans with the pain of such a headache, "It isn't really a real headache, so you don't really feel anything"? Can we say that the handsome woman with beautiful hair, who says, "I'm a mess, and my hair is just like a mop," is divorced from reality?

This ability to live another's reality with him might be considered as a description of empathy. This also means that the counselor is one who can live certainly in a world of uncertainty, one who accepts the probability in living with security. All too frequently in counseling, it really is "cases" that we are discussing, and with which we are working, whether we are in a staff conference "case" discussion, or involved in an actual counseling session. We operate with events and problems, and questions and supposed meanings, and the real-life experiencing person, either represented (and nothing more) on a piece of paper, or the flesh-and-blood person in front of us, is ignored and unseen, and we give him little help in the struggle to see who he is, because it is not "him" with whom we are relating.

In a different way, Barry and Wolf are saying much the same thing when they discuss the myths of the vocational counselor:[5]

> The word realism is essentially a mask for value judgments about the practicality and practicability of an idea, a feeling, a plan. . . . Realism is a judgement dependent upon time and the point of view of the person making it.

It is likely that thousands of students throughout the United States have sat in classrooms and offices, today, listening to their teacher or their counselor as he said, among other things, "Now, Joe, let's be realistic about this. . . ." The counselor is indeed making a value judgment, and even worse, he is imposing an absolute reality (his) upon his unfortunate victim.

The more the counselor looks at the question of reality, which in a way is like the cultural version of truth, the more likely he is to conclude, at least temporarily, that there are two broad sets of realities. There is the reality of the group, and there is the reality of the individual. The simple but questionable way in which many people have solved this dilemma is to conclude that reality must be whatever the majority says it is; according to this view, the more the individual moves away from the concept of the group, the more odd or queer or

[5] Ruth Barry and Beverly Wolf, *An Epitaph for Vocational Guidance* (New York: Teachers College, Columbia University, 1962), pp. 90–91.

the crazier he is. This concept might lead to only minor difficulty if one could live in a completely homogeneous society and never leave it, or never become aware that this is only one of many societies, each one having its own set of realities. The scientist may feel that he can easily avoid this difficulty by equating reality with truth. What has been proven empirically to be true is real, and, for the rest, we don't know whether it is real or not. But the "rest" is what daily surrounds almost everyone, and even scientists will haggle over their pitifully small set of "truths." The clergyman may equate reality with "God's truth," but if he is an intelligent clergyman he will have to admit that there are almost as many "God's truths" as there are religious denominations, or even more. As Chenault puts it:[6]

> Consensus is not a valid criterion of truth. It ignores the very personal nature of philosophy and the freedom and right to base professional practice upon it.

For the counselor, at least, it might be best to consider the concept that while there may be a broad set of realities accepted by most of those with whom we live, each individual operates on a set of personal realities. What is real to the client, but not real to the counselor, is nevertheless, as far as the counselor is concerned, *real*. The counselor relates with his client's reality, not his own. This personal reality applies to everyone—the stable, the normally neurotic, and the psychotic; and at least the first two of this trio should be able to see it in operation with themselves, if they look carefully at any time. Unhappiness because one cannot afford two cars is just as real as a people's democracy where no one has the right to vote; fear of a dark room is just as real as a state of freedom where one does what the autocratic ruler says he must do; tension over skin blemishes that no one can see is just as real as a system of student government where the faculty determines what the students can do; student despair because of getting a B now and then instead of all A's is just as real as the inferiority feelings of some individual because of his racial background. All of these things are real to some, unreal to others, but it is the function of the counselor to work with the reality of the client, and, possibly, to help him to come ultimately to a different concept of reality.

It is also real, however, to say that no one individual lives his life alone. While one may stress the need for the individual to be satisfied

---

[6] Joann Chenault, "Professional Standards and Philosophical Freedom: A Peaceful Coexistence," *Counselor Education and Supervision* 3:8–12 (Fall, 1963).

with his self, to feel that "I am doing my thing," this cannot be considered without taking into account the effect this may have on others. The way the person perceives the world around him is real, but the actuality of that world is also real. Glasser[7] feels that a common characteristic of all patients is that they deny the reality of the world around them. He goes on to say, "Therapy will be successful when they (patients) are able to give up denying the world and recognize that reality not only exists but they must fulfill their needs within its framework."

Thus while the counselor is acceptant of, and works with the reality of the client, he is not unaware of the reality of the world that surrounds the client. It is unlikely that any counselor would say that he would be happy to see the client live on in the reality of his world in which he cannot eat because he feels that various members of his family are trying to poison him. Thus in this situation the counselor can be acceptant of the reality of the client, but at the same time would try to help the client to change that perception so that his reality would mesh with that of the outer world, and he could come to see that members of his family were not trying to poison him. The stress in society today is due, not only to the imposition of society on the individual, but also to the insistence of the individual that his rights must take precedence, regardless of the price that others may pay. A society of free men, however, does not consist of those who impose on others.

School counselors sometimes find it particularly difficult to move beyond their own cultural concept of reality, and they tend, too, to associate reality with things that can be seen or touched or smelled or heard. It takes time and experience before they can go beyond their primary senses and be able to accept the concept that goblins really are in that room because a child believes they are; that big blemishes really are on the adolescent girl's face because she believes they are there; that a man really is poor, although his bank balance is over $100,000; that the student with one B and all the rest A's really is doing miserable work.

On the other hand, some counselors, such as the one below, would appear to be trying to impose the reality of the outer world on the client, giving her little chance to experience her feelings about this reality. The client (P) here is described as having a moderate to severe case of mixed psychoneurosis:[8]

---

[7] William Glasser, *Reality Therapy* (New York: Harper and Row, 1965), p. 6.
[8] Stanley W. Standal and Raymond J. Corsini, *Critical Incidents in Psychotherapy* (Englewood Cliffs, N.J.: Prentice-Hall, Inc., 1959), p. 77.

T.: So we know that under certain moods and emotional conditions our thinking is led to exaggerations. In depressive moods, for instance, reality is completely biased and the individual portrays himself far lower than he actually is. You see, you *are not* the way you told me just now; it is only because you are in such a mood that the exaggeration appears.

P.: Then I do not need to worry about the way I see myself now, since this is just the result of a mood?

T.: Right! And therefore you must never take such thinking seriously at such times: It is unrealistic.

Thus it would appear that the counselor should be aware of, acceptant, and understanding of the reality of the client, but he should also be aware of the reality of the outer world, and if the client is to live an effective life then he too must become aware of this outer reality.

COGNITION, KNOWLEDGE, UNDERSTANDING, INSIGHT

The counselor may accept his living in a relative world, but another problem that he faces has to do with knowledge and knowing and understanding. We talk about counseling as a process, a relationship, an experiencing, but at the same time we would appear to feel that clients and counselors can, somehow, come to *know* their way out of their difficulties. Certainly no one would deny the relationship between freedom and knowledge, but one can know without being wise enough to be free. As Whitehead comments:[9]

> You cannot be wise without some basis of knowledge; but you may easily acquire knowledge and remain bare of wisdom. Now wisdom is the way in which knowledge is held.

And again:[10]

> In a sense, knowledge shrinks as wisdom grows; for details are swallowed up in principles.

---

[9] Alfred North Whitehead, *The Aims of Education and Other Essays* (New York: The New American Library, 1960), p. 41.
[10] *Ibid.*, p. 48.

Much earlier, Cowper contributed a related thought:[11]

> Knowledge is proud that he has learned so much,
> Wisdom is humble that he knows no more.

The behavioral science concept of man has also tended to delude many counselors into the belief that by knowing about man they could also know man. One may learn about man by examining him, by studying him and analyzing him, but one may still be a long way from knowing the real man. Only by an experiencing and living-with can the counselor come to know the real person-in-being, the existential man.

Counselors have generally accepted the concept that the more we know about the client the better our chance of being effective with him. We might wonder, however, whether the material we use to get to "know" the client may possibly move us away from him, and help us to develop a highly distorted and biased picture. Each time a piece of information about one human being passes through another human being it comes out a little less like the original. Often, for example, we may have several reports from the teachers of a child, but we have no reports on the teachers or the circumstances under which the reports were made. Even when we have what might be called standardized test data we should keep in mind the fact that the people who administer the tests, and those who interpret the test data, are not standardized!

We might hypothesize, at least, that the client with whom we are working is the person who is now in the office with us, and this person may or may not bear much resemblance to the person as categorized in an information folder. We may also wonder about the relative importance of the degree to which the person present apparently differs from the test data person. In speaking to a group of psychoanalysts Hartmann was expressing the same general feeling when he said, "Despite what the great Plato thought about it, we do not believe in a simple correlation between the steps toward insight and the steps to moral improvement."[12]

This skepticism about the extent to which knowledge helps us to actually know a person is also indicated by Walsh when he says, "I am not at all certain that the help that they receive is a direct result of our

---

[11] James Robert Boyd (Ed.), *The Task, Table Talk and Other Poems of William Cowper*, Book VI, *Winter Walk at Noon* (New York: A. S. Barnes and Co., 1853), p. 297.
[12] Heinz Hartmann, *Psychoanalysis and Moral Values* (New York: International Universities Press, 1960), p. 91.

sophisticated knowledge of the mind, unless in the process of accumulating that knowledge we have also gained wisdom and compassion for and about people."[13] We may thus question the extent to which human understanding, and thus human communication, is dependent on the possession of didactic information, often of a highly questionable nature from equally questionable sources, and raise at least the possibility that this may pose a real hindrance to the development of a deep and basic understanding between two people.

The concept of the relationship between knowing and insight is a product of both our formal educational system and psychoanalytic therapy. In the more traditional psychoanalysis the therapist imparted insight so that the patient could understand his unconscious mind and unconscious motivations, and the imparting of knowledge to the student by the teacher has been viewed as the primary function of the school.

The "knowing about" is found in both the school curricular experience and in counseling, and in schools we usually see what we might call either an "information" counselor, or a "diagnostic" counselor. These counselors are both concerned primarily with the transmission of information *to* the client, although the typical information counselor would probably be transmitting educational and occupational information, while the diagnostic counselor would be more likely to be transmitting an interpretation of personal test data about the client. Thus the first counselor would likely find communication most difficult, since often he is transmitting, at best, information that *he* thinks the client wants and needs. The diagnostic counselor, on the other hand, is at least transmitting information *about* the client, but it is still *from* the counselor *to* the client. Often too, of course, not only is the information dubious and questionable, but the client is a rather passive or even unwilling recipient of the information. Frequently, the basic purpose of this transmission of information is the manipulation and direction of the client so that he may become more "adjusted," more able to fit easily and comfortably into the status quo, and a less curious, questioning, rebellious member of his society. These counselors see the gathering and interpretation of knowledge, and its transmission to the client, as their basic function.

The counselor who is concerned with a basic human relationship, on the other hand, is one who thinks in terms of "the client to me," rather than "me to the client." Thus his verbal communication is based

---

[13] Richard P. Walsh, "Comment," *American Psychologist* 16:712–713 (November, 1961).

on the client as he presents himself, rather than on the client as he is presented by others and by test data. He has no preconceived information to give to the client, unless it is information that the client desires, information that will be helpful in the process of communication. Since most communication, however, is not really very deep if it is at an information level, it is not too often that information, per se, enters into the relationship between this counselor and the client. The bare bones statistic of an IQ of 91 for a college freshman, who is being driven to desperation by the difficulty of his courses and the pressure of his professors and his family, is of no importance whatsoever to the counselor who sees himself involved in a warm and human relationship with another person, and in attempting to communicate non-verbally to that person his depth of understanding and acceptance.

If we are to think of man as a determined set of behaviors, then we could agree that ultimately every facet of man will be put under a microscope and examined, and prediction and control of the human race will become a part of an exact and empirical science. We might, on the other hand, hypothesize that one of the reasons why both psychology and medicine have never really got close to man, the total living being, is that they have fallen into the trap of empiricism. To medicine, man is a disease; to psychologists, he is a problem; to psychiatrists, he is a disease-problem; and to counselors, too frequently, he appears to be a profile of the results of various tests and examinations. Science has generally accepted the words "cognitive" and "meaningful" as somewhat synonymous. At least I think that science would probably say that the less cognitive a picture of man is, the less meaningful it is. My own perception would be that man—not man's behavior, since you cannot cut one off from the other, but man, the total existential being, if you will—is not really subject to empirical examination, and that both a human experience and a human being could mean very little in a cognitive sense, and yet at the same time could be overwhelmingly meaningful.

The empiricist would likely put knowing—cognition—above feeling, but we can know in an empirically cognitive sense without understanding in a feeling sense, and we can understand a fellow human without "knowing about" him, although we might consider "knowing about" to be more cognitive than "knowing." Menninger,[14] for example, shows more concern than many of his fellow psychiatrists with the total man.

---

[14] Karl A. Menninger, *The Vital Balance* (New York: The Viking Press, Inc., 1963).

It may also be that some counselors know much about the client, but have confused this knowing with self-understanding on the part of the client. They may then add to this confusion by "giving" the client more supposed knowledge, from some outer source, about himself. Roessler comments on this point:[15]

> But the term "cognitive," for me, denotes too much intellectual emphasis in the psychotherapeutic process . . . the process of change . . . is really more a function of experiencing oneself in totality.

As does Hora:[16]

> But if cognition, which is another word for understanding . . . if understanding, clarification, elucidation, seeing the light, seeing what one really is, if this is the focus of psychotherapy, then one would be careful not to say more, not to talk too much because it might hamper understanding. . . . So then, not the explicit, but the implicit will have the therapeutic value, and so there will be less and less talk.

Jung would appear to have been thinking in a somewhat similar manner when he said:[17]

> We appeal only to the patient's brain if we try to inculcate a truth; but if we help him to grow up to this truth in the course of his own development, we have reached his heart, and this appeal goes deeper and acts with greater force.

As does Gendlin:[18]

> Now that psychotherapy is widely thought to involve a concrete feeling process, we are less specific about the (still vital) role of cognitive symbols and exploration. . . . Apparently, any good vocabulary can be used as a symbolic tool for "working through" and interacting.

There are some counselors and some counselor educators who might say that the above words do not apply to them because they are

---

[15] Robert L. Roessler, "Psychotherapy: Healing or Growth," *Annals of Psychotherapy* 4:10 (1963).

[16] Thomas Hora, in *Annals of Psychotherapy* 4:10 (1963), p. 33.

[17] C. G. Jung, *Modern Man in Search of a Soul* (New York: Harcourt, Brace & World, Inc., 1933), p. 9.

[18] Eugene T. Gendlin, "Subverbal Communication and Therapist Expressivity: Trends in Client-centered Therapy with Schizophrenics," *Journal of Existential Psychiatry* 4:105 (Fall, 1963).

not involved in this "personal counseling or therapy sort of business," but rather in the "talking to, telling, information business." I would think that any form of human communication between the counselor and the client is personal, and the above words apply just as much when the client is a child who comes in to talk easily with the counselor about his job plans for the next year, as they do when the client is a child driven to desperation by his neurotic parents. They may apply even more in the former case, because it is in this talking relationship that the counselor may be most easily lulled into the false security of verbiage, just as the teacher who drones on endlessly assumes that the children *must* be learning something.

All of this, too, raises serious questions about the place of insight in the counseling process. Insight has generally been equated with self-understanding. The person who is insightful knows where he stands; he knows what he has and what he does not have. Insight usually implies, too, that not only does the individual know his assets and liabilities, but he operates with some reference to them. Thus an individual who knows that he has a low intellectual capacity but deliberately takes on a job that requires high intellectual capacity might be considered as having little insight. He knows his limitations, but he ignores them. Interestingly enough, however, despite the general acceptance of this point, it is contradicted by many school counselors who seem to feel that all that is needed for improvement is the first part of this insight—the knowing. Thus, more often than not, the use of test data in schools seems to assume that all the counselor has to do is test the students—and tell them what they have and what they do not have, and everyone will live happily ever after. Certainly for the counselor, insightfulness, if it is to be considered at all, must include the assimilation and internalization of knowledge, so that it becomes a part of the total operational individual rather than an intellectual appendage. Each of us gradually develops a basic operational self concept, and it is difficult to see how one can expect a person blithely and easily to accept a piece of information that means that this self concept has to be altered drastically.

It should be noted too, that an individual may wish, desperately, to change certain attitudes and feelings whose causes and development he has come, possibly through counseling, to understand very well. Thus the client may say, "I know all these feelings that I have are just superstitions, and that they are not really religion at all, and I know why I have believed them. But why must I still go on believing them when I don't want to and when I know they are silly?" The client must go on believing them because he still needs to go on believing them, and he will continue to do so until his self is altered.

The place of insight in the therapeutic process has tended to be downgraded in recent years. Glasser,[19] for example, in discussing Reality Therapy, says, "we emphasize behavior; we do not depend upon insight to change attitudes because in many cases it never will." Wolpe and Lazarus,[20] in indicating how behavior therapy differs from psychoanalytic therapy, say "Behavior therapists, by contrast, regard rational corrections as, in most instances merely a background to the specific reconditioning of reactions that usually belong to the autonomic nervous system." Holland[21] simply says, "We can therefore regard insight as potentially useful, but as neither sufficient nor necessary to modifications of the patient's behavior in a psychotherapeutic situation."

Counselors who see the human relationship as the crucial factor in counseling, tend to think in terms of experiencing rather than the gaining of intellectual insight. Beier[22] comments that "We speak specifically of 'experiencing' rather than of 'having insight,' because these two objectives can be most successfully realized when the patient is alerted to his own immediate behavior as it occurs . . . and not when it is discussed with him in the abstract." Corlis and Rabe,[23] in discussing a counseling session, say, "To repeat, the patient's experiencing is needed, not the explaining." Carkhuff and Berenson who view confrontation as the critical element in counseling, see insight as being of negative importance rather than of no importance:[24]

> At best, insight inundates affect with ideas and drowns it in a whirlpool of words. At worst, the person is left with the feeling of being splintered into a thousand pieces, in contact with the fact that he has no identity of his own, only fitting in relation to specific people and situations.
> . . . Thus, the alienated person who seeks *only* insights slowly decays while having the illusion of making progress.

---

19 Glasser, *op. cit.*, p. 51.
20 Joseph Wolpe and Arnold A. Lazarus, *"Behavior Therapy Techniques* (New York: Pergamon Press, 1966), p. 131.
21 Glen A. Holland, *Fundamentals of Psychotherapy* (New York: Holt, Rinehart and Winston, Inc., 1965), p. 38.
22 Ernst G. Beier, *The Silent Language of Psychotherapy* (Chicago: Aldine Publishing Co., 1966), p. 54.
23 Rahe Corlis and Peter Rabe, *Psychotherapy from the Center* (Scranton, Penn.: International Text Book Co., 1969), p. 74.
24 Robert R. Carkhuff and Bernard G. Berenson, *Beyond Counseling and Psychotherapy* (New York: Holt, Rinehart and Winston, Inc., 1967), p. 177.

The counselor is little concerned with insight as interpreted in terms of intellectual understanding. He is concerned if it is to be related with process, if it is to be an experiencing, a living, a being again with real and deep feelings. Thus the insightfulness of the client may include the experiencing again of the dreadful feeling of aloneness, but an aloneness that after a while is not the same, because there is someone this time who cares, someone who is concerned. Maybe it could be thought of in terms of a noun or a verb. If a noun, it doesn't matter too much; if a verb, it matters very much. If the client is now a person who no longer feels alone in a strange world, then insight, in terms of the traditional concept of understanding, is more than likely a by-product. In fact, the client might well say, "Of course, I know now that I'm not alone, but then I always did *know* that I was not alone, only I didn't believe it before." He knew intellectually, but he didn't believe what he knew. Now he believes, and we might say that it does not matter too much whether he knows or not.

This client, for example, did not have any clear knowledge about just what had happened when he said:

> The degree of trust I have in myself has a close relationship to how well I know myself. . . . I've learned something—about myself—in a tentative sort of way—that I didn't know even a few weeks ago—(pause)—maybe I'll talk about that. . . .

In the book by Burton that has already been referred to several times, there is a series of questions at the end of each of the fifteen case studies.[25] One of these questions is "Do you feel that this case developed significant insight? If not, can improvement be maintained?" It is of interest to note that twelve of the fifteen answers said, in varying ways, "Yes" or "No." One gave a reaction that was somewhat similar to that which has been presented in this book. The other two were as follows:

> If by insight is meant conscious insight, then the answer is "no." If by insight is meant unconscious, then the answer is "yes." In either case, the patient has maintained her improvement for a period of five years. (*Conscious* insight has the quality of intricate fact-finding or even of simple memory of related details. Through hindsight, the patient forms such details into a significant *gestalt. Unconscious* insight has a quality of experiencing in the present a previously not accepted capacity. The patient may never become aware of what has occurred in him to change his behavior.)[26]

---

[25] Burton, *op. cit.*
[26] *Ibid.*, p. 256.

Intellectual insight is no longer a *sine qua non* of improvement in psychotherapy. It may be epiphenomenal but not necessarily causal. While we know very little about emotional insight, some such experience may take place. However, this is a function of the *Begegnung* and the change in the vector forces which come about through it. Such process is largely symbolic. (I have since regretted formulating this question for the *Addendum* except that heuristically it does reveal the present state of insight in modern-day psychotherapy.) [27]

Insight, then, would appear to be an understanding that one may gain about himself, but it is a product of experiencing more than knowing. The counselor is an individual who should have achieved a high level of self-understanding, and the evidence would tend to indicate that sensitivity to others is a function of insight into oneself. [28] Nor is this self-understanding or insight something that one acquires from someone else. As Dreikurs says, "The therapist gave her strength, but no insight or reorientation." [29]

Insight, then, is a sort of an end product. It is a deep and meaningful understanding, by me, about me, and about others. These comments, from junior high school clients, are insightful, but their cognitive respectability is of little importance compared with the fact that they are understandings arrived at by the children as a result of their human relationship with an insightful counselor:

> The more pressure a teacher puts on a kid the greater the chance that the kid will resent whatever it is that the teacher is trying to do. A kid will do anything for a teacher who respects him.
>
> When are people going to start putting some of the blame on the school when a kid quits? He could be quitting because he's bored right out of his skin by subjects that have been forced on him, and have no use in his life.
>
> You learn more when you do something in class . . . when you're involved . . . when you're participating instead of watching and listening . . . like when you're in science and you do the experiments. . . . I really learn something.
>
> It's too bad the world isn't the kind of place a kid could get into trouble without getting into trouble—you know what I mean? Everybody gets so hot and bothered about delinquents and stuff like that, but if kids could have a chance to have some fun and excitement, and could do things with a little kick in them, they'd be all right. But all the adults want you to play the game with their rules. . . . The only trouble is they forget we're not adults. It's a lot more fun for us to break rules than to keep them.

---

[27] *Ibid.*, p. 280.
[28] See William J. Mueller, "The Influence of Self Insight on Social Perception Scores," *Journal of Counseling Psychology* 10:185–191 (Summer, 1963).
[29] Rudolph Dreikurs, in Standal and Corsini, *op. cit.*, p. 70.

EMPATHY AND CONGRUENCE

An empathic relationship is achieved when the counselor is able to work within the client's frame of reference, within the client's reality, responding with sensitivity to both the superficial and the deeper feelings of the client, some conscious, some unconscious. The counselor must also be able to communicate to the client his awareness of the client and his awareness of himself, and to do this he must be a genuine and congruent individual. The self that is communicated to the client must be genuine and human, and the counselor who can only repeat words or mumble, or ask clinically correct questions like a machine, or set up appropriate experiences for the client like an engineer—such a counselor is obviously going to have a difficult time establishing an empathic relationship with a client. Carkhuff and Berenson[30] put it succinctly and well when they say, "If there can be no authenticity in therapy, then there can be no authenticity in life." Corlis and Rabe[31] are equally expressive when they say, "He gave the shirt off his back and has not been heard of since. So much for the Good Samaritan."

Probably all counselors would agree that there is both a cognitive and an affective component in the achievement of an empathic relationship with another human being, but some would obviously stress one a good deal more than the other. It is interesting to note that Wolpe,[32] who sees himself as a "behavioral scientist," chides some of his fellows, who, "espousing notions of rigid behavorial engineering, imagine that one can do without such personal influencing processes."

In describing the client, Buchheimer and Balogh say:[33]

> The way he constructs his reality and the percepts he has of himself determine the way he addresses himself to his life's tasks and the goals he formulates for his life's work. It is important therefore, that the counselor allow the person with whom he is to work freedom in self-expression as well as expression of self in relation to problems and goals.

---

[30] Carkhuff and Berenson, *op. cit.*, p. 29.
[31] Corlis and Rabe, *op. cit.*, p. 37.
[32] Wolpe and Lazarus, *op. cit.*, p. 29.
[33] Arnold Buchheimer and Sara Carter Balogh, *The Counseling Relationship* (Chicago: Science Research Associates, 1961), p. 3.

382 : *The Nature of Counseling*

It is in the empathic climate that this expression of self can develop, and it is through this self-expression that one gradually comes, possibly, to perceive himself in a different manner. Man has many faces, but there is one face, for each of us, that is more basic, more real, and the client comes to sense this face when he is able to accept the current face. He can say, as has been said to me, "You know, when I actually could accept me as I was, then, right at that moment, me wasn't the same any more." As Hora puts it:[34]

> . . . if a human being attains the level of integration where he really can be what he really is, then every moment and every manifestation of his life will be a creative one.

And to be what one is, one must be a congruent, genuine, self-actualized individual. One must be able to be easily honest with oneself, and I would agree with Rosenfels that "wisdom is the product of an unfailing honesty."[35]

The congruent individual, too, is one who can perceive accurately, and Lesser[36] has reported on an interesting study, which indicated that mere feelings, by the counselor, or similarity with the client, were not conducive to counseling progress and empathic understanding. More basic was the correct perception, by the counselor, of similarity, or lack of it. In a somewhat related fashion, Buchheimer[37] has pointed out that in an empathic relationship cognitive perception of the other person becomes the capacity to perceive the counselee's frame of reference.

Thus this honesty with self, this genuineness, this self-congruence on the part of the counselor, would appear to be the crucial factor in the development of an empathic relationship in which the client also might move toward actualization and freedom. This means, too, that the counselor must be free to feel his feelings during the counseling relationship, rather than bottling them up, or presenting both to himself and to the client a blank face and pretending that he has no feelings. Since the counselor is a self-actualized individual, these

---

[34] Hora, *op. cit.*, p. 51.
[35] Paul Rosenfels, *Psychoanalysis and Civilization* (New York: Libra Publishers, Inc., 1962), p. 83.
[36] William M. Lesser, "The Relationship Between Counseling Progress and Empathic Understanding," *Journal of Counseling Psychology* 8:330–336 (Winter, 1961).
[37] Arnold Buchheimer, "The Development of Ideas About Empathy," *Journal of Counseling Psychology* 10:61–70 (Spring, 1963).

feelings will be directed at himself, rather than at the client. This point is illustrated by Roessler, when, in discussing another therapist's description of his feelings during a counseling session, he comments:[38]

> . . . we could have been annoyed, irritated, and expressed this . . . the same consequences, so long as it wasn't "Damn you for behaving this way," and instead, "I'm annoyed, I'm frustrated. Something's wrong, and something needs to be done."

This also stresses, obviously, the crucial necessity of counselor education centering on the deep and meaningful understanding *of the counselor* by the counselor, rather than on a superficial cognitive understanding of the client.

TRANSFERENCE AND COUNTER-TRANSFERENCE

Although the phenomena of transference may not be the usual experience of most counselors, particularly school counselors, as they work with their clients, they should have some awareness of what it is so that they might be more aware of its potential occurrence, and be able to differentiate it from a more psuedo sort of transference that probably occurs with all counselors. Most analytically oriented counselors would tend generally to be acceptant of the following somewhat traditional descriptions of transference. First we may note Alexander:[39]

> The principal therapeutic tool is the transference, in which the patient relives, in relation to the therapist his earlier interpersonal conflicts. Regression to the dependent attitudes of infancy and childhood is a constant feature of the transference, and, in the majority of cases, the central one. This regression in itself has a supportive effect. It allows the patient to postpone his own decisions and to reduce the responsibilities of adult existence by retiring into a dependent attitude toward the therapist which resembles the child's attitude in the child-parent relationship.

Then Hendrick:[40]

---

[38] Roessler, *op. cit.*, p. 27.

[39] Franz Alexander, *Psychoanalysis and Psychotherapy* (New York: W. W. Norton & Company, Inc., 1956), p. 154.

[40] Ives Hendrick, *Facts and Theories of Psychoanalysis* (New York: Alfred A. Knopf, Inc., 1958), p. 193.

For when a patient recounts free associations, he soon speaks of events or phantasies of vital interest to himself, and when these are told, the listener is gradually invested with some of the emotion which accompanies them. The patient gradually begins to feel that the sympathetic listener is loved or hated, a friend or an enemy, one who is nice to him or one who frustrates his needs and punishes him. The feelings toward the listener become more and more like those felt toward the specific people the patient is talking about, or, more exactly, those his unconscious "is talking about." This special case of object-displacement during psychoanalysis is called transference.

And finally, Horney:[41]

Freud observed that in the analytical situation the patient not only talks about his present and past troubles, but also shows emotional reactions to the analyst. These reactions are frequently irrational in character. A patient may forget entirely his purpose in coming to analysis and may find nothing important except being loved or appreciated by the analyst. He may develop altogether disproportionate fears about jeopardizing his relationship to the analyst. He may transform the situation, which in actuality is one in which the analyst helps the patient to straighten out his problems, into one of passionate struggle for the upper hand. For instance, instead of feeling relieved by some clarification of his problems, a patient may see only one fact, that the analyst has recognized something that he was unaware of, and he may react with violent anger. A patient may, contrary to his own interests, secretly pursue the purpose of defeating the analyst's endeavors.

The general concept held by both the medical doctor psychotherapist and the counseling psychologist is that this transference relationship takes place in psychotherapy, and that it is the working out, the explaining of these transferred feelings, including resistances and hostility, that helps the client to move ahead. It is important for the student counselor to note that when such a transference relationship does develop, it is not a case of superficial feeling, or of dislike on the part of the client for the therapist because he is like someone the client used to know. It is, rather, an infusion of feelings into the therapist, so that the therapist *is* the hated and autocratic father of twenty years ago, and the resistances that develop are as "real" as they can be. It is not that the client thinks he can now see how hostile and submissive he felt toward his father—he *is* hostile and submissive, and the therapist *is* his father. It is the gradual understanding of the why and the what

---

[41] Karen Horney, *New Ways in Psychoanalysis* (New York: W. W. Norton & Company, Inc., 1939), pp. 154–155.

and the how of this phenomenon that helps the client to greater growth. As Mowrer says:[42]

> Rather does the therapist help the patient to see what he is trying to accomplish by means of his "transference" behavior which is now just as real and just as meaningful as it originally was—and to understand the circumstances in which this type of behavior originated and why it was not earlier resolved.

Thus the client comes to feel as he once felt, but there is a difference. Although he is feeling as he did before toward a superior figure, this authority figure is now one who will be acceptant of his negative feelings, and will help him to understand them rather than reject him and strengthen his basic negative feelings.

Such authority and superiority of the "doctor" or the therapist are stressed again and again in psychoanalytic literature. This reaction is easy to understand, particularly with the medical doctor therapist. Here is a person who has had a background of education and training and work where without a doubt in the vast majority of the cases he does have the answers as to what to do about the ailments of a patient—a patient who, most often, does not know what is wrong with him, and does not know what to do about it. The doctor is in authority, and he *is* the superior figure. Nor does working in a hospital tend to diminish the feeling. There the therapist is in an environment where the patients are very often psychotic, or are assumed to be psychotic, and in the staff relationship the therapist finds himself at the top of the hierarchical ladder. Although there may be frequent reference to teamwork, it is usually quite evident who is the top sergeant of the team! Thus the phenomenon of transference is very definitely related to the authority and superiority of the therapist. If the therapist did not have such authority and superiority in the eyes of both himself and his client, then we might raise the question of whether or not transference would take place. On this point Rogers writes:[43]

> For the analyst this means that he interprets such attitudes, and perhaps through these evaluations establishes the characteristic transference relationship. For the Client-centered therapist this means that he attempts to understand and accept such attitudes, which then tend

---

[42] O. Hobart Mowrer (Ed.), *Psychotherapy: Theory and Research* (New York: The Ronald Press Company, 1953), p. 567.
[43] Carl R. Rogers, *Client-Centered Therapy* (Boston: Houghton Mifflin Co., 1951), p. 218.

to become accepted by the client as being his own perception of the situation, inappropriately held.

Corlis and Rabe are even more skeptical about the traditional ideas toward transference. They say:[44]

> What is transferred to the therapist are the patient's attitudes. If a transference relationship is to result, the therapist must then fall into the role which the patient "transfers" upon him. Traditionally, this distortion imposed upon the relationship is encouraged. In our technique we do not encourage it.

Thus, the client may have the feelings that are possible of transference in the transference relationship, but they are not transferred to the counselor if the counselor has become to the client the sort of person that the counselor can be. It is on this point, indeed, that some counselors present a most valid and reasonable criticism: can the counselor really be this sort of person, both to himself and to the client? The counselor, after all, does know more than the client about the psychology of personality disturbances. He is very frequently, in the hierarchy of values, someone who is considered to be more important than the client; and he is the one to whom the client goes to find answers, or at least to go through some experience that will make him a better adjusted person. How, then, can the counselor avoid being superior and authoritative, both in his own eyes and in those of the client?

This is a question that no counselor can answer in an absolute fashion. Certainly, more in the way of knowledge and emotional stability on the part of one individual does not mean actual or felt superiority to someone else. A counselor may feel very deeply the worth and dignity of his client. He respects him as a fellow man—not as a client, not as a disturbed person, not as a selfish creature—simply as a fellow human being. How well and how honestly does he do this? Each counselor must try to answer that for himself.

If, in either group or individual therapy, the counselor is to become completely accepted by the other members of the group (one or more), as a member of the group, it would seem that he must lose his identity as the "leader." As long as he is the leader, in the mind and in the feelings of the client or the other members of the group, he cannot be a member of the group; he remains an outsider. As an

---

[44] Corlis and Rabe, *op. cit.,* p. 95.

outsider he is suspect, and he is, needless to say, one on whom it would be very easy to transfer feelings. In a normal group session, for instance, a leader statement such as, "What one of you said there a few minutes ago made me feel sort of mad," would cause the defensive flags of most of the members of the group to rise. This would happen because the leader is still the leader. He is the *outside* critic.

But in some group sessions, and in some counseling sessions, the situation changes. The leader gradually disappears as the leader, and becomes rather a member of a group (of two or more) going through an exciting experience. The counselor may feel that while the counselor is the sort of person who is not very often threatened or disturbed, he is, nevertheless, a human being. If, at a certain point, as he is immersed with the client in the client's expression of feelings, he realizes, "This sort of worries me," then it may be better that, remaining at all times honest, he express his feeling to the client. If the counseling relationship has developed as it *can* develop, the client will not be threatened by such an expression of feeling on the part of this other person (not the boss, or the authority, or the head man) who is going through this experience with him. On the other hand, we can assume that if the counselor, in order to maintain his integrity and honesty, must be continually telling the client that he is worried or concerned by something in the discussion, then this person should be the client rather than the counselor!

It is likely, too, that there is a wide variance on the part of counselors in their ideas of just what constitutes transference. Might one not be liked or disliked by a client in a purely personal manner? Since counselors, after all, have had people fall in love with them (and vice versa) in a non-counseling relationship, we could probably assume that some clients might fall in love, or some reasonable facsimile thereof, with a counselor in his office as well as outside his office. On this question one therapist writes:[45]

> Much of what is cavalierly called "transference" by many therapists, and dogmatically interpreted to their patients as such seems actually to be the patient's becoming attached to the therapist on a fairly clear-cut reality basis. The therapist is, after all, usually quite intelligent; a sympathetic listener; fairly cultured; of good socioeconomic standing; and seemingly of a suitable age to many of his female patients. . . . This is not to gainsay the fact that in *many* instances patients fall in love with their therapists because the latter unconsciously represent father-figures, authority-symbols, and so forth. . . .

[45] Anonymous author, in Standal and Corsini, *op. cit.,* pp. 90–91.

But to insist that classic transference exists where it patently does not leads to other difficulties, including the avoidance of some of the patient's basic desires and the forcing on her of a false interpretation.

These client comments, for example, were made to counselors:

Client 1: People don't really care about people . . . you don't really care what happens to me . . . you're getting paid to sit and listen to me but you don't really give a damn whether I sink or swim.

Client 2: And then he stood there yelling at me to straighten out the wheels on the car. I clenched my fist and put it up to his face (does this to counselor) . . . and then I yelled back . . . (yells at counselor) . . . yell at me again and I'll break your neck."

Client 3: And for that brief vacation she really filled a void in my life. . . . We talked for hours and it really made me feel as if someone cared . . . like . . . like now I know . . . I have a feeling that you care for me . . . because . . . well . . . you've given me the . . . I mean . . . a chance to talk . . . a chance not to be lonely. . . .

Client 4: And I guess maybe I love you. . . . That's all right, isn't it. . . .

Client 5: All I ask is not to be interrupted when I'm saying something. . . . If there's anything I despise it's being cut off in the middle of a sentence. . . . She always did that to me and now when you do it . . . well, just don't. . . . I won't be able to talk to you if you do.

Client 6: There are just the two of you—and I love you both, but in a different way.

Client 7: Yeh . . . I could always make him anxious . . . and right now you're anxious, aren't you?

These are certainly examples of highly personal expressions of feeling by the client toward the counselor, but the counselor would not appear in these examples to be anyone other than himself. In a way, the client feelings may be being transferred to him from someone else, but in the mind of the client he still retains his identity as the counselor, rather than becoming some earlier authority figure.

These examples could be described as transference if we use the description given by Bellak and Small[46] who say, ". . . In the present discussion, transference is used broadly as comprising all the non-rational sentiments of the patient toward the therapist including hopes, fears, likes, and dislikes."

Although Borden agrees with the concept that the therapeutic process is possible without the development of the transference rela-

---

[46] Leopold Bellak and Leonard Small, *Emerging Psychotherapy and Brief Psychotherapy* (New York: Grune and Stratton, 1965), p. 40.

tionship, his reasoning that this is because of the lack of depth of counseling is to be questioned:[47]

> Because the counselor deals with relatively well-integrated individuals who are reasonably free of intense conflicts, his clients are not likely to exhibit many transference phenomena and will not readily develop intensive transference relationships unless subjected to quite ambiguous relationships over a relatively long period of time. Since most clients will not come with a profound therapeutic orientation, deep transference can take place in only a minority of instances.

Historically, the attention of therapists has been directed toward the behavior of their clients; thus it might be assumed that attention would be directed at the transference of the client's feelings toward the counselor rather than at the transference of the counselor's feelings toward the client. This phenomenon of counter-transference has been defined, like transference, as ranging all the way from an omnibus inclusion of all of the feelings of the counselor toward the client to the more subconscious and suppressed feelings of the counselor that may be brought out by the transference of feelings from the client.

Generally, however, as in transference, there is a differentiation between a surface relationship—such as a Baptist counselor's possible feeling of irritation toward a client who continually utters anti-Baptist statements—and the possible development of subtle but deep feelings of paternalism toward a younger male client who identifies with the counselor as an autocratic father figure.

These counselors, for example, have become personally involved, and their expressions are indications of their own concern about themselves, rather than about the client. Again, these are hardly examples of counter-transference in the classic sense, although the counselor is transferring some of his personal feelings over to the client.

> *Counselor 1:* I can't, Martha, I can't—you must do it.
> *Counselor 2:* Don't you realize that I really do care what happens to my clients. I care what happens to you—I always have.
> *Counselor 3:* Anxious . . . who . . . ? . . . me?
> *Counselor 4:* Well, I wouldn't say that to him. . . . You've always been sort of meek and mild and if you ever said anything like that . . . well, he might think that I encouraged you to say it . . . that I sort of encouraged you to rebel. Saying that would only lead to more trouble for you.
> *Counselor 5:* It would be nice if you mentioned to your mother how much I've been able to help you in counseling.

---

[47] Edward S. Borden, *Psychological Counseling* (New York: Appleton-Century-Crofts, 1955), p. 150.

Counselor 6: Your search for justice may not bear fruit . . . trying to find a universal kind of justice could make a person bitter because maybe it doesn't exist.

Most counselors could probably understand, and possibly see in themselves the sort of feelings described as counter-transference by Hafner:[48]

> In this phase of treatment my counter-transference for the first time became a serious problem. After several apparently fruitless hours, I felt considerable unrest creeping up in me, since I was increasingly groping in the dark in front of my silent patient. I felt pressed to do some active analyzing, but I had to concede to myself that in this situation activity on my part might well have endangered everything that had been achieved so far. Gradually, I felt a certain resignation. I feared my treatment could fail after all. Thus I recognized aggressive impulses within myself coming up against Gisels as I anticipated the frustration of my own wish for a successful completion of her treatment. I experienced these hours that apparently had passed uselessly as a waste of time.
>
> Under these circumstances I found it difficult to carry through the treatment with a persistently friendly attitude. But it seems, after all, that I succeeded in it. . . .

Although the therapist here did not verbalize to the patient his feelings about her, the fact that he can write easily about them, the fact that he could consciously be aware of them and acceptant of them, might, in a way, be a reflection of his own honesty and security; and it was to this that his patient was reacting, so that she could feel, correctly, that he was basically being kind and understanding toward her. I would tend to think of this as a human experience. If that is what is meant by counter-transference, then it would be difficult to see how any counselor could avoid being involved periodically in such an experience.

---

[48] Heinz Hafner, "A Case of Pseudo-Neurotic Schizophrenia," in Burton, *op. cit.,* p. 302.

part 4

THE COUNSELING EXPERIENCE

chapter 13

THE BEGINNING

In this final section of the book, the counseling process will be considered primarily by observation of what actually happened in a series of counseling sessions with a number of clients and a number of counselors. This is not a case book, but excerpts from various counseling sessions with different students and different clients will be used to illustrate certain phases and aspects of the counseling process. Extensive use will be made of John Bin, a high school client; Tom Ril, an adult client; the five clients, Carl, Jane, Jack, Edna and Richard, in Evraiff's case book;[1] and a number of other high school clients.

The clients presented here are basically ordinary, normal human beings facing problems of living. The children are in school, and if one is willing to accept the professional title of counselor, he should be professionally competent enough to work with them in a counseling relationship. The adults are individuals who were in school, and received little assistance and little help when they needed it. The counselors would probably use a variety of names to describe their counseling. The counselors also represent a range of experience, from those with a doctorate degree in the field and many years of professional counseling, including counseling of private clients, to student counselors who are almost at the beginning stage.

The counselors of John Bin and Tom Ril did not tape their first

---

[1] William Evraiff, *Helping Counselors Grow Professionally* (Englewood Cliffs, N.J.: Prentice-Hall, Inc., 1963).

sessions, so we will not see them until the next chapter. This initial taping poses something of a problem for some counselors in some schools, although the major difficulty is often the counselor's own uncertainty about what to do. In clinical or laboratory situations this is less of a problem, and in an increasing number of schools taping is taken as a matter of course by the students, although, as has already been mentioned, this is an ethical issue that cannot be dismissed lightly. Many counselors, particularly in schools, do feel that a tape hinders the establishment of rapport somewhat during the first session, and will withhold the use of a tape, usually bringing up the subject toward the end of the first session, and then using it, if satisfactory to the client, from the second session on.

THE SETTING FOR COUNSELING

One of the immediate problems—sometimes an overwhelming problem—that faces any counselor is the setting, the environment, the situation for counseling. Probably most schools still provide a poor setting for counseling, although the situation varies to a tremendous degree from school to school. The pressure to improve the quality and to increase the numbers of counselors is also having its impact on facilities for counseling, although we are probably getting better counselors faster than we are getting better facilities, and if we must have a choice, of course, this is the way it should be. Better a good counselor in miserable surroundings than a miserable counselor in superlative surroundings! On the whole, however, it would probably be safe to say that even in new schools the provisions that are being made for counseling facilities have not improved as much as have the facilities for other aspects of the school program, such as, for example, the teaching of foreign languages. Facilities that can be used in the education of counselors, such as counseling rooms with sound equipment for monitoring and recording, and one-way mirrors, are, other than in a few schools and laboratory institutions, practically nonexistent. Many schools have reached the point where they admit the need for a counselor, but they still do not see why he has to have anything different in the way of facilities than the teacher. This is particularly so in those schools where "counseling" is still seen as a friendly chit-chat, or the offering of some advice by a person who, even though he may have the title "counselor," is still seen as a teacher, and who, in fact, very likely actually *is* a teacher masquerading in a counselor's clothes!

Every counselor should recognize this as a two-sided question, for many sincere individuals are concerned as to just how far the school should go in the provision of various services that are only indirectly related to the educational process. Actually, it boils down to one very simple and direct question: Do you believe that every American child has the right to a chance to have that educational experience which is best for him? If the answer is "Yes," then the school must also provide those personnel services which insure that the child can benefit from the educational experience that is being provided. The most crucial of these services is counseling. There is little point in providing a group of people with a plow if we forget to provide also the means for using the plow.

The attitudinal setting is usually reflected by the physical setting. The low esteem and the complete lack of understanding of the meaning of counseling are often reflected in some schools by the fact that there is next to nothing in the way of physical facilities. Counselors may not have offices. Often, if they do, there is no secretarial service or protection, so that privacy is impossible.

Tape recorders are still considered a luxury in many schools, and there are many school counselors who have yet to hear what they sound like, and what they say, when they "counsel." Videotape is even more of a rarity.

In some schools where the actual facilities are fairly good, they are rendered ineffective by being placed cheek to jowl with the administrative offices. A student who may want to see a counselor to talk about his desire to bash the principal or perform some dastardly deed upon a teacher will naturally shy away from coming if he sees the offices together, assuming, reasonably enough, that there is a close connection between the people who are in the offices. I was once in a counselor's "office" that formerly was an anteroom to the principal's office, and the only way to the latter was to go through the former. The few clients who came to see the counselor naturally spoke in low tones, were wary of what they said, and kept a weather eye cocked on the principal's door.

If a school has a counseling suite, it should be away from the administrative offices. This is important even as a symbol of the fact that the counselor and the principal are two quite different individuals with quite different functions and responsibilities. It is important too, to have the counseling suite away from the main flow of traffic, to have a pleasant waiting room, with a secretary, to have individual counseling rooms, as well as counselors' offices, and to have at least one exit door that opens only one way. If a client has been under some stress and emotion, he naturally does not want to have to parade past many curious eyes, or to step out into a corridor swarming with fellow students.

I have recently been in several fairly new schools where the upper half of the walls of the counselors' offices were glass, giving both client and counselor somewhat of a fish in a fishbowl feeling! I have been in another school where the principal insists that the counselors keep the doors of their offices open, to convey to the students the impression of counselor friendliness!

The need for privacy, whether from other eyes or from telephones, is obvious. The office should not be austere, nor should it be a living room, although school counselors would say that while there might be some danger of the former type of office in a school, there never would be any danger of the latter type. The client, after all, will probably feel more comfortable if he has a choice of one or two comfortable chairs, and possibly even the choice of some sort of divan or couch. Some counselors, of course, particularly in schools, blanch at the very word "couch," and they immediately have sinister visions of a heavily bearded man with an Austrian accent, sitting behind the client, making copious notes and asking piercing questions about his sexual behavior. This, however, is seldom a problem, since most counselor's "offices" are hardly large enough to hold the client and the counselor!

A fairly decent office may give the client some confidence in the counselor. If all he has to sit on is a creaky chair, and all he has to look at are bare and dirty walls, he may well wonder if the counselor knows his business. One counselor has commented that he has an impressive looking library in his office so that the client may assume that the counselor is not only well-to-do but also a well educated and a well read person! In some schools, of course, the counselor would have to be wary about having too impressive an office, since this would make it stand out too much when compared with the rest of the facilities.

Thus, in a school, at least, the counselor must face the fact that he may be hired to function as a counselor in an institution that has little understanding of and even some hostility toward counseling, and in which the physical facilities for effective counseling simply do not exist. If the counselor, by being an effective counselor with students and colleagues, can come to modify the first part of this problem, then the second part may work out without too much difficulty.

The rehabilitation counselor in a state agency of a Veterans' Affairs office often has much the same impossible surroundings, in that his "office" may consist of his desk and two chairs in a large room shared with a dozen other counselors, similarly equipped. Indeed, the physical setting for so many counselors, in a variety of areas, is such that we must assume that privacy is something that many still consider an unnecessary luxury in counseling! Actually, of course, it is an absolute necessity for effective counseling, and little can be done without it.

PREPARATION FOR THE COUNSELING SESSION

The degree of preparation for the first counseling session with a new client depends on the degree of sophistication and experience of the counselor, his own particular concept of his function as a counselor, and, of course, the amount of time available. It is also true, of course, that sometimes the counselor has no chance to prepare anything, even if he wants to, since the client appears suddenly and unannounced.

If the counselor sees himself as the interpreter of test data, we can assume that he will make himself familiar with the client's test data before seeing the client. If the counselor sees his function as the presenting of information regarding what college or what job would best fit the client he is going to see, he will probably want previous information about the client so that he can accumulate accurate information for him. If, on the other hand, the counselor sees himself not so much as the provider of information, but rather as one involved in a human helping relationship with another individual, the purpose, and the need, of information changes somewhat.

Many counselors of a more diagnostic orientation would probably feel the need of information about the client so that they could understand him better, and thereby work more effectively with him. Another counselor would work with the client as he presents himself, and since he does not see himself as doing something for or to the client, he would see little or no need of previous information about him. Generally, such counselors would feel that their understanding of the client was also based on the frame of reference as it is presented to them by the client, and thus they need no previous information to develop their concept of the client's frame of reference. Some of the counselors here worked with previous information, and some with none. John Bin and Tom Ril presented themselves as they were. Their counselors had no previous information about them, other than that they wanted to see them. Other counselors referred to here had perused all the information they could about the client before they saw him.

THE ESTABLISHMENT OF RAPPORT

Rapport might be described as the ideal relationship that is developed between the client and the counselor, a relationship that is easy and comfortable and free, where each person can be honest, and in which the client can learn to be. There are many factors, some out of the control of the counselor, that might affect the kind of relationship that is established:

1. Long before the counselor ever sees the client, factors are at work that may make it easy or difficult for the counselor to establish rapport with his client. In the school situation particularly, the child gradually develops a picture of the school and the people who work in it. Although it is sometimes a very positive and pleasant picture, the odds are that the disturbed children who come to see a counselor will be those individuals who have built up a picture of the school as at best a rather unpleasant place, and at worst a regular hell-hole. The people who work there may be regarded in an equally negative manner, although, over a period of time, individual teachers and counselors may gradually come to be accepted by troubled children as different from the run-of-the-mill teacher and counselor.

Generally, however, the school counselor can assume that many of the children who have problems will regard him with suspicion, and it will be the actions of the counselor, rather than his words, that may gradually dispel this suspicion. Needless to say, of course, if the school "counselor" thinks of himself as a stool pigeon for either the school administration or the culture generally, the justifiable suspicion of the child will only be reinforced. Many of the clients described here had good reason to be skeptical about the motives of anyone who was connected with the school system.

2. The establishment of rapport will also be affected by the manner in which the client happens to appear in the counselor's office. If he appears because he has something weighing on his mind, and he feels that a talk with someone in the counseling office might be beneficial, the establishment of a good relationship will be a much simpler matter than if he has been brusquely sent down to the counselor's office to be "straightened out" or disciplined in some manner. The latter sort of situation will increase the difficulties, but one must not imply that it creates an impossible situation for the counselor. An acceptant counselor can still be acceptant even in an autocratic school; and acceptance of the client's feeling that coming to the counselor's

office is a lot of nonsense is no different from acceptance of the feeling that the experience might be something that would be good for him.

The client may, on the contrary, have too good an opinion of what the counselor can do for him. If he has been led to believe that the counselor is a medicine man who has all the answers to any problems that may beset him, it is likely that very soon even in the first counseling session, he will be disturbed to find that the counselor cannot do any of the things that were expected. Most children have come to expect domination and control and direction from school personnel. Even in counselor education departments, most student counselors take this counselor education domination for granted, and are somewhat disturbed if it is not forthcoming. Though they may, of course, pay no attention to the attempted domination, they nevertheless expect it, and thus some students may at first find the acceptant counselor "queerer" than the more old-fashioned Napoleonic type, because they are more accustomed to the latter. If the counselor is capable of helping the student to work through this confusion, the relationship that can then be established may be most worthwhile; but it is at this point that the relationship between the counselor and the client sometimes founders. The counselor should remember, of course, that if he has a forced clientele, the number of clients will be determined as much by the neuroticism of the teachers as by the neuroticism of the clients. A neurotic teacher will probably see a good deal of what the mental hygienist would consider normal behavior as indicative of a disturbed child; so the more disturbed the teacher, the more the counselor may expect to find healthy children trooping to his office "to have something done about their behavior."

The counselor's problems may also be affected by the manner in which the appointment was made. If the client talked to a secretary, for example, was she kindly and understanding, or brusque and impatient? Did she give him the feeling that his meeting with the counselor would be a nice experience, or did she imply that it would be unpleasant, and probably a waste of time for both client and counselor? Did he first hear about the counselor from a friend, and, if so, what was the picture he got? If he is a voluntary client, it is likely that the picture he got was a good one—possibly too good, since if he received a negative picture he would not have come voluntarily. He may, of course, be a quite unwilling client, going to see a counselor about whom he has a very unhappy picture. He may have met the counselor in the hall, spoken to him, and formed his impressions on the basis of this brief meeting.

3. The immediate impression that the client receives when he opens the counselor's door is also going to affect him. He should see a reasonably comfortable office, with such things as curtains on the windows, pictures on the walls, comfortable chairs, some evidence of a library, and the professional competence of the counselor. He should also be able to sit down without having a desk between himself and the counselor.

Needless to say, the client will also notice the other person in the room. The greeting of the counselor should be warm, but not effusive. The counselor who rushes around the desk, seizes the hand of the client in a death grip, gives an intimate squeeze on the shoulder, and smiles his biggest smile before his "I'm AWFULLY glad to see you," would be enough to scare me as a potential client right out of the office! Overtness is next to aggressiveness, and the super-gregarious counselor must surely pose a threat to many clients. On this point it is obvious, of course, that the uneasiness of the counselor is a paramount factor in the establishment of rapport with the client, and the beginning counselor, particularly, is going to experience sessions when he feels threatened and insecure. It is well if he is in a situation where he can work this out with the assistance of some other counselor, and it is nothing that need alarm him, since even the experienced counselor periodically runs into situations that shake him.

4. The client may sometimes immediately challenge his acceptance by the counselor, and what happens will have an important effect on their future relationship. A school counselor may find a client whipping out a cigarette, and the counselor's acceptance of this can be indicated by passing an ash tray to him. Obvious and studied verbal insolence is another means by which the counselor may be tested, and the counselor's capacity to accept such behavior is a good measure of his professional competence and personal security.

The highly colored, risqué, or just plain dirty joke may also pose an early problem for the counselor—again possibly a means of testing the counselor, or it may be just a part of the normal expression of the client. If the counselor has led such a sheltered life that he cannot understand the joke, then he will have his problems, although he might not be quite so badly off as the counselor who understands the joke, but is horrified that a child could come forth with such a statement. We can assume both that these individuals need some assistance if they are to become effective counselors, and that their relationship with the client is likely to be somewhat strained. The more mature counselor, on the other hand, can be acceptant of the client's feeling of humor in what he has said, and be neither frigid nor boisterous in his reaction. Nevertheless, some "jokes," such as those of an "anti" nature, may prove a problem for the student counselor, inasmuch as the client will be alert to detect any indication of approval or condemnation on the part of the counselor.

5. The more a counselor is attuned to the feelings of the client, the less of a problem the lack of understanding of the intellectual content of what he says will be. Some counselors may be somewhat disturbed when in the first few minutes of the beginning session the client mumbles several statements that are unintelligible. Generally speaking, it is better to refrain from asking for a repetition of certain statements, since the meaning of what has been said will usually become obvious anyway. If the counselor has to ask repeatedly for clarification, the counseling session will degenerate into a "teacher-asking-what-do-you-mean" sort of thing, a situation that will not usually help in the establishment of a good counseling relationship. If the client continually talks so softly that the counselor cannot hear him, the latter should gently point out that it is rather difficult to hear what is being said—although even here there is some question as to whether or not the counselor should take this step.

The counselor may sometimes hear a word, but lack the understanding of what it means. In this case, it is better to let the client continue. The counselor may eventually pick up the meaning of the word either by listening to a tape, or by hearing it again and using a dictionary. If he has to stop the client from an expression of feeling and say, "Pardon me, but what does that mean?" he is letting himself in for several potential difficulties. For one thing, the client may assume that the counselor must be a rather ignorant fellow if he does not understand the meaning of a word. It may also be that the intellectual explanation of the word will prove embarrassing to the client. Finally, an intellectual discussion is not the purpose of a counseling session, and there is no reason why an individual cannot function as a counselor, reacting to the feelings of the client, even though he does not understand the exact meaning of a word that is being used.

At the college level the counselor may sometimes have as a client a psychology student who is trying to impress himself with both the erudite state of his own mind and the lack of intelligence of his counselor; to this end he will deliberately use many long and complicated words quite new to the counselor. When this is obviously happening, the counselor may react to what is actually going on, and the verbalization may then develop into a more fruitful investigation, by the client, of just why he has to try to convince himself that he is more intelligent than the counselor. It is not, of course, of any importance whether the client actually is, or is not, more intelligent than the counselor; but it is of some importance to help the client to discover why he must feel as he does.

The counselor who must know the meaning of each word—and former teachers tend sometimes to be this way—may also find himself in difficulty with adolescent clients who insist on using a language all their own. Even if the counselor makes a valiant effort to find out just what some of the terms actually mean—and often even the adolescents themselves do not know—there will be further frustration in that the current language, like popular tunes, is in a constant state of flux. Thus the best thing the adult counselor can do is abandon any attempt to "know" the meaning, and rather concentrate on understanding the feeling behind the words that are being used. Possibly the real test comes when the counselor tries to establish a counseling relationship with a client who speaks another tongue. If these two can get together, it is certainly not on the basis of an intellectual understanding of what they are saying to each other!

All of these items may prove to be initial problems for the student counselor as he becomes involved in the establishment of rapport with the client in the initial counseling session. But in the long run the extent to which they prove to be continuing problems will be a measure of the counselor's professional competence and personal integrity. For some of the counselors depicted here, the establishment of rapport is still a major difficulty, as they struggle to find themselves, whereas others no longer have to *try,* and thus the relationship is better.

WHAT HAPPENS IN THE BEGINNING SESSION

The beginning session is more likely to be a testing ground for the client, and even for the sophisticated counselor there is the element of the unknown—neither person really understands the other, although the client may know about the counselor, and sometimes, of course, the counselor may know about the client. It is likely that some counselors want to know about the client in order to bolster their own feeling of security when, for the first time, they meet him.

Buchheimer and Balogh describe three phases of the beginning session: the statement of the problem, exploration, and closing and planning for the future.[2] These are reasonable enough, and very often do occur, although the student counselor should not assume that the client always follows this timetable! Some clients, for example, will spend more than the first session evading the problem in a variety of ways; some counselors will not give the client a chance to look at his problem, but will provide one for him; some clients will press the counselor for answers, for his version of who they are and what they should do; some clients will sit passively and take no overt action, verbal or otherwise; some clients will leave at the end of the first session without any plans for the future.

Often, at the beginning of a counseling session, clients do not go into any particular specific detail as to why they are coming to see a counselor. Sometimes, of course, the counselor does not give the client much of a chance. In Evraiff's book, for example, this is what happened with Carl:[3]

> Co.: Carl, I'm Mr. Williams.
> Cl.: Glad to meet you, Mr. Williams.
> Co.: Nice to know you. I see you had a little trouble last week.
> Cl.: Right.

When Jane's counselor, early in the first session, asked her what she would like to talk about, she replied:[4]

> I'm kind of sick of talking about myself, first of all, because I've had, I don't know what I should say, trouble, I guess, is the closest thing to it. Not with the police, not with anyone like that, but with my own self, and maybe with my family.

Many students come to a counselor after having been told that the counselor will give them tests or supply them with information that will be helpful to them. Jack's counselor prods him with a question about his thoughts about a future job, but all he gets is:[5]

---

[2] Arnold Buchheimer and Sara Carter Balogh, *The Counseling Relationship* (Chicago: Science Research Associates, 1961), p. 15.
[3] William Evraiff, *Helping Counselors Grow Professionally* (Englewood Cliffs, N.J.: Prentice-Hall, Inc., 1963), p. 17, dialogue entries C1–S2.
[4] *Ibid.*, p. 74.
[5] *Ibid.*, p. 167.

Well, so far about, ah, the only thing I've really thought of is welding. My father's one and I can weld a little bit. Be a good job. And, ah, I've thought of flying, something like helicopters, that would be a good job.

Edna, a twelve-year-old, gives a not uncommon reaction to the counselor who presses her by asking her what she would like to discuss:[6]

I don't know, I don't know what to discuss.

and, as her next comment:

Well, I'll, do you want me to tell you how old I am, or where I live, or something like that?

Richard reacts much the same way, when the counselor comes forth with the usual "would you like to tell me . . ." bit:[7]

I don't know what to tell you.

These reactions could be expected from children who are very likely in need of help, but frequently, when the referred child arrives at the counselor's office, his immediate feeling is that he is there because someone else told him he should be there. His problem, as he sees it, is the person who referred him, rather than the issue or action for which he was supposedly referred!

These junior high school clients (Cl) are all self-referred, and we could expect that they would wish to talk about their problems, at least as they see them, without any urging by the counselor. If, on the other hand, they had been sent to the counselor so that "he could do something about you," it is unlikely that they would have expressed themselves so easily. These are the beginning comments:

Co.: Hi, Ted, come in.
Cl.: Thanks.
Co.: What's up . . .

---

[6] *Ibid.*, p. 227.
[7] *Ibid.*, p. 317.

Cl.: Well, I wanted to see you about whether or not I should quit school.

. . . .

Co.: Hi, Jane, how are things going?

Cl.: They're not . . . things are at a standstill . . . everything's so boring.

Co.: Uh-huh . . .

Cl.: Sometimes I wonder whether I'm ever going to be happy in life. I mean . . . well . . . I seem to need excitement. I can't be content with any kind of routine.

Co.: Things have to be happening in my life in order for me to be content . . .

Cl.: Yeh. . . . I just sort of need excitement . . .

. . . .

Cl.: Hi . . .

Co.: Hi, Jim . . . you wanted to talk with me . . .

Cl.: Yeah . . . I want you to help me get out of the foster home I'm in. I'm just about fed up with the way I'm treated. What am I, an animal?

Co.: You've just about had it, eh?

. . . .

Co.: Hi, how are things going?

Cl.: Pretty good.

Co.: Pretty good . . . but not as good as they could be . . .

Cl.: Yeah, that's right. Brother, I've gotten . . . ah . . . I've gotten into a lot of trouble and my parents are going to kill me when they find out.

. . . .

Co.: Hi, come on in—have a chair . . . what's new?

Cl.: Oh . . . well . . . ah . . . nothing much, I guess . . . except I'm not friendly with Ruth any more . . . we had a fight . . . I called her some awful names . . . and we really hurt each other and well . . . I . . . uhmm . . . I don't feel too good about the whole thing . . . it's stupid . . .

Co.: It bothers me . . . I'm not happy about what happened between me and Ruth . . .

Cl.: Yeah . . . that's why I came down to see you . . . I thought if I could talk about the fight I might feel better . . . you know . . . blow off some steam . . .

. . . .

Co.: Hi, come on in. . . . You made an appointment to see me . . . what's on your mind . . .

Cl.: Well, I wanted to talk to you about math. . . . I'd like to change my math class.

Co.: Uh . . . huh . . .

Cl.: I'm not doing even fair work now . . . in fact, right now, as far as I'm concerned, math rots . . .

Co.: (Silence) . . .

Cl.: I'm fed up with math . . . and with . . . him . . .

Jane's counselor engages in a "getting to know you" sort of conversation:[8]

Cl.: It's nice here.

Co.: We've got the fan going. We're trying to make it more comfortable.

Cl.: Mm-hmmm.

Co.: On the sheet, as I mentioned before, you can take that home and finish it, and, uh, if you do come back you can bring it back or mail it back, whichever you prefer.

Cl.: Mm-hmm.

Co.: Tell me, did you have a rough time getting down here?

Cl.: Not rough, but whenever I ride the bus I just get all excited about whether I'm going to get off on time and . . .

Co.: Oh, and you just made the mistake of going up on the third floor.

Jack's counselor over-elaborates on the equipment, and shows his own nervousness:[9]

Co.: Hello, Jack; sit down. Picked a warm day to come down, didn't you?

Cl.: Mm-hmm (looking around). Two-way mirror, huh?

Co.: Yeah, that's right. Did she tell you about it? So that if there are people studying to come here to observe, they can do that. That makes you a little uneasy about it?

---

[8] Evraiff, *op. cit.*, p. 72, dialogue entries S1–C8.
[9] *Ibid.*, p. 166, dialogue entries C1–C7.

Cl.: Yeah.

Co.: Well, if there are any, there's no one around today, and if there are people who come, they will be people who are studying advanced work in college, and they're not much interested in you or me, as persons, it's just the way the counseling goes. So that's a little comfort, maybe. (Pause) It's kind of strange, isn't it, the first time?

Cl.: Yeah (Pause).

Co.: Can you tell me a little about what you, ah, came down for?

Edna is not too eager to talk with her counselor:[10]

Co.: Hello, Edna. How are you today?

Cl.: All right.

Co.: Do you mind the heat very much?

Cl.: No.

Co.: Did you come all by yourself?

Cl.: Yes, Ma'am.

Co.: Would you like to put your umbrella in the corner so you can be comfortable? And your purse you can put on the table or somewhere. Would you like to talk to me today about something? Would you like to discuss things with me? (Short pause)

Cl.: I don't know, I don't know what to discuss.

Co.: Well, maybe you could tell me something about yourself so I'd know you better. How would that be?

Cl.: Well, I'll, do you want me to tell you how old I am, or where I live or something like that?

Richard's counselor pushes and probes and dominates at the start:[11]

Co.: Make yourself comfortable. Would you like to tell me a little bit about school and the trouble you are having?

Cl.: I don't know what to tell you.

---

[10] *Ibid.*, p. 227, dialogue entries C1–S10.
[11] *Ibid.*, p. 317, dialogue entries C1–C7.

> Co.: Uh-huh. You understand the set-up here at the coun-
> seling center?
> Cl.: Uh-huh.
> Co.: Who was it that suggested that you come down?
> Cl.: My mother.
> Co.: She's concerned about how you are doing in school? Is
> that the reason she suggested it, or what?

By the end of the first session, all of these clients had indicated their willingness to return. However, one should be cautious in interpreting just what this might mean. It could mean that the client felt that at last he had found an adult who would listen to him, and with whom he felt easy and comfortable, or it might mean that he felt he had found someone who would answer his problems for him, or it could mean that he felt he was supposed to return, and he was willing to do whatever the authority figure suggested.

Some points that might be noted in the first counseling session:

1. The client is likely going to be testing the counselor to see if he fits into his preconceived image of him. If he does, this may be good or bad, depending on the image the client has of the counselor!
2. While some beginning sessions may prove to be also concluding sessions, the counselor can usually operate on the assumption that his primary function in the first session is to establish a positive climate so that the client may wish to return for further consideration of his difficulty.
3. The beginning session, like other sessions, belongs to the client, not the counselor, and the counselor's behavior should carry this message to the client.
4. If the aim of the counselor is to establish at least the beginning of a genuine human relationship, he will feel that he has no obligation to any methodology or technique, that his obligation is rather to his self integrity.
5. Toward the end of the session the counselor can indicate his interest in the return of the client without implying that the client has no choice and should return because he, the counselor, wants him to return. Some counselors give the impression of aloofness and lack of concern, whereas others imply that the client must return regardless of how he might feel.

chapter 14

THE COUNSELING INVOLVEMENT

Counseling can hardly take place unless there is an involvement between the counselor and the client, and it is equally obvious that it has to be a certain *kind* of involvement if growth is to take place. The unique characteristic of the counseling involvement is that it is centered on the client, and the counselor is one who is sensitive to, aware of, and able to operate within the client's inner frame of reference. The counselor, however, is also aware of the degree of distortion of this inner frame of reference. The individual who has a knife sticking in him, after all, has a quite different kind of problem than the individual who thinks he has a knife sticking in him!

THE INNER FRAME OF REFERENCE

The ability of the counselor to operate within the client's frame of reference should not be confused with the extent of counselor intervention or direction, and the counselor whose verbalization is limited to "You feel. . . ." is likely to be as ineffective as the one who can say no more than, "Tell me more. . . ."! Here are some examples of the involvement of different counselors in the world of the client:

> You get to a point where you sort of feel like giving up—you
> sort of wonder if you should keep trying.

> It's confusing. . . . You feel that you don't know what to expect, and since you're not sure of what's coming, you find it more comfortable just to remain silent.

> Sometimes it's hard to grow up. You get the feeling that you should act more grown up, but still, in a way, you'd rather remain a little girl.

> One day the foster home seems OK . . . another day you hate it. You wish you could have the same feelings about it instead of one day liking it and the next day hating it.

The counselor may sometimes become so involved with the other's frame of reference that he will use the first person. Needless to say, the counselor could hardly be genuine if he was using this as a "technique":

> These tests concern me, they sort of make me worry—it seems that they might have some influence on my schooling. . . . And I'm hoping that they won't have any influence, that they won't count as much as I sometimes think they will.

> I wish that people would allow me to make my own decisions. . . . I'm old enough to decide what's best for me.

> I don't like the idea that he always has to be right. . . . Why can't I be right once in a while?

> I have a choice. . . . I can continue to cheat on exams or I can stop. My only fear is that my honesty might result in my failing an exam.

> I just wish that he'd realize that I'm human . . . that I have feelings, and that I don't like being pushed around.

The use of the first person, however, is no guarantee that the counselor is operating within the client's frame of reference. A long counselor statement, first person or no, is more likely to be an intellectual summation from the counselor's frame of reference. For example:

> In other words it bugs me that everybody sort of thinks the worst of kids today when they aren't any different and they don't do any different than the kids of my parents' generation, or kids who even lived before that. I kind of feel there's nothing wrong in having a good time. My parents had their good times. . . . Why can't I without people getting so worried?

This counselor indicates his ability to be with the client:

You were too much involved in wondering about you to be able to be stimulated or excited or feel that such an attraction was . . . well, in order to be involved in such a thing. . . .

It's hard to say they were pretty good . . . how could I have had three days that were pretty good. . . .

You mean . . . ah . . . in looking at it now, it just doesn't seem as much of a test as you thought it would be. . . .

And it seems to mean . . . not so much that you can trust me, but that you can trust you. . . .

When you become what you are, then you no longer are what you were—the very act of being means that you are changing.

The possibility of others' suffering the pangs of hunger doesn't make my pangs feel any better . . . it's my inside that's hungry.

As does this counselor:

You feel that Miss Bel was being a little unfair with you.

You like it now even though at times it gets a little rough.

You kind of want to get the whole thing over with quick. You want to know where you stand.

You want to go, but you're really worried about what might happen in court.

You have an idea when you're going to get in trouble—you can sort of feel it coming.

And now you feel you have a mind of your own, and you can make decisions about what you want to do.

Many counselors will fluctuate back and forth from the client's frame of reference to the counselor's frame of reference. Note this counselor:

> Co.: What subject do you think you're failing in?
> Cl.: Literature.
> Co.: Would you like to talk about that or how you feel about it?
> Cl.: Well, I never read nothing and I don't like to read.
> Co.: There's something about reading in general that has made you dislike it?
> Cl.: Yeah . . .

Co.: Doesn't it kind of hinder your work in school?

Cl.: Well, I just read enough to get by and that's about it.

Co.: Just enough to get by.

Cl.: Yeah . . .

Co.: How do you feel about that?

Cl.: (Pause) What do you mean "How do I feel about that"?

Co.: About getting by all the time.

Cl.: I don't know.

Co.: You don't feel anything.

Cl.: Uh-hu. . . . As long as I get it done I don't care.

Sometimes the conversation would appear to be geared entirely to the counselor's external frame of reference. Jack's counselor, for example, in session eight comments as follows:[1]

Co.: I think an important thing here is that this turning it off in school, this is what happens to the school work, in some cases.

Cl.: Yeah.

Co.: This is the first real talk we've ever had.

Cl.: Yeah.

Co.: I wish we could go on.

Cl.: I'm about talked out though.

Co.: I think you're just starting now.

Cl.: Maybe we've just started on the subject, but I'm about talked out for today.

Co.: (Laughs) Yeah, I mean for today, but for the future maybe we could find out some other ways to get rid of this tension, this anger, so that it wouldn't interfere with your school work.

So the extent to which the counselor operates within the client's frame of reference varies. The student counselor must determine what is *real* for him and *effective* for the client. If he can manage to combine these two, he is probably better off than most counselors!

---

[1] William Evraiff, *Helping Counselors Grow Professionally* (Englewood Cliffs, N.J.: Prentice-Hall, Inc., 1963), dialogue entries C338–C346.

LEARNING TO BE FREE

A basic and crucial part of the counseling experience is the gradual experiencing of being free. The individual can become, in an atmosphere of security, a little more honest, both with himself and with others. This learning to be free is often painful, and although it is cathartic, there may be despair and hostility and frustration. These are feelings the client comes to be able to experience, and to live with, and to go beyond. They are necessary if there is to be growth and movement. We might assume that the more a person, young or old, has lived a lie, the more violent some of these expressions will be, whereas the moderately stable, ordinary child, living through his developmental problems, periodically needs some assistance so that he can maintain his high level of honesty and genuineness. Here are some junior school children who are receiving such assistance from their counselors. They are learning to express, and to look at, their selves.

Anxiety may be detected here:

> If he ever calls my mother I'm sunk—she'll never believe it wasn't my fault.

> I just wish she'd leave me alone . . . every time I go in her room I get a feeling like . . . well, as if I had a piece of lead in my stomach.

> I just go blank. Whenever someone says tests to me I just freeze. If someone tested me on my name I don't think I'd remember it—just because it's a test.

> School is on my mind all the time. I think about it when I get up in the morning, when I go home, when I'm in bed. I'm always planning what I'm going to do the next day, or I worry if I'll pass a test or look foolish in class . . . and yet I'm doing pretty good work. I can't understand why I'm always worrying about grades, tests and school. Really, I've got nothing to worry about . . . I mean . . . I think I don't . . . I'm all mixed up.

> I wish I could stop worrying about whether the kids like me or not. I say to myself, stop worrying, don't get so bothered, the kids like you . . . and I say it over and over again . . . but it's always on my mind, even now. The kids are friendly, and they've invited me to parties, and one girl even asked me to join her church club . . . but still I worry, I don't know why.

These children express frustration:

It's nice to be able to talk about this problem, but what can I do about it? Nobody at school can help me, you can't do anything, and I can't do anything. What's the use of even discussing it? All we're doing is running into a stone wall.

What makes me mad though . . . the teachers just keep putting on your report card "capable of doing better." How do they know? That's what I can't figure out. How do they know you're capable of doing better if you think you're doing your best now?

I wish I could get through to him. I wish I could make him listen and understand. I keep trying to make contact with him but he doesn't seem to care. It's as if I were a chair or a lamp . . . like I'm not alive . . . and all I want him to do is pay attention, to listen and understand. Even if he can't, if he'd only try.

How much am I expected to take? Do I go on letting him be sarcastic or do I put my foot down? The only trouble with putting my foot down is that he may react by shutting me off . . . sort of stop loving me. It's his favorite way of hurting me, and believe me, it hurts.

I do all my homework and study for tests and still it isn't enough. What does he want—blood? I can't spend a lifetime doing homework. How much is enough? People say study but nobody tells me how much. I really don't know how much is enough. This is me in a lot of other things too . . . not just homework. I never know how much is enough.

These clients express overt hostility:

Sometimes I wish I could choke him or push him downstairs. I sometimes just want revenge for what he's done to me.

I'll pay her back—somehow-somewhere-sometime—I'll let her know that she can't treat me like a piece of dirt.

Who does he think he is? If he thinks he can insult my mother like that and get away with it he's crazy. When I see him after school today I'm going to deck him. . . . I'll shove my fist right down his throat. . . . I don't care who sees me.

I'll never respect him, no matter what he says or does. He can never mend what he's done to me. I feel broken but not broken enough so that I'm in pieces. There are a lot of different ways that I can pay him back . . . and I want to.

This client describes one particular incident:

Cl.: I don't like Mrs. Pen, I'll tell you. No, I don't like her. When I was in Grade 7, one day I was down in the gym. I used to be a wise guy—you know me—me and a few of the other guys, you know. All the little guys now, but they were big guys then. So we were all fooling around, you know, and one of them said something to me. And I dropped a book or something. And I dropped a book on the floor and I come out with something—you know—profane language. So Mrs. Pen was standing there, and she heard it, so she said, "Who said it?" So we all just looked at her, and no one was going to tell. So she said, "If you don't tell, I'll take you all up to the office. But if you tell me, I won't say anything and I won't do anything." So I said, "Okay, I said it. I swore." So she said, "Just because you told the truth, I'm not going to take you up to the office." But the same day I had a fight with another teacher and he sent me up to the office, so I got two weeks discipline and two weeks no recess, because Mr. Dan would say, "Did you do this?" and I would say, "Yes," and he would give me two days discipline, and he'd add on every time I said something. I didn't blame him. I was being pretty wise. So then he said, "Okay, get back to your room." So this is the recess period. The next period I go into my math class with Miss Bel. What happens? I'm just sitting there, and Mrs. Pen and Mr. Dan come in. I'll never forget this, because this has bothered me quite a while. And he said, "Okay, I'm looking for a boy. All the boys in this room stand up." So I stood up and Mrs. Pen says, "That's him over there." So Mr. Dan says to me, "Take your hat and coat and get down to my office." He threw me out of school. And since that day—I don't know—I give everybody one chance. If I trust someone, I trust them. I mean it. That's the way I feel about it. I want people to trust me, and I'm here trying to get you to trust me because I want you to. That's the way I've always been. But Mrs. Pen just happened to cut my throat that day. It's not that I hold a grudge against her; it's just that I'll never trust her again.

And here in session five a client shows that he is beginning to learn to be free:

> Cl.: I grew up too damn fast. My body matured but my mind didn't. I was easily led. I wanted to show my muscles. I wanted to show how tough I was. Sometimes I slip back, but I think . . . well . . . I think my mind is starting to understand things. I'm starting to say to myself, "Who do you think you are?" I never said that before. I always thought I was somebody.
>
> Co.: You feel that you're gaining in maturity, and this is a good feeling for you.
>
> Cl.: I'm not saying that I enjoy school all the time. I mean . . . you know . . . there are things around here that are chicken. Ah, I can never change those things . . . but I am learning. I mean I'm starting to enjoy it more than I dislike it. But the thing that I really dislike . . . you know . . . those few teachers. They think they're better than other people. They look down at me. They think they're better than everybody else. Boy, that's a bad way to feel because nobody is better than anyone else.
>
> Co.: Those teachers who feel that they're better than other people kind of bother you.
>
> Cl.: Sure they do. I can't see that. Why in hell should they think that way? What makes them think that way? One thing I don't understand is why teachers don't respect certain classes and certain kids . . . I mean, who do they think they are. . . . (Pause) . . . Well, I guess time's up for now. So long, Mr. Del.
>
> Co.: So long, John.

These are periods when this client feels despair, and hostility and frustration:

> I feel terribly defeated, especially in the morning. All the dreams one makes . . . I just have to discard them and come down to earth . . . and try to accept things gracefully and with a measure of composure. . . . I'll never be able to . . . (pause) . . . and yet, having

admitted these things, you can sometimes turn around and prove them wrong.

I guess I have to go through a period of hating her . . . and after that maybe I can see her as she was. Now I hate her guts most of the time . . . the poor, neurotic, shrill, demanding woman. She did an incalculable amount of damage, and the pathetic thing is that in a way I think she knew it.

It's difficult not to be bitter . . . it was so wrong, so terribly wrong, so completely unjust. . . . They certainly instilled a degree of fear in me . . . a terrible fear.

I find myself, these past few weeks—for want of a better word—drifting. Each day is conditioned by what has to be done—structured, you might say—I feel in a way—I don't mind—and yet I feel that this isn't quite right—and yet—it seems enough to be free—relatively free of tension. . . .

You know, this is a kind of frustrating experience for me sometimes, because there are things I think about—hard things to get a hold of, dimly perceived things which I want to get a hold of—and talk about—and I cannot . . . often I just sit here and completely block—like now—I don't understand that, I just don't.

Some people are not haunted by their failures, but I am . . . a tremendous feeling of guilt. . . .

It's rough . . . I don't mean to invite your pity—but it is rough to land with your feet in the world of reality, and begin to know yourself as you are—for the first time in my entire life . . . if only it had happened years ago. . . .

This client can also be free to be honest about his feelings about the counselor, and they are not always positive:

I experienced a distinct chill when I left here last week. . . . (Long pause.) May I smoke?

If you'd been a close friend I might have said, "He's just being bitchy, so forget it. . . ." But this is a very special relationship we have, and I'm extremely sensitive to anything you might say—quite sensitive. . . .

And so the client comes to learn to experience his feelings, and to live with them, and after experiencing them, he learns, too, that somehow they are no longer the same. The ghosts are not quite the ghosts they were, the faces are not as threatening as they were, and the new face I see—the me—is stronger and more pleasing.

GROWTH AND MOVEMENT

As the person moves and grows, things become better—the individual himself becomes better, and somehow other people become better too. All is by no means, of course, sweetness and light, but the individual does gain the strength to be who he is. Often in the counseling hour the client may be talking, in a somewhat intellectual sense, about what has happened rather than what is happening, but often, too, what he is expressing is his feeling of an ongoing process. He is not simply saying positive words because they sound good, or because he feels this is what he is supposed to say; his words are truly expressive of what is, as well as he can perceive it, and experience it, happening.

Here are some comments from various high school students:

I find that I'm becoming more interested in reading just because I don't have to be angry any more.

You know, I could go on blaming others for things that have gone wrong in my life, but when I really look at it . . . I mean honestly look . . . well, I could have avoided a lot of trouble simply by using my own head.

In the past I've always reacted with anger when somebody was mad at me . . . seems that's pretty threatening for me and I have to defend myself. It must be that I've been insecure all my life, not having any real affection or love from my dad. I just have to defend myself when I'm around him or anybody like him.

Sometimes I think I enjoyed being afraid . . . but you know, I don't have to be scared if I don't want to. Before I thought that being afraid was the only way I could ever be.

Let's face it—I can stand up or I can crawl. Now I figure that once I begin to crawl, that crawling becomes a way of life; but if I stand, then standing can become a way of life. Right now I prefer standing.

Success isn't really ending up my life the way my mother wants me to. It's my life, and maybe success means sort of . . . well . . . being at ease with myself . . . sort of being satisfied with me.

The kids aren't really as bad as I thought . . . they're OK . . . I . . . ah . . . think one of the reasons I didn't get along was . . . was . . . ah . . . ah . . . because I let them bother me . . . I mean like whenever they razz me I laugh it off now . . . before I'd get excited and mad . . . that's . . . that's why they gave me the business . . . I can't be a crybaby . . . I'm . . . I'm . . . learning to take their wise cracks and give them back to . . . I don't go walking around thinking that everybody's against me.

I realize now that I can't have my cake and eat it too—I thought I could have the whole package . . . good times, girls, hanging around, and grades . . . now I'm beginning . . . ah . . . well . . . beginning to see that I've . . . ah . . . umm . . . ah . . . I've got to pick out what's important . . . you know . . . first things first.

The teachers are changing . . . they don't seem to be so rough . . . but they're changing because I'm changing. . . . I used to give them a hard time, but I don't anymore . . . it's sort of . . . well . . . ah . . . I mean . . . I don't see any . . . ah . . . umm . . . reason . . . ah . . . I'm not going to get anywhere by being a wise guy—you know what I mean. . . .

Before I thought . . . why do this or that if I don't feel like it. . . . Now I know I can't do only those things I want to . . . I mean you've got to do some things you don't want to do . . . that's life . . . and I've got to do some things in school and even at home that I don't want to . . . the world is in enough of a mess without everybody going around doing what they want. . . .

You know when I talked to you the other day about my parents fighting . . . and I . . . ah . . . umm . . . ah . . . was all shook up . . . well, since I was here last time I thought a lot about what I did . . . and the more I thought about everything the more I realize that parents must fight . . . like . . . brothers and sisters fight . . . I mean right now my parents aren't fighting and I'm happy . . . but I won't be shook up the next time . . . if people have to live close together they practically got to have a fight. . . .

I mean . . . if I fight my brother, well . . . I consider that natural . . . well, now, I say to myself if Ma and Dad fight that's natural . . . it's not the fight but the way you look at it . . . I think . . . ah . . . grown-ups are people too . . . in other words, there must be times when they get mad . . . but the next time there's a fight at home . . . I . . . ah . . . ah . . . it won't bother me as much because I won't be the same person I was before . . . I'll . . . ah . . . ah . . . I'll be the same but I won't think the same."

This client expresses his feelings of growth toward self-actualization and freedom:

And yet for some strange reason it doesn't . . . I can . . . can feel the failure of it . . . it was a failure . . . and yet it . . . ah . . . it doesn't . . . I don't seem to have taken it as hard as I thought I was going to . . . I don't understand it . . . I wish it was otherwise . . . I don't know. . . .

And also in this exchange with his counselor (Co):

> Cl.: It seems to me, looking back, that I have spent an awful lot of my life defending myself—trying to be two things—to be what I thought I was and what I wanted to be, and yet to try to conform . . .
>
> Co.: Defending yourself—to you—and to others . . .
>
> Cl.: To others—and to myself too . . . it's been an appalling struggle, consuming time and energy . . . what a waste . . . a waste . . .
>
> Co.: Do I have to spend all my time defending me . . .
>
> Cl.: But I'm less so now, and the roof does not fall in—maybe because me as I am now is more acceptable to me . . . that's kind of confusing . . .
>
> Co.: You mean . . . the me that's more acceptable isn't the me it used to be . . .
>
> Cl.: No . . . no . . . yes, yes . . .

And again:

Sitting right here now . . . I feel more like myself—whatever myself is I don't know—but I and me are both right here together—right here right now . . .

I don't have to go outside of me . . . I can stay right here and be me . . . I have less faces to meet the faces . . . but you see, when you drop the masks—and I haven't dropped them completely . . . but enough to know what it feels like to do it . . . there is a sense of loss, of not belonging anymore . . . my position in relation to other people is changed . . . I sort of feel . . . not all the time . . . but some . . . something is over and done with . . . and now . . . now I can look ahead . . . reach out. . . .

And so I felt that all these months had been a deception, and so I said "All right, this is how I feel," but as soon as I accepted the fact . . . that I felt that way . . . that this was how I felt, so all right . . . as soon as that happened, something changed . . . it was never quite the same again. . . .

And in this exchange:

> Cl.: I spent most of my time growing up trying to be what I thought others wanted me to be . . . and I spent very little time listening to my inner self—listening to

> what I really was . . . and to have the courage to *be* what I really was . . .
>
> Co.: . . . and it was hard to ever get to the "being" point . . .
>
> Cl.: Yes . . . yes . . .
>
> Co.: . . . so that you could say, "I am . . . now . . . I am . . ."
>
> Cl.: Yes . . . yes . . . (long pause) . . . a long time ago I talked about preparing a face to meet the faces . . . that's it . . . you can sum up my whole life in that phrase . . . well . . . now I *don't* . . . not any more . . . not nearly so much . . . not always maybe, but more often I am myself . . . and I'm content to be so . . .

And again:

> I've been learning to communicate more in the last few months . . . with more people . . . to take a little chance—and that pays off, you see, and you take another little chance . . . and the roof doesn't fall in on you after all . . .
>
> I thought, when I came to see you that if I changed I'd be able to stand back and watch it happen, but it hasn't worked out that way at all . . . it's been slow and gradual and subtle . . . I'm only aware of change sometimes because of what doesn't happen . . . but how . . . what happened . . . where did change take place . . . (long pause) . . . and in a way that battle is over . . . I *can* check myself . . . and of all the things that have happened to me here . . . and I suppose that catharsis is one of them—to be able to tell you all the dreadful things . . . but you know to me the most significant thing is that I've been able to sit here and explore all of my self—and to test myself, in a sense—what is real, and what am I putting on . . . and I'm convinced that it is real, it is true . . . I mean the change is that I don't feel so alien any more, I'm not so different after all, I know this, I feel this . . . and I don't feel this need to *have* to prove myself. . . .

And again:

> Cl.: It's always seemed to me in the past . . . when I've tried to reach out . . . just warm . . . relationships, you know . . . friendships . . . they've refused to be that way . . . it goes from a moderate to hostility . . .

or to something very deep and emotional . . . I can't seem to keep it in the middle . . .

Co.: It becomes a demanding sort of thing. . . .

Cl.: Uh . . . huh . . .

Co.: There can't be a closeness and at the same time a non-demanding on you . . .

Cl.: That's right, Dr. Pin, that's exactly right . . . that's just it . . . demanding is the word . . .

And movement and growth can be painful, as in these exchanges with the counselor:

Co.: Are you saying, Mr. Ril, that it's difficult to feel without wondering what's behind this—why is this—and it's difficult to accept this feeling . . .

Cl.: (Long pause) . . . I guess the . . . I guess I'm crying because one by one I've had to destroy the illusions . . . and it's hard to give them up . . .

Co.: They've been important . . . but now you're saying good-bye to them . . .

Cl.: Yeah . . . yes . . . uh . . . yes, I guess so . . .

And again:

Cl.: . . . and I suppose that's why I want to cry . . .

Co.: I want these big things . . . excellence . . . but I can't. . . . I won't be in first place. . . .

Cl.: No, I won't be in first place . . . there's a wide gap between fact and fancy . . . (long pause) . . . boy, it's a long fall. . . .

Co.: . . . back to the company of other humans . . .

Cl.: To hell with them . . . I don't care . . . about most humans . . . I care about me . . .

Co.: Uh . . . huh . . .

Cl.: Their concern is their concern, not mine . . . (long pause) . . . that sounds conceited, doesn't it . . . but I don't care . . . that's how I feel . . .

Co.: You care more about you . . .

Cl.: I do . . . I do . . . I do . . . but I want to separate caring from an excessive preoccupation . . . you see . . . . there is a difference there.

And again:

> Cl.: I just couldn't accept the whole thing, so I had to re-
> arrange it, didn't I, I had to reconstruct it, and bring
> it here, and lie to myself, and lie to you, so that it
> could become something I could accept . . . and I felt
> so ashamed of myself . . . ashamed that I couldn't
> listen to myself . . . ashamed that I had to come here
> and lie to myself and to you . . . and I'm frightened
> . . . I had to work so hard to change it . . . it was
> such a feverish effort . . .
>
> Co.: You just had to make it into something good. . . .
>
> Cl.: I couldn't accept it the way it was . . . and yet, I did
> have to tell you—I just couldn't sit here and lie to
> you. . . .

And so these clients are growing and moving. For some, the
growth and the movement is not too difficult, for they are young, and
change is easier. For others, it is harder, but all are having an involvement with another human being in a therapeutic experience. Their
movement is toward greater individual freedom and greater individual
responsibility, and in becoming more aware of their own self they also
become more aware of and more sensitive to their fellow humans.
Only the strong and the secure can truly live with the other in a
condition of love and trust and respect.

chapter 15

THE ENDING

The ending of a series of counseling sessions should, of course, be only the beginning of a newer, brighter, freer life for the person who has been known as the client. This brighter life comes to be usually because the individual has become able to do what he felt he could not do before, and he has found that he does not have to do what he once felt he had to do. The two faces have come closer together, and living with self has become easier, more comfortable, more satisfying. This can occur, in a modest and undramatic fashion, when a child sees a counselor for only a single session, as well as at the end of a long series of painful and traumatic sessions.

The ending of a single session should pose no particular problem for the counselor in that a time limit should be agreed upon, and it should be held to, except in the most unusual circumstances. In a school, a counseling period usually fits in with a class period, and most students assume that a counseling session will last the same amount of time as a class session, although in some schools the two do not necessarily coincide. The inexperienced counselor may sometimes feel pressed by the client to continue for a longer period of time, but this is usually unwise, and it is beneficial neither for the client nor for the counselor. One indication of progress in counseling might be the assumption by the client of the responsibility for indicating that the time is up, rather than waiting for the counselor to take the initiative. Often, of course, a client might be emotionally involved and quite unaware of time; in such a situation the counselor, obviously, should not cut the person off right in the middle of an expression of feeling, but somewhere within the general time limit he should take the initiative in gently suggesting that the time is just about up.

In the ideal situation it is the client who determines, correctly, that he no longer has any need of the counselor's help, and that he can get along very well without him. This, however, does not always happen, and the "ending" may come in a variety of ways. Let us note a few of these.

1. In a school situation the counseling sessions usually end with the end of the school year. In many ways this is beneficial, in that the client knows in advance that, come May or June, he is going to have to go it alone. With some children, of course, who may be in more serious difficulties, referral would be a necessity if the counselor was not available during the summer months. Clients should know in advance if they have only a certain time available for counseling, and if a school counselor takes on a client for what would appear to be a series of counseling sessions during the month of May, he should point out that he will be available only until, say, the middle of June.

2. In most cases, when the client indicates his desire to terminate the counseling, the counselor will see no reason why he should not be acceptant of this desire. These clients in a high school, for example, would appear to know where they are going:

> I really don't feel that it's necessary for me to come back. I feel that I'm able to . . . well . . . sort of . . . able to think for myself and decide just what I should and shouldn't do. . . .

> Things have worked out. I went back to her and told her how I felt . . . I mean I let her know that I didn't like what was developing. After that talk things seemed to ease off . . . I sort of got it out of my system. I don't think it will be necessary for me to continue with counseling.

> I've kind of tried out this new person that I've decided to become and it feels real good. I mean I think that there's definitely a sort of a change in me . . . I don't think I'll be seeing you for a while . . . I want to be on my own. . . .

Some counselors, after comments like these, would probably indicate their availability if and when they were needed. Others would feel that this determination should be made by the client without what might be considered as possible counselor encouragement to return for further counseling. The counselor, they would say, should not say,

426 : The Counseling Experience

"Don't come back again," but neither should he say, "I'd be glad to see you again if you wish."

3. The counselor, however, may not always honestly feel that the client is wise in terminating. If the counselor is honest and genuine, he will relate these feelings to the client. He may feel that the client is terminating because of his distaste for the counselor, and suggest another counselor with whom the client might be able to relate more effectively. He may feel that the client is terminating because of his feeling of despair that nothing is happening, or possibly because of his feeling that too much is happening. In any case, it would seem that if the counselor is to be congruent, and genuine, then his "unconditional positive regard" for the client can include his expressing his feeling that the client is unwise to choose to terminate. The final choice, of course, would be left to the client, although even here there is potentially a sticky ethical problem. What if the client has disintegrated even more, and is presenting real evidence of almost totally disorganized, psychotic behavior—does the counselor still say to the client, "The choice is yours . . . ?"

4. Some clients, of course, terminate without any previous notice or warning. They just don't come back. The counselor must be concerned with the part he had to play in this abrupt termination, and tapes of such final sessions can sometimes provide valuable leads as to why the client terminated. Some school counselors may have colleagues attempt to find out the "why" of the termination, since in such cases the client is usually still in school. Others would feel this unwise, and would not interfere with the client's right to terminate—abruptly or not.

5. Some counselors will take the initiative and pose the possibility of termination before it has been suggested by the client. Here again, if this is the honest feeling of the counselor, and if he is genuine, then it would seem that he should pass this feeling on to the client. Many counselors, of course, would say that they were simply reflecting or interpreting the feelings that the client was conveying to them. This would likely be the case, for example, with these counselors:

> It seems that there's nothing more to talk about, eh. . . . If you feel that there might be more to talk about, feel free to make an appointment.

> It appears that you're now able to handle this problem. You're free to continue with counseling if you wish . . . or you can try to get along without it . . . the decision is up to you. . . .

> We've been getting together now for a period of four months,
> and you feel that you've changed . . . you don't feel the need to be
> angry at the world any more . . . you're able to take things in stride.
> You can continue to come here if you want . . . the decision as to
> whether or not to continue with counseling is, as always, up to you.

Sometimes, too, the counselor may feel that he is being ineffective, that he and the client are simply going around in circles, and that
nothing positive is happening. Again, if he does have this feeling, and
if it appears to him that the client would receive more effective help
from another counselor, then he should probably pass this feeling on to
the client. This may be even more of an ethical problem when this is a
private situation, and the client is paying a fee. The client, of course,
will not always agree with the counselor, and may indicate his feeling
of satisfaction with what is happening, whether the counselor agrees
with him or not. What then—does the counselor continue in a relationship that he feels is ineffective? And to what extent does this reflect on
his own integrity, and on the value he places on his self?

6. Finally, realistically, it is likely that if the service was available, and if money was not a factor, there would be a large number of
individuals who, periodically, off and on, would avail themselves of
the services of a counselor as the pressures pushing in on them became
too much to take alone. This is already happening to some degree, and
as it becomes more culturally acceptable, and people can more easily
avail themselves of such services without having the tab of "mentally
sick" put on them, then there may be some decrease in the dreadful
things that so many individuals must do to themselves, and, inevitably
then, to others.

And what of the two clients to whom we have referred frequently
in this section, Tom and John? Tom is now able to walk alone, without
the counselor. His world is not freed of anxiety, and fear and pain, but
they will mean less, because he is stronger, and more able. He has
achieved a higher level of freedom, and he is more the determiner of
the meaning of his existence than the victim of fate.

For John, too, the counseling is over. In his last session he is
looking ahead, and talking about what he now can do, and what he
will do. This is approximately the last half of that session, and for John
it is the beginning, not the ending:

> Cl.: I can talk free with Martha. I mean I like to do that.
> I don't like to hide anything. I think that when a boy
> takes out a girl and tries to act like a phony, he's just

going to get caught; and the more he lies to her, the deeper he goes and he can never get out of it. All of his lies just mix him up—jumble him up, if you know what I mean. And with Martha it's good—I don't have to lie to her.

Co.: Uh . . . huh . . . you feel that with her you can be truthful. . .

Cl.: I can say anything I want to without being ashamed. I can eat any way I want to eat. If I want to eat six hamburgers, I can—Martha won't say anything. I don't have to worry if Martha will think I'm a pig, or something like that.

Co.: You kind of feel free with Martha. . .

Cl.: Yeh . . . I can act myself. I don't have to pretend. I don't have to be a phony. Some guys have to be phonies with their girls, but I don't have to be with Martha. I can just say what I want and do what I want and be what I want.

Co.: Uh . . . huh. . .

Cl.: I can trust Martha with my life. She's the only girl I could trust it with . . . well . . . besides my mother and aunt. I mean she's the only person who's not a relative, the only girl that I could trust . . . (pause) . . . I'm getting older now . . . I think about getting married—I think about having kids of my own, and I enjoy thinking about it.

Co.: Marriage seems to be a part of your future—it's normal to think about it. . .

Cl.: I figure I'd like to have three or four kids, and I'd like to be able to pick out a girl that I want—not have a girl pick me out, and not have anything to say about it. Maybe what I mean is this . . . maybe I want to be able to pick the girl out, and I want the girl to pick me. I want us to want each other. I don't want a girl to put a chain around my neck and drag me around.

Co.: You feel that the girl should want you as much as you want her.

Cl.: Martha's really okay . . . (pause) . . . I'm not going steady with her any more. I take her out once in a while, but nothing steady. She wanted to go steady, and I know that when she goes steady, she just wants to go out with me and nobody else. Well, I don't see it that way. I figure okay, I'd like to go out with Martha and I'd like to go steady, in fact. Okay, so we do go steady, but I like my freedom. I like to be able to go out with another girl when I please. I mean if I meet another girl that I like, to figure that I can take her out, and that I'm not cheating or something like that. I wanted her to go out with other guys, but she wouldn't. She said she only wanted to go out with me. So I figured that was too much. I mean she's young. I don't want to tie her down. So I told her maybe we'd better stop going steady. Maybe it's better if we just went out and didn't go steady.

Co.: You don't want to go steady with Martha, because this restricts you—you still like the freedom to go out with other girls.

Cl.: I don't like to lose my freedom. I like it. I like to be able to meet a new girl and go out with her. In fact, maybe I've been spoiled. I've always been able to get whatever I wanted from girls. All I have to do is call a girl up and she goes out with me. I don't know what it is, but I guess it's just been too easy for me. There's too many girls that I can take out, and I like the idea of meeting a new girl and taking her out. I like this kind of freedom. I've done a few bad things with some of the girls I've taken out, and I'd like to be able to tell Martha about it. But I'm afraid to. Sometimes I want to, and I try to, but I just can't get it out. I'm afraid to.

Co.: You'd like to tell Martha about these other girls but you just can't bring yourself around to telling her.

Cl.: How am I going to tell her that I was out with another girl? I just can't bring myself around to it, especially since she thinks that we're supposed to go steady. . . . But I straightened that part out—I told her that I didn't want to go steady. And I told her it's not because of me, but because of her. I tried to turn it around a little bit, but I figure this . . . she may as well go out with other boys, and then if she really likes me, she can always come back to me. And I figure I should be able to go out with other girls, and if I really like Martha, I'll come back to her. Then we'll really know that we're meant for each other.

Co.: You want to tell Martha about these other girls, but still. . .

Cl.: I think I'll call her up tonight and ask her to go out, and then I'll explain the whole thing to her, just what I've done, because I owe it to her. I'll feel better about it too. She'll be mad. She'll probably want to drop me, but I figure it will be better that way. I'd rather be honest with her, especially if I want to be serious about her. I'd like her to go out with other boys. I'd like her to know it's not a crime, just like I'd like her to know it's not a crime for me to go out with other girls.

Co.: Uh . . . huh . . . (pause) . . .

Cl.: I want to be able to bring my kids up right. I want to be able to let them make up their own minds as to what to do. I mean I can give them advice, but I want them to make up their own minds about their own lives. I just hope they make the right decisions. Like me . . . like I figure now that I'm starting to make the right decisions, and it feels good inside. It really does. Boy, I've got that confidence in me. You can't beat it . . . and it's what I need. I've got the feeling that I'm going to amount to something because . . . I don't know . . . I figure that a lot of things that were bothersome to me before, I can handle now. I want to make out good in life, Mr. Del, and I figure I can. I really do . . . I don't know . . . I've got that . . . somewhere, in my stomach some place, or in my chest some place . . . I've got that good feeling. The feeling that things are going to be okay for me if I use my head.

(*It doesn't matter that John does not say, "This is what counseling has done for me. . . ." The important thing is that he has that feeling, "in his stomach," or somewhere. With Mr. Del, he has come to learn that he is somebody, and that he can do things.*)

Co.: You have the feeling that there's a right future ahead for you. . .

Cl.: I'm in school for a purpose. I know that. I realize it, but sometimes I don't know what the purpose is. I mean I know I'm here to make something for myself. I guess that may be it, but still, I'm not sure. I don't know what I mean exactly.

Co.: You feel that there's a purpose for your being here, but you're not really sure what it is.

Cl.: I've got the ambition now, but I want to be sure that I use the ambition in the right way. I want to be sure that I don't . . . you know . . . go backwards again. I want to make something of myself, but I'm not sure just what. I mean I want my future to be there, but I don't know what I want it to be in.

Co.: Uh . . . huh. . .

Cl.: What I mean is this. I want to get something out of my education, but I'm not sure what I exactly want to get out of it. I mean I want to get a job, but I think I'd want it to mean more than just a job. I think I want something to happen inside of me. . . . That's it, I guess . . . I want to feel educated inside. I want my education to mean something to me.

Co.: You want your education to do something internal, rather than just the completion of a certain amount of work.

Cl.: Something like that, I guess. I want to build on what I've got now. I mean I think I know the direction that I have to go, and I want to be able to add to what I have. If I'm a good person now . . . and it's hard to say that, because I don't think I'm really a completely good person yet, but if I'm on the road, I want to keep on the road. If I'm going to get there, the only way I'll make it is to keep building . . . not to look over my shoulder, but just to look ahead. I don't know . . . I don't know if I'm making myself clear. . .

Co.: Uh . . . huh. . . You feel that since you have this good feeling inside of you, you don't want to lose it. You want to hang on to it, and add to it . . . kind of build it up.

Cl.: I'm going to be whatever God will let me be, but I'm going to be somebody. The only thing is that I hope that my bad record doesn't go against me. I mean I hope that if I decide that I want to become a doctor or something like that, they're not going to hold my record against me. It's stupid. I was found not guilty, but I'm afraid that some people won't understand this. They'll figure that just because I was in court on a charge, then I must be a bad kid, a bad character— that must be immoral or something like that.

Co.: You feel that your bad record might be held against you some day when you're looking to further your education. . .

Cl.: I hope it isn't held against me, but I just get that kind of a feeling, 'cause I know how people are. I know how they are when they hear you've been in court . . . they don't like you.

Co.: You feel that people won't be very understanding.

Cl.: I don't see how they can be. You don't know how those words "in court" affect people. You don't know how they act when they hear it. I mean I've seen people, I've seen how they acted when they heard about it. I'm just afraid that these people who will be making decisions about whether or not to let me into a certain place—I just hope these people won't act like the rest of the people. I hope they are older and smarter. I hope they won't hold it against me.

Co.: This really worries you. . .

(*The counselor does not give false reassurance to John. John's fears are well grounded, and while this counselor will help him to think things out, he is not the "things will be better" type.*)

Cl.: I hope that they can look at my later record and decide that I need—I mean that I deserve some sort of chance. I hope that they just don't look at certain things, and decide that they don't want me. I hope that they look further. I hope they look at what I've done this year, and what I'm going to do from now on.

Co.: Uh . . . huh. . .

Cl.: And another thing—I want to stand on my own two feet. I don't want to depend on anybody. I don't want you to think I'm selfish, but I just want to be able to stand up and say, "I'm John—this is me." I don't want to have to say, "This is John," and then hide my face because I'm ashamed.

Co.: You want people to accept you and not to look down at you.

Cl.: Nobody can change my life but me. I've made some changes so far, but I still want to make more. Nobody can do it but me. John's the only one who can do it.

Co.: Uh . . . huh. . .

Cl.: I just feel that there's something ahead for me. I just feel it inside of me. I mean I can come to school now and enjoy it. Don't get me wrong. I don't love school; I don't think anybody loves school. But it isn't such a hard place to take. I can get along better. I enjoy it. I'm more interested in what I'm doing.

Co.: You feel better about school now than you did in the past. . .

Cl.: Well, now I'm steady about school. I mean I don't have my ups and downs. Everything can go along pretty good. Like I said, I don't love it, but it isn't like before. I used to hate it, and then I'd like it and then I'd hate it, and then again I'd like it. I mean I had crazy feelings—crazy ideas about school. I mean I didn't know why I was there, and what I was supposed to do. But now I know—now I know I'm here because I want to make something of myself.

(A major task of some school counselors is to help a child to adjust to, and to live through, an unrealistic school experience, a school experience that has little or no relationship to his totality as a person, but one that he must, according to the law, endure.)

Co.: Uh . . . huh. . .

Cl.: I can take school now. I never could take it before. Every little thing bothered me, but now I can take it. I don't have to be mad at the world any more; I don't have to be mad at teachers. Before, all a teacher had to do was cross me just a little bit, just enough to tip me off, just enough to let me show my temper, and boy, I'd show it. But now I figure that I don't have to show it. I don't have to prove anything to anybody. I can just—well—I guess I can just be myself.

Co.: You feel more comfortable about being in school now, because you don't have to fight everything like you used to. You can just take things in stride, and be comfortable about the whole thing.

Cl.: I'm dying for the next few years to go by. It's funny —I don't want them to go by, but still I do want them to. I'm dying to see what I can make of myself. I'm dying to see if that thing inside of me is real or if it's just there for a little while. I'm dying to see that I can make something of myself. There's nothing holding me back now. The only thing that can hold me back is me—myself. If I started thinking like a jerk again, then maybe I wouldn't make it. But I think that I can take care of myself. I think that I can make it. I just want to stay on an even keel, and then maybe I'll be okay. If I can just keep my mind on what I'm doing, then I think I'll be okay. I mean if I can just think before I act, then I think everything will be okay.

Co.: If you can only hang on to what you've found, you feel that things will work out okay—that you'll make something of your future.

Cl.: The thing to do is hang on to it, and I think I can. The more I think about it the more I can. Like I say, it depends on me. It doesn't depend on you. It doesn't depend on my aunt. It doesn't depend on my parents. It's me. If I'm going to make it, I've got to decide what I've got to do. No one can decide that for me. If my future isn't important to me, why the hell should any one else worry about it? If I'm going to have anything, I'm only going to get it because of me.

Co.: You feel that your future really depends on you—you alone. It doesn't depend on anyone else.

Cl.: If I said it depends on somebody else, then I'd probably never make it, but if I decide that my future depends on me, then there's a good chance that I can make it . . . because I think I can handle my future better than anyone else.

Co.: Uh . . . huh. . . .

Cl.: Sometimes I get nervous about next year, but at other times I think of it as a challenge. I'd like to really see if what I've found out about myself is going to stick, or is it going to rub off in the first rain storm. See, I don't know—I won't really know until next year, and the year after, and so on. Maybe I'll never know. Even if I did go to college, I'd probably never really know if I made it. I don't know. How does a person know when he's made it?

Co.: You feel that you may never know whether or not you've made it. . . .

(Note that even here, when both counselor and client know that their experience together is just about over, the counselor does nothing to hold the client to him; and he gives nothing in the way of nice, but possibly false reassurance. What the client has done, he has done, in a way, because of the counselor, but only because the counselor has helped him to do it himself. The counselor has respected his own integrity, and that of the client. Even here, in the last few comments, he is still saying to the client, with compassion and understanding, and with the underlying insistence on the strength of the client: "It always has been, and it still is—up to you.")

Cl.: Maybe not . . . (long pause) . . . Well, I guess . . . (long pause) . . . I won't see you again, Mr. Del, for a long time . . . I'll see you to say "Hi" to, of course . . . but not like this . . . (long pause) . . . So long then, Mr. Del, and thanks, thanks for everything that you have done. . . .

Co.: So long, John.

And so John leaves Mr. Del. Mr. Del, being human, probably feels a bit sad, and a bit proud. For John's sake, he no doubt hopes that John will not have to see him again, and the final client comment, indicating counselor success, might well be, "Thank you—but I hope that I don't have to see you again."

The evidence, as these words are written, is that the strength that John gathered was not just a passing phase. He did become more capable of standing on his own feet; he did become more of a responsible individual, capable of standing up and answering for himself, and willing to do so. He was given no medicine, he was given no cure, but through a warm and human relationship with a skilled and educated person who respected him and understood him, he was able to marshal the strengths that he always had, and become a stronger and better person. This, then, is the experience known as counseling.

index

439